Armand A. Maurer, CSB

Medieval Philosophy

In this outline of the history of medieval philosophy from St. Augustine to the Renaissance, Part One, "The Age of the Fathers," is devoted to St. Augustine, Boethius, Erigena, St. Anselm, Peter Abelard and the School of Chartres. Part Two, "The Coming of the Schoolmen," introduces the reader to scholasticism, Arabian and Jewish philosophy, and early philosophers at Paris and Oxford. Part Three, "The Age of the Schoolmen," describes the philosophies of Roger Bacon, St. Bonaventure, St. Albert, St. Thomas Aquinas, Latin Averroism and Duns Scotus. Part Four, "The Modern Way," studies the new logic and physics, Ockham, Eckhart and Nicholas of Cusa. Part Five, "The Middle Ages and Renaissance Philosophy," links medieval philosophy with the Renaissance philosophers Ficino, Pomponazzi and the Renaissance scholastics.

The study shows the continuity of philosophical thought through the Middle Ages and the contribution made to it by the most eminent minds of the time. An effort has been made to present their ideas as clearly and accurately as possible for the use of undergraduates and the general reading public.

With the exception of a few minor modifications and corrections, this updated reprint of *Medieval Philosophy*, first published in 1962 as the second volume of the series *A History of Philosophy* edited by Etienne Gilson, is identical with the original. An appendix has been added containing corrigenda and addenda and a bibliographic supplement of notable works on medieval philosophy published in recent years. The volume includes copious notes, general and special bibliographies, and an index of names.

D1219331

The Etienne Gilson Series 4

Medieval Philosophy

Second Edition
With Additions, Corrections and
A Bibliographic Supplement

BY

ARMAND A. MAURER, C.S.B.

With a Preface by
Etienne Gilson

PONTIFICAL INSTITUTE OF MEDIAEVAL STUDIES

The publishing program of the Pontifical Institute
is supported through the generosity of the
De Rancé Foundation.

Canadian Cataloguing in Publication Data

Maurer, Armand A. (Armand Augustine), 1915-
   Medieval philosophy

(The Etienne Gilson series, ISSN 0708-319X; 4)
First ed. published: New York: Random House, 1962.
Bibliography: p.
Includes index.
ISBN 0-88844-704-3

1. Philosophy, Medieval – History. 2. Philosophy, Renaissance – History.
I. Pontifical Institute of Mediaeval Studies. II. Title. III. Series.

B721.M39 1982   189   C81-095151-7

B
72 (
.M37
1982

Couverture: Bibliothèque Nationale, Paris (MS fr. 95, f. 254)

First edition, © 1962
Second edition, © 1982 by

Pontifical Institute of Mediaeval Studies
59 Queen's Park Crescent East
Toronto, Ontario, Canada M5S2C4

Printed by Universa, Wetteren, Belgium

JESUIT - KRAUSS - McCORMICK - LIBRARY
1100 EAST 55th STREET
CHICAGO, ILLINOIS 60615

To my Mother

To my Mother

Contents

Part Two

The Coming of the Schoolmen

Part Three

The Age of the Schoolmen

Part Four

The Modern Way

Part Five

The Middle Ages and Renaissance Philosophy

AUTHOR'S FOREWORD
TO THE SECOND EDITION

Medieval Philosophy first appeared as volume two in the series *A History of Philosophy* edited by Etienne Gilson and published by Random House. Since the publisher has discontinued the printing of the series and since there remains a demand for *Medieval Philosophy*, it was decided to reprint it as a separate volume. The text, with a few minor modifications and corrections, is the same as the original. The General Bibliography has been brought up to date and a Bibliographical Supplement has been added.

AUTHOR'S FOREWORD

Within the last fifty or so years there has been a remarkable growth of interest in medieval philosophy. Formerly the domain of a small group of historians specially trained to read the Latin documents of the Middle Ages, it is now attracting the attention of a wider circle of historians, students of philosophy, and even the educated public. This growing curiosity in medieval philosophy is but one aspect of a more general awakening to the riches of medieval culture and of an appreciation of the historical roots of our civilization in the Middle Ages. More particularly, it is due to the growing awareness of the influence of medieval thought upon modern philosophy. Hitherto it was commonly believed that one could pass from the philosophy of ancient Greece and Rome to classical modern philosophy with but a cursory glance, if any, at the thought of the intervening centuries. This prevalent attitude was summed up in the statement of O. Hamelin, that Descartes "is in succession with the ancients, almost as if—with the exception of the physicists—there had been nothing but a blank between." [1]

These words are understandable from the pen of a rationalist like Hamelin who failed to find his own ideal of the separation of reason and faith in medieval thinkers. The rationalism of Descartes was bound to appear to him as in continuity, not with the Middle Ages, but with the classical period of Greece and Rome. An examination of the contents of the Cartesian philosophy, however, shows the great debt of its author to the Middle Ages. [2] From this point of view, Cartesianism does not continue the thought of the ancients as though there were no speculation in the intervening centuries. Indeed, the philosophy of Descartes, like that of Malebranche, Leibniz, and Spinoza, is incomprehensible without a knowledge of St. Augustine and the great medieval schoolmen. [3]

If this is true, we are led to the conclusion that medieval thought,

under the influence of Christian faith, created ideas that have passed
into the philosophical heritage of the West. We are not here concerned with the nature of medieval speculation or with the question in what sense, if any, it can be called philosophical. We shall
let the men of the Middle Ages explain their own views on the
nature of their intellectual activity and reserve our general observations on this subject for the conclusion of the book. At this point
we simply wish to stress the fact that the Middle Ages was a vital
and creative period in Western thought and that it cannot be
ignored if we wish to understand the development of modern
philosophy.

This book is designed as an introduction to medieval philosophy
for the educated public and undergraduate students. It traces the
history of philosophical speculation from St. Augustine to Suarez,
laying stress upon the main figures and currents of thought en-
countered during this period. Many details and many minor men
are omitted or scarcely mentioned, and certain aspects of medieval
thought receive slight attention, notably political philosophy. It
is hoped that the reader will be stimulated to advance beyond this
book to the more complete histories of medieval philosophy, particularly Etienne Gilson's *History of Christian Philosophy in the
Middle Ages,* and beyond all histories to the works of the medieval
philosophers themselves.

The general plan of the book is clear from the table of contents.
Part I, entitled "The Age of the Fathers," is devoted to medieval
writers from the fourth century to the twelfth. This period witnessed the fall of the Roman Empire and the gradual rebuilding
of a new, Christian civilization in western Europe. In calling it the
Age of the Fathers we are extending this phrase beyond its ordinary meaning, but not without reason. The Fathers of the Church
were theologians, living in the early centuries after Christ, who
were outstanding for the depth and orthodoxy of their teaching
and for the sanctity of their lives. The greatest among the Greek
Fathers were St. Gregory of Nazianzus, St. Basil, St. John Chrysostom, and St. Athanasius; and among the Latin Fathers St. Ambrose,
St. Jerome, St. Augustine, and St. Gregory the Great. Historians
generally consider the Age of the Fathers to be closed with the

death of St. Gregory in 604, but in a broader sense they extend it to the twelfth century and include St. Bernard (d. 1153), traditionally called the "Last of the Fathers." This early period of medieval speculation owed its spiritual, cultural, and intellectual ideals to the Fathers, especially to St. Augustine. Its prevailing philosophical ideas were drawn from Plato and the Neoplatonists, as were those of St. Augustine. During this period little was known of Aristotle's philosophy except minor logical treatises and some secondhand information contained in the writings of other men.

In the twelfth and thirteenth centuries important changes took place in medieval culture. Urban life flourished with the growth of large cities, and the intellectual life became scholastic with the establishment of the universities and the discovery of the major works of Aristotle and his Arabian commentators. In Part II we describe the advent of scholasticism, the factors that entered into its formation, and its early progress at the Universities of Paris and Oxford. Then in Part III we examine the great scholastic syntheses of the thirteenth-century schoolmen.

Although we distinguish the Age of the Fathers from that of the Schoolmen, we do not mean to imply that they were historically separated from each other or that the characteristics of one are not also to some extent found in the other. History is a continuous and complex process that does not lend itself to neat divisions into periods and epochs. The Fathers of the Church did not cease to influence philosophical thought in the later Middle Ages, although their influence was modified by the coming of Aristotelianism. So, too, scholasticism did not spring up unheralded in the thirteenth century. Boethius and St. Anselm already show certain scholastic traits with their tendency to systematize and to express themselves in terse formulae, and Abelard was one of the founders of the scholastic method. The fact remains, however, that a profound change took place in Western thought with the discovery of the works of Aristotle, and a new intellectual climate was created that differentiates the Age of the Schoolmen from that of the Fathers.

In the fourteenth century the vitality and creativeness of scholasticism began to decline and men turned to new ways of thought described in Part IV. The title we have given to this portion of

the book—"The Modern Way"—was used in the fifteenth century to designate the nominalist movement, whose leading figure
was William of Ockham. We have let it stand for all the new aspects of medieval speculation in the late Middle Ages. Once again,
however, we must beware of departmentalizing history. Scholasticism did not cease to dominate the medieval mind in the late
Middle Ages even though it came under increasing criticism. Moreover, some of the most advanced thinkers of this period began
to look back to the pre-scholastic age for philosophical and theological inspiration. Some of the best minds of the late Middle
Ages consciously returned to the Neoplatonism of the Fathers in
preference to Aristotelianism. What appears to be new in their
teachings is often but a rediscovery or development of older ideas
that went out of fashion in the thirteenth century.

The extension of the present History beyond the recognized
limits of the Middle Ages is to show the continuity and development of medieval philosophical ideas in the Renaissance and early
modern times.

It is a pleasure to express my gratitude to those who have helped
me in the writing of this book: to Etienne Gilson, whose writings,
lectures, and conversations have been a constant source of historical
and philosophical wisdom; to Anton C. Pegis, who invited me to
write the book and made many valuable suggestions; and to Fr.
Frederick Black, C.S.B., and my other Basilian confreres, who read
the manuscript and improved its style.

PREFACE

ETIENNE GILSON

The creative period of Greek philosophy came to an end in the third century A.D. with Plotinus, whose teaching deeply influenced the course of philosophical speculation for more than fifteen centuries. Even before the early diffusion of Christianity, Greek philosophy had begun to undergo a striking transformation under the impact of religious forces from the Near East. Plotinus himself, whose philosophy appears as a belated burst of energy after a long period of speculative inactivity, is proof of this. Practically all the Greek philosophers before him *ended* their work by positing one or several divine principles of the universe; in the doctrine of Plotinus, everything *starts* from the divine Triad, from which all the rest proceeds and to which it aims to return. Not only is the philosophical world of the pagan Plotinus centered upon God and the One, it is also a way for man to rejoin the divinity.

It is therefore probable that, even without the rise of Christianity, Greek philosophy would have become a predominantly religious interpretation of the world; but it is a fact that the teaching of the Gospel of salvation among Gentiles of Greek culture hastened that evolution and brought philosophy under the controlling influence of Christian doctrine. Thus there arose, even before the death of Plotinus, a new type of philosophical speculation, rational in its method and religious in its inspiration, which aimed at conferring upon Christian truth the maximum of intelligibility it could bear without ceasing to be an essentially religious knowledge, that is, a doctrine of salvation through faith.

Medieval Philosophy, the second volume of our *History*, describes the more important doctrines born of this cooperation between the new Christian faith and the Greek philosophical tradition. In this sense, it can be said that there never was any break in continuity in the development of Western philosophy. Less than one century after the death of Plotinus, such Christian scholars as Saint Ambrose and Marius Victorinus were already at work assimilating as much of his doctrine as could help to build a rational interpretation of Christian faith. The long period during which this cooperation between religion and philosophy took place without meeting any insurmountable opposition coincides roughly with what we call the Middle Ages, and the type of philosophical speculation distinctive of that period is called "medieval philosophy." From one point of view, medieval speculation can be seen as a development of Greek philosophy, for the Christian philosophers used techniques inherited from the Greeks. Principles, methods of demonstration, and, as often as not, demonstrations themselves, were soon considered by Christians as their rightful property. Since their God was the source of the truth of reason as well as that of revelation, those early Christian converts felt entitled to the whole truth. For this reason the new religion, instead of repudiating the Greek philosophical tradition, worked for centuries to keep it alive, and to assimilate it as far as was possible. The summit of this historical evolution was reached around the middle of the thirteenth century, when Thomas Aquinas undertook to express the religious truths of Christianity in the philosophical language of Aristotle. With the *Summa Theologiae* as a vantage point, the whole philosophy of the Middle Ages assumes its true meaning.

Such a course was not inevitable. In the Islamic world, instead of striving to put philosophy to good use, the theologians mistrusted it to the point of opposing it. The two greatest Moslem philosophers, Avicenna and Averroes, are two cases in point. Held in suspicion, refuted, and even, in the case of Averroes, persecuted by the Moslem theologians, these philosophers were attentively studied by the Christian theologians of the thirteenth century. In fact, it is among the Christians that these two Moslem philosophers found their philosophical posterity.

From another point of view, however, the philosophy of the Middle Ages implied a breaking away from the Greek tradition. Instead of depending solely on rational knowledge, it called on the light of revelation to fortify and perfect the natural light of

reason. The Christian philosophy of the Middle Ages is characterized by its recognition of this two-fold source of knowledge and
by its absolute trust in the fruitfulness of the cooperation of faith
and reason. Indeed, medieval thinkers trusted faith more than
reason, but considered it as inevitable for faith to make use of
reason as it was profitable for reason to avail itself of all it could
derive from revelation.

Medieval philosophy came to an end when the conditions that
had brought it about ceased to exist. Born of the confluence of the
early Christian faith with the philosophical traditions of the Greeks,
it was bound to die when Christians of a later day decided that
philosophy should again be cultivated for its own sake, apart from
theology and independent of revelation. Francis Bacon and René
Descartes were primarily responsible for that epoch-making decision, which is considered to mark the birth of "modern philosophy."
The fifteen centuries of philosophical speculation that extend from
the end of the Greek period to the beginning of modern philosophy
constitute the subject matter of this volume.

The fact that medieval philosophical thought is often called
"Christian philosophy" is enough to warn the reader that he is
about to enter controversial ground. Though history as such has
no business in controversy of this kind, it is, on one point, entitled
to go a step beyond mere factual narration. It may, and even must,
take stock of the wealth of philosophical knowledge accumulated
by generations of medieval theologians and later received by modern philosophers either as immediately evident or as demonstrated
by philosophical reasoning. It is at least puzzling to see so much
modern philosophy flow from doctrines supposedly innocent of
philosophical speculation and even at times presented as barring
and opposing such speculation from the start. In this sense, despite
the philosophical revolution discussed at the end of this volume,
the following volume will not break the continuity. For without
a knowledge of the history of Western philosophy during the
Middle Ages, we cannot interpret correctly the history of philosophy from the sixteenth century to our own day.

1 THE AGE OF THE FATHERS

I

St. Augustine

WISDOM THE GOAL OF LIFE

ST. AUGUSTINE'S LIFE, so dramatically related in his *Confessions*, was a long quest for wisdom.[1] At the age of nineteen he read the *Hortensius* of Cicero, an exhortation to philosophical wisdom. This work awakened in him a love of truth that remained with him for the rest of his life. For almost ten years he sought wisdom from the Manichaean religion, which boasted that human reason by itself could make men wise.[2] His eventual disillusionment with Manichaeism led to a short period of skepticism. He then chanced upon some works of the Neoplatonists Plotinus and Porphyry, who introduced him to first-rate philosophical thinking. These philosophers helped to free his mind of materialism and at the same time stirred him to purify his moral life. But the liberation was still imperfect; his quest could end only with his conversion to Christianity. Then was the goal in sight, and the means to reach it at hand. He saw clearly that conversion to wisdom is conversion to Christ, the Wisdom of God, who is both light to our mind and strength to our will.

St. Augustine's approach to philosophy was thus a highly personal one. He was concerned with his own unhappiness, the fruit of his disordered thinking and moral life. Evil weighed heavily upon him. His struggle to bring order into his mind and morals led him to God as the source of all order and happiness.

Philosophy for St. Augustine is consequently inseparable from religion. The philosophers, he says, aim at happiness, as do also

Christians. But only Christians know man's true happiness and they alone possess the means to attain it. True philosophy, accordingly, is identical with true religion.*3*

FAITH AND REASON: THE MEANS TO WISDOM

SHORTLY AFTER his conversion to Christianity St. Augustine outlined his program for finding wisdom. He writes in his treatise *Against the Academics:* "Let me tell you my whole program briefly. Whatever may be the nature of human wisdom, I see I have not yet perceived it. But though I am now in my thirty-third year, I don't think I ought to despair of sometime reaching it. So I have turned away from all the things that mortal men consider to be good, and I have set myself the goal of serving the pursuit of this wisdom. The arguments of the Academics [that is, the skeptics] used to hold me back seriously from such an undertaking; in the present disputation I have, as it seems to me, defended myself sufficiently against those arguments. Furthermore, everyone agrees that we are impelled to learning by the double urge of authority and reason. From this moment forward it is my resolve never to depart from the authority of Christ, for I find none that is stronger. However, I must follow after this with the greatest subtlety of reason. For I am so disposed now that I have an unbounded desire to apprehend truth not only by believing it, but also by understanding it. In the meantime, I am confident that among the Platonists I shall find what is not opposed to the teachings of our religion." *4*

In this program there are two guides to wisdom: the authority of Christ and human reason. St. Augustine's own experience convinced him that human reason, left to itself, is not enough. Faith in Christ must come first to prepare the way for understanding. He likes to quote Isaias: "Unless you believe, you shall not understand." *5* But once we have accepted the truths of faith, reason intervenes to help us understand better what we believe. In the eleventh century St. Anselm will give classic formulation to this ideal in his motto: *Faith seeking understanding.*

This is the concept of Christian wisdom St. Augustine gave to

the Middle Ages and which became its intellectual ideal. As understood and practiced by St. Augustine and his authentic followers,
this is no abstract, cold speculation, but a loving study and meditation on sacred Scripture, aiming at a mystical experience of God
and an ultimate vision of him. All the resources of the human mind
are brought into its service. All the truths discovered by the
pagans—the treasures of philosophy, science, history, and grammar
—are considered to belong by right to Christians and to be for
their use. St. Augustine never thought of developing a philosophy
for its own sake, independent of theology. True, he philosophized
abundantly and profoundly, but always in the service of Christian
wisdom.

Our concern is not with the properly theological notions of
St. Augustine—for example, his doctrines of the Trinity and grace
—but rather with his philosophical views expressed in the context
of his theology. We are forewarned by St. Augustine himself that
these are Platonic in inspiration. Has he not told us, at the beginning of his career, of his confidence in the agreement between
the Platonists and Christianity? Later he regretted this confidence
to some extent and found it necessary to modify Platonism on
important points. Nevertheless, his basic philosophical views always remained deeply indebted to Platonism. St. Thomas expresses
this with his customary precision: "Whenever Augustine, who
was imbued with the doctrines of the Platonists, found in their
writings anything consistent with the faith, he adopted it; and
whatever he found contrary to the faith, he amended." [6]

THE PROBLEM OF CERTITUDE

BEFORE HIS CONVERSION St. Augustine was a follower of the
New Academy and its skepticism. At this time he was also a
materialist. His intellectual conversion was a transition from
skepticism to certitude and from materialism to the recognition of
spiritual reality.

St. Augustine was haunted by the questions: Can we be certain
of anything? If so, of what can we be certain? The Academics,
for example Carneades and Cicero, thought that certitude was

impossible. In his treatise *Against the Academics,* written against Cicero's *Academics,* St. Augustine sets out to show the absurdity of this position. We can know many things with certainty even about the physical world; for example, that there is either one world or many, and that if there are many the number is either finite or infinite. We are certain, moreover, that the world either had a beginning in time or it did not. Of course we may not be sure which of these alternatives is true, but the disjunctive propositions themselves are true. Suppose the skeptic replies that we cannot even be sure the world exists because of the untrustworthiness of the senses. Well, we are at least sure that the world appears to us as we perceive it. We may be wrong in judging that an oar in water is really broken, but not that it appears to be broken. The senses are indeed trustworthy. They report things to us just as they should, even though the mind sometimes judges incorrectly that reality is just as it appears to be.

The wise man will realize, with the Platonists, that sense knowledge yields only opinions about reality and not truth. To know the truth, one must discriminate between reality and false images of reality. It is clear from dreams and states of madness that the senses are incapable of this. So we must conclude that we cannot expect the certitude of truth from the senses. The "judgment of truth" is rather to be found in the intellect and interior mind.[7]

Granted that the senses do not give us certitude, truth is still possible. Indeed, a state of absolute doubt is contradictory. At least we are certain that we are and that we think. But suppose that we are mad or asleep and what we think is an illusion. If we are mistaken, at least we exist and are alive. "For we are," Augustine says, "and we know we are, and we love our being and our knowledge of it. In these three things that I have mentioned there is no falsehood, parading as truth, to disturb us. For unlike things which are outside of us, we do not touch these by any bodily sense; . . . but without any deceptive representation or phantasms, I am absolutely certain that I am, and that I know and love this. These truths stand without fear in the face of the arguments of the Academics."[8]

Descartes in the seventeenth century met the skepticism of

Montaigne in a similar way. Both St. Augustine and Descartes had to overcome skepticism at the beginning of their careers, and both did so by establishing their own existence as the first and most certain of all truths. But the comparison should not be pressed too far. Descartes' celebrated "I think, therefore I am" is the starting point of a philosophical system. Augustine, as we have seen, had no intention of establishing such a system. He was seeking a wisdom beyond that of philosophy, and his victory over skepticism opened his mind to the infinite possibilities of that wisdom.

One of the most characteristic features of St. Augustine's thought is revealed by his manner of overcoming skepticism; namely, his *interiorism*. We find in him not only the interiorism common to all deeply religious thinkers and mystics, but also a philosophical, and more exactly a Platonic, interiorism. According to St. Augustine, the act of knowing goes inward toward oneself, not outward toward material things. To discover the truth, one must enter into himself and know himself. "Do not go abroad," St. Augustine admonishes us. "Return within yourself. Truth dwells in the inward man." 9

When a man looks inward upon himself, not only is he certain that he exists and knows; he also finds other truths there. He is certain of mathematical truths (for example, that 3 plus 7 equals 10), as well as ethical laws (for example, that the eternal is to be preferred to the temporal). Apprehending these objects, we do not see sensible things, but eternal, intelligible, and necessary laws.

How are we to explain the presence of this true knowledge in our souls? Is it caused by sensible things? Hardly, for they are changing and contingent, whereas truth is unchanging and necessary. Neither can my own mind be the source of this knowledge, for it is also subject to change. In fact, my mind submits to truth and is ruled by it. Truth is in my mind, but it is also above my mind. Moreover, truth cannot be caused by my individual mind, for truth is public and open to the gaze of everyone, just as a sensible object can be seen by all who look at it. When I say something true and you agree with what I say, where do we see that it is true? You do not see it in me, nor do I see it in you. We both see it in the truth which transcends us. We are sure, then, that truth exists above the human mind and that it is necessary, immutable, and eternal. Now these qualities are attributes of God. To prove the existence of truth is thus at the same time to prove the existence of God, who is Truth.[10]

This is St. Augustine's preferred path to God: from the exterior world he turns inward upon himself, where he discovers truth, whose sole sufficient reason he finds in a transcendent God. He himself marks out the stages in this journey with his usual precision. The way to God leads "from the exterior to the interior, and from the inferior to the superior." [11]

THE SOUL

IN USING THE METHOD OF REFLECTION in order to discover the truth, St. Augustine is not denying the existence of the external world of sense, but focusing his attention upon what he considers to be truly real and intelligible; namely, God. This method also puts him in contact with his soul, which is man's true center. At the moment of escaping skepticism, therefore, he also throws off materialism, because in discovering truth he finds himself as a thinking being or mind transcending matter. The soul knows itself directly as an intelligence and hence as incorporeal, like truth itself. It also knows itself as immortal, for it is the bearer of truth, which is immortal.

God and the soul: these are St. Augustine's main concern. He writes: "I desire to know God and the soul.—Nothing more?—Nothing whatever." [12] And he prays: "O God, who art ever the same, let me know myself and thee." [13] To know himself: is that not to know his soul? He often uses expressions like the following: "I, that is, my soul." And he defines man, with Plato and Plotinus, as "a rational soul, using a mortal and earthly body." [14] Again, he calls the soul "a certain substance, sharing in reason and suited to the task of ruling the body." [15] In short, the true man is the soul, and the body is its instrument.

St. Augustine, however, is well aware that man is a composite of soul and body. He has no doubt that the body is a part of human nature. He writes: "Anyone who wishes to separate the body from human nature is foolish." [16] To understand his identification of man with his soul, we must realize that his approach to man is chiefly that of a moralist and religious thinker, concerned above all with man's happiness and the means to achieve it. We do him an injustice if we judge his doctrine in terms of the scholastic metaphysics of man of the thirteenth century. The problem of man's unity in being will then be a burning issue; it is not so for St. Augustine. His problem is rather to know how man should be ordered and governed in order to reach his final end. What is the highest and most perfect part of man from this point of view? Obviously his soul, for it is through his soul that he arrives at truth and the enjoyment of truth, which is his happiness. In this sense man truly is his soul.

How is the spiritual substance of the soul united to the material substance of the body? To this difficult question St. Augustine replies that the union is one of vital attention. The soul is the guardian of the body and constantly watches over it. It is, moreover, present as a whole in all parts of the body. This is shown by the fact that the whole soul perceives what is going on in any part of the body. It senses as a whole in each part, consequently it must be present as a whole in each part. "When there is a pain in the foot," he writes, "the eye sees it, the tongue reports it, the hand reaches toward it. This would not be unless the soul were present in these parts . . . The soul is, therefore, at one and the same time as a whole in each part of the body, just as it senses as a whole in each part." [17]

In this view, the soul's presence in the body is for the sake of the body. The soul has a natural desire to watch over the body, to vivify it, and to bring to it the beauty, harmony, and order it itself has received from God. But the body tends to be a weight upon the soul, and it longs to be rid of it. In his early works St. Augustine, like Plotinus, describes the body as the prison of the soul. He does not mean, however, that the body is intrinsically evil or that the soul's union with it is evil in itself. As a Christian he knows that matter is good, because it has been created by God. So even the body is good, although the soul can become evil by giving the body too much care, to forgetfulness of itself and God.

KNOWLEDGE

ST. AUGUSTINE'S CONCEPTION OF MAN has important consequences for his doctrine of knowledge. We see a body that is colored and hear one that is struck. How are we to account for these sensations? We should not think that the body impresses its image upon the soul. This is impossible, for the soul is spiritual, whereas the body is material. Matter cannot act upon spirit, nor can the inferior act upon the superior. We must not suppose that the body produces any effect upon the soul, as though the latter were material and receptive of the body's influence. In short, the soul is not passive and receptive in sensation; rather it is active.

What, then, is sensation? We have seen that the soul animates the body and is present to it by vital attention. It keeps a constant vigil over the body. When other bodies act upon our body and change it, this does not escape the notice of the soul. The soul modifies its attention according to the modifications of the body. Sensation is the soul's special concentration of attention arising from disturbances in the body. Consequently, sensation is a spiritual act of the soul; it is not a passive reception of images from the external world. Sensory images, and the intellectual notions corresponding to them, are caused by the soul itself, which fashions them out of its own substance. "When we see a body," St. Augustine writes, "and its image begins to exist in our soul, it is not the body that impresses the image in our soul. It is the soul itself that produces it with wonderful swiftness within itself." [18]

We are here far from a doctrine of abstraction of ideas from sensible things. We are equally far from a doctrine of innate ideas. Augustine recalls Plato's famous proof that learning is remembering ideas known in a previous life, but he does not accept this explanation of knowledge. "We ought rather to believe," he writes, "that the nature of the intellectual mind was so made that, by being naturally subject to intelligible realities, according to the arrangement of the creator, it sees these truths [for example, of geometry] in a certain incorporeal light of a unique kind, just as the eye of the body sees the things all around it in this corporeal light." [19]

St. Augustine is here substituting for Plato's theory of reminiscence a doctrine of the discovery of truth through divine illumination. As the eye is naturally bathed in physical light, so the mind is bathed in intelligible light, and in this light it sees the truth. It cannot be doubted that God is the source of this light. Scripture tells us that God is the "Father of lights," and that the Word of God "enlightens every man who comes into the world." [20] The Platonists also call God the sun of the intelligible world.

Three elements must be taken into account in St. Augustine's doctrine of knowledge: 1] God is spiritual light and he illumines all men. This illumination is given to all men, although in varying degrees. 2] There is a world of intelligible truth illuminated by God. 3] There are minds that know this world of truth under the divine illumination. As Augustine puts it: "There is present in [men], insofar as they can grasp it, the light of eternal reason, in which light the immutable truths are seen." [21]

It is a persistent difficulty for interpreters of St. Augustine to know precisely the nature of these immutable truths. They cannot be creatures, because creatures are mutable and truth is immutable. Neither can they be God himself or his Ideas. For we see the truth, but outside of extraordinary states, such as ecstasy, we cannot see God or his Ideas, which are identical with himself. Divine illumination of truth, however, functions through the divine Ideas. When we know the truth, these Ideas act upon our mind by impressing their images upon it, as a ring leaves its image upon wax. Does this impression give us our ideas? Augustine touches only briefly on the question of the origin of our ideas. He says that the mind gathers its knowledge of corporeal things through the bodily senses. As for non-empirical ideas (for example, the notion of wisdom or justice), these it acquires through itself. [22] Later medieval philosophers will be greatly interested in solving the problem of the origin of our ideas. St. Augustine's problem is different. What interests him is not so much the origin of our ideas or the distinction between ideas and judgments involving them, but how we, contingent and mutable creatures, can make necessary and immutable judgments. The divine illumination is meant to explain this extraordinary fact. Through this illumination, whenever we make a true judgment our mind is in contact with the immutable and necessary truths in God's mind, and although this contact does not enable us to see the divine Ideas, it accounts for the immutability and necessity of our knowledge.

THE NATURE OF GOD

THE PRESENCE OF TRUTH in our intellect assures us of the interior presence of God. For truth is eternal and immutable, and God alone has these qualities. In short, God is Truth. God, then, is within us, but he is also above us, transcending and ruling our minds. We know he is present to us, otherwise we could not have true knowledge; but his nature escapes our grasp. It is easier for us to know what he is not than to know what he is. In fact, we know him best when we realize our ignorance of his nature. He is not only superior to our mind; he is that to which nothing is known to be superior.[23] Later St. Anselm will exploit this notion in his famous proof of the existence of God.

One name, however, designates God better than any other. This is the name revealed to us by God himself in the book of *Exodus* (3:14). When Moses asked God his name, he replied: *I Am Who Am*. This means that God is being itself (*ipsum esse*). But what is the meaning of being? We should pay close attention to St. Augustine's answer, for it reveals his profoundest metaphysical view of reality. True being is something that endures without change. Consequently, to say that God is Being is to say that he is unchangeable. He is always the selfsame and his years do not fail. He is in fact eternal. Indeed, the very substance of God is eternity. Moreover, because God exists in the highest possible way, he is the highest entity (*essentia*), and that is why he is immutable.[24]

From this it is clear that being, in the true sense of the term, means for Augustine that which is immutable and self-identical.

Whatever changes is not truly being because it contains an element of non-being; it both is and is not. It is what it is at the present moment, but it is not what it will become in the future. Anything existing in time lacks authentic being; it can better be described as *becoming*.

St. Augustine inherited this notion of being from Plotinus. He differs from the great Neoplatonist, however, in ascribing being to the First Principle of the universe. According to Plotinus, the First Principle is the One, and it is above being. Plotinus posited a trinity of universal causes: the One, from which all the rest proceeds; the Intellect or Being, which flows immediately from the One; and the World Soul, which is the cause of the material world. St. Augustine's Trinity, inspired by sacred Scripture, is quite different. It embraces the Father, the Verbum or Logos of the Father, and the Holy Spirit. The Persons of the Trinity are one in substance, or *ousia*, so that they share the same being.

CREATION

THE SENSIBLE WORLD and the soul itself cry out to St. Augustine that they have been created. Listening attentively to them, he hears them say: "We did not make ourselves, but he made us who abides forever." [25] Their very mutability demands an eternal, immutable being as their cause. This is the constant direction of St. Augustine's thought. His gaze never remains fixed upon the changing world but glances off at once to a transcendent world which is its stable and eternal ground.

The very forms and perfections we discover in creatures are but fleeting reflections of eternal Ideas in the mind of God. These are the models according to which God created all things. There are divine Ideas not only of species but also of all the individuals within a species; for example, of individual men. All things thus pre-exist in God in the shape of intelligible Ideas, somewhat as a work of art pre-exists in the mind of the artist. St. Augustine does not probe deeply the problem of reconciling the unity of God with the multiplicity of his Ideas. This is one of the many problems he bequeaths to later medieval speculation. Plotinus himself was

so acutely aware of the difficulty that he refused to attribute ideas
or knowledge to the One, because the One transcends all multiplicity. Augustine sees no difficulty in ascribing many Ideas to
God and in identifying them with God.

God created the universe not only through his Ideas—that is
to say, intelligently—but also freely. Why did he choose to create
the universe? He did so because of his goodness and his desire to
share with creatures a measure of that goodness. But, absolutely
speaking, he did not have to create. On this point, too, St. Augustine opposes Neoplatonism. For Plotinus the universe emanates
necessarily from the One; it is not created through God's free
choice. It is an eternal diffusion of the One. Not so for Augustine.
Intelligent and free, God created the universe out of nothing.
Matter itself is a creature of God. He did not merely impose form
on matter in creation, but brought out of nothing the very stuff
from which things are made. Consequently, matter is good, for
nothing created by God is evil. As a result, there is an optimism in
the thought of St. Augustine in contrast to the pessimism of the
Manichees, who considered matter to be substantially evil, and
of the Neoplatonists, who regarded matter as a principle of evil
and imperfection.

Like the Neoplatonists, St. Augustine distinguishes between an
unformed and a formed matter; but for him both have been created from nothing. Unformed matter is something in between being
and non-being. It is "almost nothing," or "not entirely nothing." [26]
It has minimal reality, but reality nonetheless. God did not create
this unformed matter by itself but endowed it immediately with
the various forms that give it order, harmony, and beauty. Besides
the corporeal matter of the visible universe, St. Augustine suggests that there is spiritual matter in angels and human souls.

Because the world was created, it had a beginning in time. For
time itself is a creature, and no creature is eternal. St. Augustine
never conceived the possibility of a created world eternal in time.
Does not Scripture tell us: *In the beginning God created heaven
and earth* (*Gen.* 1:1)? The obvious conclusion is that the universe
had a temporal beginning, and reason agrees with this. It is understandable why theologians and philosophers of the thirteenth cen-

tury who were nurtured on Augustinism were shocked by the Aristotelian doctrine of the eternity of the world and by the attempt of some scholastics to reconcile it with Scripture.

In commenting on *Genesis*, St. Augustine asks what Scripture means when it says that the world was created in six days. Was God's creation not complete on the first day? Did he have to add to his original work and perfect it little by little? According to St. Augustine, God created everything at once, although not in the same perfect state. In the beginning some things existed in perfect form, while others were created in embryo or in "seed," and only later reached their full development. Originally, then, the world was filled with "seeds" of things to come.[27] These Augustine calls "seminal principles" (*rationes seminales*)—a notion borrowed from the Stoics through Plotinus. Some historians consider this an anticipation of the modern doctrine of evolution. But St. Augustine has no notion of evolution in the modern sense, according to which one species has evolved from another. In St. Augustine's view, God implanted the seminal principle of each species in matter, so that in the course of time, under favorable circumstances, each might come, as it were, to full flower.

From a philosophical point of view the doctrine of seminal principles is significant for its bearing on the problem of causality. What exactly is the role of God and creatures in producing an effect? In the Augustinian view, all natural forms have been created by God and pre-exist in matter in their seminal principles. A created agent has no power to introduce forms into nature; it can only excite already existing forms to come into perfect being. The gardener plants and waters his garden, but in reality he does nothing; it is God who gives the increase. For St. Augustine, this Pauline dictum [28] holds good not only in the order of grace but also in nature. Parents, for example, who beget a child are nothing; God forms the infant. The mother who nourishes her child does not count for anything; God gives the increase. God is working continually in nature, activating seminal principles to develop the visible forms we see around us. There is no question of a secondary cause drawing a form from the potency of matter, as St. Thomas will teach. Creatures simply uncover forms planted in nature by

God at the moment of creation. Augustine's constant tendency is to minimize as far as possible the efficacy of creatures in order the more to exalt the power and creative activity of God. We have seen this tendency already in his account of knowledge: the divine action of illumination, not the human mind, is the real cause of truth. The doctrine of seminal principles shows the same concern to insure the supremacy and power of God and to emphasize the frailty and nothingness of creatures. We shall observe this same tendency in Augustine's ethics.

ETHICAL NOTIONS

THE PREDOMINANTLY ETHICAL CHARACTER of St. Augustine's thought has already been pointed out. He is concerned above all to find happiness, which he describes as "joy in truth." All the resources of his mind and heart are concentrated on this enterprise. That is why every discussion he begins leads spontaneously to God, who is Truth. Here is the center of his interest. Everything else has meaning and value only insofar as it draws him toward God and reveals him more clearly. The force attracting him to this center is love. Physical bodies are drawn to the center of the earth by their weight; Augustine is drawn to his center—God— by love. As he puts it cryptically: "My weight is my love." [29]

The reader of St. Augustine is often at a loss to find any system in his thought. There is none in the scholastic sense. He does not develop in a systematic and independent way the topics relevant to metaphysics, epistemology, the philosophy of nature, or ethics. All of these interest him, but only insofar as they recall the focal point of his interest—God—and excite in him the love uniting him to this center. It is the common reference to this center that gives order and unity to his many speculations and reflections. The unity of St. Augustine's thought is thus a unity created by love. Love and an ethics based on love are at the core of Augustinism.

The love that unites us to God is not simply a natural one; it is a supernatural gift bestowed on us by God himself. St. Augustine's personal experience with evil proved to him that we need God's grace in order to be good and to direct our love to its proper object. Fallen man has no strength of his own to choose the good. By himself, he is enslaved to his passions and to the sensible world, which distract him from his own soul and from God. St. Augustine does not deny that man in the state of sin retains his freedom of choice (*liberum arbitrium*), but he insists that in this state man does not enjoy liberty (*libertas*) because he cannot use his freedom as he should: he does not will the good, or, if he does, he cannot do the good that he wills. Liberty in the true sense is incompatible with sin; as Scripture tells us, he who sins is the slave of sin (*John* 8:34). Having lost his liberty by original sin, man can regain it only by the grace of God. But even then man can sin and lose at one stroke both grace and liberty. He enjoys perfect liberty only in the next life when he will be confirmed in grace and incapable of sinning.

Love, then, is at the center of the moral life of man—a fact that is hardly surprising when we remember that God himself is love (*I John* 4:16). Through the gift of love, God draws us to himself, and at the same time he implants in us all the other moral virtues that rectify our will with regard to God and our neighbor, for example the cardinal virtues of prudence, fortitude, temperance, and justice. In the doctrine of St. Augustine the problem of the origin of the moral virtues is similar to that of the origin of truth in the intellect. We have seen that the intellect, because of its changeableness, is incapable of knowing the truth without the illumination of the divine Ideas. So, too, the will, because of its weakness, is incapable of pursuing the good without an illumination of the divine virtues. In short, man requires a moral as well as an intellectual illumination. Let us see how this moral illumination is brought about.

God has given each of us a conscience by which we are aware of the moral law. In God himself resides the eternal law containing the prescriptions of divine reason, or the divine will, commanding that the natural order be preserved and forbidding that it be disturbed.[30] For example, it is the natural order that the lower be subject to the higher: that in man the body be subject to the soul, and that within the soul itself the senses be subject to reason, and reason to God. In order for us to be aware of these necessary rules, the immutable eternal law must illuminate our conscience and leave upon it its impression. The primary prescriptions thus imprinted upon us make up the natural law.[31]

But it is not sufficient for our conscience to be aware of the law; our will must be rectified so that it will yield to it and put it into practice. This rectification of the will is brought about by the illuminating action of the divine virtues. The virtues of prudence, fortitude, temperance, and justice are present in God, and they shine like lights upon our souls, establishing within them a similar moral order.[32] Through this moral illumination God truly becomes the life of the soul, vivifying and ordering it from within, as the soul in its own way gives life and order to the body.

THE CITY OF GOD

THUS VIVIFIED BY GOD, men are united to him by love. At the same time, through their common love of God, they are united to each other. They form a society or people which St. Augustine defines as "an association of rational beings united by a unanimous agreement upon the things they love." Love, then, is at the basis of a society, and the kind of love defines the society and makes it different from every other. Now basically there are two loves: love of God, and love of self and the world. These two loves produce two societies. The love of God unites men into a City of God, the love of the world unites them into a City of the World.[33]

The theme of St. Augustine's *The City of God* is the history of these two Cities from the dawn of creation to the end of the world. The occasion of its composition was the sack of Rome by the Goths in A.D. 410, an event of far-reaching significance, for it marked the end of the great Roman Empire. The pagans blamed the Christians for the fall of Rome. Did not Christianity teach renouncement of the world and turn citizens away from service to the state? Did it not inculcate forgiveness of enemies and thus weaken patriotism? Furthermore, the pagans argued that the destiny of Rome was bound up with the worship of her gods. These gods had abandoned her since the empire became Christian under Constantine, and the Christian God had failed to protect the city.

In 413 Augustine took up his pen and wrote his reply: *The City of God*. In the first part he answers the pagan charge: Rome perished because of the Christians. He shows that the fate of Rome is not unique in history; all great empires have fallen in the past. The decline and fall of earthly empires are due to their vices. In the case of Rome, it was corrupt before the coming of Christianity, as Roman authors like Sallust and Juvenal attest.

St. Augustine also argues that Christian doctrine, far from making bad citizens, produces good ones. It does not forbid giving oneself to the service of the state or dying in defense of one's country. As for Christian virtues, even pagans like Sallust and Cicero taught forgiveness of injuries. No, Christianity is not to blame for the downfall of the empire; dying paganism itself must shoulder that responsibility.

In the second part of *The City of God*, St. Augustine comes to his main point. He examines the nature of society (*civitas*) and traces the history of the two great societies found among men from the beginning of the world to the end: the City of God and the City of the World. It will be recalled that a man belongs to one City or the other, depending on his love. The City of God is a spiritual society whose head is Christ. Its members are all those—both men and angels—who love God in Christ and are predestined to reign eternally with him in heaven. The City of the World, on the other hand, embraces those who love the world and self rather than God and who are to suffer eternal punishment with the demons.

With the two societies thus defined, the opposition between them is absolute. In this life, however, their members are intermingled; we must wait for the last judgment for their complete separation. The City of the World is not identical with the state or civil society; members of the City of God also belong to temporal societies. Nor is the City of God identical with the Church; some members of the Church may fall away from faith and never reach heaven. True, St. Augustine sometimes includes certain historical empires in the City of the World, like Rome in its decadence. He also calls the Church the incarnation of the City of God, for it never ceases to aspire after the goods of heaven. But this is not meant to be a strict identification. It seems to depend on the prevailing and dominant will of a society whether it can be reckoned a part of one City or the other. Augustine's aim is not to distinguish between Church and state nor to define their relations. It is the more basic one of marking out, in the light of eternity, the two societies to which men and angels are committed by what is deepest in them; namely, their love.

The direction of St. Augustine's thought is always the same. Whether he examines nature or human history, it is not for itself in its temporal dimension, but from the viewpoint of the supratemporal and eternal. Seen in this light, the City of God appears as the very reason for creation. The whole of history is the unfolding of God's plan to build up the heavenly City until its final triumph at the end of the world.

The City of God had an enormous influence. It set the pattern for a theology of history; that is to say, a total view of history in the light of Christian doctrine, which many future historians would follow. It also inspired men to organize the earth into a single society made to the image and likeness of the heavenly City. Four centuries after St. Augustine, the Emperor Charlemagne founded his empire as the embodiment of the City of God on earth. And down through the ages men have dreamed of a perfect society for men, whether it was a religious ideal as in the case of Roger Bacon or Leibniz, or a secular one as in the case of the utopias of Campanella, Thomas More, or Karl Marx.[34]

CONCLUSION

MORE THAN ANY OTHER SINGLE WRITER, St. Augustine molded the medieval mind. Not until we meet St. Thomas Aquinas will we find a comparable intellectual giant; and St. Thomas himself is in a true sense a disciple of the bishop of Hippo. It is difficult to compare the two because their points of view are so different. From the standpoint of philosophy, what strikes one immediately is the Platonism of St. Augustine and the Aristotelianism of St. Thomas. Each found one of the two great Greek philosophies ready at hand to be used in the work of Christian wisdom. But each modified and transformed his Greek philosophical instrument through his own genius and in the light of Christian doctrine.

No Christian ever Platonized more courageously or cautiously than St. Augustine. His sound theological sense enabled him to use Platonism while avoiding the pitfalls it presents to less prudent Christian thinkers. St. Augustine seemed to know instinctively which Platonic insights are of value to Christian wisdom, which need to be modified and corrected, and which need to be rejected. It must be added, however, that many of the uncertainties, unresolved problems, and difficulties we find in Augustinism are due precisely to the weaknesses in his philosophical instrument.

A student approaching St. Augustine with some acquaintance with the scholastic theologians and philosophers of the thirteenth century will look in vain for their distinction between theology and philosophy, and between the various branches of philosophy itself. The student must be warned that the clear-cut distinctions of the scholastics will be achieved only under the influence of Aristotle in the thirteenth century. St. Augustine's own view of God and the world is not measured by these distinctions. It is more simple because more lofty. He sees all things, not in the specific light of philosophy or even of theological science, but in the light of the highest Christian wisdom and of charity.[35]

II

Boethius

WHEN ST. AUGUSTINE DIED in 430 the Germanic tribes from northern Europe were rapidly subduing the Roman Empire. Fifty years later they were its masters. Italy was then under the rule of the Ostrogoths (East Goths), who had been converted to Arian Christianity. This was the world Boethius was born into in the year 480.[1]

A student of Greek philosophy and a master of the Greek language, he was one of the most important channels by which Greek philosophical ideas were passed on to the Middle Ages. He was an orthodox Catholic but was shown favor by the Arian King Theodoric, who raised him to a high position at his court. There Boethius soon learned the fickleness of fortune. Accused of treason, he was imprisoned and executed on the orders of the king. Happily for the Middle Ages, his long imprisonment gave him an opportunity to set in order his thoughts on human happiness, chance, freedom, and God's foreknowledge of our free acts. The fruit of his meditation was the *Consolation of Philosophy*, one of the most popular books in the Middle Ages.

PHILOSOPHY AND ITS DIVISIONS

IN THE BEGINNING of his *Consolation of Philosophy*, Boethius paints an allegorical picture of philosophy. While he was languishing in prison, complaining of his bad fortune, the muses of poetry surrounded him and inspired him to write verses to drive away his melancholy. Suddenly philosophy appears to him in the guise of a noble lady. Her every detail is significant. Of venerable countenance, she appears above Boethius, with eyes of more than human keenness (philosophy transcends human nature). She is lively and vigorous; mature, but not of Boethius' own age and time (philosophy is perennial). Her stature is difficult to judge; she pierces the heavens and yet is on the level of mankind. Her garments are imperishable, finely woven by her own hands (philosophy is indestructible and independent). They have lost some of their luster (philosophy has become somewhat decadent), and they have been torn (by factions in philosophy). The Greek letter *pi* (π) is embroidered on the bottom of her dress (practical philosophy), the Greek letter *theta* (θ) at the top (theoretical philosophy). There are steps leading from one to the other (the two kinds of philosophy communicate with each other).

But Boethius is not content to describe philosophy allegorically; he also defines it and classifies its parts. The word "philosophy" means the love of wisdom. By wisdom is meant not simply a practical or speculative knowledge but the highest of all realities; namely, God. He is subsistent Wisdom, causing all other things to exist, illuminating men's minds with truth, and drawing them to himself by love. In short, for Boethius as for St. Augustine, philosophy is the pursuit and love of God.

Boethius divides philosophy into two kinds: theoretical, which is knowledge for its own sake, and practical, which is knowledge for the sake of action. He classifies theoretical philosophy in several ways. In the *De Trinitate*, 2, he adopts the Aristotelian division into natural philosophy, mathematics, and theology (not the theology based on sacred Scripture, but theology in the Aristotelian sense). These are distinguished by their objects, which are forms more or less separated from matter. Natural philosophy studies the forms of physical bodies along with the matter to which the forms are conjoined in reality. Since these bodies are in motion, their conjoined forms are also in motion. Mathematics studies the forms of bodies (for example, lines and triangles) without matter and motion, although these forms cannot really exist apart from bodies. Theology studies forms that are separate from matter and motion, such as God, angels, and human souls before their descent into bodies.[2]

To each of these three branches of philosophy Boethius attributes a distinct method of procedure. Natural philosophy uses the method of reason (*ratio*), mathematics the method of "learning" (*disciplina*), theology the method of intellect (*intellectus*).[3] Theology rises above the play of imagination and apprehends pure form, which is being itself and the source of all being, namely God. St. Thomas will use and transform all these notions in his commentary on Boethius' *De Trinitate*.

Boethius adopts the post-Aristotelian division of practical philosophy into three parts: ethics, politics, and economics. The first part teaches man how to conduct himself virtuously as an individual. The second teaches how the state is to be ruled according to the virtues of prudence, justice, fortitude, and temperance. The third sees to the virtuous conduct of the family.[4]

The position of logic is ambiguous in Boethius' scheme of the sciences. He considers it a necessary instrument for all the sciences, because it teaches us how to reason correctly and to arrive at true conclusions. But from another point of view he calls it a science and a branch of philosophy, because it has its own subject matter and it can be studied for its own sake apart from the use to which other sciences may put it. Logic is like a hand, which is both a part of the human organism and its instrument. Grammar and rhetoric, Boethius adds, are also of use in the sciences, not for the acquisition of knowledge but for its proper expression.[5]

Logic, grammar, and rhetoric are three of the liberal arts that formed the basis of Roman education and were passed on to the Middle Ages by Boethius. In the Carolingian period they were called the Trivium. Boethius gave the name "Quadrivium" to the other four liberal arts: arithmetic, geometry, astronomy, and music.[6] He wrote treatises on all the arts of the Quadrivium, with the exception of astronomy. His pupil Cassiodorus (*c.* 480–575) wrote extensively on all the seven liberal arts,[7] as did also Martianus Capella (*c.* 400–439),[8] and Isidore of Seville (d. 636).[9]

GOD

IN HIS *Consolation of Philosophy* Boethius offers a description of God and a brief proof of his existence. God is the being who is supremely good and the source of all good things. We are sure that such a being exists, for anything is called imperfect because of the privation of some perfection. So whenever some imperfection is found, there must be a corresponding perfection. "Nature," Boethius writes, "does not make a beginning with things mutilated and imperfect; she starts with what is whole and perfect and falls away later to these feeble and inferior productions." [10] We cannot doubt, then, that God exists and that he is the most perfect of all beings—a conclusion that agrees with the common belief of mankind.

Since God is supremely good, he is supremely happy. For happiness is that perfect state in which everything good is united. God is happiness itself, for he is goodness itself. And just as no being can be good except by sharing in God's goodness, so no being can be happy unless he shares in God's happiness. The theme of Book III of the *Consolation of Philosophy* is that man's natural desire for happiness cannot be fulfilled by any partial goods, such as fame, riches, or pleasure, but only by the total good or God. Only by participating in God, and in a sense becoming divine, can man possess all that is good, and only then is he happy.

THE SOUL AND KNOWLEDGE

BOETHIUS ACCEPTS Plato's doctrine of the pre-existence of souls and their fall into bodies. Souls previously existed with the angels, but they entered bodies, thereby losing their happiness and purity of intelligence.

Several poems of the *Consolation of Philosophy* are inspired by this Platonic doctrine. Boethius compares the soul to a bird shut up in a cage. Previously the bird sang in the lofty trees. Men try to make up for her loss of freedom by offering her sweet foods. But when she sees the outdoor meadows she forgets her food and yearns to be free again. The soul is also compared to a tender plant forcibly bent down to the earth. When released, it springs back toward heaven (III, poem 2).

Another poem has for its theme Plato's doctrine of reminiscence. He who pursues the truth must search for it within himself by the interior light in deep meditation. If he is to possess the true treasure of his soul, he must repress the tendency to turn his gaze to the sensible world. Truth lies hidden within the soul; its light has been darkened by the soul's contact with the body, but not completely extinguished. Learning consists in recovering this lost treasure by the soul's reflection upon itself. The poem concludes: "If Plato's teaching erreth not, We learn but what we have forgot" (III, poem 11, see prose 12).

In still another poem Boethius opposes the notion that the mind is passive in knowing and that it receives its knowledge from the sensible world. The Stoics, Boethius says, taught that the living mind is like a written page whose letters have been inscribed by sense experience. In fact, the mind is an active power, dividing and combining, grasping each whole presented by the senses and analyzing it into parts. This is hardly consistent with the Stoic description of mind as a mirror passively reflecting the external world (v, poem 4).

The senses, however, do have a role in knowledge. The body through the senses stirs the soul's intelligence. "The qualities of external objects," Boethius explains, "affect the sense-organs, and the activity of the mind is preceded by a bodily movement that calls forth the mind's action upon itself and stimulates the forms until then lying inactive within" (v, prose 5). Far from being a blank sheet on which the sense world inscribes its message, the mind is filled with hidden ideas that need only the stimulation of the senses to become objects of our knowledge. Ideas are not abstracted from the sense world; we are born with them as memories of a previous existence.

In our present state reason is our highest power. Below it in the scale of cognitive faculties are sense and imagination; above it is intelligence, which is a divine faculty. The object of sense is a figure clothed in matter; for instance, the shape of a man in the human substance. Imagination pictures the human figure alone without matter. Reason transcends the figure and contemplates the universal nature contained in the individual; for instance, humanity in individual men. The eye of intelligence sees beyond all these powers. Transcending the whole universe, it beholds simple forms in themselves. The human soul, once capable of such intellectual intuitions of pure forms, is now forced to use the faculty of reason because of its confinement to the body and the senses. Occasionally, however, it receives brief glimpses of its true home and mode of knowing and it longs to return to them.

THE PROBLEM OF UNIVERSALS

FROM THE *Consolation of Philosophy* it is clear that Boethius' doctrine of knowledge is Platonic. He does not agree with Aristotle that universal ideas are abstracted from the sense world; rather, we are born with them as impressions of pure forms seen in the divine mind in a previous life.

In this work, however, Boethius does not raise the problem of the nature of universals. His classic formulation of this problem is found in his second commentary on Porphyry's *Isagoge* (Introduction to Aristotle's *Categories*). All later medieval philosophers will be indebted to him for the terms in which he states it.

Following Porphyry, Boethius asks three questions about universals. First, are genera and species and other universals realities or simply conceptions of the mind? Second, if they are realities, are they corporeal or incorporeal? Third, if they are incorporeal, do they exist apart from sensible things or in union with them? Porphyry himself refused to answer these "more lofty questions" in his work designed for beginners in logic. Boethius does not show the same restraint but attempts to satisfy the reader first by explaining the difficulty of the problem and then by resolving it.

The central problem concerning universals is whether they are real or simply conceptions of the mind. These appear to be the only alternatives, and yet both seem to be impossible. If the species "man" or the genus "animal" were a reality, it would be one single reality, for everything real is one in number. But "man" and "animal" are common to many at one and the same time: "man" is common to many individual men, "animal" to many species. We should notice, too, the way in which they are common: each individual possesses the species entirely (each man is wholly man), and each species possesses the genus entirely (each species of animal is wholly animal). The universal is not common to many by parts, as though each possessed only a part of the genus or species. Neither is it common as a servant or horse is used by many at different times or as a theater is common to all who attend it. The species and genus constitute the very substance of the things to which they are common. Since by definition a universal is common to many in this way, it cannot be one, and hence it cannot be a reality.

It seems equally impossible for universals to be simply concepts in the mind. For if they are concepts, they either correspond to some reality or they do not. The first supposition is ruled out because, as we have seen, there cannot be a universal reality. The second possibility is equally to be rejected, for if no reality corresponds to our universal concept, it does not represent reality as it is, and consequently the concept is false. It appears, then, that universals are neither realities nor concepts.

In order to escape from this dilemma, Boethius turns to Alexander of Aphrodisias (c. A.D. 200), a Greek commentator on Aristotle. Alexander assures us that in order to be true, our concepts need not represent things as they are in reality. We can form, for example, a true concept of a line apart from a body, although a line cannot exist separate from a body. Falsity arises only when we combine in our mind what is not combined in reality, as when we join horse and man in our imagination and construct a centaur. Now the senses present things to us in a state of mixture and confusion. They transmit, besides bodies themselves, all the incorporeal realities present in them, such as lines, surfaces, and other qualities. Our mind has the power to abstract these incorporeal realities from bodies and to consider them in themselves.

Now genera and species are realities of this sort. Incorporeal in themselves, they exist in sensible bodies, but they can be understood apart from them. How is this possible? We observe the substantial likeness of several individuals, and when this likeness is conceived by the intellect, it becomes a species. A species is the concept formed from the substantial likeness of individuals unlike in number. For example, observing individual men we see they are alike in being human, and this likeness conceived by the mind is the species "man." A genus, in turn, is the concept gathered from the likeness of different species. In individual things these likenesses are sensible, but when they are conceived by the intellect they become intelligible. Consequently, universals have two modes of being: in reality and in thought. In reality they exist in sensible bodies, but in the mind they can be thought of apart from these bodies.

This is Aristotle's solution of the problem of universals as interpreted by Alexander of Aphrodisias. It differs from that of Plato, Boethius says, because Plato taught that genera, species, and other universals are not only *known* separately from bodies but also *exist* outside of them. In his commentary on Porphyry's *Isagoge* Boethius refuses to judge which of these views is correct, reserving this for a loftier branch of philosophy than logic. He explains that in the present work he has set forth Aristotle's doctrine at some length, not because he especially approves of it, but because the book on which he is commenting is an introduction to Aristotle's *Categories*.

Boethius' refusal to accept the Aristotelian doctrine of universals does not come as a surprise, in view of the Platonism of the *Consolation of Philosophy*. The conception of knowledge in this work is not Aristotelian but Platonic. Boethius denies that the intellect is passive and receptive of ideas from the sensible world and adopts the Platonic doctrine of innate ideas. Through the power of reason we recognize universal natures in individuals, but through the power of intellect we can contemplate pure forms existing outside the universe in the divine mind. This shows that Boethius does not accept the Aristotelian doctrine of abstraction, nor does he limit the existence of universal forms to sensible reality. But even though he rejects Aristotle's doctrine of universals, his explanation of it (in the interpretation of Alexander of Aphrodisias) was destined to have a considerable influence on medieval philosophy. It gave the early Middle Ages some conception of the Aristotelian doctrine

of universals, pending the discovery of Aristotle's own works in
the twelfth and thirteenth centuries.

THE STRUCTURE OF REALITY

BOETHIUS, LIKE PORPHYRY, realizes that the problem of universals is more than a logical one; it is fundamentally metaphysical,
since its solution rests upon the nature of being or reality.

In the *De Trinitate*, 2, Boethius tells us that everything owes
its being (*esse*) to form. For instance, a statue is not a statue on
account of the brass which is its matter, but on account of its likeness to a living thing which is its form. So, too, earth is what it is,
not because of primary, formless matter, but because of dryness
and weight, which are forms. So nothing is said to be because it
has matter, but because it has a distinctive form. Form determines
a thing to be the kind of thing it is, and in so doing gives the thing
its being (*esse*).

God is pure form without matter; he lacks all composition and
hence is absolutely one. Creatures, on the other hand, are constituted of parts. Man, for instance, consists of both soul and body.
He is neither soul nor body taken separately. Boethius expresses
this by saying that creatures are not "what they are"; that is to say,
they are not identical with any of their parts. God, however, is
absolutely simple, and so he is identical with what he is.

Boethius goes further into the distinction between God and creatures in his *De Hebdomadibus*. In a creature, being (*esse*) is different from "that which is" (*id quod est*).[11] "That which is" is a
concrete individual, constituted of parts. An individual man, for
example, is compounded of animality, rationality, as well as many
accidental characteristics differentiating him from other men. All
of these together constitute the concrete existing individual. His
being (*esse*) is his humanity, for humanity is the form that makes
him to be essentially what he is, namely a man.[12] Consequently, the
specific essence of a creature differs from the concrete individual.
God, on the other hand, is absolutely simple: his being and that
which he is are identical.

St. Thomas will use the Boethian formula, "Being is different

from that which is," to express the real distinction in creatures between their act of existing and essence, in contrast to God, in whom
these two are identical. In Boethius' own mind, the formula expresses the distinction in creatures between their specific essence
and individual substance.

An individual thing is a substance because it underlies (substands)
accidents. If the individual substance is of a rational nature, it is
a person. Subsistence is not identical with substance. A thing has
subsistence if, unlike an accident, it does not need a subject in which
to exist. Genera and species have subsistence; they do not require
a subject in which to exist. But they are not substances, for they
do not underlie accidents. The species "humanity," for example,
is a subsistent reality, but it is not a substance. Peter, on the other
hand, is a substance, because he is the subject of accidents.[13]

A substance can be the "same" in three different senses. It can be
the same as another substance in genus; a man, for example, is the
same as a horse because of their common genus "animal." It can be
the same in species, as Cato is the same as Cicero because of their
common species "man." Finally, it can be the same in number, as
Tully is the same as Cicero, these being two names for the same
individual. Similarly, things are "different" in three ways: in genus,
species, and number. Numerical difference is the result of a variety
of accidents. Three men are the same in genus and species, but they
are different in number because of their distinctive combinations
of accidents. They differ at least by the accident of place, for no
two bodies can occupy the same place.[14]

In an individual substance, accordingly, there is a combination
of several subsistent forms and accidents. To be more precise,
Boethius calls these "images" rather than forms. Strictly speaking,
forms cannot exist in matter, but only their reflections or images.
Pure forms are Ideas in the divine mind; the forms we see in the
sensible world are participations of the divine Ideas.[15]

We are now in a position to understand Boethius' answer to the
problems Porphyry raised concerning universals. 1] Universals
are not simply concepts of the mind; they are subsistent realities.
2] They are incorporeal, because in themselves they have no matter
and they are not extended in three dimensions. 3] They do not

subsist outside individual things, except as Ideas in the mind of God
and in our mind.

FREE WILL AND PROVIDENCE

WHILE BOETHIUS WAS IN PRISON, Lady Philosophy consoled
him by telling him that he would be happy if he accepted the will
of God. His sufferings were a part of God's providence. If he
accepted them freely, he would still enjoy liberty even though he
were confined to prison. We are most free when we submit ourselves to God's providence. We are slaves to the degree that we
turn to the sensible world and let our souls be dominated by the
passions of the body.

But how are we free if God exercises providence over all things,
including our actions? If he infallibly foresees what we will do, how
are we free to choose otherwise? Can human freedom be reconciled with God's providence? This is the problem Boethius takes
up in Book V of the *Consolation of Philosophy*.

Boethius first asks Philosophy if chance exists, and if so, what it
is. Philosophy replies that there is no chance if we mean by that
something that occurs without a cause. Everything has a cause;
nothing comes from nothing. God is the first cause of everything
that happens, so that in relation to him nothing happens by chance.

Boethius then asks whether chance has any meaning at all. Philosophy replies that it does have meaning in relation to us. Suppose
a man digs into the earth and finds buried gold. His finding the
gold was accidental and by chance, but it was not uncaused. It was
caused by the hiding of the money and the digging in the earth. It
was a chance occurrence because of the unintended meeting of these
two causes. With respect to us, then, there is chance, but not with
respect to God, who disposes all things in their due times and places.

But how can man be free if God foresees and disposes all his actions? The fact of man's freedom is clear from his possession of
reason. By nature man has the use of reason and hence he can discriminate in judgment. He can distinguish between what is to be
avoided and what is to be desired. Consequently, he can seek out
what he judges desirable and avoid what he thinks undesirable. It

is clear from this that beings endowed with reason also possess the faculty of free choice. But it seems contradictory that man is free and yet that God foreknows everything that he will do. If God foresees infallibly everything that will happen, it seems that it must necessarily happen.

The root of the difficulty is that we think that God's knowledge is like our own. We can foresee with certainty only what necessarily happens. For us there can be no certain foreknowledge of a free action, because the action is not yet determined. Neither, therefore, can our knowledge of it be certain and determined. God's knowledge is different from ours. He does not know in time, just as he does not exist in time; he lives and knows in the eternal present. Eternity is the total, perfect, and simultaneous possession of unending life. So there is no before and after in God's life or knowledge. Strictly speaking, he does not foreknow; he simply knows or sees. All events in time are eternally and simultaneously present to him. He sees in the eternal present some things happening necessarily and others happening freely or by chance. We see the sun rising, but this does not make it rise or make the event necessary. Similarly, God sees all events together in the eternal present, and his knowledge of our free acts does not impose necessity on them.

CONCLUSION

BOETHIUS SET OUT to translate into Latin the complete philosophical literature of the Greeks. He fell far short of his goal, for he translated only the logical works of Porphyry and Aristotle, and not even all of these continued to be known in the early Middle Ages. However, his translations and commentaries were important, for they taught the Middle Ages the rudiments of Aristotelian logic and many philosophical terms and definitions that became part of the intellectual heritage of the West. Boethius' ambitious task was taken up by others in the succeeding centuries, and by the middle of the thirteenth century an impressive part of Greek philosophy, including the complete works of Aristotle, was made available to the Latin world.

Boethius' stature as a philosopher must be judged not only by these logical works but especially by his *Consolation of Philosophy* and theological treatises. These are works of a fine speculative mind that influenced the whole history of medieval thought. It is interesting to note that the *Consolation of Philosophy* had a considerable influence upon English literature. As early as the ninth century King Alfred translated it into Anglo-Saxon, and in the fourteenth century Chaucer translated it and used some of its ideas in his *Canterbury Tales.*

III

John Scotus Erigena

AFTER THE DEATH of Boethius three centuries elapsed before another philosopher of outstanding genius and originality arrived on the scene. He was John Scotus Erigena, the only Irishman we shall meet in our history of medieval philosophy.[1] In the middle of the ninth century he was the master of the Palace School of the Emperor of the Franks, Charles the Bald. A speculative thinker of bold and comprehensive views, he produced one of the greatest theological and philosophical syntheses in the early Middle Ages—a forerunner of the immense *Summae* of the thirteenth century.

Erigena was not the first schoolmaster to cross the English Channel to teach on the Continent. He was preceded by a number of both Irish and English, the greatest of whom was Alcuin.[2] In 782 Alcuin came from York to become the headmaster of Charlemagne's Palace School. Through his genius as a teacher and organizer he enabled Charlemagne to realize his ambition of restoring the school system of western Europe, which for centuries had been overrun by waves of barbarian invaders. Alcuin was not gifted with a genius for philosophy, but he was a man of vision with extraordinary ability as a reformer and organizer. Through his initiative, schools were opened attached to monasteries and cathedrals. These were to be the great centers of learning in the eleventh and twelfth centuries, until they were supplanted by the universities in the thirteenth. Alcuin was thus one of the creators of medieval culture and civilization. He knew and loved pagan classical literature and passed it on to the later Middle Ages. In his own

view, he was building a new Athens, more excellent than the old
one because it was ennobled by the teaching of Christ. The classical culture of Greece, after passing to Rome, had been transferred
to England and Ireland through Roman missionaries like St.
Augustine of Canterbury. Finally it returned to the Continent with
men like Alcuin and Erigena. Medieval writers referred to this
journey of classical thought from Athens to western Europe as the
"transference of learning" (*translatio studii*).

PHILOSOPHY AND FAITH

THE DECISIVE EVENT in Erigena's philosophical career was his
reading and translating of some writings of Greek Neoplatonist
theologians: Gregory of Nyssa (*fl.* 379–394), Maximus the Confessor (*c.* 580–662), and especially Dionysius the Pseudo-Areopagite.
Throughout the Middle Ages this obscure Dionysius was thought
to be—as indeed he pretended to be—the Dionysius converted by
St. Paul at the Athenian Areopagus (*Acts* 17:34). We know now
that he was greatly influenced by the Neoplatonist Proclus (410–
485) and that he was probably a Syrian monk who lived about
A.D. 500.

Through these writers Erigena received a Neoplatonist philosophical formation. In this regard his case is similar to that of St.
Augustine, who imbibed Neoplatonism through the writings of
Plotinus and Porphyry. However, Erigena's use of Neoplatonist
ideas is more daring and spectacular than Augustine's. A less profound theologian than the Bishop of Hippo, he sometimes allows
his Neoplatonism to distort rather than to illuminate the teachings
of faith.

Erigena's purpose, however, is not essentially different from St.
Augustine's. For both of them the goal of life is joy in knowing
the truth revealed in sacred Scripture. "O Lord Jesus," he writes,
"I ask of you no other reward, no other happiness, no other joy,
than to understand your words, inspired by the Holy Spirit, correctly and without any error of deceiving speculation." [3] Philosophy is nothing else than understanding sacred Scripture. "What
else is philosophy," he writes, "except the explaining of the rules

of true religion, by which God, the highest and principal cause of all things, is both worshipped humbly and investigated rationally?" [4]

Like St. Augustine, then, Erigena identifies philosophy with religion. No wonder he can write: "No one can enter heaven except by philosophy"! [5]

Erigena describes three stages in man's search for truth. Before the coming of Christ, reason was obscured by original sin. In this stage men were limited to the rational investigation of the world and demonstration of the existence of its creator. After Christ's coming, reason is not our only source of truth; we have revelation, which must be accepted on faith. Reason now has the task of exploring rationally the content of revelation and of making faith effective in our lives. Reason must bow to the authority of Scripture, but this is not a humiliation for reason; on the contrary, it is of the greatest assistance to it. Nor can right reason contradict true authority, because they both come from the same source; namely, divine reason.

Erigena illustrates the relation of faith and reason by the following allegory. We are told in Scripture that after the resurrection of Christ both Peter and John ran to the tomb. The tomb is Scripture; Peter is faith; John is reason. John outruns Peter and gets to the tomb first, but Peter is the first to enter. So, too, faith must precede the understanding of Scripture; reason comes after and helps us to explore its contents.[6]

The third stage of man in his search for truth is heaven, where he shall see Christ, who is the Truth. Faith will then disappear and vision will take its place.

The aim of philosophy is thus wholly spiritual and religious: it is the illumination of faith through human reason, moving toward the vision of Christ's divinity. What makes the journey so adventuresome is that the means chosen to achieve this completely Christian end are the techniques of Neoplatonic philosophy.

THE DIVISION OF NATURE

ERIGENA'S CHIEF WORK, the *Division of Nature*, is a vast synthesis of Christian thought organized by Neoplatonic dialectic.

God, the cause of all things, is presented as supreme Unity. Creation is the procession of the many from this Unity. It is a process of *division*, by which reality descends from the divine unity, unfolds in a cascade of essences of decreasing universality and increasing multiplicity until individual things are reached. Creatures are finally described as retracing their path and returning to God by a process called *analysis*.

Division and analysis are well-known methods of handling our concepts. By division we derive many less universal concepts from a more universal one. For example, we can divide "substance" into "corporeal" and "incorporeal," "corporeal substance" into "living" and "non-living," "living corporeal substance" into "rational" and "irrational," and "rational substance" into "Peter," "Paul," and so on. By analysis we can resolve these concepts back into the unity of "substance." For Erigena, however, division and analysis are not simply methods of ordering our concepts among themselves; they are the laws of nature itself. Division is the process by which the universe with its vast multiplicity proceeds from the unity of God; analysis is the process by which it returns to that unity. Thus Erigena, like Hegel, identifies the laws of reality with the laws of thought.

Following these laws, nature falls into four divisions: 1] nature which creates and is not created,   2] nature which is created and which creates,   3] nature which is created and does not create,   4] nature which does not create and is not created. These four divisions can be reduced to two: God and creatures. The first division is God considered as the creator of all things. The fourth is the same God considered as no longer creating but drawing all things back to him. The second division covers the divine Ideas, which are created by God and which in turn create individual things. The third division embraces the individuals created by the divine Ideas.[7]

Erigena calls this a division of *nature*, not of *being* or *reality*. The reason for this is that "nature" is a broader term than "being"; some things are included in nature that are not beings in the strict sense of the term.[8] A being is anything that can be understood by the intellect or perceived by the senses. This excludes God, for he cannot be the object of intellect or sense. Sensible things can be perceived by the senses, but, unlike ideas, they cannot be grasped by the intellect. So they too are not being, relative to the divine Ideas.[9]

After this preliminary explanation of terms, we can proceed to examine in detail each of the four divisions of nature.

GOD AND CREATION

THE SOURCE OF REALITY is an incomprehensible and ineffable God. Owing to the excellence of his nature, he is beyond the reach of man's senses and intellect and cannot be expressed or defined in human terms or categories. This is hardly surprising, since God infinitely transcends creatures. But Erigena goes farther than this. God is not only incomprehensible to us; he is incomprehensible to himself. The divine nature, he says, is unknown even to itself: *sibi ipsi incognita.*[10] Erigena's reason for saying this is not too difficult to see. Anything comprehensible can be circumscribed within limits or defined. But God is infinite; that is to say, without limits. And this is true not only with regard to us but also with regard to God himself. So he cannot comprehend or define himself any more than we can. This, of course, is not to impute any imperfection to God, but to insure his absolute transcendence and infinity. Erigena writes: "How can the divine nature understand what it is, when it is no-thing? For it transcends everything that is. God does not know what he is because he is not a 'what.' Both to himself and to every intellect he is incomprehensible in anything." [11]

This line of reasoning is valid if we accept the implied notions of being and knowledge. A being is a limited "something," definable in definite terms. Knowledge is the comprehension or definition of such a being. From this it follows logically that God rises above being and knowledge because of his infinity.[12]

But how can we talk about God if we do not know what he is? What is the meaning of the many names given to God in sacred Scripture? In solving the problem of the divine names Erigena is faithful to his Neoplatonic sources, especially to Dionysius. We first affirm names of God. We say, for instance, that he is a substance and that he is good and great. In doing this we affirm certain categories of God. But we know that in fact he is not confined to any category. So we must immediately deny these names of him. We must say that he is not a substance and that he is not good or great.

These affirmations and negations are equally justified. In a sense God is all things, for he created them. As works of art can be attributed to the artist who made them, so all creatures can be attributed to God. Yet he is superior to his creations, and so we should deny that he is any one of them.

The superiority of God to creatures is expressed by the word "super." We can say that God is good because he is the author of all good things. But since he is not identical with any of these, we must deny that he is good. He is in fact more-than-good. This last assertion includes the other two, but it is really a negative, not a positive, statement. It may appear to assert something of God, but the affirmation is only apparent. In saying that God is super-good we do not say what he is, but rather what he is not.[13]

The divine self-incomprehensibility is the reason for creation. In his innermost depths God dwells in obscurity and darkness. In order for him to know himself there must be something that will reveal him, and this must be something finite and comprehensible; in short, a creature. Creation is thus required in order that God may become known to himself. It is God's self-manifestation. It is also his self-creation, for through creation God begins to be some *thing*, whereas before he was no-*thing*.

THE DIVINE IDEAS

THE FIRST CREATURES OF GOD, or divine manifestations, are the divine Ideas. Erigena writes: "The divine nature is created by itself in the primordial causes [i.e., the divine Ideas]. In this way it creates itself, that is, it begins to appear in its theophanies [i.e., divine appearances], for it wishes to emerge from the most hidden recesses of its nature in which it is unknown even to itself. I mean that it does not know itself in anything, because it is infinite and super-natural and super-essential and above everything that can be understood. But it descends into the principles of things; and as it were by creating itself it begins to be in something."[14]

The divine Ideas are the primal exemplars or prototypes of all things. They exist in God—more precisely in the Second Person of the Trinity, the Word or Wisdom of the Father. Like the number one, which is simple and yet contains implicitly all numbers, the divine Ideas in the Word form a unity that embraces an infinite multiplicity of Ideas arranged according to a definite hierarchical order. This order, however, does not appear or unfold until the Ideas are realized in the universe. According to this order, the first Idea created by God in the divine Word is that of goodness; then follow the Ideas of essence or being, life, reason, intelligence, wisdom, virtue, beatitude, truth, and so on.[15]

As existing in God the Ideas are eternal, for he was never without them. But they are not absolutely coeternal with God, for they depend on him as their cause. What is truly eternal has no beginning. The divine Ideas have a beginning in their creator, and hence they are not truly eternal but participate in eternity.[16]

Why does Erigena teach that the divine Ideas are creations of God? Why does he not identify them with God, as St. Augustine and St. Thomas Aquinas do? His reason is clear. Each Idea is a limited form or essence, different from every other Idea. To say that God is identical with his Ideas is to place limitation and multiplicity in him. If God is one, he cannot be identical with his Ideas, which are manifold. Again, if God is infinite, he cannot be identical with his finite Ideas. As a Christian, Erigena knows that the Ideas are in God and not in a world apart, but he does not see how they can be identical with God without destroying his unity and infinity.

We are now in a better position to understand why the divine nature is incomprehensible. Since God transcends his own Ideas, he also transcends knowledge, of which Ideas are the medium. He must descend to create Ideas in order to know himself. Furthermore, we can understand why he transcends being. Being is one of the divine Ideas. It is not the first of the Ideas, for in Platonic fashion Erigena places goodness before being, but it is none the less a created Idea. Being is found, therefore, only at the level of creatures; and since God rises above his creatures he also rises above being. He is super-being as he is super-good.

In this, the God of Erigena bears a striking resemblance to the One of Plotinus. He is that One dressed up in Christian garb. Like the Plotinian One, he is the source of being and knowledge while transcending both in his innermost nature.[17]

Erigena has been accused of being a pantheist because of his daring statements identifying God with the being of creatures. For example, he calls God "the being of all things." [18] But in fact he does not identify God with his creatures, not even with the divine Ideas. He raises God so far above beings that no confusion between them is possible. When he calls God the being of all things, he means that God gives being to everything. But God himself is not identical with his creation. "God is not the whole of his creation," Erigena writes, "nor is his creation part of God; and conversely creation is not the whole of God, nor is God a part of his creation." [19]

MAN AND THE UNIVERSE

CREATION IS A CONTINUOUS PROCESS, beginning with God and ending with individual things. Some of these individuals are pure spirits (angels); others are material; and still others combine both spirit and matter (human beings). With individuals, creation comes to a close: they are the natures which are created and do not create. The direction of creation is always from the one to the many and from the more universal to the less universal. This is true even among the divine Ideas. The most general Ideas are divided into genera, genera into sub-genera, sub-genera into species. Individuals flow in turn from species. The whole process can be compared to the radiation of light from a central source. As the light diffuses it becomes more widespread and also weaker, until it can no longer illuminate. Matter is the point at which this illumination, which started with God, comes to an end.

Among the Ideas created in the divine mind the Idea of man is of special importance. The Idea of man is Humanity in all its perfection and excellence. The true man, Erigena says, is "an intellectual notion eternally produced in the divine mind." [20] Thus the true substance of man exists in the second division of nature among the divine Ideas.

How did man begin to exist in the third division; that is to say, divided into individual human beings? If he had not sinned, he would have multiplied like the angels, whose division took place in a purely spiritual manner. No division of sexes would have been needed for the multiplication of the human race.[21] In fact, we know from Scripture that man did sin. He was created in Paradise, which signifies, not an earthly garden, but the beauty of the divine image in man. But he ceased to contemplate the divine truth and separated himself from God. With this, he lost the perfection of the divine image and sank to the level of an animal. As a result, the division of the sexes arose, as well as the vast diversity of qualities, thoughts, customs, times, and places which now characterize human beings.[22]

The fall of man had a further consequence: it brought with it the fall of the whole universe. The world as we now know it, divided into myriad individuals, all of which are subject to generation and corruption, is the result of original sin.

The reason for this is that the universe originally existed in man; hence its fate was bound up with his. When God created the ideal man in the divine mind, he endowed him with the knowledge of all things. Knowledge is thus innate in man; it is only because of his alienation from God by sin that he must acquire knowledge gradually. The whole intelligible and sensible universe existed in man before it became externalized in the present world. Moreover, in that ideal condition the universe was more perfect than in its present state of division and dispersal.[23] When man fell from God, individual human beings came into existence, and as a consequence the other species existing in man became divided as well. The sensible world as we now know it came into being.

What is a sensible substance? It is a certain nature existing in space and time and subject to generation and corruption. It also has quantity and quality. It is therefore composed of several parts; namely, a nature and several accidents. The formed body can be perceived by the senses, but each of its component parts is solely an object of the intellect.[24] So the analysis of a material thing leads us to the surprising conclusion that it is composed of immaterial parts. In fact, material bodies are formed by the coming together of certain incorporeal and intelligible realities. "Visible matter joined to form," Erigena writes, "is nothing else than the coming together of certain accidents." [25]

In what sense, if any, is a sensible substance real? Erigena compares it to a shadow caused by light and a body.[26] A shadow, he says, is not nothing; it is something. To be more precise, it is an appearance. When light and a body come together the shadow appears; when they are separated the shadow disappears, but it still remains in its causes. So, too, a visible body is an appearance caused by the coming together ("coagulation") of certain causes, each of which is immaterial and intelligible. It ceases to appear when these causes no longer converge, but it still remains in them potentially. In the last analysis, then, the material world is reduced to an appearance of reality. Reality itself is immaterial and intelligible, and it is found in the realm of Ideas. We have seen that God rises above reality because of his unity and infinity. We can now see that visible matter falls below the level of reality because of its confusion and lack of intelligibility.

Basically immaterial, the universe of Erigena is well designed to fulfill the function he demands of it; namely, to reveal the invisible God. It is a vast system of symbols, all of which are apt subjects of religious contemplation. And this is indeed Erigena's main concern. He is not interested in studying the nature of the physical world for its own sake. He is looking rather for the traces of God in nature so that he can mount the ladder of creation and return to God.

THE RETURN TO GOD

UP TO THE PRESENT we have been considering the process of division by which creatures proceed from God. We shall now turn our attention to the reverse process—analysis—by which they return to him. With this, we reach the fourth division of nature: God as the end of all things.

As soon as creatures leave the unity of God they aspire to return
to it. Away from that unity, they are deficient and restless. This
is true not only of intelligent creatures, like men, but also of the
material universe, which unconsciously aspires to God. The soul
itself can be called "a movement toward God" (*motus circa Deum*).
So the whole process of division and analysis has the same starting
point and goal. "For the end of the whole movement," Erigena
writes, "is its beginning, since it is terminated by no other end
than its principle, from which its movement begins and to which
it constantly desires to return, that it may halt and rest in it." [27]

The return to God begins with man's death—the point beyond
which no further dispersal of man is possible. The next step will
be the resurrection of bodies, which will return to their souls and
be spiritualized in them. Fallen man, however, cannot bring about
his own resurrection. For this he needs Christ, his savior, whose
resurrection is a pledge of our own. Grace as well as nature is
thus required for man's complete return to God. [28] After the resurrection, man's soul will return to the unity of the Idea of man
from which it came forth. At the same time the whole material
universe will go back to the unity of man from which it came. As
all things were created in man and have fallen with him, so they
will be saved through him. In the end all things will be absorbed
in God: "For God will be all in all when there will be nothing but
God alone." [29]

The return of man and the universe to God does not entail their
annihilation in God. Air does not cease to be air when illumined
by the sun, nor does iron cease to be iron when it glows in the fire.
So, too, the body remains a body when spiritualized in the soul,
and the soul retains its identity when transfigured in the light of
God. The return of man to God does not result in a mingling of
their substances, but in a reunion without change or confusion. [30]
In this way Erigena attempts to preserve the individual personalities
of men in God.

Moral evil will disappear when the cosmic return is complete,
and physical suffering will end when men are spiritualized in God.
All men will then become pure spirits; yet the wicked will be punished eternally. Their punishment will not be physical, however,

but adapted to their spiritual condition. The only real punishment for a spirit is ignorance of the truth. Some men will be damned because they will never know Christ, who is the Truth.[31]

Erigena's *Division of Nature* enjoyed a considerable popularity in the Middle Ages, although it begot no school or movement to keep its ideas alive. There are traces of its influence in the early thirteenth century, when Amaury of Bène made use of its rather unguarded and fantastic language. It was condemned in 1225 by Pope Honorius III for teaching the following errors: 1] all things are God; 2] the divine Ideas are created and create; 3] at the end of the world the sexes will be abolished.

Erigena made a quite uncritical use of Neoplatonism, which did not always serve the purpose of Christian wisdom. Revealed doctrine fits poorly in the Procrustean bed of Neoplatonic dialectic. However, his work constitutes a landmark in medieval thought. Through his translations of Dionysius, Gregory of Nyssa, and Maximus, and through his original writings, he passed on to the Latin world Greek theological and philosophical ideas that became part of its permanent heritage.

IV

St. Anselm

THE REFORM BEGUN by Charlemagne did not long outlast his death. His empire was divided among his sons, and France once more became the scene of war and violence. The Viking invasions in the ninth and tenth centuries made any serious intellectual life extremely difficult, if not impossible. It is amazing that despite these bad conditions there were some who kept alive interest in the humanities and in classical culture, like Eric of Auxerre (*c.* 841–876), Remi of Auxerre (*c.* 841–908), and Gerbert of Aurillac (*c.* 940–1003). During this period the papacy itself was dominated by secular powers, and it was hardly in a position to foster spiritual and intellectual interests. In the tenth century, however, there was a gradual movement toward reform in all departments of life. The re-establishment of the empire by Otto I in 962 brought some political unity into western Europe, and monastic life was reborn in the monasteries of Cluny, Gorze, Auxerre, and Fleury. Reformers lashed out at abuses in religious life and organization and recalled men to Christian ideals.

One of these reformers, St. Peter Damian (1007–1072), merits our attention. His attitude toward philosophy and secular learning in general was typical of certain devout spirits in the Middle Ages as well as in our own day. Like Tertullian earlier, and St. Bernard, Thomas a Kempis, and Erasmus later, Peter Damian looked upon philosophy as a compromising influence in Christian life.[1] For him, Jesus Christ has spoken, and his saving Word should not be adulterated by curious speculation. The important thing is to save one's soul, and the surest way to do that is to become a monk. A monk

needs to know sacred Scripture, and will also find the writings of
the Fathers of the Church helpful. But Plato and the other pagan
philosophers have nothing to teach him. Rather, they are tools of
the devil. Indeed, the first grammarian was the devil, who taught
Adam to decline *deus* in the plural! [2]

The suspicion toward philosophy shown by Peter Damian and
others in the eleventh century was not without provocation. There
were theologians at the time who exalted reason above the mysteries of faith and submitted them to the laws of human logic, leading to questionable and even heretical conclusions. Berengar of
Tours (*c.* 1000–1088) was one of them. "Unless a man is stupidly
blind," he writes, "he will not contest that in the search for truth
reason is undoubtedly the best guide. It is characteristic of a great
mind always to have recourse to dialectics." [3] When Berengar himself used dialectics to explain the Eucharist he denied transubstan-
tiation.[4] He was opposed by Lanfranc (*c.* 1010–1089), the teacher
of St. Anselm, for abandoning "sacred authorities" and turning
to dialectics.[5] Lanfranc himself did not deny the utility of dialectics, but he objected to its indiscreet use in interpreting the mysteries of faith. In fact, all the theologians of the period made use
of dialectics. The conflicts between them concerned its value in
theology and its precise application to the mysteries of faith. In the
eleventh century reason was awakening and beginning to stretch
its wings. Its flight at first was erratic and feeble, but exhilarating
and breath-taking. Under the circumstances it is not surprising that
reason sometimes ran out of control when it tried to interpret the
teachings of faith.

St. Anselm stands out as having the best-balanced mind among
his contemporaries.[6] A staunch traditionalist, he wanted to be
nothing else than a loyal follower of St. Augustine; and indeed
he captured admirably the spirit and doctrine of his great master.
But he was a man of the eleventh century, in love with dialectics
and endowed with a keen, logical mind, which he put to such
original use that he has a high rank among medieval thinkers.

FAITH AND REASON

LIKE AUGUSTINE, Anselm was convinced that we have two sources of knowledge: faith and reason. Faith must be the starting point in the search for truth. He writes in his *Proslogion:* "For I do not seek to understand in order that I may believe, but I believe in order that I may understand. For I also believe this, that unless I believe, I shall not understand." [7] Unlike the extreme dialecticians, he upholds the primacy of faith and refuses to subordinate Scripture to reason or dialectics. But once a Christian is firmly established in faith, he can legitimately try to understand what he believes. How far can he go in understanding the mysteries of faith? St. Anselm does not think that he can comprehend them—in this life they will always remain mysteries—but he is confident in the power of the mind to give necessary reasons for them. For example, he thinks it possible to prove the necessity of the Trinity and the Incarnation. He thus combines a humble attitude of belief in Scripture with an almost unbounded optimism in the ability of reason to demonstrate its truths. St. Thomas Aquinas will be more discriminating in assigning limits to the demonstration possible in theological matters.

THE EXISTENCE OF GOD

ST. ANSELM is best known in the history of philosophy for his so-called "ontological" argument for the existence of God. [8] Before the *Proslogion*, however, which contains this proof, he wrote another treatise, the *Monologion*, in which he proves God's existence by another method. We shall consider these proofs in their chronological order.

The *Monologion* was written at the request of the monks of Bec, where St. Anselm was Prior. His monks asked him to write a model meditation on God, in which everything would be proved

by reason, with absolutely nothing depending on the authority of
Scripture. This is surely a strange meditation for monks, but the
request reflects the extraordinary interest at the time in rational
speculation.

In reply to his monks' demand St. Anselm sets out to give a rational proof of God's existence. Our senses and our reason make
us aware of a great number of good things. Are all these good
through some one thing, or is each good through something different and peculiar to itself? Clearly the former is the case. For
it is absolutely certain that if a number of things are said to possess
an attribute in greater, less, or equal degree, they are said to possess
it through some one thing that is understood to be the same in all.
Thus things called just in any degree, whether greater, less, or
equal, can be understood to be just only through justice, which is
the same in all. Hence all true goods have the character of goodness through the same being, through which all goods exist. This
being is not good through something else; it is good through itself.
Hence it alone is supremely good, surpassing all others. It is indeed
the most excellent of all beings; in a word, it is God.⁹

Using the same method, Anselm then offers two more proofs
of the existence of God. He shows that all beings exist through
one being which exists in virtue of itself, and that all perfect beings
are more or less perfect insofar as they participate in a supreme
perfection. Supreme goodness, being, and perfection are but three
names for the same reality and this is God.¹⁰

It is not difficult to recognize the Platonic character of these
proofs. They all begin with the observation of a multitude of
things united in the possession of a common perfection, whose
source is outside them and in which they participate in equal or unequal degrees. But the use Anselm makes of Platonic participation
carries him beyond Platonism itself. It leads him in fact to the
Christian God. We find in these proofs a typical instance of what
can be called Christian Platonism.

In the preface to the *Proslogion*, Anselm relates that after writing the *Monologion* he cast about in his mind for a simpler proof
of God's existence. The desired proof came to him suddenly, the
fruit of long meditation and prayer. In Chapter One he invites

the reader likewise to prepare himself for the proof by prayer. "Enter into the inner chamber of your mind," he exhorts, "shut out all things save God and whatever may aid you in seeking God; and having barred the door of your chamber, seek Him." [11] It is clear from this exhortation that the new proof will follow the interior path marked out by St. Augustine. It is also clear from what follows that Anselm, like Augustine, is seeking God in love and faith, endeavoring to understand what he already believes with his whole heart: "I confess and give thanks, Lord, that you have created in me this your image, so that I may remember you, that I may think of you, that I may love you.[12] But your image has been so worn away by the continued corruption of vices, it has been so clouded by the smoke of sins, that it cannot do what it was made to do unless you renew and reform it. I am not seeking, Lord, to penetrate your heights, for I do not in any way consider my understanding equal to this; but I desire only a little understanding of the truth which my heart believes and loves. For I do not seek to understand in order that I may believe, but I believe in order that I may understand. For I also believe this, that unless I believe, I shall not understand." [13]

With this introduction St. Anselm proceeds to his proof. We believe that God is a being than which none greater can be thought. Is it possible that this being does not really exist? Some in fact have denied God's existence. We read in the *Psalms* (13:1): *The fool has said in his heart: There is no God.* And yet when the fool hears the words, "a being than which none greater can be thought," he understands them, and what he understands exists in his intellect, even though he does not think that such a being exists in reality. For it is possible for something to exist in the intellect without understanding that it really exists. When a painter thinks over in advance what he is going to paint, he has this in his intellect, but he is conscious that it does not yet exist in reality. But when he has painted it, he both has it in his intellect and understands that what he has produced really exists. Even the fool, then, must be convinced that there exists at least in his intellect a being than which none greater can be thought. But—and here is the crux of the argument—it is greater to exist in reality than to exist in the intellect alone. Hence it would be contradictory to say that the being than which nothing greater can be thought could exist in the intellect alone: a being greater than this could always be conceived existing in reality. Without doubt, therefore, there exists both in the intellect and in reality something than which a greater cannot be thought.[14]

The stages in this proof must be clearly distinguished. Anselm begins with a lively faith in God's existence. The demonstration raises his mind, with the aid of divine illumination, to an understanding of it. At the end he exclaims: "I thank you, good Lord, I thank you, because through your illumination I now so understand that which, through your generous gift, I formerly believed, that, were I to refuse to believe that you exist, I should be unable not to understand it to be true." [15]

GAUNILON'S OBJECTIONS

ST. ANSELM'S PROOF has always found critics in philosophical circles. The first was one of his own contemporaries by the name of Gaunilon. This astute Benedictine monk from Marmoutier (Tours) wrote a remarkable pamphlet, "In Defense of the Fool," in which he raises two objections to St. Anselm's argument. First, he denies that he really has in his mind the idea of a being than which a greater cannot be thought. He hears the spoken words, but he cannot conceive of this being any more than he can conceive of God himself. He does not know the reality which is God, and he cannot form a notion of him from other realities because, as St. Anselm himself says, there is no reality like him.[16] Gaunilon's second objection is that, even if we could conceive of a being than which none greater can be thought, it does not follow that this being exists in reality, but only in thought. We can think of any number of unreal things, and even impossible ones, which certainly have no existence outside the mind. For example, we can form the notion of an earthly paradise, the Isles of the Blessed, but that does not warrant our concluding that the islands really exist.[17]

In reply, St. Anselm explains in what way we can conceive God. We form a notion of him beginning with the knowledge of less perfect things and raising our mind to the notion of a most perfect being. Gaunilon claims that we neither know such a being in itself, nor can we form an idea of it from anything like it. Obviously this is not true. For everything that is less good, insofar as it is good, is like the greater good. It is therefore evident to any rational mind that by ascending from the lesser good to the greater we can form a considerable notion of a being than which a greater is inconceivable.[18]

Anselm meets Gaunilon's second objection by pointing out that we can reason from existence in thought to existence in reality in one case only. For there is only one being which cannot be thought not to be; namely, the being than which none greater can be thought. This being alone necessarily implies existence in reality. The idea of the Isles of the Blessed does not resemble it in this respect, for there is nothing in the notion of these Isles that compels us to affirm their real existence.[19]

Ever since St. Anselm proposed this proof, philosophers have been concerned with it. Many accept it, at least with modifications; for example, St. Bonaventure, Duns Scotus, Descartes, Leibniz, and Hegel. Others agree with Gaunilon that it should be rejected; for example, St. Thomas Aquinas, Locke, and Kant.

Why do some accept the proof and others deny it? Those who deny it agree that all our knowledge begins with sense experience and that we can know the existence of anything only through the perception of sensible things. On the other hand, those who accept it think that the mind can know real being by turning inward upon itself. Real being is not given to us through sense experience—at least not exclusively—but through our ideas.

We should not be surprised to find St. Anselm in the latter group of philosophers. All the great medieval thinkers who preceded him —Augustine, Boethius, Erigena—adopted the interior route to knowledge of real being, which they identified with truth, the intelligible object of our thought. We see now that Anselm is following the tradition they established.

In Anselm's own day there were two main groups of philosophers: nominalists and realists. We shall have more to say about them in the next chapter. For the moment it will suffice to explain that the nominalists identify the content of thought with words, whereas the realists identify the content of thought with things (*res*). Anselm belongs to the second group, the realists. He points out that when we think of fire or water we can understand either words or things. If we think simply of the words, nothing prevents our saying that fire is water. But if we think of the things signified by the words, this is impossible.[20] The same is true of God. If we think simply of the word "God," we can say that he does not exist. In other words, a nominalist can deny the existence of God; his position is precisely that of the fool mentioned in Scripture. But if we think of the being signified by the word, we cannot say that God does not exist. For he is the being than which none greater can be thought, and it is impossible to think of such a being and to deny its existence. The very being conceived compels the mind to assert its existence not only in thought but in reality.

TRUTH

IT SHOULD BE CLEAR by now that Anselm's proofs of God's existence in the *Proslogion*, as well as in the *Monologion*, rest upon a certain conception of knowledge and truth. Unfortunately, he has left us only scattered suggestions as to the origin of our knowledge, but these point to his fidelity to Augustine's doctrine of divine illumination. With regard to universals, he opposes the nominalism of some of his contemporaries and insists on the reality of genera and species.[21]

More helpful for understanding St. Anselm's doctrine of knowledge is his treatise *On Truth*. The purpose of this short work is to set forth the nature of truth. It begins by examining certain instances of truth. Truth is found most obviously in propositions. A proposition is true when it says that what is is, and that what is not is not. In other words, a proposition is true when it expresses what it ought to express. So the truth of propositions and of thought itself consists in "rectitude." [22]

Truth is also in the will and consists in its rectitude. For the will is true when it wills what it ought to will. Actions also have truth; we do the truth when we do what we ought to do. Even non-rational creatures can be said to do the truth. When fire burns, it does the truth, for that is what it was made to do and ought to do. Man, of course, does the truth freely; fire does it necessarily.

Moreover, truth resides in the essence of all existing things, for they conform to their Ideas in the divine mind. They are what they ought to be in relation to God's knowledge, and so they are true.[23]

Truth, then, is rectitude found in propositions, thought, will, actions, and things. And since this rectitude is not the object of any of the senses, but only of the intellect, truth can be defined as "rectitude perceptible to the mind alone." [24]

Above all particular truths or rectitudes there is the highest truth, which is God. He is not rectitude in the sense that he owes something to another. Everything else is indebted to him, but he is indebted to nothing. There is no reason for his being what he is except that he exists. Uncaused in himself, he is the cause of all other truths or rectitudes. He is the cause of the truth of things, and their truth in turn is the cause of the truth of thought and of propositions.

We say there is truth of things, of thought, and of propositions, but this is an improper way of speaking. There is indeed but one truth, God, who causes and measures all things, just as there is only one time that is the measure of all temporal events. Truth is not varied or diversified according to the diversity of the things measured by it, any more than time varies with things existing in time.[25]

Thus the universe in which we live is governed by truth, and truth, wherever we find it, leads us to God, who is subsistent Truth. This is a theme we have already met in St. Augustine. It reappears in his disciple, St. Anselm. The truth of propositions is founded upon the truth of thought, the truth of thought upon the truth of things, the truth of things upon the divine Ideas, which are one with God.

The "ontological" argument for God's existence is at home in a universe of this sort. When we think of a being than which none greater can be conceived, we are faced with a truth whose message is clear and undeniable. This is a being unlike all others in that it is its very nature to exist in reality. To deny its real existence is to go counter to the very "rectitude" of the notion, which is guaranteed by its Idea in God's mind; that is, by God himself.

THE WILL AND LIBERTY

AS WE HAVE SEEN, there is a special kind of truth in the will, which St. Anselm calls the will's rectitude. He also calls this rectitude justice, because it makes a man just and upright in the sight of God. What is the nature of this moral rectitude and what is its relation to freedom?

The term "will," St. Anselm tells us, has three meanings.[26] First of all it means the power or faculty of willing, as "sight" means the power of seeing. In this sense the will is a natural endowment of the soul and the instrument by which we exercise the acts of loving, desiring, willing, and choosing. Like the power of sight, the will is inseparable from man; he possesses it even while not actually using it, as when he is asleep. The will is a self-determining power; it moves itself to its own decisions and turns itself to what it desires most. And it moves not only itself, but also the other parts and faculties of man like the hands, tongue, and sight, as well as external instruments like a pen or an axe.

In the second sense the word "will" means the inclination, propensity, or affection of the power of will. For example, a mother is always inclined to will the well-being of her children so that this can be called her permanent will. The will is inclined to two kinds of objects: the useful and the just. It is permanently inclined to what is useful, but not to what is just. The inclination to justice is inseparable from the power of will only in the angels and saints. In the present life the will of man may be inclined to justice, but it is always possible to lose this inclination through sin.

The inclination to justice is always good and cannot lead to sin, but not so the inclination to what is useful. This latter inclination must be brought under the control of the inclination to justice; otherwise it will get out of hand and destroy man's propensity to justice. The correct balance between these two inclinations was upset by original sin, when man, by a free decision of his will, let his desire for the useful gain the upper hand, with the result that he lost his inclination to justice. And once lost, this inclination could not be regained by man's own efforts but only by God's grace. Justice is a gift of God, which man can lose by himself but which he cannot gain by himself.

In the third sense the term "will" means the act of willing, as "sight" means the act of seeing. This act is the exercise and manifestation of the power and inclination to will. Among the acts of the will is choice, which is a judgment (*judicium*) or decision of the will (*voluntatis arbitrium*).[27] Although an act of the will, choice presupposes knowledge, for the will chooses or rejects objects according to the evidence of reason. The ability to choose is natural to man and inseparable from his powers of will and reason.

St. Anselm devotes one of his treatises to the problem of freedom of choice and liberty (*De Libertate Arbitrii*). He recognizes the fact that the human will has the natural power to choose or not to choose, to choose to act in this or that way, and even to choose to sin. But like St. Augustine, he distinguishes between free choice in this broad sense and liberty. Liberty does not include the power of sinning; otherwise God and the angels, who are incapable of sinning, would not be free, whereas they possess liberty more perfectly than man. In St. Anselm's view, sin is incompatible with liberty, for he who sins is a slave of sin (*John* 8:34). Certainly the power to put oneself in bondage is not the mark of true liberty. For this reason St. Anselm refuses to include this power in the definition of liberty. The true definition of liberty is "the power of preserving rectitude of will for the sake of rectitude itself." [28] St. Anselm includes in this definition the phrase "for the sake of rectitude itself" because a man who is truly free does not act right for any selfish motive, but because he knows his act is right.

Man was created with freedom of choice, but he chose to commit sin, thereby giving up his liberty and becoming a slave of sin. His choice was free, though it cannot be said to have come from his liberty, since this inclined him to act right. He was like a man who freely chooses to become another's slave; he made his choice freely, but in abdicating his freedom he did not act like a free man. Men are now slaves of sin, but they have not destroyed their natural freedom of choice. They are simply unable to use it properly without the grace of God. Only when liberated by grace are they truly free and capable of making good use of their freedom of choice.

In his study of the will, St. Anselm, like St. Augustine, is not interested in defining its nature or in analyzing the act of free choice. His problem is not psychological, but moral and religious; namely, how is man's will to be rectified in order to insure the fullest freedom and happiness for man? He replies that the human will is most free when it has, over and above its natural freedom of choice, the divine gift of liberty. The will is then what it ought to be and its actions are always just. Moreover, the will is then on the way to finding the happiness it desires, and which is inseparable from its liberty.

V

Peter Abelard

THE FAME OF PETER ABELARD rests upon achievements in several fields.[1] He has a prominent place in the history of medieval theology, which he helped to organize as a science. His controversies with St. Bernard and William of St. Thierry on such subjects as the Trinity and Incarnation do not concern us here, although they loomed large on the theological horizons of the twelfth century. Abelard's letters, including his account of his life and calamities and his correspondence with Héloïse, make him stand out as one of the most concrete and colorful figures in the Middle Ages.

All of his purely philosophical writings are concerned with logic. In this field he continued the speculation of Aristotle, Porphyry, and Boethius, although in his usual manner he deepened and extended the ideas handed down to him by his predecessors. Most striking is his nominalistic approach to logic. In the Middle Ages only William of Ockham will go farther in tying logic to a nominalist philosophy.

FAITH AND REASON

IT HAS BEEN SAID that Abelard was a rationalist, but this is not true if it means that he put reason above faith or separated the two. Writing to Héloïse toward the end of his life, he protested against the charges laid against him of being more expert in logic than in the knowledge of St. Paul and of subverting the faith. "I do not want to be a philosopher," he wrote, "if it is necessary to deny Paul. I do not want to be Aristotle if it is necessary to be separated from Christ. For there is no other name under heaven whereby I must be saved (*Acts* 4:12)." [2] St. Bernard criticized him for putting faith on the level of mere human opinion, but Abelard did not deny the truth of Christian faith. As a professor of theology, he was interested in teaching Christian doctrine to pupils so that it could be understood. Nothing revolted him more than a lecture consisting of meaningless words. He knew well enough that the limited human mind cannot hope to comprehend the mysteries of faith; but words are meant to convey a meaning, and he sought the human meaning of sacred Scripture. That is why he was so concerned with words and their meaning and why he studied logic so passionately. His so-called rationalism was really a growing awareness of the domain of human reason and the world of nature. In the twelfth century the school of Chartres was furthering this awakening by its studies in cosmology. Abelard contributed to it particularly in the field of logic and human reason. Thus he marks an important step forward in medieval philosophy.

Abelard did not teach in the monastic schools, which flourished in the tenth and eleventh centuries, but in the newer urban schools of the thriving towns of the twelfth century. The atmosphere of these schools was quite different from that of the schools of the monasteries. The urban schools showed a new spirit of independence and freedom and an insatiable curiosity in contrast to the conservatism of the earlier schools. Abelard absorbed this spirit, while making his own contribution to it.

He was also a pioneer in the formation of the scholastic method. In his lectures and writings he aimed to lead his pupils by an orderly method to a rational grasp of the subject matter. When he lectured in theology, for example, he was not content to read sacred Scripture and state the varying opinions of the Fathers of the Church on a given subject. After citing their statements pro and con, he tried to solve the problem in a way conformable to all the best authorities. This is the method of his theological work entitled *Sic et Non* (*Yes and No*), which was to contribute to the formation of the scholastic method.[3] Abelard, like all Augustinians, sought to understand what he believed, but the type of understanding he aimed at was new. His goal was not the monastic contemplation of a St. Anselm or St. Bernard, but an orderly, rational understanding, worthy to be called scientific. In this he was the harbinger of a new age: the Age of the Schoolmen, or of scholasticism.

DOCTRINE OF UNIVERSALS

IN THE ELEVENTH and twelfth centuries the ruling doctrine of universals was that of Boethius, who considered them to be realities. This traditional realism was then under attack by nominalists, who looked upon universals as simply words. All through the twelfth century the battle raged between the realists (*reales*) and the nominalists (*nominales*), with Abelard in the thick of the fray.

One of Abelard's first teachers, Roscelin (*c.* 1050–*c.* 1123), was the leader of the nominalists. Little is known of him or of his doctrine. St. Anselm almost certainly had him in mind when he refers to certain modern heretical dialecticians who called universals *flatus vocis;* that is, vocal utterances.[4] John of Salisbury (*c.* 1115–1180) tells us that Roscelin considered universals to be merely spoken words (*voces*), adding that in his own day this opinion, along with its author, Roscelin, had already passed almost completely into oblivion.[5] From the testimony of these men we know that Roscelin identified universals with the sounds we make when we speak. He was convinced that only individual things are real and that the universal terms by which we signify them are nothing but words. For example, we use the general word "man" to designate all men.

At the Council of Soissons in 1092, Roscelin was accused of heresy for applying his nominalism to the doctrine of the Trinity. If only individual things are real, it would seem to follow that the three Persons of the Trinity have no real divine nature in common, and consequently they are three gods. Roscelin, however, denied that he taught this, and he was not formally condemned.[6]

Another of Abelard's teachers, William of Champeaux (*c.* 1070–1121), was one of the outstanding realists, holding, with Boethius, that universals are substances common to many individuals. Humanity, for example, is a common substance totally present in all individual men. All men are essentially one in being human. So, too, all animals are essentially one in possessing the common substance of animality. Individuals in the same genus or species differ by the variety of their accidental characteristics. Thus Plato and Socrates have the same substance of humanity, but this substance is individual in each through their personal qualities, quantities, places, and so on.

This was William of Champeaux's teaching when Abelard first studied under him. But Abelard's persistent criticism—to be considered shortly—forced him to shift his position. After Abelard's attack he no longer said that individuals are essentially one in possessing a common substance, but that they are "indifferently" one. This does not mean that two individuals in the same species are the same because they share the same essence, but that they are the same because they do not differ from each other. For example, Plato and Socrates are the same in being men because they do not differ in the nature of humanity. According to this position, the same humanity is not present in both men; each has his own humanity, but each resembles the other in his humanity.[7] Abelard considered this doctrine a mitigated form of realism, closer to the truth than William of Champeaux's former doctrine, but only verbally different from it.

Abelard levels a long series of arguments against William of Champeaux's realism. If humanity is a reality simultaneously present in all men, it is either partly or wholly in any one. If it is only partly present, this individual is not truly and wholly man. If it is wholly present, no other man can exist. Furthermore, William of Champeaux says that all things are one in their substance and different only by their accidents. But then all things are identical in substance and they have the same substance as God. Moreover, individuals in a species or genus cannot be the same in their substance and differ simply by their accidents, for each accident is itself a universal just like substance. At bottom, all qualities are the same and so, too, are all quantities, just as are all substances. So the addition of accidents to substance does not result in an individual. Universals may be added to universals, but no individuals will result. The sum of universals is a universal, not an individual. Lastly, if the substance animal really exists in two of its species, man and horse, the same animality that is rational in man is irrational in horse. Thus one and the same thing is both itself and its contrary, which is impossible.

These and similar arguments forced William of Champeaux to abandon his first doctrine and to hold that two individuals are the same in that they do not differ from each other. But Abelard was quick to point out the weakness of this position. The non-difference in question has either a negative or a positive meaning. If its meaning is simply negative, the problem of universals is not solved. It is true that Socrates does not differ in any way from Plato as a man, which they both are; but neither do they differ in any way as stones, which they are not. If, on the contrary, the non-difference has a positive meaning, William of Champeaux's second position coincides with his first, which has been refuted.[8]

Another type of realism criticized by Abelard is that of Joscelin of Soissons (d. 1151), who claimed that a universal is a collection of individuals. Joscelin taught that all men taken together are the species "man," and that all animals taken together are the genus "animal." Abelard replies that this is impossible, for a species or genus is predicable of each individual in it, but a collection cannot be predicated of each individual in the collection. Obviously the whole class of men cannot be predicated of each individual in the class. Plato is not the sum total of all men. If only a part of the collection is predicated of each individual, then the collection itself is not a universal, for a universal is predicable wholly of many individuals.[9]

The conclusion of these criticisms is that a universal is not a reality or a thing. Every thing is individual; there are no universal realities. What, then, is a universal? For the answer to this question, Abelard turns to the grammarians and logicians. Grammarians distinguish between common and proper nouns, logicians between universals and individuals. A common noun or universal is one that is predicable of many things; a proper noun is predicable of only one. For example, "man" is a universal noun because it can be applied to all individual men, while "Socrates" is a proper noun because it is applicable to only one.[10]

In describing universals as a certain class of words, Abelard follows in the footsteps of Roscelin, who called them vocal utterances. But Abelard goes beyond his teacher in recognizing that universals are not simply words; they are words with meaning. They are not simply *voces*, but *sermones;* that is, names that function as signs. It is because words have meaning that we cannot predicate any word we wish of any other. For example, we cannot say "Man is a stone." This is a correct sentence from the point of view of grammar; it is wrong, however, because it disregards the meaning of the words. In his account of universals, therefore, the logician must go beyond grammar and take into consideration not only words but the fact that they have meaning.

How is this fact to be explained? Do universal words derive their meaning from things? It would seem that they do not, for, as we have seen, there are no universal realities or essences that they could signify. There are only individual realities, and no universal word signifies precisely any one individual. "Man" does not mean precisely the individual Socrates nor any other particular man. Since only individual men exist, it would seem that universals have no meaning based upon real things.

In order to escape this difficulty, Abelard points out that even though individuals have no essences in common, they do have common likenesses that serve as a ground for our universal names and concepts. Socrates and Plato have no real humanity in common, but they are alike in being men, as a horse and an ass are alike in not being men. Another way to put it is that they are in the same state or condition of being men. Abelard is careful to explain that a state is not a "thing"; it is simply the individual itself in its likeness to other things. And it is this state or resemblance that is the common cause of our imposing universal names on things.

Abelard is aware of the obvious objection to this. If a state is not a thing, how can it be a cause? Surely a cause is a thing, and a common cause is a common thing. Are not the realists correct, then, in assigning a common reality or essence as the cause of our universal words and concepts? Not at all, according to Abelard. We often assign as a cause what is not a thing, as when we say: "He was lashed because he did not wish to appear in court." We call his not wishing to appear in court a cause, yet it is not a thing. Similarly, we can call the states of things the cause of universals even though they are not things.[11]

Accordingly, Abelard rejects the realism of his contemporaries who maintained the presence of a common essence in individual things. In his view, each individual differs from every other by its essence or form and not simply by its accidental properties. Things are substantially and not only accidentally different. But because individuals are more or less like one another, they can be classified into genera and species.

Abelard has now explained the foundation in reality of our common names. He has not yet told us what corresponds to them in our mind. Do universals exist in the mind, and if so, what are they? In order to answer these questions we must examine Abelard's doctrine of knowledge.

KNOWLEDGE

SENSE PERCEPTION AND UNDERSTANDING are two distinct actions of the soul. The senses use bodily organs and have for their objects bodies and their properties. For example, sight perceives a tower and its visible qualities. Understanding, on the other hand, does not use a bodily organ, nor does it need a material thing as its object. The mind constructs and retains within itself the likenesses or images of things, which serve as its object in the absence of the things themselves. However, understanding has no need of these mental constructs in the presence of real objects.

Now there are two types of images constructed by the mind. Some are general and confused, representing no one individual in a class distinctly, but all generally. Others are particular and detailed, representing one individual alone. Confused images are evoked in the mind by common names like "man," particular images by proper names like "Socrates."

Universal concepts are nothing else than confused mental images.

Abelard draws no distinction between images and concepts; indeed he defines an image as a "confused conception of the soul." [12] This implies that the distinction between imagination and understanding is not one of kind but only of degree. They correspond to different degrees of attention on the part of the soul. Imagination comes before thinking. By imagination, we grasp an object weakly and confusedly, without distinguishing its parts or properties. By understanding, we give greater attention to the same object, grasping it more distinctly by analyzing its properties. For example, by imagination we picture to ourselves the confused, general image of man; by thinking we analyze it by fixing our attention on some property, like rationality or animality. As a result, we gain a clearer and more distinct notion of man by understanding than by imagination.

Universal concepts are formed by abstraction. By abstraction Abelard means simply the concentration of attention upon one aspect of a thing to the disregard of other aspects of the same thing. It is in this way that we conceive the concept "substance" when thinking about a man. Man is at once substance, body, animal, and so on. When we think of him only as a substance, we disregard the other forms that exist together in him. These abstractions do not represent their object fully, but they are not false or empty. We are not in error if we consider separately the gold and silver joined together in a statue. Neither do we err if we consider separately the form and matter in man. We would be in error only if we considered them to be actually separated. Even our concepts of individuals are formed by abstraction, as when we conceive an individual man as *this* substance, *this* body, and *this* animal. Each one of these concepts is the result of a special act of attention bearing upon one individual man who is at once a substance, body, and animal.[13]

This notion of abstraction has little in common with that of St. Thomas. Abelard reduces abstraction to the well-known psychological fact that we can turn our attention to various aspects of one and the same object. He has no conception of St. Thomas' doctrine, according to which the intellect abstracts an essence, existing individually and materially in the world of nature, and gives it a new mode of universal and immaterial existence within itself. Abelard possessed neither the metaphysics of being nor the doctrine of the agent intellect required for the elaboration of the Thomistic notion of abstraction.

According to Abelard, there are abstract conceptions in God as well as in us, for God conceives beforehand the Ideas of the things he creates, as an artist forms in advance the idea of his work of art. But God's universals are different from those we form through the senses. By means of them God knows clearly all the individuals he creates in the same state. We, who receive our knowledge through the senses, achieve a simple and perfect knowledge of this sort scarcely ever, or never at all.

The ultimate explanation of universals is consequently to be found in the divine Ideas. We give things common names and form universal concepts of them because they resemble one another. But there is nothing intrinsic to them to account for their common likeness. They resemble one another simply because God, through his Ideas, created them in the same state. In the last analysis, then, Abelard finds an objective basis for our universal names and concepts in the divine Ideas.

In conclusion, Abelard summarizes his doctrine of universals by replying to the questions raised by Porphyry.[14]

1] Do genera and species exist? Abelard replies that as concepts they exist only in the intellect, but they signify real things. In fact, they signify the same individuals represented by particular concepts, although they signify them confusedly and indistinctly.

2] Are universals corporeal or incorporeal? Abelard replies that, insofar as they are words, universals are corporeal and sensible, but their capacity to signify many similar individuals is incorporeal.

3] Do universals exist in sensible things or outside them? Abelard replies that inasmuch as universals signify the forms of sensible things they exist in them, but inasmuch as they signify abstract concepts, like those in the divine mind, they are beyond the sensible world. Thus both Aristotle and Plato were right: Aristotle because he insisted that universals exist in sensible things, Plato because he held that universals exist independently of the sensible world.

4] Abelard himself raised a fourth question: If all the individu-

als signified by a universal ceased to exist, would the universal
retain its meaning? Would a rose still be a rose if no roses existed?
Abelard answers: In that case a universal would lose its character
as a universal, for it would not be predicable of many individuals.
But it would still keep its meaning in our intellect, for it would
still make sense to say: "No roses exist."

ETHICS

ABELARD'S NOMINALISM, which stresses the reality of the
individual, has important repercussions on his ethical theory. His
main concern is with the individual—in this case with the individual
moral agent and his personal guilt and responsibility.

Abelard's ethical views are contained in a treatise entitled *Ethics,
or Know Thyself*. The aim of this little work is to determine the
basis of good and bad acts. Why are some acts called good and
others bad? More simply, what is a sin? Sin must not be confused
with a weakness of the mind or disposition to evil. It is a defect
in a person to be prone to evil, but he does not commit a sin if he
withholds his consent to a bad act. Indeed, if the weakness is con-
quered he gains merit. Neither is sin the mere desire or will to do
evil. As long as consent is withheld, no sin is committed. Neither
is pleasure sinful, even if it accompanies an evil act. Since pleasure
in itself is natural, it cannot be a sin or increase the sinfulness of an
act. What is more, sin is not a human act considered in itself. No
act is good or bad in itself. Killing a man is not in itself a sin, for it
might be accidental and without consent, in which case it cannot
be called a sin. Some acts are "unseemly" in themselves; for example, mistakes in grammar or logic. But these defective acts are
not sins in the proper sense, for they imply no contempt of God
or his laws.

What, then, is a sin? It is simply consent to evil. To sin is to
despise God and his laws intentionally.[15] The morality of an act
depends solely on the intention with which it is done. An act done
with a good intention is always good; an act done with a bad intention is always bad. The act itself, or the result of the act, adds
nothing to its own goodness or badness. Intention alone determines

its moral character. God does not weigh what we do, but the spirit in which we do it. Two men put a criminal to death, one out of zeal for justice, the other out of hatred. Their action is the same, but their intentions differ: in one the act is good, in the other it is evil. Did not God command Abraham to kill his son and then revoke the command? In both cases God's action was justified, for his intention was good. In short, it was good for the same action to be prescribed and also to be prohibited.[16]

This shows that acts themselves are morally neutral. "An action is good," Abelard writes, "not because it contains within it some good, but because it issues from a good intention." Similarly, an action is not bad in itself; it is bad because it issues from a bad intention.[17]

Sin in the proper sense, then, consists solely in bad intention. It can never come about without personal guilt. As a consequence, original sin is not a sin for us, but only for Adam and Eve. We share in the punishment of the sin but not in the guilt. In adopting this position, Abelard parts company with the realists, who taught that, since humanity is the same in all men, the same humanity that contracted the guilt of original sin in Adam is present in all his successors. As a result, all men are guilty of original sin. Abelard, however, does not admit the reality of a universal humanity. In his view, individual persons alone are real, and they alone can be guilty of sin through their bad intention.

If sin consists in bad intention, we have still to discover what makes an intention good or bad. Abelard explains that for an intention to be good it is not enough for it to seem good; it must be really good by corresponding to God's will and intention. God has revealed his laws to Christians, who must conform their wills to them.[18]

This would seem to exclude pagans from the ranks of the morally good and to deny them a chance of salvation. But Abelard thought that non-Christians as well as Christians have access to God's laws. In his *Christian Theology* he teaches that God granted a revelation to the great pagan philosophers who lived holy lives and came very close to Christian truth. Through them, pagans were enlightened concerning God's will, and hence moral goodness and salvation were within their reach. In any case, if a person is ignorant of God's will and acts contrary to it in good faith, he does not sin. This is true of the persecutors of Christ and the martyrs. Because they did not know what they were doing, they did not sin. On the contrary, they would have sinned if they had acted against their conscience and permitted their victims to go free. This was one of the doctrines of Abelard condemned in 1141 at the Council of Sens.[19]

Abelard's ethics is a radical subjectivism, for the only criterion of morality it recognizes is intention. Human acts, for him, have no intrinsic moral nature as an objective basis for the morality of our intention. The only criterion by which we can judge our intention is conformity to the divine intention.

In thus stressing the importance of intention in moral theory Abelard is in continuity with the ethics of St. Augustine, but in denying an objective moral order determining certain acts as intrinsically evil he parts company with him. It was left for later medieval theologians, like St. Thomas Aquinas, to work out a balanced moral doctrine, taking into account both the subjective and objective sides of morality.[20]

Abelard's ethics is consistent with his doctrine of universals. Since there are no essences or natures in things, universals have no objective basis in them but only in the divine Ideas. Similarly, the morality of human acts is not founded upon an objective moral order in nature but upon the will or intention of God. In both cases the solution of the problem is not found in the nature of things but in God.

VI

The School of Chartres

BESIDES ABELARD'S ITINERANT SCHOOL there were two outstanding educational centers in the twelfth century: the
school of St. Victor founded by William of Champeaux at the
Augustinian Abbey of St. Victor at Paris, and the school of
Chartres attached to the famous cathedral of that name. The Victorines, the most celebrated of whom were Hugh and Richard of
St. Victor, belong more properly to the history of theology and
mysticism than to that of philosophy, although their speculation
contains a philosophical element.[1] Of greater philosophical interest
is the school of Chartres. While Abelard was examining human
reason and logic, which is reason's tool, this school was probing
nature and raising cosmological problems. It cultivated not only
the trivium: grammar, rhetoric, and dialectic (sciences of *voces*),
but particularly the quadrivium, including not only mathematics
and astronomy but also physics and theology (sciences of *res*). The
masters of Chartres had a lively appreciation of nature as a *cosmos*;
that is, as a universe or ordered whole, whose causes can be sought
out rationally. They did not have the help of Aristotle's treatises
in natural science, which were translated into Latin only at the
end of the twelfth century and the beginning of the thirteenth.
But a number of scientific and mathematical works of the Greeks
and Arabians were made available at this time, stimulating interest
in these fields. Philosophically, the school of Chartres was chiefly
indebted to Platonic sources, including a portion of Plato's *Timaeus*,
translated and commented upon by Chalcidius, and to the works
of St. Augustine, Boethius, Macrobius, and Apuleius. Frequently

the speculation of the masters of Chartres takes the form of a commentary on the works of Boethius. At this period the influence of Aristotle was still restricted mainly to logic.

The course of studies at Chartres emphasized the value of the Latin classics and the cultivation of literary taste and style. It was the center of classical learning and Christian humanism in the twelfth century.[2]

The school of Chartres [3] was founded by Fulbert, bishop of Chartres, who died in 1028. The first important master and chancellor was Bernard, whom John of Salisbury describes as "the foremost Platonist of our time." [4] Bernard died about 1130. His pupils include Gilbert of Poitiers (Gilbert de la Porrée), who succeeded him as chancellor and who died in 1154 as bishop of Poitiers; and William of Conches, who died about 1154. Bernard's brother, Thierry (d. before 1155), succeeded Gilbert as chancellor. Also associated with the school were Bernard Silvester (fl. c. 1145–1153); Clarenbaud of Arras, a disciple of Thierry, who died after 1170; and John of Salisbury, who died as bishop of Chartres in 1180.

DOCTRINES

THE MEN OF CHARTRES do not form a school in the sense that they rigidly adhered to the same philosophical principles and were content with exploring their implications. They shared certain philosophical allegiances (for example, to Platonism) and in some cases identical doctrines. But each was an individual thinker —some more so than others—and worthy of separate consideration. All that can be done here is to set forth some of their most significant ideas.

Typical of the school of Chartres is Thierry's fourfold division of the causes of the universe. God, he says, is its efficient cause, the wisdom of God is its formal cause, the goodness of God is its final cause, and the four elements (earth, water, air, fire) are its material cause. This fits in neatly with his doctrine of the Trinity. The Father is the efficient cause of the universe, creating the elements from nothing; the Son is its formal cause, bringing order and beauty into matter; and the Holy Spirit is its final cause—the love prompting God to share his perfections with creatures. We shall examine in turn each of these four causes of the world.[5]

Efficient Cause

Thierry of Chartres and William of Conches prove the existence of God by the fact of the order in nature. The wonderful harmony of the universe and its parts is evident. Witness, for example, the marvelous arrangement of the parts of man's body. The author of this order in nature must be a wise architect whom we call God.

Is God, however, the cause simply of the order of nature or also of its very existence? The men of Chartres read Plato's account of the formation of the universe from primitive chaos by the god Demiurge. They also read the book of *Genesis,* according to which God created the world from nothing. Between the two accounts of the origin of the world there is an important difference, for Demiurge does not create matter but simply introduces into it harmony and beauty, while the Christian God is a true creator whose causality extends to everything in nature, including matter.

The men of Chartres were not very concerned with the differences in the Platonic and scriptural explanations of the origin of the world. They considered the *Timaeus* as a mythical account of creation, which was more clearly revealed in *Genesis.* They pointed out, moreover, that even the *Timaeus* (28a) lays down the principle that everything coming into being owes its being to a cause. Since everything in the world comes into being and passes away, it must have an efficient cause of its being. Hence the universe as a whole and in all its parts has been created from nothing by God.

Creation, as taught in the school of Chartres, is thus not simply the introduction of order into previously existing matter. It is the giving of total being to the universe, which previous to creation did not exist.

The God of the Bible is eminently suited to the role of creator, for, unlike the Demiurge of Plato, he is Being itself. Thierry of Chartres points out that God revealed his name to be "He Who Is" (*Exod.* 3:14). Since he is Being, he exists through himself; he does not have to receive being from another in order to exist. All other things, however, exist only because they have received being from God.

Thierry and his pupil Clarenbaud express this by saying that God is the form of being (*forma essendi*) of all things. This does not mean that the divinity is a form existing in matter, like the form of a triangle or a square. It means simply that every being derives its existence from Being itself and participates in Being. So closely is the being of creatures bound up with the divine Being that the presence of the divinity in all creatures is their total and unique being, so that even matter itself owes its being to the presence of divinity. The divinity itself, however, has its being neither from matter nor in matter.

This is not pantheism, for Thierry insists on the transcendence of God with respect to his creatures. No single creature, nor the sum total of creation is God; every created being is but a participation in the divine Being, which is infinitely superior to the whole of creation.

Thierry also explains the relation of God to creatures in terms of unity and plurality. Unity precedes and generates number; thus one comes before two, which is made by adding one to one. Now every creature has a plurality of parts; it is indeed a number, and the universe itself is a vast system of numbers. As the source of the universe of numbers, God must be pure Unity, or the One. The creation of things is in fact the creation of numbers, all of which owe their being to their participation in Unity; that is to say, in God. Like all Platonists, Thierry favors a mathematical approach to the universe as the key unlocking the secret of its very being and ultimately the secret of God himself.

Formal Cause

The universe has not only a creator who is its efficient cause, but also a formal cause, which the men of Chartres identified with the Wisdom of God, the Second Person of the Trinity. Since God created the universe intelligently, he must have created it through his wisdom, using an intelligible model or plan for its execution. Hence there must be Ideas in the divine mind according to which all things have been created. These Ideas are the exemplary or formal cause of all creatures, determining them to be what they are.

What is the exact status of these Ideas in God? Bernard of Chartres describes them as being, in a sense, products of the divine mind. From the very beginning, he says, God conceived the universe within his mind. The Ideas of creatures, thus conceived, are subsequent in nature to God because they are his effects. But they are not subsequent to him in time, for he conceived them from all eternity. Hence Bernard calls the divine Ideas eternal but not co-eternal with God. Only the three Persons of the Trinity are coequal and coeternal, for there is absolute parity among them. The divine Ideas are less than God, having been produced by him.[6]

This doctrine, which closely resembles that of Scotus Erigena, was not universally accepted by the men of Chartres. Thierry and William of Conches speak of the conception of the Ideas in the divine mind without denying their coeternity with God. Thierry holds that the Ideas come forth from God, but they constitute a unity in the divine mind; they are in fact identical with the divine form itself.

The divine Ideas are stable and eternal, according to Bernard of Chartres. Enclosed in the sanctuary of the divine mind, they remain undisturbed by the changes constantly occurring in the world. They themselves do not enter into composition with matter. The forms uniting with matter to make up individual things come from the divine Ideas, but they are not identical with them. As Boethius says, they are only images of the divine Ideas: copies that have lost the stability and perfection of their originals through contact with matter.

Gilbert of Poitiers calls these forms in matter "inherent forms" (formae nativae) and bases his solution of the problem of universals upon them. John of Salisbury sums up Gilbert's doctrine of universals as follows: "An inherent form is sensible in things perceptible to the senses, but insensible as conceived by the mind. It is singular in singular things, but universal in all [of a kind]."[7] The point to be noticed here is that Gilbert maintains at one and the same time the singularity and universality of an inherent form in matter.

He knew the traditional Boethian position on universals, according to which all the members of a species have the same substantial form but differ in number through their accidents. In his own day that was being taught by Thierry of Chartres and Clarenbaud of Arras. To Gilbert's mind, however, this is not an adequate explanation of an individual. It is true that all men share in humanity, so that the form of humanity is common to all. But individual men do not differ solely through their accidental characteristics; each man possesses his own humanity, so that there are as many humanities as there are individual men. This had also been Abelard's position against William of Champeaux, but it had led Abelard to deny the reality of universals. Gilbert's aim is to save the substantial difference of individuals within a species while at the same time safeguarding the presence in them of a common form. Let us see how he does this.

Following Boethius, Gilbert claims that both universals and particulars subsist; that is to say, they exist through themselves without the need of accidents. In addition to subsisting, particular things also support accidents, so that they are substances. The difference between universals and particulars is that only particulars are substances; both are subsistent realities. How are subsistent universals multiplied in singular things? How, for example, does the universal humanity, subsisting in Cicero and giving him his subsistence as a man, take on the individuality of Cicero? What, in short, makes Cicero to be the individual man that he is? Gilbert's answer is that the uniqueness of an individual is the result of the totality of the forms within it. All the elements of which an individual is composed are common, being shared with other individuals in the same species or genus. What is not shared, and hence unique in any individual, is the collected totality of forms within it. Gilbert says: "Individuals are so called because each one of them is made up of such characteristics that when they are all collected together by thought, they will never be duplicated by natural conformity in any numerically different particular thing. That is why the total form of Plato (*Platonis tota forma*), being in nature like no other creature, is truly individual." [8]

Like Abelard, Gilbert realized that there is something unique in each individual that will never be duplicated in any other. This total unlikeness is the result of the unique combination of forms—specific, generic, and accidental—which go to make it up. In themselves, however, these forms are not individual; many individuals can share them. Hence they are universal.

Gilbert shares with Boethius the tendency to explain created things in terms of a graduated series of forms capable of an indefinite number of different combinations. This formalism will enjoy considerable popularity all through the thirteenth and fourteenth centuries.

Final Cause

The final cause or purpose of creation is the divine goodness. The men of Chartres liked to quote Plato's saying in the *Timaeus* (29e) that, because the maker of the universe was good and without jealousy, he desired that all things should be as like himself as they could be. William of Conches points out that God is all-perfect and has need of nothing. Hence he did not create the universe because of any need on his part, but simply because in his liberality and goodness he wanted to share his perfections with creatures. In particular, he created intelligent beings, angels and men, who are capable of knowing and loving and thus of sharing in his happiness.

Accordingly, man has a special place in the physical world. God created it for man, to serve as his dwelling place and to minister to his needs. The rest of the universe is for the sake of man and was created for him. Indeed it is only by serving man that the universe as a whole attains its end. Next to God, then, man is the final cause of creation. The dominant position of man in the universe is indicated by the fact that the world in which he lives is at the center of the universe. Man has also something in common with everything else in the world. He shares existence with non-living things, life with the vegetable world, sensation with animals, and intelligence with angels. He is thus the universe in miniature, or a microcosm. In him, moreover, are found in perfect equilibrium the four elements scattered throughout the universe.

Is this the best possible world God could have created? Abelard thought God made all things as good as they could be made and

as good as God himself could make them. Not so for William of
Conches, who was of the opinion that, while the universe is excellent, God could make it better either by increasing its elements or
adding to their perfection. In any case, God created nothing evil
by nature. True, nature does not exclude the possibility of evil,
which is a corruption of good rather than a positive reality. Because material things are contingent and mutable, they are in constant danger of losing what good they have. And the will of man,
created as a good, can always be turned in the direction of sin.
But God does not bear the responsibility for this. The universe
as he created it is indeed a reflection of his goodness.

Material Cause

According to Thierry of Chartres, the material cause of the
universe is the four elements. In his interpretation, when *Genesis*
says that in the beginning God created heaven and earth, "heaven"
means air and fire, while "earth" means earth and water. In the
beginning earth was hardly distinguishable from water, or air
from fire. There was a quasi-formlessness and uniformity among
the elements which the philosophers (Plato) described as *hyle* or
chaos. But this does not mean that matter was created prior in
time to form or to the four elements.

Motion was imparted to the universe by fire, which because of
its lightness tends to be unsteady and naturally moves in a circle
at the rim of the universe. The heat and light from fire were imparted to the air below it, which in turn solidified the earth and
condensed the surrounding waters.

The details of Thierry's cosmology are of greater interest to
the history of science than to that of philosophy. Of philosophical
importance, however, are the mechanistic tendencies of that cosmology, which explains the development of the universe in terms
of the movement of the elements and the transference of movement through an impulse (*impetus*). Thierry knew nothing of
the Aristotelian physics, according to which lightness and heavi-
ness are qualitative forms of bodies moving them to their proper
places in the universe. In Thierry's cosmology, the lightness of
fire and air is simply their movement, and this movement is the

primary factor in the formation of the universe. Movement is transferred from one body to another by means of an impulse given to the moved body by its mover: an impetus which is in proportion to the power of the moving body. We shall see these primitive mechanistic ideas reappear in the fourteenth century after the heyday of the qualitative physics of Aristotle in the thirteenth.

John of Salisbury

JOHN OF SALISBURY followed the speculations of his contemporaries with a rather detached and critical attitude. His own tastes were those of a humanist seeking a well-rounded intellectual and moral education enabling him to live a good life and to express himself learnedly and eloquently on all important matters. He studied under many of the famous teachers of his day, including Abelard, William of Conches, and Gilbert of Poitiers, and his itinerant career brought him into contact with all the major centers of learning. As secretary of Theobald and Thomas à Becket, archbishops of Canterbury, he made frequent diplomatic missions to France and Italy, where he was a keen observer of the political and educational scene.

Nurtured by the humanism of Chartres, John mastered the large body of Latin literature of his day, including Virgil, Cicero, Seneca, Ovid, Horace, Juvenal, and Terence. He found in them not only models of Latin style, which he cultivated with taste, but also philosophers and moralists of great value to a Christian thinker. The classical writer he admired most was Cicero. Like Cicero, he considered himself an Academic, or moderate skeptic, in philosophical matters. He writes: "I feel no shame in proclaiming myself a member of the Academic school, and I am faithful to their rule in all matters that appear doubtful to the sage. For although this sect is supposed to introduce an element of obscurity in all discussions, none is more devoted to the critical examination of truth, and we have it on the authority of Cicero, who in old age took refuge in this school, that none is more friendly to progress. In statements made from time to time in regard to providence, fate, freedom of the will, and the like, I am to be regarded as a disciple of the Academy rather than as a dogmatic exponent of that which is still a matter of doubt." [9]

John of Salisbury was not a complete skeptic; faith, the senses, and reason he considered sources of truth. But on most philosophical issues he was content to maintain a modest reserve and to withhold final judgment. This was his attitude toward the dispute over universals. He surveys the current opinions about universals and concludes that all of them miss the point. All of their proponents profess to follow Aristotle, and yet they all misunderstand him. Aristotle says that genera and species do not exist but are only understood. Now if a universal does not exist, how can we determine its nature, quality, quantity, or origin? We cannot describe what does not exist. Yet this is what philosophers try to do when they identify universals with words, concepts, ideas, inherent forms, or collections. For all of these doubtless exist.

But if universals do not exist, what foundation in reality has our knowledge? John of Salisbury replies by pointing out the various ways in which we know. Sometimes we understand a thing simply as it is; for example, when we consider an individual man like Plato. At other times we make up something in our imagination, as when we picture a centaur to ourselves. At still other times we understand by abstracting, as when we consider a line or a surface apart from matter. When our intellect thus abstracts, it thinks of a line without matter, but it does not judge a line to be a reality apart from matter. So, too, we can think of a genus or species by considering the substantial mutual resemblances of certain individual things. But these universals are not realities separate from the individuals. They are simply shadowy likenesses of them, reflected, so to speak, upon the mirror of our intellect.

Hence universals are not substances or accidents in reality, nor are they causes of real things as the Platonists of Chartres would have it. John of Salisbury sees them as belonging to an entirely different class; namely, to the signs by which we know and discourse about things. [10]

John of Salisbury's main criticism of his contemporaries is that they look to logic for the solution of philosophical problems, confusing logic with philosophy.[11] He himself valued logic as an aid to the other disciplines, but he thought it barren and lifeless by itself. Its categories are not to be transposed from the world of knowledge to the world of reality, nor are they to be taken as constitutive of the real world.

2   THE COMING OF THE OF THE SCHOOLMEN

VII

Introduction
to Scholasticism

WITHIN THE SPACE of about a hundred years—roughly from 1150 to 1250—a large number of Greek, Arabian, and Jewish philosophical writings were translated into Latin, profoundly transforming Christian theology and philosophy. Thus began a new chapter in Western culture called "scholasticism." During this period the basic aspiration of Christian thinkers remained the same as before. The greatest among them, like the Fathers of the Church before them, dedicated themselves to a deeper understanding of the truths of faith. But the discovery of the new philosophical literature put fresh ideas and methods at their command, giving birth to new types of theology and philosophy. By stimulating both theological and philosophical speculation, the new literature led to some of the finest products of medieval thought.

By far the most important of these new writings were the works of Aristotle, of which only a few minor logical treatises were previously known. With the translation into Latin of his *Topics* and *Analytics*, the schoolmen learned the Aristotelian methods of disputation and science, and these became their own techniques of discussion and inquiry. Theologians like St. Thomas Aquinas adapted the Aristotelian notion of science to theology, which now became the "science" of sacred doctrine. In 1255 the works of Aristotle were made the core of the curriculum of the Faculty of Arts at Paris, displacing textbooks and classical works of a humanist bent. The triumph of Aristotle was now secure. He was not to go unchallenged, as we shall see. Opposition to him arose almost from the start, and some of the greatest schoolmen (for example, St. Bonaventure) rated Plato above him. But during this period no one remained outside the sphere of his influence; for everyone he was *the* Philosopher.

THE NEW TRANSLATIONS [1]

THE NEW TRANSLATIONS were made chiefly in Mediterranean countries (especially Italy, Sicily, and Spain), where Christians, Moslems, and Jews mingled freely and spoke each other's language.

About 1128 James of Venice translated from Greek to Latin Aristotle's *Topics, Prior* and *Posterior Analytics,* and *Sophistical Arguments.* These became known as the New Logic (*Logica Nova*), in distinction to the Old Logic (*Logica Vetus*), which included the *Categories* and *De Interpretatione.* John of Salisbury was the first to show a knowledge of all these logical writings.

Before 1162 Henricus Aristippus, archdeacon of Catania in Sicily, translated from the Greek the fourth book of Aristotle's *Meteors.* He also translated Plato's *Phaedo* and *Meno.*

In the first half of the twelfth century in Toledo, Spain, John of Spain translated from Arabic the *Logic* of Avicenna. Also in Toledo, Dominicus Gundissalinus, with others, translated Avicenna's *Physics* (*Sufficentia*), *De Caelo et Mundo, On the Soul* (*Liber Sextus Naturalium*), and *Metaphysics.* The same group also translated from Arabic the *Metaphysics* of Algazel and *The Source of Life* (*Fons Vitae*) of Avicebron (Ibn Gabirol).

Another important member of the Toledo school of translators was Gerard of Cremona (d. 1187). He translated (from an Arabic translation) Aristotle's *Posterior Analytics* with Themistius' Commentary, the *Physics, De Caelo et Mundo, De Generatione et Corruptione,* and the first three books of the *Meteors.* He also translated *On the Intellect* by Alexander of Aphrodisias, as well as Alkindi's treatise of the same name, and he may have been the translator of Alfarabi's *On the Intellect* and of the *Book of Causes* (*Liber de Causis*).

In the first half of the thirteenth century at Toledo, Michael Scot (d. *c.* 1235) rendered into Latin Aristotle's *De Anima, De Caelo et Mundo,* and the treatises on animals, as well as some of Averroes' commentaries on Aristotle.

Aristotle's *Metaphysics* was translated in part from the Greek as early as 1210. Another translation, from Arabic, lacking books K,M,N, was made by Gerard of Cremona. About 1260 William of Moerbeke translated all but books M and N from the Greek. Aristotle's *Nicomachean Ethics,* Books I–III, was translated from the Greek around 1200. Shortly afterward Robert Grosseteste translated the whole work.

William of Moerbeke's contribution to this work of translating is worthy of special notice.[2] A Flemish Dominican and friend of St. Thomas Aquinas, he lived at the papal court in Italy and also in Greece and Asia Minor. He died as bishop of Corinth sometime before 1286. At the request of St. Thomas he undertook new and more faithful translations of Aristotle's Greek texts to be used by the Angelic Doctor for his commentaries. Scholars are still trying to identify the exact extent of his translations and to distinguish which are new and which are simply revisions of earlier versions. His translations are extremely—indeed crudely—literal, but there is no doubt as to the value of the service rendered by the Flemish Dominican. He also translated from the Greek some of the commentaries of Simplicius, Alexander of Aphrodisias, Philoponus, and Themistius, as well as some of the works of Proclus, including the *Elements of Theology* (1268).

As the work of translating progressed, the scholastics gained a more complete and accurate knowledge of Aristotelianism and learned to distinguish it from Neoplatonism. This was the more difficult, as Aristotle's Greek and Arabian commentators freely mingled Neoplatonic ideas with his own. Indeed, the Arabian philosophers considered Plato and Aristotle as exponents of the same philosophy. Under these circumstances it is understandable that they could attribute to Aristotle two Neoplatonic treatises, the

Book of Causes and the *Theology of Aristotle*. The former is largely taken from Proclus' *Elements of Philosophy* and the latter from Plotinus' *Enneads*. The *Book of Causes* was translated from Arabic into Latin in the twelfth century; the *Theology of Aristotle* was not available in Latin until the Renaissance. When William of Moerbeke translated Proclus' *Elements of Theology*, St. Thomas was quick to realize the true parentage of the *Book of Causes*. In recognizing the Platonic character of this work and dissociating Aristotle from many of the Neoplatonic accretions of his commentators, St. Thomas helped the Middle Ages achieve a sounder understanding of Aristotelianism.

Through the new translations the medieval world came into possession of some of the greatest treasures of the Greek philosophical genius and the truly remarkable systems of the philosophers of the Islamic countries. In these writings Christian philosophers were confronted with a scientific and philosophic vision of the universe far superior to any they had known before. By this new standard the early Middle Ages was philosophically poor and immature. The Greeks and Moslems taught the schoolmen the meaning and method of philosophy. Since their writings were products of the human mind unassisted by revelation, they opened up unexpected reaches of reason and gave the schoolmen enormous confidence in the power of the human mind. This confidence was to sustain them all through the fruitful period of the thirteenth century, when they would reach the peak of their own philosophical achievement. It was to wane in the later Middle Ages, when distrust of Aristotle and the philosophers of Islam went hand in hand with distrust in reason itself.

ECCLESIASTICAL PROHIBITIONS [3]

THE NEW LITERATURE was bound to be welcomed by those anxious for a more satisfying scientific and philosophical conception of the universe; but there were elements in it that inevitably shocked and scandalized more conservative Christians, who found difficulty in reconciling it with the teachings of their faith. Did not Aristotle teach the eternity and necessity of the world? How could this be squared with the biblical doctrine of creation? St. Bonaventure's shock on first learning Aristotle's philosophy must have been a not uncommon experience at the time. "When I was a student," he wrote, "I heard it said that Aristotle posited the world as eternal, and when I heard the reasons and arguments quoted to that effect, my heart began to beat, and I asked myself: how is this possible?" [4] This was about 1245, when St. Bonaventure was a student of philosophy at the University of Paris. Before this time Aristotle's natural philosophy was not even allowed to be taught at Paris. In 1210 a local council forbade the public or private teaching of Aristotle's writings on natural philosophy or the commentaries on them. In 1215 the statutes of the university, approved by the papal legate Robert Courson, forbade the teaching of Aristotle's metaphysics and books on natural philosophy with their commentaries. The study of Aristotle's logic and ethics, however, was not prohibited.

These prohibitions applied only to the University of Paris and not to other universities, such as Oxford or Toulouse, where the teaching of Aristotle's works was ahead of Paris. Moreover, there was no prohibition against the private reading of these books. Aristotle's cause continued to gain ground, and in 1231 Pope Gregory IX, while renewing the earlier prohibitions, set up a commission to censor the prohibited books so that they could eventually be taught. This commission does not seem to have effected its work of censorship, possibly because of the death of William of Auxerre, its most distinguished member. By 1255 the tide had turned so strongly in favor of Aristotle that all his known works were being taught at Paris.

The entrance of Aristotelianism into Christian thought was now an accomplished fact. The question that remained was whether it would be a useful servant of the faith or its master and destroyer. That Aristotle in fact became an ally of Christian wisdom was largely due to St. Thomas Aquinas. In 1263 Pope Urban IV summoned St. Thomas to Italy, where he began his voluminous commentaries on Aristotle, based upon the new translations of William of Moerbeke. This serious effort to present Aristotelianism in its own light, undistorted by Arabian interpretations, turned a potentially hostile doctrine into an ally of the faith and made possible a vital and fruitful assimilation of Aristotle's thought.

SCHOLASTICISM [5]

THE EARLIEST of the medieval universities grew out of twelfth-century schools and developed to full stature in the thirteenth century.[6] "Scholasticism" is simply the name for the theological and philosophical teachings of these schools. Since there was no one theology or philosophy taught by all the university masters, scholasticism does not designate one uniform doctrine. St. Bonaventure, St. Thomas Aquinas, Duns Scotus, and William of Ockham—to mention four outstanding examples—were all scholastics; yet each was highly original and frequently in disagreement with his contemporaries. What did the scholastics have in common to warrant our giving them the same name?

Most noticeably, their works have in common certain peculiarities of style, owing to the fact that the scholastics were university teachers and their writings are, on the whole, products of their profession. Their works tend to be impersonal in style, specialized and limited in vocabulary, abounding in abstract formulae, and somewhat rigid in the structure of their argumentation. We must remember the special audience to whom they were addressed and the purpose they were meant to serve. By contrast, the writings of the Fathers of the Church are more varied in style and less abstract and impersonal, but they were written for a more general public and without pretensions to being "scientific." Some of the earlier medieval writers already reveal "scholastic" traits (for example, Abelard and Gilbert of Poitiers) but their works were also products of the schools. Although the scholastic style degenerated into dullness and pedantry at the end of the Middle Ages, in the hands of its masters it was one of the most remarkable instruments philosophers have ever had. Moreover, it was capable of great variety, from the warmth of feeling of St. Bonaventure to the wonderful precision and lucidity of St. Thomas.

The teaching methods current in the universities greatly influenced the thinking and writing of the scholastics and made for uniformity in their style. Teaching was done mainly by lecture and disputation. A lecture (that is, a *lectio*, or "reading") consisted of the reading of a prescribed text by a bachelor or master, followed by his commentary on it. In the Faculty of Theology the text was the Bible or the *Sentences* of Peter Lombard, a twelfth-century compliation of extracts from the Fathers on theological subjects, conveniently arranged for teaching purposes. In the Faculty of Arts the text might be a work of the grammarians Donatus or Priscian, or a work of Aristotle.

Besides lecturing, masters also conducted disputations on chosen subjects. There were both regular classroom disputations held throughout the school year (*disputationes ordinariae*) and solemn or extraordinary ones held before Christmas and Easter, in which a master undertook to dispute any question proposed to him (*disputationes de quolibet*).[7]

In these disputations a question was raised on which negative and affirmative sides might be taken. In ordinary disputes the master or his students might uphold the negative side, while a young teacher with the Bachelor's degree (but not yet the Master's) would give arguments for the affirmative and answer the question. Throughout the debate the master was in charge, and it was his duty to settle the question according to his opinion and to reply to objections.

In these disputes the rules of dialectics expounded in Aristotle's *Topics* were put into practice. Students were trained to see both sides of a problem, to learn the viewpoints of the ancient philosophers (the "authorities") with regard to it, to argue in behalf of their own opinion, and to answer objections to it.

The scholastics found the "question" form an excellent one in which to express their views. They published individual disputed questions or groups of them relating to a particular topic; for example, St. Thomas' *Disputed Questions on the Soul.* They also arranged questions in larger syntheses or *summae*, as St. Thomas did in his *Summa Theologiae.* Even their published commentaries, which are sometimes literal expositions of the prescribed text, frequently took the question form, the commented text serving simply as the occasion for raising certain problems. The masters also wrote continuous treatises, divided into chapters, as well as sermons; but the most typical expression of the scholastic method is the medieval "Question."

VIII

Arabian and
Jewish Philosophy

O NE OF THE MOST important events in the development of
scholasticism was the contact of the Christian West
with Arabian and Jewish thought in the twelfth and thirteenth
centuries. The Moslem world possessed the main works of Aristotle
long before the Christian West, and many of the first Latin translations of these writings were from Arabic manuscripts. Along
with the Aristotelian treatises, Arabic scholars passed on to the
Christians their own commentaries on them and original philosophical works. Jewish thinkers of the twelfth century also pro-
vided Christians with new ideas and approaches to philosophical
and theological problems. If we are to understand the evolution
of medieval philosophy, therefore, we must have some acquaintance with the main representatives of Arabian and Jewish thought.

ARABIAN PHILOSOPHY

WHAT is generally called Arabian philosophy was one of the cultural products of the vast Moslem empire, which by the eighth
century extended from Persia to Spain.[1] This empire had been
created by the Arabs under the leadership of Mohammed (d. 632)
and his successors, the caliphs. The Arabs' conquest of the Middle
East placed them in contact with the cultural centers of Syria and
Persia, to which scholars had brought the riches of Greek science

and philosophy after A.D. 529, when the Emperor Justinian closed
the schools of philosophy at Athens. Philosophy came into its own
in the Moslem empire under the Abbassid Caliph al-Ma'mūn (813–
833), who founded a school at Baghdad devoted to the translation
of Greek scientific and philosophical literature. It was here that
some of the greatest scholars of the Moslem Empire lived and
wrote, notably Avicenna. Another important center of Moslem
culture was Cordova in Spain. In the tenth century this city was
the most civilized in Europe. In 1126 it witnessed the birth of another great philosopher of Islam, Averroes. It is to be noted that
neither Avicenna nor Averroes was an Arab by descent; Avicenna
was a Persian and Averroes a Spanish Moor. Both, however, belonged to the Moslem religion and wrote in Arabic.

The Moslems were culturally superior to the Christians during
these centuries. The Moslems' knowledge of Greek science, mathematics, and philosophy, and their original creations in these areas,
were far in advance of the Christian West. In mathematics alone the
Western world owes to the Moslems such important discoveries as
the cipher and Arabic numerals, algebra, and trigonometry.

Avicenna

AVICENNA (Ibn Sina) (980–1037) drew upon many sources, including Aristotle, the Neoplatonists, and his predecessors at Baghdad,
Alkindi (d. 873), and especially Alfarabi (d. 950).[2] For all that,
his philosophy is a highly personal achievement, ranking among
the greatest in the history of philosophy. He was never far from
the minds of the schoolmen in the thirteenth century, who either
found inspiration in his profound speculation or attempted to refute
his ideas that clashed with Christian faith.

Avicenna passed on to the scholastics many metaphysical notions
that became part and parcel of their own metaphysics. St. Thomas,
for example, was fond of quoting his statement that the notion of
"being" (ens) is the first conceived by our intellect. To this primary notion Avicenna adds those of "thing" (res) and "necessity"
(necesse). The meaning of these notions is immediately evident;

there are none simpler by which they can be known or explained. A being is something that exists. A thing is an object about which a truth can be enunciated. Every thing has an essence or quiddity by which it is what it is. For example, a triangle has an essence by which it is a triangle. Avicenna calls the essence of a thing its "certitude," for it is the truth of the thing known by the intellect and expressed in speech. Necessity is the opposite of possibility, both of which are primitive notions that can be defined only by each other. Every being involves necessity, for it has an essence through which it is necessarily what it is; for example, a being with the essence of a triangle is necessarily a triangle.

Metaphysics is the primary science because its subject is primary: being *qua* being. This science studies the necessary properties of being, such as unity, and its primary divisions, such as substance and accident. It also proves the existence of God, the first cause of every being besides himself. Because the goal of metaphysics is to know God, it is called "divine science."

Avicenna's proof for the existence of God appealed to many scholastics as a model metaphysical approach to the divinity, and they adapted it in various ways to their own philosophies. The proof can be summarized as follows. Whatever begins to be must have a cause of its being. The terms of this statement must be carefully noted. Avicenna is not saying that whatever moves or changes must have a cause of its motion or change. A cause of motion is not the same as a cause of being. The latter gives a thing its very existence, whereas the former gives it only its motion. The maker of a work of art originates the change in his materials that ends in the finished product, but he does not give that product its very existence. In fact, its existence so little depends on him that it continues to exist when he has stopped working upon it. This is not the case with a cause of being. This cause must be simultaneous with its effect as the reason for its very existence.

Now whatever begins to be is in itself simply a possible being. It can exist, but only under the influence of its cause. The reason for its existence is found in a cause that gives it existence. If this cause is itself only a possible being, it too must have a cause of its existence. But the series of such causes cannot be infinite. There must, then, be a First Cause which is not in itself a possible but a necessary being, receiving its existence from no prior cause. This is God.

An essential element in the proof is the assertion that an infinite series of causes of being, or "essential" causes, is impossible. This assertion needs to be proven. There can be an infinite series of moving causes; for example, a father can beget a son, who in turn begets a son, and so on to infinity. But the series of the causes of being must be finite, for otherwise all the members of the series will be simply possible beings and there will be no reason why they actually exist. Their actual existence is explained only by a Being who is in no sense possible but simply necessary.

Avicenna determined the number in the series of causes of being in line with the cosmology of his day. God is the First Cause and Necessary Being. Because he is One by essence, he can create directly and immediately only one effect. This is according to the Neoplatonic principle that what is one can produce only one being. This one effect is a superior kind of angel called an Intelligence. This Intelligence is possible in itself but necessary in relation to its cause because it necessarily comes from God. And since, according to another Neoplatonic principle, thinking is creating, the first Intelligence by knowing God creates another Intelligence. By knowing itself as necessary in relation to God, it produces the soul of the first sphere; by knowing itself as possible, it produces the matter of that sphere. By a similar process of reflecting upon the preceding Intelligence and upon itself as both necessary and possible, the second Intelligence creates a third Intelligence and the soul and body of the second sphere. In this way are created nine Intelligences and nine spheres, the last of which is the sphere of the moon. The Intelligence governing this sphere creates a tenth and final Intelligence, which is the Agent Intellect. The Agent Intellect in turn creates the four elements in the sublunary world and individual souls. Avicenna calls this cosmic Intellect the "giver of forms" (*dator formarum*) because it constantly emits all possible forms, which are received in matter suitably disposed to receive them and also in human intellects disposed for their reception.[3]

The creation of the Intelligences and of the physical universe is necessary and eternal. Only individual things in the sensible world are contingent, in the sense that they come into existence and pass away in time; and their contingency is not due to the will and providence of God but to matter. God transcends not only the world but the whole series of the Intelligences. He knows himself and, in so doing, knows all possible beings; but he knows them in general and not in particular. Hence his providence does not extend to the details of creation. Scholastic theologians will strenuously oppose these doctrines of Avicenna, as indeed orthodox Moslem theologians did in Islam. Many scholastics would have echoed the statement of a famous Moslem philosopher who recanted his rationalist doctrines on his deathbed with the words: "Almighty God has spoken the truth and Avicenna is a liar!"

One aspect of Avicenna's doctrine of creation, however, was of momentous importance for the development of scholasticism; namely, the distinction between essence and existence in creatures. This doctrine was not original with Avicenna; he took it from Alfarabi, who appears to have been its author. Alfarabi points out that we can conceive what something is (for example, humanity), without knowing whether it exists. From this he concludes that existence is not contained in the essence of things but is an accessory accident of them. Before Alfarabi, Aristotle had distinguished in his logical writings between the notion of what a thing is and the fact that it exists. Alfarabi took this logical distinction as a sign of the real distinction in creatures between their essence and existence.

No doubt the impulse to extend Aristotle's logical distinction to the order of reality came from the revealed notion of creation, which was unknown to Aristotle. For Alfarabi and Avicenna, a creature in itself is a possible being; that is to say, it is an essence which can exist when given existence by its cause. Its existence, then, is not identical with its essence, nor is it one of the essential properties following upon the essence, as the ability to laugh is an essential property of the essence of man and a necessary concomitant of it. Existence is a separable concomitant or accident of essence. At least this is true of created existence. In God there is no distinction between essence and existence. Indeed, Avicenna denies to God an essence, properly speaking, for an essence is communicable to many, whereas God is unique. He alone exists necessarily through himself; he alone is pure existence.

Not only is the essence of creatures distinct from their existence; the same essence can simultaneously take on different modes of existence in reality and in the intellect. Humanity, for example, can exist in several ways: in the real world (for example, in Socrates and Plato), and in the intellect where it is known. In the intellect the essence exists as a universal—that is to say as a concept predicable of many subjects; in the real world the essence exists as a singular thing, with accidental characteristics differentiating it from every other individual with the same essence. In itself, however, the essence is neither universal nor individual but is simply itself. For example, in itself humanity is simply humanity; universality and singularity, like existence, are outside its essence and are added to it as supervening accidents.

Avicenna's analysis of essences aims at isolating them in all their purity, stripped of everything extrinsic to them. He denies that they exist as such. They exist only in the mind and in things. Yet he ascribes to them a being that belongs to them in themselves (*esse proprium*), which is not an existential being but the essential being reached by the mind when it considers an essence in abstraction from everything that is not itself. Scholastic philosophers like Henry of Ghent and Duns Scotus will see in this pursuit of essences in all their purity the proper function of metaphysics and, like Avicenna, they will attribute to essences as such a being of their own called the "being of essence" (*esse essentiae*).[4]

We can see Avicenna's analysis of essences at work in his psychology. What is the essence of man? Avicenna asks us to imagine a man created in empty space and incapable of perceiving anything with his senses, not even his own body. Would this hypothetical man know anything? Yes, Avicenna replies, he would know his own existence as a spiritual soul. But he would not know of the existence of his body, for he could not perceive his body. This shows that man's body is extrinsic to his essence. It also shows that the body is a substance distinct from the substance of the soul. The latter is a spiritual being independent of the body and hence capable of surviving its death. In short, it is immortal. It is the form and perfection of the body, giving it life and movement, but this relation to the body is not of the essence of the soul. By its essence it is a spiritual substance; its function of animating the body is extrinsic and accidental to its nature. We call the soul a form as we call man a worker, designating by this, not the soul's essence, but a function it performs; namely, that of animating a body.

According to Avicenna, each man possesses his own spiritual soul endowed with vegetative, sensitive, and intellectual powers. The highest of these powers is the intellect. Created devoid of knowledge, this intellect is capable of knowing (hence its name of "possible intellect"), but it actually knows only through the cooperation of man's sense power and the Agent Intellect. It will be remembered that this latter Intellect is a separate intelligence which not only creates men but constantly radiates forms that are impressed upon human minds capable of receiving them. The work of preparation for this reception is accomplished by the external and internal sense powers, whose functions Avicenna describes in detail. Through the external senses we perceive sensible things, the images of which remain in our internal faculties of imagination, common sense (*sensus communis*), and the cogitative power. The purpose of knowing is to grasp essences in their purity, stripped of all accidental characteristics. This is done through abstraction, which lays bare the essence of an individual sensible thing, whose image is preserved in the internal senses. Abstraction, however, is not the work of the human intellect but of the separate Agent Intellect which, like the sun flooding our eyes with light, so illumines our mind that it can see pure forms.

From this it is evident how closely the destiny of human souls is bound up with the Agent Intellect. This Intellect is not only their immediate creator but is the source of their purest perfection and joy; namely, intellectual knowledge. What is more, souls after death find their salvation, not in God but in this Intellect, being united to it forever in proportion to the intellectual progress they have made in this life.

The schoolmen found much in Avicenna's philosophy to reject and also much to adapt to their own use. Since both Avicenna and St. Augustine came under the influence of Neoplatonism, there are certain resemblances in their notions of the soul and of knowledge that made some thirteenth-century followers of Augustine look upon the Arabian philosopher with sympathy. In particular, their doctrines of illumination were united in a theory of knowledge aptly called Avicennian-Augustinianism.[5]

Averroes

THE GREATEST of the philosophers of the Moslem Empire after Avicenna was Averroes (Ibn Rochd) (1126–1198).[6] His influence was strong throughout the thirteenth and fourteenth centuries and even into the Renaissance. So highly esteemed were his commentaries on the works of Aristotle during this period that he was given the name of "the Commentator."

Averroes' ambition was to understand and to teach the philosophy of Aristotle, whom he considered the greatest of the philosophers. He wrote: "I believe that this man was the rule in nature and the model that nature produced to show the ultimate in human perfection." [7] Even if allowance is made for oriental hyperbole, this is an extravagant eulogy. In fact, Averroes wrote as though the philosophy of Aristotle were identical with philosophy itself. He had little conception of philosophy as an intellectual discipline capable of progress; and indeed the Averroist school of philosophy which he inspired in the Christian West was one of the least creative and progressive.

Averroes had to defend Aristotle's philosophy against two groups in the Moslem world. The first were philosophers like Alfarabi and Avicenna, who he thought had distorted the Aristotelian philosophy by mingling it with religious doctrines; for example, the doctrine of creation. Against these men he set out to expurgate all traces of religion from philosophy and thus to restore it to its rational purity. The second group were the Moslem theologians who attacked philosophy as an enemy of religion. The greatest of these was Algazel (d. *c.* 1111), whose treatise "The Incoherence of the Philosophers" is an attempt to refute the doctrines of Aristotle and Avicenna opposed to the Koran, such as the eternity and necessity of the universe and the unicity of the Agent Intellect. Against the attack of Algazel, Averroes upheld the truth of philosophy in a work entitled "The Incoherence of the Incoherence." [8]

While defending philosophy as the highest truth, Averroes considered religion a social necessity and indeed as basically in agreement with philosophy. In order to appreciate the respective roles of religion, theology, and philosophy, he considered it necessary to understand the three classes into which all men are divided: 1] The first class, comprising the vast majority of people, live by imagination rather than by reason. This class must be induced to live virtuously by eloquent preaching which stirs the imagination rather than the mind. The philosopher is virtuous for rational motives and so does not need religion. Religion and philosophy thus work for the same end and are basically in accord. Religion is but truth made accessible to those whose imagination is stronger than their reason.   2] The second class are the theologians. They have the same beliefs as the vast majority of people but want reasons for what they believe. Reason is beginning to awaken in these men, and they look for a rational justification for their beliefs. But they are incapable of reaching the absolute truth; their conclusions at best are probable.   3] The third class is made up of a small number of philosophers, the elite of mankind. They perceive the nucleus of truth contained in the fancies of men of faith and in the dialectical probabilities of the theologians; but they rise above them and know the truth in all its purity.

These three groups of people use different approaches to the same truth and they ultimately agree with one another. The beliefs of the common people and the teachings of the theologians are simply philosophical truths adapted to inferior minds. Averroes did not despise religion or faith, for he recognized their civilizing force among the masses. It was the theologians who bore the brunt of his attack because of their infelicitous mingling of faith and reason. The Koran he considered a miraculous book and divinely inspired, for it is more effective than philosophy in raising the people to the level of morality. Moses, Jesus, and Mohammed were true prophets and messengers of God to mankind. But their religions were only popular approaches to the truth found in its purity in philosophy.[9]

Avicenna offered a metaphysical proof of God's existence that locates God above the Intelligences moving the heavenly spheres. In contrast to him, Averroes, like Aristotle, thought it possible to prove the existence of God in natural philosophy through an analysis of movement. The divinity whose existence is thus proven is not the transcendent God of Avicenna but the Intelligences themselves, the chief of which is the Prime Mover.

Averroes points out that there are beings that move and thus pass from potency to act. Now whatever moves is moved by something else which is in act. Since there cannot be an infinite series of such movers, there must be a primary cause of motion which is itself not capable of being moved and hence is purely in act. How many primary causes of motion are there? As many as are needed to account for the primary movements in the universe, which astronomers calculate to be thirty-eight. Hence there are thirty-eight pure Acts or Intelligences, each of which is divine. The first in the hierarchy of these Intelligences is the Prime Mover, who is the ultimate cause of all motion.

According to Averroes, all the Intelligences are eternal and uncreated, as is also the universe which they move. The notion of creation was to his mind a teaching of religion, having no place in philosophy. According to philosophy (that is, Aristotelianism), the Intelligences move the celestial spheres, and through them the sublunary bodies, as *final* causes. The souls of the spheres, which are endowed with knowledge, love the Intelligences and aspire by the circular movement they communicate to the spheres to imitate their perfection to the extent that this is possible.

Having rejected creation, it was only natural for Averroes to deny the real distinction between essence and existence. For him, the distinction is only a logical one between the notions expressing what a thing is (that is, its essence) and the fact that it exists. His argument against the real distinction will often be quoted by scholastics agreeing with him on this point. If existence is distinct from essence, coming to it from outside to make it exist, then another being must be added to existence to make it exist, and this being requires still another to make it exist, and so on to infinity. The fact that Aristotle knew nothing of this distinction is conclusive evidence for Averroes that it has no place in philosophy.

Averroes' own metaphysical notions follow those of Aristotle. Being, in the primary sense of the word, is substance; that is to say, an individual existing thing. Universals exist only in the intellect, which is the cause of universality. Secondarily, being is an accident, which exists only in a substance. The primary substances are the Intelligences, which are immaterial forms and pure Acts. In material things, forms are united to matter, but the essence of these material substances consists in their forms alone. Hence all beings are either substances or accidents; there is no other being besides them called "existence."

The substantial form of the human body is its soul. The soul is not a spiritual substance endowed with its own possible intellect, as Avicenna thought. It is a corporeal form essentially tied up with the body and hence incapable of surviving after death. Its highest power is a corporeal one called the passive intellect or imagination, by which an individual human being is capable of union with the Agent Intellect. This Intellect, as Avicenna taught, is the last of the celestial Intelligences and the ruler of the sublunary world. It illuminates the passive intellects of men disposed to receive knowledge from it. Since it makes human knowledge possible, it is also called the possible intellect. Avicenna had conceded to each individual man his own spiritual soul and possible intellect—a spiritual power by which he could personally know the truth and enjoy eternal happiness. The Agent Intellect alone, and not the possible intellect, is one for all men. Averroes goes farther and denies to individual men their own possible intellects. The result is that he conceives man as a superior type of animal whose highest individual powers are corporeal and corruptible with the body.[10] Man's dignity consists in his special union through knowledge and love with the Agent Intellect.

The rationalism of Averroes put him at odds with his fellow

Moslems, who accused him of heresy and banished him from Cordova. However, he was restored to favor before his death. Among Christians his reputation for impiety grew as his influence became stronger. Duns Scotus calls him "that accursed Averroes," and Petrarch dubs him a mad dog barking against Christ and the Catholic religion. In fact, Averroes did not openly attack even the Moslem religion, which he thought a social necessity. Such hostile epithets were prompted by the destructive influence of the philosophy of Averroes in Christian circles.

History credits St. Thomas Aquinas with stemming the influence of Averroes in the Christian West. The triumph of St. Thomas over Averroes was celebrated in art by Renaissance painters like Benozzo Gozzoli and Andrea of Florence, who depict St. Thomas enthroned with Averroes groveling under his feet. While there is some truth in this picture, it does not adequately represent St. Thomas' relation to the great Arabian philosopher. St. Thomas effectively refuted the errors of Averroes, but he also learned much from him. One has the impression that St. Thomas had Averroes' commentaries constantly by his side, so frequently does he refer to them and draw light from them. For St. Thomas, as for all the schoolmen, Averroes was "the Commentator" on Aristotle and an inexhaustible source of information on philosophical subjects.

JEWISH PHILOSOPHY

THE influence of Jewish philosophers upon the scholastics was considerably less than that of the philosophers of Islam. However, at least two of the greatest among them must be mentioned for their contributions to Christian philosophy.[11]

Ibn Gabirol

SOLOMON IBN GABIROL (*c.* 1020–*c.* 1070), known to the scholastics as Avicebron or Avencebrol, was a Spanish Jew who wrote his chief work, *The Source of Life* (*Fons Vitae*), in Arabic.[12] Although the scholastics knew this work well, they did not realize that its author was a Jew. They mistook him for an Arab or a Christian.

Gabirol was best known among the scholastics for teaching that all creatures, both corporeal and incorporeal, are composed of matter and form. Only God lacks this composition. There are two kinds of matter: the gross corporeal matter in our own bodies and in those surrounding us, and an invisible, spiritual matter belonging to angels and human souls. The presence of spiritual matter in incorporeal creatures explains how there can be many of them in the same species (more technically, it is their principle of individuation), and it also accounts for the possibility of change in these creatures. Almost all the Franciscan schoolmen adopted this thesis, which fits in well with St. Augustine's suggestion of the existence of two kinds of matter, spiritual and corporeal. St. Thomas Aquinas, on the other hand, rejected the notion of spiritual matter as contradictory, and substituted for the hylomorphic composition in all creatures the composition of essence and act of being (*esse*).

According to Gabirol, God creates a universal being composed of universal matter and a universal form. This being is immediately clothed with added forms which diversify it and thereby cause the various types of beings in the universe. Each particular being is thus made up of matter and a number of forms which establish that being in its genus and species. For example, the form "corporeity" places all bodies in the genus "body." Less general forms are then added, such as "animality" and "humanity," resulting in a human being. The purpose of rational analysis is to discover the structure of a particular being by distinguishing the various forms which go to make it up. These forms are arranged within it according to a definite pattern and hierarchy, depending on their degree of generality. The more general forms are inferior to the more particular ones that are added to them. Lower forms, moreover, are contained within higher forms (for example, "body" is contained in "animal" and "animal" in "man"). The higher the form, the more numerous are the inferior forms it contains, but this does not entail loss of unity on the part of the higher form. It is a general law that the higher the form, the more unity it has. Thus the form "humanity" has a greater unity than the form "corporeity."

The scholastics called this the doctrine of the plurality of forms, and many adopted it as the most reasonable explanation of the metaphysical structure of created being. It is obviously an attractive doctrine to philosophers with a leaning toward Platonism, because it presupposes a close parallelism between the structure of our logical thought and of reality.

Gabirol's philosophy owes much to Neoplatonism, although the influence of the Old Testament upon it is also evident, as is clear from its doctrine of creation *ex nihilo*. At the beginning of *The Source of Life*, Gabirol establishes knowledge as man's highest good. Self-knowledge is most important. From a knowledge of self, man proceeds to know other things and finally God, who is their cause. But owing to God's infinity, our limited minds cannot know him in himself but only in his creatures.

Man is the world in miniature, or the microcosm, and hence he contains within himself all forms, the knowledge of which leads him back to his creator. He is born into the world with a soul filled with ideas that have only to be stirred to full consciousness in order to be known. The sensible forms of things are capable of doing this if man only turns toward them. Gabirol compares the sensible world to a book whose symbols awaken the mind of the reader to understand their meaning. So, too, the world of sense stimulates the human mind to an understanding of the intelligible ideas lying dormant within. More than one scholastic thinker of Neoplatonic and Augustinian tendencies found this comparison an apt one to express his doctrine of knowledge.

Moses Maimonides

MOSES BEN MAIMON, the greatest medieval Jewish theologian and philosopher, was born in Cordova in 1135 and educated by his father and Arabian masters. At an early age he traveled east, settling in Cairo, where he died in 1204. St. Thomas and the other scholastics knew him as Rabbi Moses. The fact that they frequently referred to him by his own name instead of by the anonymous "someone" (*quidam*)—their usual appellation for contemporaries or near contemporaries—indicates their respect for him and the authoritative position they accorded him.

The meeting of Greek and Arabian philosophy with Judaism brought about a conflict between philosophers and theologians similar to that which occurred in the Moslem and Christian worlds. How were Greek science and philosophy to be reconciled with the Jewish faith? Maimonides wrote *The Guide for the Perplexed* to answer this question.[13] He maintains that there neither is nor can be any conflict between reason and faith. Any apparent conflict between them arises from a misinterpretation of Scripture or the writings of the philosophers. Scripture abounds in anthropomorphic passages that are not to be taken literally. For example, God is often described in terms applicable only to a material being, whereas in fact he is incorporeal. On the other hand, because philosophy, and especially metaphysics, is so difficult, it should not be taught to the young or to the common people. Instruction should not begin with metaphysics: faith should come first, and it suffices for the guidance of children and ordinary persons. St. Thomas makes use of this notion in his *Summa Contra Gentiles*, I, 4, when proving that it was fitting for God to reveal truths within the reach of human reason.

A subject of apparent conflict between Scripture and Aristotle is the duration of the world. Scripture teaches the creation of the world in time, while Aristotle would have us believe that it always existed. Maimonides shows that creation is reconcilable with philosophical principles and that the Aristotelian arguments for the eternity of the world are not conclusive, because they do not take into account the omnipotence of God, who can freely create a universe of whatever duration he wishes. St. Thomas adopted the same attitude toward this problem.

Maimonides also anticipates St. Thomas with his proofs for the existence of God as First Mover and First Cause of the universe and as the Necessary Being. St. Thomas, however, opposed his doctrine of the divine attributes, for which he was perhaps best known among the scholastics. For Maimonides, an attribute of God is either affirmative or negative. Affirmative attributes do not apply to God literally; otherwise he would not be one and indivisible, for he would be his essence along with the superadded attributes. When Scripture describes God by many attributes it does not mean that he contains any plurality, but simply that he accomplishes many actions without in any way impairing his strict unity. For example, when the prophets call God powerful or wise they do not mean that he possesses qualities distinct from his essence. Power and wisdom do not exist in God himself; these attributes are to be understood as different relations between God and his creatures. They signify that God has power to create things and wisdom to know what he created. Only negative attributes—for example, immutability—are true with reference to God himself; but these tell us what God is not rather than what he is.

Scripture, however, reveals one positive divine name that is not derived from God's action in relation to his creatures but that designates his very substance. This is the sacred name God revealed to Moses (*Exod.* 3:14) called the Tetragrammaton, because it was written in four Hebrew letters. Maimonides says that the meaning of this word, long kept secret by the priests, has been lost, but he thinks that it means "absolute existence." If this is true, by this name God revealed himself to be pure and necessary existence. In him there is no duality of essence and existence, for the two are identical. They are distinct, however, in all creatures. Following Avicenna, Maimonides calls the existence of creatures an "accident" superadded to their essence by their cause.

Maimonides takes most of the details of his cosmogony from Avicenna, including the notion of celestial spheres with motor Intelligences, which he identifies with the angels of Holy Scripture. He shows his Jewish spirit in insisting, against Avicenna, that God knows and provides for every individual man in the world. Like Avicenna, he identifies the last of the Intelligences with the Agent Intellect, and he assigns to it the function of illuminating human minds.

In the closing chapter of *The Guide for the Perplexed,* Maimonides takes up the problem of human perfection, which he divides into four kinds: The first and lowest is the acquisition of wealth and property; the second is the perfection of the body; the third is moral excellence; and the fourth is speculative knowledge of God. The first three types of goods do not perfect man as man. Even excellence of character does not concern a man in himself but in relation to other human beings. Only intelligence, leading to a metaphysical knowledge of God, is man's true perfection. It gives him immortality and on its account he is called a man. Nothing shows better than this notion of salvation by metaphysics how deeply the Greek intellectual spirit penetrated the mind of Maimonides.

IX

Early Philosophy at Paris and Oxford

THE DEVELOPMENT OF SCHOLASTICISM went hand in hand with the growth of the universities in the thirteenth century, the greatest of which were Paris and Oxford.[1] Without exception, the scholastics we shall be concerned with studied and taught at one or both of these two universities. There was constant traffic and communication between the two schools, but each had its own typical intellectual attitudes and interests. In general it can be said that Aristotelianism triumphed at Paris, whereas Platonism and Augustinism had the upper hand at Oxford, although this is a broad statement admitting of exceptions and qualifications. In any case, Aristotle and the Arabian philosophers never gained the popularity at Oxford that they did at Paris. This difference between the two universities can be seen even in their scientific interests. Paris generally followed the biological approach of Aristotle, while Oxford favored the mathematical study of nature more congenial to Platonism.

The Universities of Paris and Oxford were formally constituted at the beginning of the thirteenth century, although they grew out of earlier schools in these towns. The University of Paris developed from the cathedral schools of Paris, receiving its charter from the King and Pope in 1200. It consisted of four Faculties: Arts, Theology, Law, and Medicine. Students first enrolled in the Faculty of Arts, usually about the age of fifteen, to obtain the degrees of Bachelor and Master of Arts. After that they could enter one of the higher Faculties of Theology, Law, or Medicine. By the end of the twelfth century Oxford was rapidly progressing toward the status of a university. Its earliest colleges, Balliol and Merton, were founded respectively in 1263 and 1264.

Other universities sprang up in the thirteenth century, notable among which were the University of Toulouse in France, the University of Naples in Italy, and the University of Cambridge in England. None of them, however, was a serious rival to Paris or Oxford. These two universities, and especially that of Paris, were the intellectual centers of the Christian world. It was there that the newly translated works of the Greeks, Arabs, and Jews aroused the greatest intellectual ferment, stimulating philosophical and scientific thought, and raising critical problems in minds anxious to preserve the Christian faith and the heritage of the Fathers of the Church. We shall observe the reaction of two of the earliest and most intelligent theologians to this crisis: William of Auvergne at Paris and Robert Grosseteste at Oxford.

William of Auvergne

WILLIAM OF AUVERGNE'S CAREER AT PARIS, as student, teacher, and bishop, extending over the first half of the thirteenth century, coincided with the period when the university felt the full impact of the philosophies of Aristotle and Avicenna.[2] Averroes was just beginning to be known in the 1240's, and a generation would elapse before Christendom grappled with his philosophy. William of Auvergne was concerned chiefly with the implications of Avicenna's philosophy for Christian thought. Firmly established in the tradition of St. Augustine, Boethius, and St. Anselm, he considered Avicenna's philosophy a serious threat to the faith, and his numerous writings were designed to offset its pernicious influence. He was well aware, however, that in order to refute a philosopher one must himself be a philosopher. The challenge of Avicennianism stimulated him to deeper philosophical reflection and led him to ask new questions and to rethink old problems in new terms, which were often those of Avicenna himself.

CRITICISM OF AVICENNA

WILLIAM OF AUVERGNE'S CRITICISM of Avicenna centered around his notions of God and creation. In Avicenna's world there is a First Cause and ten Intelligences, all of whom are creators. The First Cause creates only one immediate effect, the first Intelligence, who in turn creates the second Intelligence, and so on. This series of creations ends with the tenth Intelligence, who is the creator of human souls and matter. According to Avicenna, then, the First Cause, or God, is not the immediate creator of the world. Neither is he a free creator; like all the Intelligences, he creates necessarily as a result of his self-knowledge, not freely as a result of a decision of his will.

The radical error in this view of creation, according to William of Auvergne, is that it ignores the omnipotence and freedom of God. It limits God's creation to one immediate effect, on the ground that from one being, inasmuch as it is one, only one effect can come: *ab uno, inquantum unum, non est nisi unum*. Since God creates through the knowledge he has of himself, and he knows himself only in one way, being absolutely one, Avicenna argued that only one creature could proceed from him. William retorts that this places limits upon the intellect of the creator, confining it to the knowledge of only one thing. This makes God the most foolish of beings. In fact, God, the infinite and perfect being, knows everything by knowing himself. Moreover, he does not know one thing better than another, but all equally. In this respect he is like an architect, who knows many buildings and not one rather than another. So, too, God through his self-knowledge knows all possible ways in which creatures can participate in his perfection, and hence he knows all creatures without exception or preference. What is more, he is not forced to create one to the exclusion of others. Like a builder, who is free to make whatever building he chooses, God is free to create any creature he wishes.[3]

William of Auvergne thus championed the Christian notion of God as a free creator against the Greco-Arabian doctrine of God as a limited and necessary cause of the universe. Avicenna, in his view, exalted the unity of God at the expense of his other attributes, particularly his wisdom and liberty. As a consequence, the Moslem philosopher did not see how God could directly produce a multiplicity of creatures. William of Auvergne would have us understand the actual, infinite perfection of God, and see that he is the sole and immediate creator of the universe. In particular, there are no Intelligences separating the human soul from God. A direct creation of God, the soul is intimately joined to him and is destined to see him face to face in the next life.

William was also critical of the cosmological role Avicenna assigned to the Intelligences. Avicenna thought that the heavenly spheres surrounding the earth were animated by souls which moved them in circles as a result of their love of the Intelligences. William considered this not only impossible but ridiculous. Surely, he exclaims, the souls of these spheres could pass their lives more usefully than in dragging the immense bulk of the spheres in dizzy rotation, like horses or donkeys harnessed to mill wheels!

GOD AND EXISTENCE

ONE OF THE MOST remarkable achievements of thirteenth-century philosophy is the notion of God as pure existence, or existence itself. This notion finds its best expression in St. Thomas Aquinas, but Avicenna helped to shape it, as did also William of Auvergne.

According to William of Auvergne, there are two types of being: being that receives its existence from another, and being that exists by itself because its existence is underived. We know that there are beings of the first sort, and since there cannot be an infinite series of such beings, one receiving existence from another to infinity, there must be a First Being who exists by himself. This being is God.

What, however, is the meaning of being? William of Auvergne replies that being (*esse*) has two meanings.[4] First, it means the substance or essence of a thing, when that essence is considered in itself and stripped of all its accidents. In this sense, being is that which a thing's definition signifies. Second, being means a thing's existence, which is designated by the verb *is* in a proposition. Now we can define what any creature is without saying anything about its existence. For example, we can define the essence of a man or a donkey without affirming or denying their existence. In the case of God, however, this is impossible, for God and his existence are identical. As Scripture tells us, God is "He Who Is" (*Exod.* 3:14). This means that there is no distinction in God between his essence and his existence: he is existence itself in all purity, so that he has no essence or definition. On the other hand, every creature has an essence distinct from its existence. Its existence is accidental to it, for it is not necessary that it exist. It exists or not, depending on God's will to create it. In all creatures, then, existence is really distinct from essence by reason of their radical contingency and dependence on God's creative will.

William of Auvergne anticipates St. Thomas not only in teaching the real distinction between essence and existence in creatures but also in attributing greater value to existence than to essence. Existence, he says, is of greater worth than any substance or accident.[5] As an indication of this he points out that a being will cling to its existence at all costs and will refuse to give it up despite the injury it may receive to its essence. By the love and desire it reveals for its existence, the whole universe proclaims the superiority of this aspect of its being to every other. And the reason for this love of existence is evident. Is not God existence itself? No wonder the universe he created treasures and prizes existence above everything else; this is but to treasure and prize God himself. In clinging to existence, creatures are in fact clinging to God.

God is most intimate and present to a creature precisely through its existence. Mentally strip from Socrates, for example, the form that makes him the individual he is. Then take from him the specific form by which he is a man and the generic forms by which he is an animal, a body, and a substance. After this, being still remains as the innermost garment, so to speak, with which the creator has clothed him. His being or existence, then, is the closest point of contact between himself and God.[6]

So close indeed is God to creatures at this point that William of Auvergne tends to substitute the divine presence for created existence. God, he says, is the being of all things. This is not meant in a pantheistic sense, as though creatures were confused with God. William of Auvergne simply wishes to stress the existential dependence of creatures upon God, but in so doing he tends to deny creatures any existence proper to themselves. This can be seen from his statement that God is related to creatures as the soul is to the body: as the soul gives the body life, so God gives existence to his creatures.[7] St. Thomas will explain that God is the *efficient* cause of the existence of creatures, whereas the soul is the *formal* cause of the existence of the body, which in fact has no other existence than that of the soul.[8] William of Auvergne makes no such clarification, leaving the relation between God's existence and that of creatures ambiguous. He describes the existence of creatures as potential, flowing, and false. God alone possesses true existence, and creatures exist only insofar as they participate in it.[9]

This depreciation of the created world and exaltation of God as the sole true being is in line with early medieval philosophy, which reduced the universe to a reflection or image of God, or to a book of symbols in which God can be read. This is also the world described by William of Auvergne. Against Aristotle and Avicenna, who were above all concerned with establishing the stability and eternity of the universe, he argues for its essential instability and non-eternity. Indeed, he considers created being so empty and deficient that it cannot exercise true causality. As God is the sole true being, so is he alone truly a cause. It is only by an abuse of the term that a creature is called a cause. In reality it is but a channel or window by which the divine causality is communicated to the world.[10]

In contrast to William of Auvergne, one of the chief aims of St. Thomas Aquinas will be to reconcile the total dependence of creatures upon God with their status as true beings and causes within the created order.

THE SOUL AND KNOWLEDGE

WILLIAM OF AUVERGNE'S NOTION of the soul is Platonic and Augustinian. He describes the soul as a spiritual substance residing in the body as a pilot in a ship or a ruler in his kingdom. The body is a prison in which the human soul is held captive all during the misery of this present life. Again, he compares the body to a garment worn by the soul; the soul on the other hand is the whole being and essence of man. This he proves by Avicenna's hypothetical experience of a man suspended in air in such a way that he has no sensations. A man in this situation would at least know his own existence as a soul. His true self, then, is his soul; the body is simply the instrument by which he acts. Properly speaking, the arts are located in the human soul. True, it is man who writes, builds, and knows, using his body as an instrument; but these are really operations of the soul and not, as Aristotle thought, of the composite of soul and body.[11]

If man is essentially a soul, why does the soul reside in the body? William of Auvergne accounts for its presence there by its weakness and imperfection. Spiritual substances, such as angels, command bodies and move them without residing in them. The human soul must live in the body in order effectively to move it and use it as its tool. The soul must be in the body, then, because of the imperfection and weakness of the soul's power of commanding.

Following St. Augustine, William of Auvergne maintains that the soul vivifies and operates in every part of the body. He acknowledges that the soul does not perceive itself doing this, although it should be able to do so. "No knowledge," he says in true Augustinian fashion, "is more natural to the soul than the knowledge of its own self." The unnatural ignorance of the human soul regarding its union with the body must be a consequence of original sin. He writes: "Perhaps when the soul has been liberated from the oppression of this present misery and from the shadows enveloping it in this life, it will with the greatest clarity see itself vivifying all the parts of the body and exercising life in them. It seems to me too that in the state of natural purity and liberty the souls of our first parents saw this, or could see it if they wished to turn their minds to it or advert to it." [12]

The darkening shadow of original sin has altered our knowledge in still other ways. While confined to the body, the human soul finds itself located on the boundary of two worlds: the world of sensible things which it contacts through the body, and God to whom it is akin by nature. Both worlds play a role in the genesis of knowledge. The senses have for their object the accidents of things; namely, their color, sound, taste, and so on. The intellect's task is to penetrate to the substance of things, of which the accidents are the external coverings. For example, from the movements and actions of the body, it knows the human soul. But in the present life our intellect never attains a clear-sighted view of the substances of things so as to know them distinctly and individually.

In order to illustrate this point William of Auvergne uses the following example. Suppose someone paints so exact a portrait of Socrates that anyone knowing him would clearly recognize it as his likeness. Looking at the picture from a distance, however, he would see it only vaguely as a likeness of a man. It is in the latter way that our intellect knows the particular objects of sense. Tied to the body, the intellect is so short-sighted that it sees them only indistinctly and abstractly. It lacks knowledge of the substances of things by which they differ numerically from each other (for example, the substance of Socrates as distinct from that of Plato), and so it must distinguish them by their accidental characteristics. If, however, the soul were released from the body or given a special divine illumination, it would know the substance of things, but this is impossible so long as it is asleep in the body.[13]

Abstraction for William of Auvergne is thus nothing but the short-sightedness of the intellect (*brevitas intellectus*) owing to its present wretched state in the body. He saw that for abstraction of this sort an agent intellect is not necessary. Aristotle attributed to man both an agent and possible intellect, but William of Auvergne considered this distinction not only unnecessary but opposed to the simplicity and indivisibility of the soul. The soul has no faculties distinct from its substance; what we call the intellect is simply the soul exercising its knowing activity. This activity takes place on the occasion of the body's being stimulated by the sensible world. The intellect then instantaneously conforms itself to external things, producing within itself abstract ideas of them. It does this by a sort of natural mimicry, as a monkey imitates those around it or a chameleon adapts its color to its environment. By a similar instinct the intellect acts out within itself the drama of the external world in order to inscribe it within itself and thus know it.[14]

The origin of this innate capacity of the intellect to give birth to ideas is God, who illuminates and fecundates it by his own Ideas. William of Auvergne compares God to a mirror or a living book in which the intellect can read intelligible truths and the rules of morality. "The creator himself," he writes, "is the natural and proper book of the human intellect." [15] By this he does not mean that our intellect enjoys a direct vision of the divine Ideas in the present life. Like St. Augustine, he means that all our knowledge of the truth presupposes the immediate action of God upon the soul as its interior light and teacher.

By ascribing to God the light by which the intellect knows, William of Auvergne makes it as completely dependent upon God for its knowledge as every creature is for its being. The intellect by itself is empty and passive; only through the action of God is it moved to know. Not only does this eliminate from man an agent intellect whereby he is the cause of his knowing; it removes every intermediary between God and the soul in the production of knowledge. No created Intelligence, like the Avicennian Agent Intellect, illuminates man's mind; God himself does so directly. As far as we know, William of Auvergne did not call God the agent intellect of man's soul, but in fact his description of God's role in producing man's knowledge is similar to that of Avicenna's Agent Intellect. It is only a short step from this to affirm that God is the agent intellect of the soul, and we shall see that there were some Augustinians—for example, Roger Bacon—who did not hesitate to take it.

Robert Grosseteste

IT IS FITTING to introduce philosophy at Oxford with Grosseteste, for he was the university's first great scholar as well as its first chancellor.[16] His influence in shaping its intellectual atmosphere and educational ideals lasted beyond the Middle Ages. It is surely no coincidence that so many of his predilections—the classics, linguistic studies, logic, mathematics, and experimentation—should have become characteristic of the University of Oxford and its close associate, the University of Cambridge. Owing largely to him, scholasticism at Oxford was noticeably different from that at Paris. Oxford never espoused Aristotelianism so completely or enthusiastically as the French university. Despite the influence of Aristotle, Platonic and Augustinian philosophical ideas always held first place.

If we are to believe Roger Bacon, Grosseteste completely disregarded the works of Aristotle and their methods and relied upon his own experience and other authors.[17] However, this is hardly an exact statement of Grosseteste's relationship to Aristotle. Grosseteste wrote the first extensive commentary on Aristotle's *Posterior Analytics* (between 1200 and 1209), and he always remained indebted to the theory and method of science proposed in this work. Besides this, he commented on Aristotle's *Physics* and *Metaphysics*, and in later life he translated the *Nicomachean Ethics* from Greek to Latin. The point to Bacon's statement is that in many of Grosseteste's own philosophical and scientific treatises (Bacon mentions specifically those on the rainbow and comets) he relies not upon Aristotle but upon his own observations and the mathematical method of the Arabian scientists and it was for this that Bacon chiefly admired him. Grosseteste was in fact one of the originators of the scientific method, both describing it in theory and applying it in practice in his study of such topics as heat, the stars, and comets.

SCIENTIFIC METHOD

WE ARE NOT HERE concerned with Grosseteste's scientific theories as such, but his views on scientific method are of importance in the history of philosophy.

Science, according to Grosseteste, uses both the inductive and deductive methods. It begins with particular observable events and advances by induction to the statement of a general law that accounts for them. To use one of his own examples: Let us suppose someone frequently notices that the eating of scammony happens to be accompanied by the discharge of red bile. Constantly observing the conjunction of these two events, he begins to form in his mind the idea, itself unobservable, that scammony is the cause of the discharge of bile. To verify this supposition, he then begins to experiment. He isolates and excludes all other causes of the purging of red bile. When scammony is administered many times under these conditions and the same result occurs, he leaps to the conclusion that all scammony of its nature discharges red bile. A law of this sort, called by Grosseteste a "universal experimental principle," goes beyond a simple empirical generalization to state something about the very nature of things.[18]

After the law has been discovered, particular occurrences can then be deduced from it, so that the law explains them and gives their cause. The role of experiment in scientific research is to verify or falsify a theory by testing its empirical consequences. Basic to Grosseteste's notion of experimentation are the principles that nature operates uniformly and in the simplest possible manner.

According to Grosseteste, our knowledge of causes in natural science is always incomplete. By induction we cannot know all the relevant facts or all the theories that might account for them. So even though the facts we know may appear to verify a particular theory, we cannot be sure that the discovery of new facts may not prove it false or that some other theory may not equally well account for the known facts. In short, in our knowledge of the physical world there are science and demonstration, but not in the strictest sense.[19] Our most certain knowledge is mathematics. It is more certain even than metaphysics. The objects of metaphysics are nobler than those of mathematics, but owing to the impediment of the body and the disturbance of the imagination, the mind is ill-equipped to make progress in this lofty science. As we shall see, certitude in metaphysics is possible only for a purified elite with the help of divine illumination.

Grosseteste insists on the necessity of mathematics for a knowledge of the physical universe. He writes: "There is the greatest utility in considering lines, angles and figures, because without them it is impossible to know natural philosophy. . . . For all causes of natural effects must be expressed by means of lines, angles and figures." [20] The reason that nature can be properly understood only through mathematics is that physical motion is simply the propagation or diffusion of light, and this diffusion takes place according to geometrical laws. Hence the behavior of light must be studied by means of mathematics. This science, however, contributes only to our knowledge of the formal causes, or definitions of events. It gives us no knowledge of their efficient and final causes. Grosseteste insists that the mathematical study of nature be supplemented by a physical study that takes these latter causes into account.

The aim of natural science is to arrive at the laws by which things operate in accordance with their natures or forms. Natural science discovers and defines as accurately as possible the common natures of things that determine their mode of behavior. These universal natures exist in things as reflections of the eternal Ideas in God's mind. The human mind, however, is so defective that in its present condition it cannot grasp the natures of things with certitude. Is certainty about nature possible? Yes, but only by the help of divine illumination. The truth of anything is its conformity to its Idea in God's mind. So if we are to know the truth we must see it in the light of its archetypal Idea. This is possible for an intellect purified of the corrupting influence of the body and illuminated by God. Then "the intellect and science apprehend a thing in the purity of its essence, as things are in themselves." [21]

In this way Grosseteste unites the empiricism of Aristotle with the Augustinian doctrine of the knowledge of truth through contact with the divine Ideas. Despite his borrowings from Aristotle, however, his epistemology is basically Augustinian. The only reason he assigns for the necessity of sense knowledge and experimentation is that our intelligence is darkened and weighed down by the body. Our intelligence is not the form or actuality of the body. The soul, of which the intelligence is the highest part, is the body's mover and ruler. If the soul were separated from the body, it would at once, like the angels, possess perfect science through divine illumination. In its present condition of union with the body, the stimulation of sensible things is required for knowledge, but knowledge and certitude are gained by the soul's awakening to the light of the divine Ideas operating within it.

THE METAPHYSICS OF LIGHT

THE NOTION OF LIGHT is central not only to Grosseteste's epistemology but also to his metaphysics and cosmology. He conceives God as the primal, invisible, and uncreated light, and the hierarchy of creatures, embracing angels, human souls, the heavenly bodies, and the physical beings in the lower world, as a series of lights of diminishing splendor. In Grosseteste's world, light thus furnishes the bond between God and creatures. Indeed, the illuminative power of God accounts for creation, just as it does for all knowledge, angelic and human.

In his short treatise *On Light or the Beginning of Forms*, Grosseteste describes how in the beginning of time God created unformed matter and a point of light, which, diffusing itself in the form of a sphere, produced the spatial dimensions of the universe and all the physical beings within it. Light by its nature tends to diffuse itself in all directions unless hindered by an opaque object. Thus it naturally tends to form a sphere. As light diffuses itself, it becomes weaker and more rarefied until its force is spent. That is why matter at the extremities of the universe is more rarefied, whereas the earth, which is at the center, is denser and thicker.

Grosseteste argues at length to prove that the diffusion of the original point of light must produce a finite and not an infinite universe. Light, as originally created, is an unextended simple force. It naturally tends to multiply itself and to extend matter to which it is joined. It must multiply itself an infinite number of times, for a finite multiplication of an unextended force does not produce a quantity. However, an infinite multiplication of something simple and unextended will produce a quantity, but one that is finite and not infinite.[22]

When light (*lux*) reaches the limit of its diffusion, producing the finite sphere of the universe, it is reflected back toward the center. This reflected light Grosseteste calls *lumen*. The action of this reflected light produces the nine heavenly spheres and below them the four elements of fire, air, water, and earth.[23]

The basic constituents of all material things are thus matter and the form of light. Each of these Grosseteste calls a simple or un-extended substance. Matter is potential to the form of light, which actualizes and completes it by giving it extension in space. Both matter and light are unextended in themselves, but light spontaneously diffuses itself in all directions, so that it extends matter in three dimensions. The light thus described by Grosseteste is not the physical light that we see. In itself it is an unextended point of energy manifesting itself in visible light and in all the processes of nature. Although he calls matter and light substances, suggesting that each has a reality of its own, he adds that neither can be separated from the other.

Because light is the form that extends matter in three dimensions, thus producing a body, Grosseteste calls light "bodiness" or "corporeity." On this point he shows the influence of the Jewish philosopher Ibn Gabirol, who called corporeity the first form of matter and identified it with light.[24] Like Gabirol, he thought that one substance can have several substantial forms. Bodies are first informed by light, and then by the forms of the elements, plants, and animals, and finally by the intellectual souls of men.[25]

Grosseteste's reason for identifying the first form of bodies with light is a metaphysical one. The first corporeal form, he says, is nobler and more excellent than all subsequent corporeal forms because of its closer resemblance to forms existing apart from matter; namely, God and the angels. Light fits both of these descriptions. It is more exalted and excellent than all corporeal things and it is most similar to immaterial forms. Consequently, light is the first corporeal form.[26]

As has been said, light not only gives bodies their extension in three dimensions; as their primal energy it is also the source of their manifold activities. Matter itself is passive. Form, and principally the first form, or light, is the intrinsic principle of the movement and action of bodies. This is why the scientist who studies the movements of bodies must be principally concerned with light. This is also why the science of light, which was called optics even in the Middle Ages, is the most important of all the sciences. And since light diffuses itself in a straight line and by angles of reflection and refraction, a knowledge of geometry is all-important for the scientist. The mathematical study of nature is thus required by the very structure of the physical universe.

Grosseteste's metaphysics of light, which has its roots in Neoplatonism and Arabian philosophy, was destined to be widely influential not only at Oxford but also at Paris. His theory of science, with its emphasis on experimentation and mathematics, had a decisive influence upon the succeeding generations of natural philosophers at Oxford, and particularly upon Roger Bacon.

3 THE AGE OF THE SCHOOLMEN

X

Roger Bacon

ROGER BACON is a paradoxical figure in the Age of the Schoolmen.[1] In his youth he lectured on Aristotle's works at Paris and wrote philosophical Questions, but the scholastic style did not suit his unconventional and independent spirit. He became disgusted with Parisian scholasticism because of its neglect of linguistic and literary studies, and he turned back to the Age of the Fathers, and especially to St. Augustine, for his ideal of wisdom. A constantly recurring theme in his writings is the decadence of contemporary thought and the lost glories of the past. He had nothing but contempt for the commentaries on the *Sentences* and the *Summae* of theology of scholastics like Alexander of Hales, Albert the Great, and Thomas Aquinas.

This, however, was only one side of Bacon's complex personality. He not only looked back with nostalgia to the past, but through his scientific interests he helped to prepare the way to the future. At Oxford he devoted himself to science, enthusiastically joining the scientific avant-garde inspired by the genius of Robert Grosseteste. He saw in the mathematical and experimental methods not only the key to the understanding of nature but also the necessary tools for the universal science he aimed to establish. Bacon's fascination for us comes from this mixture of the old and the new, the presence in one mind of outmoded ideas and dreams that would shape the future.

THE CRITIC

BACON BEGINS HIS CHIEF WORK, the *Opus Majus*, with a description of four causes of error which he considered prevalent in his day: 1] submission to unworthy authority, 2] the influence of custom, 3] popular prejudice, 4] the concealment of one's own ignorance accompanied by an ostentatious display of knowledge. These are the "four chief hindrances to the understanding of truth that stand in the way of every man, however wise."

Bacon's criticism of authority must be rightly understood. He does not reject "solid and sure authority," such as that of the Church, or saints, or "perfect philosophers and other men of science." [2] What he inveighs against, not without spite and jealousy, is the presumptuous claim to wisdom he thinks he detects among some of his contemporaries, and the popular adulation they receive. Chief among these is Richard of Cornwall, whom he describes as "the worst and most stupid [author] . . . with the greatest reputation in that stupid crowd." [3] He criticizes the masters at Paris, especially the "boys of the two Orders," likely a reference to Franciscans and Dominicans, such as Albert and Thomas Aquinas, who entered religion as boys. These men presume to teach without having a solid foundation of knowledge. Alexander of Hales is falsely credited with having written a *Summa* of theology, which in any case is "more than a horse-load." Albert writes as though he were an author on a level with the greatest thinkers of old; moreover, he is ignorant of language, optics, and experimental science. [4]

Even those whom Bacon calls the "perfect philosophers" do not go uncriticized. Aristotle, he claims, was ignorant of many things and is to be taken to task for his doctrine of the eternity of the world. So, too, Aristotle's greatest followers, Avicenna and Averroes, made false statements in both philosophy and science. If these great men fell into error, what can we expect from their inferiors! Even the sacred writers, such as Augustine and Jerome, had to retract some of their statements; and they did not always agree with each other! [5]

This should warn us against relying uncritically upon human authority. It should also make us cautious about the correctness of our own views. In general, we should prefer good authorities to weak ones, reason to custom, and the opinion of the wise to popular prejudice. If the common people hold something to be true, it is likely to be false; they are the worst guides to wisdom.[6]

Bacon thought his contemporaries particularly prone to disregard these rules. He considered the philosophy and theology of his day in need of thorough reform. The current movement in theology was especially repugnant to him, for he thought it neglected the Bible in favor of the *Sentences* of Peter Lombard. His own ideal of theology was that of St. Augustine: a universal science, or wisdom, embracing all knowledge useful for an understanding of Scripture and for the guidance of life. He writes: "There is only one perfect wisdom, which is contained wholly in the Scriptures, and is to be unfolded by canon law and philosophy."[7] Like St. Bonaventure, Bacon conceives philosophy simply as a step toward this wisdom; in itself it "leads to the blindness of hell, and therefore by itself it must be darkness and mist." Christians who philosophize can complete the philosophy of the pagans and advance far beyond them. So long as they do not transcend the bounds of philosophy and restrict themselves to subjects common to believers and unbelievers, they are philosophers and not theologians. However, they have the duty to subordinate their philosophy to theology so that it may be its servant. In itself, philosophy has no value; indeed, it is essentially harmful.[8]

We could not wish for a clearer notion of Christian philosophy nor for a more resolute denial of the value of secular learning divorced from the all-embracing science of theology.

Bacon has a theoretical reason for bringing philosophy within the orbit of theology: like Scripture, philosophy comes to us as a divine revelation. God is the light of our understanding and our Agent Intellect, and it is through his inner illumination that we acquire science. This was true even for the wise men of old, such as Solomon and Aristotle. "The third reason," he writes, "why the wisdom of philosophy is reduced to divine wisdom is that God not only enlightened their minds to acquire wisdom, but they received it from him and he revealed, presented, and gave it to them." [9]

The revelation here referred to by Bacon does not exclude the need of experience and experimentation. God reveals the *principles* of philosophy to us, but these have to be completed by experience. In this way Bacon makes room for experimental science, one of the central features of his proposed reform.

THE REFORMER

BACON'S PROPOSED REFORM of education is divided into several parts, to each of which he devotes a section of his *Opus Majus*. In the first place, he stresses the need of studying languages, especially Hebrew and Greek, so that the Bible can be read in the original. Both Greek and Arabic must be learned so that the philosophical and scientific works in those languages can be read correctly. He insists that translations are never exact; especially faulty are the current Latin versions of Aristotle and the other philosophers. A further reason for a knowledge of languages is the conversion of unbelievers—a project dear to Bacon's heart and closely connected, as we shall see, with his dream of bringing all men within the unity of the Church and Christendom.

The second feature in Bacon's reform is the absolute necessity of mathematics. His respect for the value of mathematics was inherited from Robert Grosseteste. Mathematics, Bacon claims, is the gate and key to all other sciences, human and divine. Its neglect in the last thirty or forty years has destroyed the whole educational system among the Latins. Anyone ignorant of mathematics can know neither the other sciences nor the affairs of the world. It is, in fact, the foundation of all knowledge, preparing the mind and elevating it to a certain knowledge of all things. As an illustration of this he cites the cases of Robert Grosseteste and Adam of Marsh, "who by the power of mathematics have learned to explain the causes of all things and to expound adequately things human and divine." [10] Bacon gives examples to show how mathematics is required for a knowledge of both celestial and terrestrial bodies and their movements. As Grosseteste pointed out, the forces in nature act according to geometrical laws and hence cannot be understood without this science. Mathematics is also necessary for the theologian, who must understand the numbers in Scripture and calculate dates. Sacred music must also be based on mathematics.

After explaining the importance of languages and mathematics, Bacon turns to the "very beautiful science" of optics. This he describes as the science of visual perception and of light.[11] It deals with the physiology of perception, colors, the behavior of light in reflection and refraction, and the errors of the senses. In this connection Bacon describes various types of mirrors and lenses that can be made to aid vision. Mathematics is important in optics for calculating the angles of reflection and refraction of light and for constructing lenses. The Arabian scientist Alhazen (965–1038) was Bacon's chief authority in this field, but he himself did original work in it.

Important as mathematics is for true wisdom, it cannot take the place of experience, for "without experience nothing can be sufficiently known."[12] Experimental science occupies the central place in Bacon's proposed reform of learning. The term itself, *scientia experimentalis*, Bacon attributes to Ptolemy,[13] but it was through Bacon himself that it gained currency among western thinkers. For Bacon, experimental science is not a special science. It is any knowledge gained by experience, and since there is no certainty without experience, it is the basis of all sure knowledge.

There are two ways of acquiring knowledge: reasoning and experience. By reasoning we draw conclusions from premises, but the mind is not satisfied without experience. A man who never saw a fire may be able to prove by adequate reasoning that fire burns, but this will not satisfy him, nor will he avoid fire until he places his hand or some combustible material in the fire. Only the actual experience of fire will convince him of the truth that fire burns. Even mathematical truths, which are the most convincing of all, fail to satisfy the mind without experience. Only when we have drawn the appropriate figures and have actually experienced them do we accept without question the conclusions of geometry.

Experience is of two kinds. The first is gained through the external senses, whether it concerns objects seen upon the earth or celestial phenomena observed through instruments made for that purpose. Things lying beyond the range of our personal observation we can know through scientists living in other parts of the world who have experienced them. Bacon calls this sort of experience human and philosophical, but he insists that it is not sufficient. Owing to the difficulty of knowing the material world with certitude and to the fact that the spiritual world lies beyond the scope of sense perception, man's intellect must be raised to another and higher type of experience through divine illumination. Bacon describes the seven stages of interior illumination, beginning with that required for the natural sciences and concluding with supernatural raptures and ecstasies. It is not difficult to see the influence of St. Augustine when Bacon makes certitude in philosophy depend upon divine illumination.

Experience gained by sense perception has several roles to perform in science. As we have seen, it confirms the conclusions reached by reason. It also provides new knowledge of nature both through ordinary observation and as a result of planned experiments. The man most admired by Bacon as an experimentalist was the French scientist Peter of Maricourt (*c.* 1269), whom he calls the "master of experiments." Little is known of this man who combined the mathematical method with experimentation in his study of nature. Manual dexterity in devising instruments of research was for him an important part of the experimental method. His chief work is a treatise *On the Magnet*, which is described by the historian of science George Sarton as "a splendid and rare exemplar of the experimental method" and as "one of the greatest monuments of experimental research in the Middle Ages." It was the best work on magnetism up to the seventeenth century, when it was used by Gilbert.[14]

Bacon himself was not a great experimentalist, although he carried out some notable experiments. In his enthusiasm for experimenting with lenses he sent one to the Pope so that he too could become a scientist! Bacon's most famous use of the experimental and mathematical methods is in his study of the rainbow, to which he devotes several chapters of his *Opus Majus*.[15] His own accomplishments in science, however, do not equal his prophecies of future scientific achievements. In a remarkable passage he foresees the day when boats will move swiftly by mechanical means, men will fly through the air in machines, cars will travel with unbelievable rapidity, heavy weights will be raised by a tiny engine, men will walk on the bottom of seas and rivers, and bridges will span rivers without piers or other supports. These and other "mechanisms and unheard-of engines" would result from the application of the mathematical and experimental methods to the study of nature.[16]

The practical advantages of science were never far from Bacon's mind. These advantages, as he saw them, were not just material but chiefly moral and religious. With his practical turn of mind—so common among English philosophers—he subordinates all human knowledge to moral philosophy. He describes this branch of philosophy in the final part of the *Opus Majus*. Its purpose is to guide man's conduct in relation to himself, his neighbor, and God. It concerns man's happiness and salvation. This practical end of moral philosophy makes it the noblest of the sciences, for "all speculative philosophy has moral philosophy for its end and aim." The nobility of moral philosophy is further shown by its close relation to theology, which is also practical in its end, since it leads man to salvation.[17]

Theology is a universal wisdom embracing all the sciences as its servants. It is the one perfect wisdom, revealed to man by the one God, who also founded one Church to bring mankind to a single end; namely, eternal life. If this is so, should there not also be one temporal society—a "Christian republic"—embracing all men? Bacon's whole reform of morals and education was aimed at making such a universal society a reality. Science would provide the instruments by which Christians could ward off the attacks of the Saracens and Tartars threatening Christendom. Meanwhile the study of languages would equip missionaries to go forth to convert unbelievers to the true faith. Christendom would then extend to the whole world, and all men would be united in a commonwealth of the faithful ruled by one head, the Pope.

Bacon's great dream of a totally Christian world, united by a common faith and ruled by one man, was inspired by St. Augustine's *City of God*, although it altered the Augustinian notion of the heavenly City by locating it on this earth and by directing it, at least partially, to worldly ends. As we have seen, Augustine himself conceived the City of God as a society whose nature and end are wholly spiritual, since it is directed to man's eternal salvation. Bacon brought this ideal down to earth; but it remained a religious ideal none the less, for the basis of his universal society was faith and theology.

This conception of Christendom, absorbing all states in the Church, as all secular learning is incorporated into theology, gave definite shape to the profound aspiration of the Middle Ages for world unity. It was not the only crystallization of this ideal. Others, such as Dante (1265–1321), proposed to separate the temporal and spiritual orders, the Holy Roman Emperor to rule the earth and the Pope to rule the Church. It was left to the Renaissance and modern times to propose the unification of the world by purely secular means and by human reason.[18]

THE PHILOSOPHER

BACON WROTE a long series of philosophical works that contain his views in physics, psychology, metaphysics, and ethics. These are not his most original writings. In them he generally follows Aristotle and Avicenna, whom he considered the greatest philosopher after Aristotle. Through St. Augustine, the philosophers of Islam, and Ibn Gabirol, Bacon's philosophy inherited a Neoplatonic strain which, like so many of his contemporaries, he tried to harmonize with Aristotelianism.

The influence of Ibn Gabirol is evident in Bacon's conception of every creature as a combination of matter and several substantial forms, each of which gives to the creature some generic or specific perfection. The union of matter with the most general of all forms results in a substance. A further form determines substance to be corporeal or incorporeal. Other forms must be added to make corporeal substance living and human. Each being thus contains a hierarchy of forms, the lower forms preparing the way for subsequent ones. The last form completes the being and unites within itself all the lower forms. These lower, preparatory forms do not disappear with the coming of the last form. They enter into it and make up a part of it. For example, the human soul, which is the ultimate form of man, contains within itself the inferior substantial forms of animality and substance. It is thus through its ultimate form that a being is unified and made to be *one* being.

If universal matter is joined to universal form, the result is a universal; if individual matter is joined to individual forms, the result is an individual. No combination of universals will produce an individual, nor can anything be added to a universal to make it an individual. Bacon criticizes those philosophers who think there is something within an individual being that makes it individual. These is no intrinsic cause of individuality, but only the efficient cause, which in the case of natural beings is God. He makes individuals to be individual. At the same time, God is the cause of universality, for he creates individual forms such that they resemble one another. The mind is not the cause of universality, for even if we did not apprehend things they would be like one another. For Bacon, universality is as much a feature of the real world as individuality, and it has the same cause: God, the author of nature. Averroes claimed that the intellect is the cause of universality, but he was talking about our universal ideas and not about the universality in nature.[19]

The human soul is described by Bacon as an individual substance composed of spiritual matter and form.[20] In this respect it resembles an angel; but, unlike an angel, it has a natural aptitude to be the form of a body. The soul has many powers that are its spiritual and "potential" parts; they are not accidents of the soul, as St. Thomas Aquinas taught. By this Bacon means that the faculties of the soul differ in nature from each other: the will, for example, is essentially different from the intellect, and the intellect from the senses, as is evident from their operations. But they are all powers of the one substance of the soul and are consubstantial with it.[21]

Because the soul is both the form of the human body and a substance in its own right, it has two avenues of knowledge. As the form of the body, it draws its knowledge from the external world as recorded by the senses. The soul is passive in this operation, for its role is to receive impressions from the outer world. When the intellect knows in this way, it is called the "possible intellect." As a spiritual, immortal substance, however, the soul is independent of the body and the sensible world. It can turn inward upon itself and behold there, in a confused way, innate ideas which are the traces of God's own Ideas within itself. When the intellect knows in this way, it is called the agent intellect.[22] However, even in its role as a possible intellect, drawing its information from the sensible world, the agent intellect is required to illuminate the images in the imagination, thus abstracting those images from their material conditions and placing them in the possible intellect.[23]

Bacon is here attempting to unite the Aristotelian notion of abstraction with the Augustinian doctrine of illumination. In his *Opus Majus* he makes it clear that, in relation to God, our intellect is totally receptive and "possible," receiving from him the illumination required for knowledge. In this perspective the agent intellect of our soul is not one of its powers but God himself. "The active principle illuminating and influencing the possible intellect is a separate substance, namely God himself." [24] Bacon assures us that this is the true teaching of both Aristotle and St. Augustine and all the greater philosophers. He tells of hearing William of Auvergne twice express this opinion at Paris at university convocations, and he gives it as the teaching of both Robert Grosseteste and Adam of Marsh at Oxford. The following chapters will show how burning a question this was at the time and how diverse were the solutions to it proposed by the schoolmen of the thirteenth century.

XI

St. Bonaventure

The Early Franciscan School

WHILE ARISTOTELIANISM continued to gain ground in the thirteenth century, Augustinism sprang into new life and experienced its second spring. The growing popularity of Aristotle contributed to this revival of St. Augustine's thought. Theologians, disturbed by the success of Aristotle's doctrines, some of which were startlingly novel and even contrary to faith—at least as interpreted by his Arabian commentators—extracted from St. Augustine's writings philosophical notions with which to oppose Aristotle's. The resultant Augustinism was not identical with the doctrine of St. Augustine himself, for it grew in a new soil and fed upon new sources, among which was Aristotle himself, as well as Arabian and Jewish philosophers. Nevertheless, St. Augustine left his mark upon this new synthesis of theology and philosophy, so that its true parentage is unmistakable.

The Augustinism of the thirteenth century flourished particularly in the Franciscan Order. St. Francis (d. 1226) had no intention of founding an Order devoted to study and teaching, but circumstances and the pressing needs of the Church turned it in that direction almost from the start. An Englishman, Alexander of Hales (c. 1185–1245), was an important factor in this development. He was already a professor of theology at Paris when he became a Franciscan in 1236. He continued to teach as a Franciscan, and after his death it became the custom to appoint a Franciscan to his chair. An immense *Summa* of theology, which

Roger Bacon described disparagingly as "more than a horse-load," is traditionally ascribed to him. Bacon added that Alexander was not really its author—a statement substantially confirmed by modern historians. It appears to be a compilation of extracts from the works of Alexander of Hales, John of Rochelle, St. Bonaventure, and others. Its compiler or compilers are not known for certain.[1] In some respects a precursor of St. Thomas' *Summa* of theology, it contains many doctrines typical of the Franciscan school, for example the existence of spiritual matter in human souls and angels, the plurality of substantial forms in man, the synthesis of Augustinian illumination with Aristotelian abstraction, the doctrine of seminal principles (*rationes seminales*), and the notion of God as supreme Entity (*essentia*).

St. Bonaventure

THE early Franciscan school produced its finest flower in St. Bonaventure.[2] A true son of St. Francis, he brought into his theology and philosophy the poor man of Assisi's ardent love of God and burning desire for contemplative union with him.

According to tradition, St. Bonaventure was a friend of St. Thomas Aquinas, with whom he taught for a time at the University of Paris. Both saints have been declared Doctors of the Church, and their writings have been recommended by popes to the Catholic world. In his encyclical *Aeterni Patris*, Pope Leo XIII particularly recommends the doctrine of St. Thomas Aquinas, but he also gives special mention to St. Bonaventure.

I. PHILOSOPHY IN THE SERVICE OF LOVE

IT IS DIFFICULT to compare St. Bonaventure and St. Thomas, so different are their approaches to theological and philosophical problems. Both were theologians who developed and used philosophical ideas to further their theological work. Hence their philosophical ideas are to be found within their theologies; neither separated his philosophy from his theology or his faith. But their specifically philosophical notions are often opposed. In general, St. Bonaventure depends upon St. Augustine rather than upon Aristotle, while St. Thomas owes a greater debt to Aristotle and the Arabian philosophers.

We are fortunate in having St. Bonaventure's own estimate of his great predecessors. He admired Aristotle as the master of science and described him as "the more excellent among the philosophers." [3] Plato rated higher in his estimation, as a master of wisdom, for Plato turned toward heavenly things, whereas Aristotle centered his attention upon the earth. Above both these philosophers is Augustine, who, by the grace of the Holy Spirit, was the master of both science and wisdom. [4]

Nowhere is St. Bonaventure's allegiance to St. Augustine more evident than in his placing all learning in the service of love. Devotion and love were always his primary concern; knowledge and science came second. This accounts for his frequent use of affective language. Like those of all the great mystics, his works abound in the language of the heart. More perfect than rational investigation is knowledge through love (*dulcis cognitio*), in which the mind savors the divine sweetness. "The best way to know God," he writes, "is through the experience of sweetness; this is more perfect, excellent and delightful than through rational inquiry." [5]

St. Bonaventure saw this emphasis on love as a characteristic differentiating Franciscans from Dominicans. Dominicans, he says, give themselves first to speculation and study and second to devotion (*unctio*), while Franciscans give themselves first to devotion and second to speculation. [6] St. Bonaventure never considered science or knowledge as ends in themselves but as means to the building of character and to the experimental knowledge of God through love, to be consummated in the Beatific Vision. This is the theme of his *Reduction of the Arts to Theology*, which concludes:

"And this is the purpose of all the sciences, that in all of them faith is strengthened, God is honored, character is formed, and consolations are derived consisting in the union of the spouse with her Beloved: a union that takes place through love, to the attainment of which the whole purpose of sacred Scripture, and consequently, every illumination descending from above, is directed—a union without which all knowledge is empty."

Thus for St. Bonaventure the true purpose of philosophy is to foster devotion and to help us reach a mystical union with God. This does not entail a confusion of philosophy with theology. Philosophy is knowledge of the things of nature and the soul naturally innate in man or acquired by his own efforts. Theology, on the other hand, is knowledge of heavenly things based upon faith and the revelation of the Holy Spirit.[7] But St. Bonaventure is vehemently opposed to any practical separation of philosophy from theology. He considers that our reason is so darkened by original sin that without the light of faith it is bound to fall into error.[8] Aristotle is a perfect example of this. Having limited himself to explaining the sensible world, he denied the divine Ideas as intermediaries between God and the world. From this a whole series of errors followed: ignorance of exemplarism, divine providence, and the divine governance of the world. This triple error of Aristotle involves a triple blindness, for he teaches the eternity of the world, the unity of the agent intellect for all men, and the denial of rewards and punishments after death.[9] Other philosophers, like Plato and Plotinus, avoided these errors, but they could achieve only a deformed and stunted truth because they lacked the help of faith. Their basic defect was ignorance of original sin. Because they did not know the disease, they could not apply the remedy. These philosophers of pure reason are like ostriches, whose wings do not enable them to fly but only to run more quickly. Faith alone preserves man from error and gives him the power to mount to God.[10]

When philosophy renounces its self-sufficiency and allows itself to be guided by faith, it enters into the all-embracing synthesis of Christian Wisdom. It then becomes simply a stage toward higher knowledge: "Philosophical science is a way to the other sciences; but he who wishes to halt in it falls into darkness." [11] Correct order demands that faith should come before philosophy. After philosophy comes theology, then the gift of the Holy Spirit called knowledge, and finally the light of glory. All knowledge, then, whether philosophical or theological, is simply a step forward in the journey of the mind to God.

II. CHRISTIAN METAPHYSICS

THE TRUE METAPHYSICIAN, St. Bonaventure tells us, will understand that he has come forth from God by creation and that, with God's help, he is now returning to him. There are, accordingly, three main themes in St. Bonaventure's metaphysics (*nostra metaphysica*): *creation*, or the procession of creatures from God; *exemplarism*, or God as the exemplar of his creation; *consummation*, or the journey of man back to God by means of divine illumination.[12] We shall consider St. Bonaventure's metaphysics according to his own division.

1. Creation

The doctrine of Aristotle that perhaps most affronted the medieval Christian mind was that of the eternity of the world. To St. Bonaventure this was a denial of the creation of the world from nothing, as taught by sacred Scripture in accord with human reason. On this subject he thought the simple man of faith wiser than the most learned philosophers, no one of whom arose to the Christian doctrine of creation. But not even the least intelligent of the philosophers claimed that the world is both eternal and created from nothing. These notions, which according to St. Thomas are compatible, St. Bonaventure considers mutually opposed. If the world is created from nothing, he reasons, it receives existence after non-existence; hence it cannot always have existed.

St. Bonaventure offers the following arguments for the non-eternity of the world: 1] If the world had no temporal beginning, an infinite time has already passed. Yet each day adds a unit to the temporal duration of the world. But it is impossible to add to the infinite. Therefore, the eternity of the world supposes an infinity capable of being increased, which is absurd. 2] If the world had no beginning, an infinite number of revolutions of the heavenly bodies must have already taken place. But this is clearly impossible, because an infinite series cannot be traversed. On the supposition of a world without a beginning in time, the present could not have been reached.　3] If the world is eternal, men would always have existed, and there would be an infinite number of immortal souls. But it is impossible for an infinite number of things to exist simultaneously. For these reasons St. Bonaventure holds that the revealed doctrine of the temporal beginning of the world agrees perfectly with human reason.[13] On this point he differs from St. Thomas, who taught that reason alone cannot settle the question; revelation alone assures us that the world began in time.

Since the world is God's creation, St. Bonaventure attributes its total being to him. It does not exist by itself, but by God who gave it existence. Moreover, it must be constantly held in existence by God. If left to themselves, creatures would lapse into the nothingness from which they were created. The world is thus radically contingent upon God's will. It has no natural stability, for there is nothing in its nature to make its existence necessary. St. Bonaventure calls the tendency of every creature to lapse into nothingness its "vertibility." Creatures are saved from sinking into nothingness only by the grace of God.[14] This notion of the natural "vertibility" of all creatures was opposed by St. Thomas, who, while maintaining God's power to annihilate his creatures, taught the *natural* indestructibility of human souls, angels, the heavenly bodies, and the material universe as a whole.

THE PHYSICAL WORLD. In explaining the nature of the physical world, St. Bonaventure adopts the metaphysics of light taught at Oxford by Robert Grosseteste and Roger Bacon. According to them, all bodies are composed of matter and the basic form of light. Light is not simply an accidental form of bodies but the noblest of all substantial bodily forms.[15] It is the universal active principle in bodies, giving them their basic energy and activity. Other substantial forms perfect matter subsequent to this form; for instance, the forms of the elements (fire, air, water, and earth) and the forms of plants, animals, and men.

In itself the form of light is imperceptible. Visible light is not the form itself but simply a striking manifestation of it. God is pure light, dwelling in light inaccessible (*I Tim.* 6:16). Light in the created universe is a participation in God's light. All the activities of bodies, plants, animals, and men stem from the basic energy of light. Even knowledge, sensible and intellectual, takes place through light, or illumination. This doctrine enables St. Bonaventure to stress the analogy between the universe and God and the beauty of creatures as a mirror of the divine beauty.

SEMINAL PRINCIPLES. St. Bonaventure adopts St. Augustine's doctrine of seminal principles (*rationes seminales*) to explain the origin of new beings in the universe. In the beginning God created the universe filled with the "seeds" of all things that would later develop. All their forms—with the exception of the human soul, which is created *ex nihilo*—existed in matter in an embryonic or virtual state, waiting for the proper circumstances to arise in order to come forth into perfect being. As a rosebud becomes a rose, so do all things develop from their primitive embryonic forms.

This implies that no created agent can impart forms to matter; God alone can do that by creation. All that creatures can do as secondary causes is to bring forms existing in matter in an imperfect state to a perfect state. Thus a secondary cause does not produce in its effect a form similar to its own, as St. Thomas teaches, but simply gives a new disposition or mode of being to a form already created in matter. "This is the sum and substance of our position," St. Bonaventure writes, "that a created agent produces absolutely no quiddity, either substantial or accidental, but gives a being a new disposition." [16] In this way he strictly limits the efficacy of secondary causes, in line with his principle that it is better to enhance the power and glory of God than to risk attributing too much to creatures.

THE HUMAN SOUL. The soul must not be confused with God or with the body to which it is joined. It is created out of nothing as a composite of matter and form. This composition is a necessary result of the fact that it is created and given life by God. Its life is a participation in the life of God. So there must be something in the soul that gives life to it (namely, form), and something that receives life (namely, matter). Furthermore, the soul changes and in so doing receives new qualities. So it must be partly passive and receptive; it is not wholly active. In short, it has matter in its make-up. This matter, however, is not like that we see around us; it is spiritual matter similar to that of the angels.[17]

Since the soul is made in the image of God, we can be certain that it bears within itself the image of the Trinity. This image resides in the faculties of the soul. As St. Augustine taught, the soul has three main faculties: understanding, will, and memory. These are not identical with the substance of the soul, yet they are not simply accidents of it. They are consubstantial with the soul.[18] As in the Trinity there are three Persons sharing in the same substance, so there are in the soul three faculties consubstantial with the soul.

Composed of form and matter, the human soul is a complete substance, capable of subsisting apart from the body. It is therefore immortal. Its immortality, however, is not that of a simple substance, incapable of being dissolved into parts, as in the philosophy of St. Thomas. Neither does it have the natural necessity of continuing in existence forever which St. Thomas attributes to it. St. Bonaventure principally bases the soul's immortality upon its dignity as the image of God. If the soul resembles God, who is incorruptible, surely it too must be incorruptible. God would not condemn to nothingness a soul made to his own image and likeness. Furthermore, man desires to be happy, and true happiness requires the possession of a perfect good without fear of losing it. This would be impossible unless man's soul were immortal.[19]

Although the soul is superior to and independent of the body, it nevertheless has a natural desire to be united to it. As God by his grace gives life to the soul, so the soul in its turn reaches below itself to vivify and perfect the body. The union of soul and body is thus no accidental one. They are united substantially to form the composite substance, man.

The human soul is thus the substantial form of the body, but it * is not its only substantial form.[20] The body must be disposed to receive the soul by prior substantial forms (for instance, the form of

* See Addenda, p. 427.

light and the forms of the elements). The human soul adds a further substantial perfection, forming the complete and perfect man. Unlike St. Thomas, St. Bonaventure can maintain a plurality of substantial forms in man because in his view no one substantial form by itself gives man his total substantial being. Each gives him but a part of his substantial perfection.

2. Exemplarism

The second theme of St. Bonaventure's metaphysics is God as the exemplar or model of creatures. God has created all things intelligently—that is to say, through divine Ideas—and so they all mirror him to a greater or lesser extent. This likeness of creatures to God is not incidental to them; it is at their very core, permeating their very substance.[21] So without a knowledge of exemplarism it is impossible to penetrate deeply into the created world.

It is here, St. Bonaventure points out, that the metaphysician makes his most valuable and specific contribution. The philosopher of nature, like the metaphysician, considers the origin of things and rises from creatures to God, their uncreated cause. The ethician or moralist, like the metaphysician, concerns himself with man's last end or happiness. But only the metaphysician considers God as the exemplar of all things. Consequently, he is most truly a metaphysician when he treats of this theme.

As a result, St. Bonaventure denies that Aristotle was a true metaphysician. He was a philosopher of nature, and a better one than Plato; but because he attacked Plato's doctrine of Ideas and denied exemplarism he cannot claim the loftier title of metaphysician.[22]

According to St. Bonaventure, the Ideas through which God fashions his creatures are not really distinct from himself. They are distinct only according to our way of conceiving and naming them. More exactly, the Ideas are contained in the Word, the Second Person of the Trinity, who is the expressed Image of the Father and the Wisdom by which the world was created. The divine Ideas are simply the infinite possible ways in which God's perfection can be imitated by creatures.

All creatures, accordingly, come forth from God bearing some

degree of likeness to him. Some are merely shadows of him, some
are vestiges, still others are images. A shadow is a distant and confused representation of God, a vestige is a distant but distinct representation, an image is a distinct and close representation. St. Bonaventure considers material creatures shadows and vestiges of God.
They are shadows in their being and life, vestiges in their goodness and power. Only spiritual creatures—for example, human souls
—are images.

It is typical of the Seraphic Doctor to see traces of the Trinity
everywhere in creation. The Triune God created the universe and
so it should bear its stamp. A vestige of the Trinity is found in the
union of form with matter in every creature. We find in this union
the elements of matter and form along with their composition.
Matter is the original principle or foundation, form is its comple-
tion, and the composition is the union of the two. These correspond
respectively to the Father who is the origin of the Trinity, the Son
who is the image of the Father, and the Holy Spirit who is the bond
of love between Father and Son.[23] As we have seen, the image of
the Trinity is also found in the trinity of faculties of the soul united
in its substance.

In this way all creation is filled with intelligible likenesses leading
us to God. "The created world," St. Bonaventure says, "is like a
book in which the creative Trinity shines forth, is represented,
and read . . ." [24] Before original sin it was easy for man to see God
in everything. After the fall the book of creation was closed to him;
it became like Greek or Hebrew to one who does not know the
meaning of the written symbols. Man saw only signs and could
not decipher their meaning. A perfect example of this is Aristotle's
Physics, which studies the physical world for its own sake without
grasping its deeper message. But when the understanding is enlightened by faith, the book of nature once more becomes intelligible to
us and it becomes a path leading us to God.

So clearly does the universe reveal God to the purified mind that
it is hardly necessary to formulate elaborate proofs for his existence. St. Bonaventure has the typical Franciscan feeling for God's
presence in nature and he delights in pointing out how different
creatures proclaim God to us. Even before we begin to devise

proofs for God's existence based upon the sensible world, our mind possesses notions revealing what we are attempting to prove. Suppose, for example, we begin with the fact that sensible things are contingent, and reason that God must exist as the necessary being who causes this contingent world. Our knowledge of the contingent already implies a knowledge of the necessary, and this is God. Indeed all men possess an innate idea of God as a being who is immutable and necessary, and this notion implies his existence. As St. Anselm pointed out, it is impossible to think that God does not exist.[25] In a bold simplification of the ontological argument for the existence of God, St. Bonaventure proclaims, "If God is God, God exists." [26] St. Anselm's point could not be put more neatly. *
The very notion of God assures us of his existence. In saying this, St. Bonaventure, like St. Anselm, does not leap from the idea of God to his real existence, as the critics of the ontological argument assert. Our innate idea of God is simply his way of being present to our mind. Consequently, there is no bridge to cross between the idea of God and his real existence. As St. Bonaventure puts it, nothing is closer to the soul than God, and so he is knowable by himself. This knowledge of God's existence, however, does not extend to a comprehension of his essence. St. Bonaventure likes to quote Hugh of St. Victor to the effect that God has so measured out our knowledge of him in this life that we can never fully comprehend *what* he is nor be entirely ignorant *that* he is.[27]

3. Consummation: The Road Back

God made man upright when he created him to his own image and likeness. But through original sin man became estranged from his creator. He must learn to walk upright again and recover the divine image in his soul in all its splendor. Only faith and grace can bring about the full return of man to God. Philosophy, however, is a useful help on the way. It is one of the lights leading man back to God.

St. Bonaventure outlines the main stages of man's return to God in his little masterpiece, *The Journey of the Mind to God*. He pictures the universe as a ladder by which we mount to God. We must begin with the corporeal and temporal traces of God in the

* See Addenda, p. 427.

visible world outside us. Next, we must enter into our mind, which is the spiritual image of God within us. Finally, we must rise above ourselves to God, the eternal cause of all things. In short, man's journey to God must be "from the external to the internal and from the temporal to the eternal." [28] The student will recognize this as the same route to God traveled by St. Augustine.

Each stage of this journey is made possible by an illumination from God aiding the six powers of the soul: sense, imagination, reason, intellect, intelligence, and the apex of the mind or spark of conscience. If we examine St. Bonaventure's doctrine of knowledge and morality, we shall see how these illuminations function.

KNOWLEDGE. St. Bonaventure's doctrine of knowledge is largely Augustinian, although Aristotle's influence is also present. Like St. Augustine, he describes two ways in which the soul can gain knowledge. With its "lower face" it can turn toward the sensible world and acquire knowledge through sense perception. With its "higher face" it can also look inward upon itself and discover there, independent of sense knowledge, a spiritual and intelligible world. In describing the first way of knowing he follows Aristotle; in describing the second he draws upon St. Augustine.

In sense knowledge a material object acts upon a sense organ, producing within it its sensible likeness. Through this likeness the material object then acts upon the soul itself, causing sensation. More exactly, it acts upon the man, who is a substantial composite of soul and body. This is contrary to the Augustinian explanation of sense perception, which does not admit an action of matter upon the soul. St. Bonaventure is willing to agree with Augustine's principle that lower substances cannot act upon higher ones, but he does not think that this applies to the present case. For inasmuch as the soul is the form of the body it is brought to the level of the sensible world, and so it can be modified by it.[29] Thus, contrary to St. Augustine, the soul does not form the content of sensation from its own substance but receives it from the external world. Sense perception itself, however, is not the reception of the sensible likeness of a material object by the soul, but the act whereby the soul, stimulated by the sense object, judges it. In man this sense judgment differs from that of brute animals. The divine illumination extends even to this low level of cognitive activity. In the simple act of sense perception there already shines forth the light of the divine beauty.

Following upon sense knowledge, our intellect knows the natures of material things. This knowledge comes about by abstraction. St. Bonaventure agrees with Aristotle that we have both an agent and possible intellect, but for him these are not separate faculties of the soul; they are simply different functions of one and the same intellect. When it functions as the possible intellect, it extracts the intelligible content from the data furnished by the senses and forms universal concepts which it then receives within itself. The possible intellect is thus receptive of information drawn from the senses; but it is not wholly passive, it is also active. It is not so active, however, that it can abstract and judge intelligible objects without the cooperation of the agent intellect. The function of this intellect is to illuminate the possible intellect and make it capable of doing its work. Thus the two functions of the agent and possible intellects are mutually dependent: the agent intellect makes abstraction possible by its illuminative activity; the possible intellect carries out the work of abstraction and judgment under the energizing activity of the agent intellect.[30]

All our knowledge, however, is not acquired by abstraction from sensible objects. Our soul knows itself and God without the help of the senses. St. Bonaventure would have been quite willing to agree with Leibniz that there is nothing in the intellect that was not previously in the senses, with the exception of the intellect itself. By its superior faculty of reason, the soul can directly scrutinize itself, its spiritual perfections such as knowledge and love, and God, in whose image it has been made.[31]

Whether knowledge is gained by abstraction through the senses or through the intellect itself, it has a quality for which man himself cannot account: certitude. Two factors are required for certitude: immutability on the part of the known object and infallibility on the part of the knower. Now sensible objects are constantly changing, and no one will doubt that the mind itself is mutable. Hence the certitude of our knowledge can be accounted for only by God, who is by nature immutable and infallible. Whenever we know the truth, our mind is in contact with God, who supplies the deficiencies of our nature. He illumines our mind, moving and regulating it by his divine Ideas so that it can know with certitude. Of course we do not clearly see the divine Ideas functioning in this way, but we can be certain of their active cooperation with us in all knowledge of the truth.[32]

This divine light is not the sole or total cause of our knowledge. Our own faculties of sense and intellect must cooperate with it; hence they are partial causes of knowledge. But by themselves they are not sufficient. We already participate in the divine light through our agent intellect, but since this is a created light, it cannot by itself account for our knowledge of the truth. An added divine light is needed.

What is the nature of this divine help? It is not an instance of God's general cooperation with nature in its activities. Truth is too precious and intimate to man to be given in the same way that life, for example, is given to plants and animals. Neither is it a special help, for then it would be a supernatural grace, and knowledge of the truth would not be a natural achievement but an infused one. The divine illumination is between a general and special help of God without being either.[33] A disciple of St. Bonaventure, Matthew of Aquasparta (*c.* 1240–1302), tried to be more precise. It is, he says, more special than the general influence of God upon all creatures, but still a general influence. In any case, it is not a special grace.[34]

The Bonaventurian school expended a good deal of effort in attempting to solve this problem without advancing much beyond the point where St. Bonaventure left it. The stakes were serious, for man's natural power of knowing the truth was in question. Furthermore, if, as St. Bonaventure held, we know the truth *by* and *in* the divine Ideas, how important is the existence of the sensible world for knowledge? Is not the object of our intellect the same whether sensible things exist or not? What basis in reality, then, do our concepts have? These were questions that seriously disturbed Matthew of Aquasparta. After attempting to answer them philosophically, he was forced to admit the inadequacy of the

principles of philosophy and to have recourse to theology.[35] The
certitude and objective ground of our knowledge is assured, not
by our natural powers of knowing and the stability of the sensible
world, but by the divine illumination and the mind's contact with
the divine Ideas. It was inevitable that philosophical skepticism
should gain ground as theologians of this school began to realize
more fully the implications of their position. But we shall have to
wait for the fourteenth century before its full consequences become evident.

MORALITY. A similar problem arises in the field of
morality. Can man do good without the help of God? Can he acquire the moral virtues by his own natural powers, or is an added
assistance from God needed? St. Bonaventure's solution to this
problem is exactly parallel to his solution of the problem of knowledge. Our will by itself is too weak and fluctuating to acquire virtue, just as the intellect by itself is too unstable to judge the truth.
So we need a moral illumination to be established in virtue, just as
we need an intellectual illumination to know the truth.

How does this moral illumination function? To act morally, we
must make practical judgments, guided by the virtue of prudence.
Prudence is thus the central virtue in the moral life. There are four
cardinal virtues: prudence, justice, fortitude, and temperance. Prudence guides us in all our moral acts by enabling us to apply the
laws of our moral conscience to the particular acts we have to perform. But we have already seen that our intellect is unstable, and
this instability contaminates the conclusions of our practical intellect, by which we make moral judgments, as well as those of our
speculative intellect. Hence our soul must be illuminated by the
divine virtues. God has the four cardinal virtues and all the others
following upon them. He has supreme rectitude (justice), stability
of being (fortitude), practical wisdom (prudence), and purity
(temperance). Through these divine virtues God strengthens the
soul by leaving traces of them within it. In this way the good life
of man requires constant contact with the divine virtues, just as his
knowledge of the truth demands the continual influence of the
divine Ideas.[36]

CONCLUSION

ST. BONAVENTURE's thought is basically a continuation and development of St. Augustine's. No one in the thirteenth century captured the Augustinian spirit and doctrine more exactly or adapted it more successfully to the Age of the Schoolmen. It has been claimed that St. Bonaventure was an Augustinian in his theology, but in his philosophy basically an Aristotelian, influenced by Neoplatonism.[37] This is hardly an accurate estimate. True, St. Bonaventure uses many Aristotelian terms, such as act and potency, form and matter, agent and possible intellect, but this was the common terminology of the time. When we examine the meaning he attaches to the terms, we usually find an underlying Augustinian idea.

As early as the 1250's, when St. Bonaventure wrote his *Commentary on the Sentences*, he had a comprehensive knowledge of Aristotle's philosophy and opposed it on almost all the major philosophical issues of the day. Later, in the 1270's, when the danger of Averroism was acute, the tone of his condemnation of Aristotelianism was sharper, but his fundamental criticism was the same. Because Aristotle rejected divine Ideas and exemplarism, he was bound to fall into serious error regarding God, his relation with the universe, and the destiny of the human soul. The impious errors of the Arabian Aristotelians were a necessary consequence of this. It was inevitable that St. Bonaventure should prefer Plato and Plotinus to Aristotle, for they, with all their faults, at least accepted the divine Ideas. But in making his choice in favor of the Platonists, St. Bonaventure once more reveals his basic allegiance to St. Augustine.

XII

St. Albert the Great

T HE MIDDLE AGES gave St. Albert the titles of "Albert the
Great" and the "Universal Teacher" for his extraordinary breadth of learning and his excellence as a teacher.[1] He was
called "the amazement and miracle" of his day and was quoted as
an authority equal to the greatest philosophers—an unparalleled
honor which, as we have seen, piqued Roger Bacon.

An examination of the thirty-eight volumes of Albert's collected
works makes this admiration understandable. They are the work of
an intellectual giant, whose interests extended to almost all the areas
of theology, philosophy, and science cultivated in his day. St. Albert was perfectly at home with the vast philosophic and scientific
literature recently translated from Greek and Arabic, and he was
one of the first to recognize its immense value for the development
of the human mind and the deepening of Christian thought. While
others were banning the works of Aristotle and denouncing the
errors of the philosophers, he embraced all their works with a
characteristic open-mindedness, convinced of their basic sound-
ness and confident in the ability of Christians to refute any errors
they contained. He was also aware how difficult it was to understand these works in translation, and he undertook to teach them to
his contemporaries. In particular, he set out to make Aristotle,
whom he rated the greatest of the philosophers, understandable to
them. After that he proposed to write original philosophical works
to fill up the lacunae in the Aristotelian system. His success was
so great that in no small measure the triumph of Aristotelianism in
the thirteenth century was due to him.

ATTITUDE TOWARD PHILOSOPHY

ST. ALBERT'S ATTITUDE toward philosophy was different from that of St. Bonaventure and Roger Bacon. They did not value secular learning for its own sake but only as an aid to theology. St. Albert's mental horizon was broader. He loved and esteemed every achievement of human reason, whether in the order of theology, philosophy, or science. Nothing intellectual was alien to him or failed to arouse his curiosity. He classified minerals and plants, described animals and insects with the same ardor with which he solved theological and philosophical problems. His harshest words were directed against those obscurantists who denied the value of philosophy. "There are ignorant men," he writes, "who try in every way to combat the use of philosophy, above all among the Preachers [i.e., Dominicans], where no one opposes them. Like unreasoning animals they blaspheme what they do not understand." [2] This passionate love of human reason and unshaken confidence in its powers were not the least legacy of St. Albert to his pupil Thomas Aquinas.

An important result of St. Albert's studies in philosophy was a clearer appreciation of its distinction from faith and theology. Not only did he distinguish between them in a theoretical way by showing that they differ in definition, but he marked out more clearly than his predecessors the field within which the philosopher is competent to work. Reason and philosophy enter into the doctrines of St. Anselm, Abelard, and Scotus Erigena, but these men did not always realize the limited scope of reason. As theologians, they believed in order to understand; but they frequently acted as though they could understand everything they believed. St. Anselm, for example, thought he could demonstrate (although not completely understand) the mysteries of the Trinity and Incarnation.

With St. Albert we reach an important moment in medieval thought, when the domains of philosophy and theology begin to be marked out in a practical way and the scope of reason becomes progressively limited. This was crucial for the development of philosophy as a kind of knowledge distinct from theology. St. Thomas was to play an important role in this matter, but St. Albert paved the way for him.

We have seen that Roger Bacon was captivated by the scientific literature of the Greeks and Arabs, chiefly that dealing with mathematics and optics. St. Albert was attracted rather by Aristotle's biological works. He learned and taught all they had to say and then went beyond them with his own researches and discoveries. The historian of botany, E. Meyer, says that Albert stands out as the solitary representative of a truly scientific theory of botany in the period between Aristotle and the sixteenth century.*3* In his *De Plantis* he describes the plant life in Germany which he had himself observed. His *De Animalibus* contains keen observations on mammals, fish, birds, and insects. He was the first to note nerve fibers in the stomachs of insects, and he gives good descriptions of the ostrich, spider, ant, and bee. A comment on the ostrich is worth quoting: "It is said of this bird that it swallows and digests iron; but I have not found this myself, because several ostriches refused to eat the iron which I threw them. However, they eagerly devoured large bones cut into small pieces, as well as gravel!" *4* His treatise *De Mineralibus* shows that he did personal research in chemistry, in connection with alchemy.

His method in natural science was to rely first of all on his own observations and then on the observations of others. In describing the various plant species he writes: "What I have to say is partly proven by experience and partly taken from the reports of those whom I have discovered do not readily make statements that are not proven by experience." *5* One could not wish for a more correct scientific procedure.

In philosophy, St. Albert does not show the creativeness and originality of St. Thomas. He was well acquainted with the philosophies of Aristotle, Avicenna, Averroes, Ibn Gabirol, and Maimonides, and he drew upon all of them. Among Christians, St. Augustine, Boethius, and Dionysius were particularly influential in shaping his ideas. From all these writers he gathered material for his vast encyclopedia of knowledge, without, however, fully harmonizing and unifying his different sources. Aristotle holds the first place in his estimation, but he generally saw Aristotle through the eyes of Avicenna and Averroes. The result was a genial, if not always coherent, synthesis of Aristotelianism and Neoplatonism.

MAN AND HUMAN KNOWLEDGE

ST. ALBERT'S ATTEMPT to harmonize Aristotle and Plato is well exemplified by his conceptions of the human soul and knowledge. Plato defined the soul as a spiritual substance moving the human body, while Aristotle defined it as the form and perfection of the body. St. Albert did not think these definitions contradictory if rightly understood; as Avicenna already had pointed out, they simply present the soul under two different aspects. Plato defined the soul in itself, as a substance separable from the body; Aristotle defined it by its external relation to the body. "Considering the soul in itself," St. Albert concludes, "we agree with Plato; considering it as the form animating the body we agree with Aristotle." [6]

This rather facile reconciliation of the two Greek philosophers had been rejected long before Albert's time in a work entitled *On the Nature of Man,* written about A.D. 400 by Nemesius but attributed by St. Albert and other medieval writers to St. Gregory of Nyssa. Nemesius pointed out that the definitions of the soul proposed by Plato and Aristotle cannot both be true. If we define the soul in the Aristotelian manner as the form of the body, it cannot be a separate and immortal substance, as Plato rightly thought it to be. For, according to Aristotle, a form is essentially bound up with matter and cannot exist outside it. [7]

St. Albert grants to Nemesius that this would be true if Aristotle defined the soul as a form from the standpoint of its essence. In fact, he says, Aristotle's definition is in terms of the soul's relation to the body. This leaves room for Plato's definition of the soul in itself as a spiritual substance.

There are, however, two difficulties with St. Albert's position. First, it does not do justice to Aristotle's notion of the soul as a form. Nemesius was correct in insisting that a form, in the Aristotelian sense, is inseparable from matter. Second, Albert's position makes it difficult to account for the substantial unity of man. It leads inevitably to a dualism of soul and body. St. Albert, following Avicenna, describes the soul as present in the body like a sailor in his ship, as though soul and body were two distinct substances. At the same time he recoils from a sharp dualism and insists that the soul is the substantial form of the body, composing with it a substantial unit. The reason for the substantial unity of soul and body is the natural inclination of the soul to animate the body. There is a natural aptitude in the soul to give existence and life to the body. Without the soul, the body would not be truly an organic body, any more than a dead man is a man. In this respect the soul is different from an angel, who has no natural inclination to inform a body. Even after death the soul keeps its natural desire for the body and cannot be perfectly happy without it.[8]

Although the soul's relationship with the body is natural, St. Albert did not think this relationship entered into the very essence of the soul. In its essence, the soul is an incorporeal substance, complete in itself and independent of matter. This is clear from the fact that the soul is basically an intellect. The soul has some powers that are exercised through bodily organs and hence are dependent upon the body, but this is not true of the intellect. The intellect is essentially independent of matter, as we shall presently see. The whole intellectual soul must as a consequence be separate in essence from the body.[9]

As a spiritual substance the soul cannot be produced by natural forces but is a special creation of God. The mark of its creaturehood is its internal composition, for only God lacks all complexity. It does not contain matter, as St. Bonaventure thought, for it is entirely spiritual. Hence it is not composed of matter and form. There is a distinction in the soul, however, between the individual soul and the nature it possesses in common with other souls. Following Boethius and Gilbert of Poitiers, St. Albert calls this a distinction between *quod est* (that which is; namely, the individual being) and *esse* or *quo est* (the essence or nature of the individual). St. Albert explains that this distinction is similar to that between matter and form. As matter receives form, so the individual receives the nature that gives it its specific essence. However, the distinction between the individual and its nature is found in all creatures, including the angels, whereas the distinction between matter and form is present only in material things.[10]

The soul has two intellectual powers corresponding to and based upon the two metaphysical components St. Albert has just described. Corresponding to the passive and receptive part of the soul (its *quod est*), it has a possible intellect enabling it to receive knowledge. Corresponding to the soul's active part (its *quo est*), it has an agent intellect by which it actively acquires knowledge. Each individual soul has its own possible and agent intellects: there is not one intellect for all men, as Averroes taught. Our agent intellect, which is a participation in God's own intellect, is the light whereby we understand. It is man's special glory, for it is the image of God in the soul. God is closest to the soul at this point and he bestows upon it successive illuminations, culminating in the light of glory in the Beatific Vision. We have a possible intellect, not because the soul is the form of the body and abstracts its knowledge from sense data, but simply because the soul is receptive of knowledge. Since angels are in the same condition, they too have an intellect of this sort. But owing to the soul's contact with the body its possible intellect is slightly immersed in matter, and this is why, unlike the angels, it receives knowledge through the senses.[11]

The intellect, however, is not so immersed in the body that it must gain all its knowledge through the senses. The intellect knows physical and mathematical objects by turning to the senses and the imagination and by abstracting data from them. But St. Albert denies that our knowledge of metaphysical or "divine" objects is acquired in this way; our intellect receives this higher knowledge by divine illumination and not by abstraction. He writes: "The union of man's intellect to matter and time does not exclude its capacity to be raised to the pure and clear light of understanding, in which it can receive knowledge of intelligible objects [that is, objects beyond the level of physics and mathematics] because in this case it does not turn back to the senses." [12]

Knowledge by abstraction is a lower form of knowledge preparing the way for divine illumination. But even abstraction is impossible without the illuminating help of God. The light of the agent intellect alone does not enable us to know the truth even concerning the physical world. It must be brightened by God's own light, or by the combined light of the angels and God, "as the sun's light is added to that of a star." [13] St. Albert calls this divine illumination a grace in the broad sense, for it is a gift added to our natural endowments. However, it is not a supernatural grace on the level of faith or the light of glory.[14]

Consequently, St. Albert sees a continuity in knowledge, from sense perception and abstraction to the highest reaches of divine illumination. As we have seen, it is not essential for the soul to be joined to the body, nor is it necessary for it to gain knowledge through the bodily senses. The primary function of the agent intellect is to receive illuminations from above and to illuminate in turn the possible intellect so that it can abstract forms from material things. It is only because of the presence of the soul in the body that it must first know by abstraction. The goal of knowledge is the full illumination of the possible intellect by the agent intellect. In the angels this takes place instantaneously; in man the intellect grows luminous by degrees. The human possible intellect, immersed as it is in the body, is somewhat darkened and cannot at once receive the full flood of light from the agent intellect. It must receive this light gradually and, as it were, piecemeal. The body and the senses play a role in this. They enable this light to be broken up by forms abstracted from the data of the senses, somewhat as physical light is broken up and diversified into the various colors by different kinds of opaque objects. Only after a long period of study and preparation is the possible intellect ready to receive the complete illumination of the agent intellect.[15]

The ultimate goal of man in this life is the possession of an intellect perfected in this way and capable of contemplating divine things. When his intellect is thus sanctified, he rises to a knowledge of his own spiritual nature, the angels and God, which are the fitting objects of his knowledge. At the same time he is prepared for eternal happiness, for the intellect thus perfected is the foundation of immortality (*radix immortalitatis*).[16]

St. Albert's noetic was inspired by St. Augustine and Dionysius among Christian writers, as well as by Aristotle and the Moslem philosophers. He sometimes speaks the language of Aristotle, but here as elsewhere his outlook is better described as Neoplatonic than Aristotelian. His true successor was not St. Thomas Aquinas but the Neoplatonic school of German mystics, whose leader was Master Eckhart.

METAPHYSICAL NOTIONS

ST. ALBERT'S METAPHYSICAL LANGUAGE is rather confusing owing to the variety of sources from which it is drawn. Nowhere is his syncretism more evident than in the different meanings he assigns to metaphysical terms such as "being." Nevertheless, a fairly consistent metaphysics can be gleaned from his works. Here we shall limit ourselves to a few of his more important metaphysical notions.

St. Albert considers Aristotle's doctrine of being imperfect because it does not take creation into account. Being, for Aristotle, is the concept reached at the end of an intellectual analysis of reality; it is not the primary effect of God the creator. Following Aristotle, we can analyze a composite notion into its component parts; for example, "man" into the genus "animal" and the sub-genus "substance." "Substance" in turn can be analyzed into "being," which is the most universal of all concepts. In its complete indetermination it is like primary matter, which is devoid of all form.

The Fathers of the Church had a deeper insight into being than Aristotle, for they recognized God as the primary Being and the intelligent and free creator.[17] As primary Being, it is only to be expected that his first effect should be being. As Dionysius and the Neoplatonic *Book on Causes* say, being is the first of all creations. St. Albert did not think this to be a separate being, like the *Nous* of Plotinus. Being is the most primitive and indeterminate of all perfections bestowed by God upon creatures, serving as the foundation for all the others. God gives being to all creatures, but over and above this he endows some with life and intelligence. This shows that even though being is the most fundamental of God's effects, it is the least perfect of them all. It is more perfect to exist and to live than only to exist, and it is still more perfect both to live and to understand.[18] To exist (*existere*) means simply to

stand outside (*sistere ex*) a cause. To say that God gives existence
to creatures is to say that they proceed from him as from their
first cause.[19] This is as general and indeterminate as the Aristotelian
notion of being, but it is more intelligible, owing to the Christian
notion of creation.

God gives to some creatures special perfections such as life and
intelligence; to all he gives, besides being, the attributes of goodness, truth, and beauty. These notions are as general as the notion
of being, for every being is good, true, and beautiful. Unlike the
notion of being, however, they are not simple notions. The good
is defined as being ordained to an end. It is thus a complex notion
comprising being and its relationship to an end. Every being is
good, for God has assigned a purpose to everything in the universe.[20] Being is a more primitive notion than that of goodness
because it is simpler. However, if we consider the goodness of
God and the existence of creatures, goodness is prior to being, for
creatures exist because of the divine goodness. As St. Augustine
says, "We exist because God is good, and we are good insofar as
we exist." [21]

The notion of truth is also complex and posterior to that of being, for truth adds to being a relation to the form by which the
being is what it is, and by which it is knowable.[22] The notion of
beauty is even more complex. Like the Neoplatonists, St. Albert
defines beauty in terms of light, which is present in every being as
a reflection of the divine light. Beauty is the radiance of form
(either substantial or accidental) shining upon the proportioned
parts of matter or upon a diversity of powers or actions.[23]

These and all other created perfections stem from God, who is
their model and exemplar. They all exist most perfectly in him,
without introducing any complexity or composition into his being.
Every creature, on the other hand, is composite, being made up
of a concrete subject (for example, Peter) and a nature possessed
by the subject (for example, humanity). God's being alone is simple (*simplex essentia*). This is why his proper name, revealed in
Scripture, is "He Who Is" (*Exod.* 3:14). St. Albert thought the
simplicity of the divine being well expressed by this simplest of
all names. Another reason that being properly belongs to God is

that he alone exists independently of a cause. Existence is accidental to creatures, for God alone exists necessarily, whereas creatures are possible beings, depending for their existence on the creative power of God.[24]

St. Albert here blends together ideas taken from his favorite Christian, Moslem, and pagan sources. His own contribution consists mainly in the synthesis he made of them. In insight into philosophical problems and creative originality in solving them, he was far inferior to schoolmen such as Thomas Aquinas and Duns Scotus.

St. Albert outlived St. Thomas and continued to write after the death of his pupil. There is a tradition that when some of St. Thomas' doctrines were condemned in Paris in 1277, St. Albert made the long journey from Cologne to defend his favorite pupil. However this may be, he never became a Thomist. He was the first to appreciate St. Thomas' genius, and he foretold that one day his pupil's words would be heard throughout the world. Many centuries elapsed before this prophecy was fulfilled; but like so many of his contemporaries and successors, St. Albert never seems to have heard St. Thomas' voice. It is understandable that the master clung to older ways of thinking and did not accept the revolutionary views in metaphysics advanced by his young pupil. However, his complete silence concerning them is remarkable.

XIII

St. Thomas Aquinas

THE OFFICE OF A WISE MAN

IN THE OPENING CHAPTERS of his *Summa Contra Gentiles,*
St. Thomas sets forth the ideal of wisdom which he constantly held before him as his goal in life.[1] Wisdom, he explains, is
bound up with order. This can be seen most clearly in practical affairs, in which the wise man is he who brings about order by ruling
others and by directing them to a desired end. Examples are the ruler
of a state, the leader of an army, and the architect of a building. The
same is true in the realm of theoretical knowledge, with the difference that here the wise man does not create order in human
affairs but discovers and contemplates the order in the universe.
Now this order cannot be understood without knowing the end to
which the universe is directed, and this is identical with its origin;
namely, God. The universe can also be said to be ordained to
truth, because God is an intellect, and the end or good intended
by an intellect is truth. Consequently, the wise man is he who
pursues the knowledge of God or truth. St. Thomas could find no
better words to express his goal in life than those of St. Hilary
(which are thoroughly Augustinian): "I am aware that I owe this
to God as the chief duty of my life, that my every word and sense
may speak of him." [2]

In directing wisdom to the contemplation of God, St. Thomas
was conscious of following in the footsteps not only of the Fathers
of the Church but also of the great philosophers. Did not Aristotle
call primary philosophy theology; that is to say, the study of God?

He also described it as the science of truth, and especially of the divine truth, which is the first cause of the universe. The philosophers, however, knew God only by natural reason. Christians are in a more advantageous position, because they have access not only to truths about God demonstrated by philosophy but also to truths surpassing the powers of reason and known only through revelation. Revelation, however, is not limited to those truths about God completely surpassing human reason. God has seen fit to reveal some truths about himself that reason by itself can attain. Did not God reveal to us his very existence, which is also demonstrable in philosophy? St. Thomas thought this eminently fitting, for even though reason by itself can reach some knowledge of God, few men have the ability, leisure, and interest to become metaphysicians. Moreover, even those who eventually do attain this lofty state will have had need in their youth—a time unsuited to metaphysics—to be certain of the basic truths about God; and having later become metaphysicians, they may still fall into error without the unshakable certitude given by faith.[3]

As a Christian, St. Thomas availed himself of both revelation and natural reason in his approach to God. He considered natural reason and philosophy useful not only in understanding better what he believed but also in refuting the errors of the pagans, who do not accept the authority of sacred Scripture.

The science of theology, or sacred doctrine—to use St. Thomas' preferred term—contains all truths about God, whether they are known by natural reason or only by revelation. But for him this does not exhaust the content of sacred doctrine. If we wish to see how vast the horizons of this science are in the eyes of St. Thomas, we have only to glance through his two major theological works, the *Summa Contra Gentiles* and the *Summa Theologiae*. They are replete with philosophical and even scientific information and demonstrations; but because all this contributes to St. Thomas' work as a theologian and serves the ends of theology he considered it to be part of theology.

Today we are accustomed to a narrower view of theology, as embracing only those truths actually revealed or deducible from revelation. St. Thomas' perspective was quite different. For him,

any truth of natural reason can be included in theology if it sub-
serves the understanding or defense of revelation. It may not actually be revealed (*revelatum*), but if it is related to revelation it
comes under the formal object of theology as revealable (*revela-
bile*) and is part of that science.[4]

St. Thomas' vocation was that of a theologian, but the fulfillment of his calling, as he understood it, demanded intense philosophical inquiry. He wrote long commentaries on the works of
Aristotle, as well as a few short philosophical treatises. But all this
was to aid his theological studies. What is more, his most original
and profound philosophical ideas are not found in his Aristotelian
commentaries but in his theological writings. What is today called
"Thomistic philosophy" is that part of St. Thomas' theology which
he considered rationally demonstrable and which has been taken
out of its theological context. In justice to St. Thomas, however,
we must not forget the theological setting in which his philosophical ideas flowered. Obviously he did not think faith a hin-
drance to philosophical studies, but rather an indispensable aid to
the Christian who philosophizes.

The mingling of rational and revealed truths in St. Thomas'
theology does not indicate any confusion in his mind between the
methods of philosophy and theology. He learned from the Greeks
and Arabs the nature of philosophy and of rational demonstration,
and he had a clear conception of the limits of such demonstration,
particularly in regard to God. These limits can best be seen in the
Summa Contra Gentiles, whose first three books are devoted to
truths about God and creatures accessible to human reason, while
the fourth book concerns truths about the Incarnation, Trinity,
and Sacraments, held by faith alone. This work, like the other
theological and philosophical writings of St. Thomas, contains
abundant philosophical analyses and inquiries, so that we can form
a clear notion of what he conceived such an inquiry to be, as
well as its limitation in respect to revealed truth. In particular,
he makes it clear that philosophy must begin with data furnished
by the senses and analyzed in the light of principles, the first of
which is being. Only at the end of his inquiry does the philosopher
attain some knowledge of God as the first cause of being. The

theologian, on the other hand, begins with the data concerning God furnished by revelation, and he considers creatures only insofar as they are related to God and throw light upon him.[5]

THE EXISTENCE OF GOD

THE FIVE WAYS of proving the existence of God found in the *Summa Theologiae*[6] provide a good example of St. Thomas' use of philosophy in his theology. These proofs are not original; each can be traced back to the philosophers of antiquity or the Middle Ages. But in his hands they are transformed and lead to the existence, not of the God of Aristotle or the Arabian philosophers, but of the God of Christianity.

The first and most evident way of proving God's existence is from motion. It is clear that some things are in motion. Now whatever is moved must be moved by something else. For a being in motion is in potency with respect to that toward which it moves, whereas a being moves insofar as it is in act. For motion is nothing else than the reduction of something from potentiality to actuality. A being cannot be brought from potentiality to actuality except by a being in act. For example, wood that is potentially hot can be made actually hot only by something actually hot, such as fire. At first sight the self-movements of living beings seem to be an exception to this rule, but on closer examination we see that they have parts, one of which moves the other. If the cause of motion is itself moved, it must be moved by some other mover, which in turn is moved by another, and so on. But there cannot be an infinite series of movers, because then there would be no first mover and consequently no other movers. For subsequent movers move only inasmuch as they are moved by the first mover, as the staff moves only because it is moved by the hand. Therefore, there is a primary cause of motion which is moved by nothing, and this everyone understands to be God.

The second way begins with the observation that there are efficient causes producing effects in the world about us. Now it is impossible for anything to be its own efficient cause, because an efficient cause is by nature prior to its effect, and nothing is prior to itself. Every efficient cause therefore presupposes another, which in turn presupposes another, and so on. But it is impossible to regress to infinity in a series of efficient causes arranged in a hierarchy of perfection, for intermediate efficient causes depend for their very causality on a first cause. Without a first cause, there would be no intermediate causes, and the effects we observe would not take place. Hence there must be a first efficient cause, and this we call God.

The third way rests on the evident fact that some beings come into existence and pass away; in other words, it is possible for them to be or not to be. Now what is possible cannot account for the fact that it exists. Indeed, if all beings were merely possible, nothing would actually exist. The fact that some possible beings exist points to the existence of a necessary being as their cause. This necessary being is either caused by another necessary being or it is uncaused. And since there cannot be an infinite series of necessary beings, there must be a being that is necessary in itself and whose necessity is uncaused. This everyone calls God.

The fourth way to God starts with the degrees of perfection in things. We observe that beings are more or less good, true, noble, and so on. But things are said to be more or less only inasmuch as they resemble in various degrees some maximum. Hence there must be something truest, best, and noblest and consequently being in the highest degree, for according to Aristotle what possesses truth in the highest degree is the maximum being. This noblest and most perfect being, which is the cause of all other beings with their relative perfections, we call God.

The fifth way is based upon the order of the universe. Although natural bodies lack knowledge, they act for an end. This is clear from the fact that they regularly act in the same way and achieve the same result. This cannot be due to chance but to an intelligence directing these bodies to act as they do, as the arrow is directed by the archer. Consequently, there is an intelligent being directing all natural things to their end, and this we call God.

Each of St. Thomas' five ways of proving the existence of God has a different starting point, but they all exhibit the same structure. To begin with, each is based upon an empirical observation of the sensible world, and hence it has an existential foundation from which the mind ascends to the existence of God. Secondly, each proof makes use of the notion of causality by showing that God is the ultimate cause of the sensible beings with which the proof begins. St. Thomas considers the notion of causality to be derived from sense experience. The mind is not equipped with an innate principle of causality which we apply to empirical data furnished by the senses. Indeed, he tells us that it must be proved that anything in motion must be moved by something else.[7] This he does by showing that a being in motion is potential to the terminus of its motion. In order to be brought into act with respect to that terminus, it must be moved by a being already in act.

The second point to be proved, St. Thomas continues, is the impossibility of an infinite series of movers or causes. It should be noted that he does not deny the possibility of an infinite series of causes on the same level, one succeeding the other in time; for example, a man begetting a son, who in turn begets his own son, and so on. As we shall see, he did not think human reason could disprove the eternal duration of the universe, and in this hypothesis an infinite succession of individuals in the various species would be possible. St. Thomas' proofs for the existence of God are valid, even supposing the eternal duration of the universe. The series of causes whose infinity he deems impossible is one whose members are arranged in a hierarchy of perfection, so that the lower causes are instruments of the higher, and all contribute simultaneously to bring about an effect. Since the causality of an instrument depends upon a first cause (a stick can cause an effect only if moved by a hand), if all causes were instrumental they could bring about no effect. Beyond all instrumental causes, therefore, there must be an absolutely first cause to account for the causality of secondary causes and for their effects.[8]

OUR KNOWLEDGE OF GOD

EACH OF THE ABOVE WAYS to God adds something to our knowledge of him. As the prime mover, he is immovable and unchangeable, and consequently he is not passive or material. As the first cause, he is endowed with unlimited power to cause other beings, while he himself is uncaused. As the first necessary being, he does not derive his existence from anything else but exists through himself. As supremely perfect, he is being, truth, and goodness to the highest degree. As the cause of order in the universe, he is its intelligent director and provider.

This knowledge of God, however, does not enable us to penetrate to his essence so that we know *what* he is. St. Thomas insists that in this life we know God only through negation and through his relation to creatures. Since God is all-perfect, we can deny of him anything implying an imperfection, such as change, passivity, and composition. We can then attribute to him immobility, perfect actuality, and absolute simplicity. Besides this negative knowledge of God, we can know him by analogy with his creatures. As effects of God, creatures must bear some resemblance to him, even though it be very remote. We can be sure that what exists in the effect pre-exists in its cause, although in a more perfect way.[9]

Now two kinds of perfections are found in creatures. Some by their very nature imply a defect or limitation; for example, humanity and animality. These cannot be attributed to God in their proper sense but only metaphorically, as when we say that God is the "light" of our intellect or that he "walked" in the Garden of Eden. Other perfections of creatures are absolute, implying no defect or limitation; for example, wisdom, being, and goodness. These are present in both God and creatures, although in God they exist in a more perfect manner. Hence we can say that God is supremely good, perfect, one, intelligent, free, and powerful. However, we do not know the divine goodness or perfection itself, any more than we know his essence. We know that God's goodness and other attributes are proportionate to his being, as those of his creatures are proportionate to their being.[10] But in saying this, we acknowledge that the divine being infinitely escapes our grasp, for that being is infinite, whereas created being is finite.

When all is said and done, therefore, our judgments of analogy between God and creatures do not yield a positive concept of

God in himself. Because of the infinite gulf between what we
know of God and what he is, St. Thomas agrees with Dionysius
that "man reaches the peak of his knowledge of God when he
realizes that he does not know him, understanding that the divine
reality surpasses all human conceptions of it." [11]

One of the most significant negative attributes of God established by St. Thomas is the divine simplicity; that is to say, the
absence in God of all composition. This follows from the fact
that a composite is made up of several elements, one of which is
potential and the other actual. Moreover, the elements of a composite are potential with respect to their union, and they require
a cause to bring them together. But it has been shown that God is
completely actual and uncaused. Hence he is not a composite being. [12]

St. Thomas draws several conclusions from this fact. To begin
with, the divine being is not composed of matter and form or
substance and accident. Moreover, owing to his simplicity, God is
identical with his essence. In this respect he is unlike everything
in our experience. A man, for example, is not humanity. He
possesses humanity as his essence, but he has other characteristics
belonging to him as an individual. This implies that, unlike God,
he is a composite being. [13]

An even more important consequence is that God's essence and
being (*esse*) are identical. The word "being," St. Thomas tells
us, designates an act, for a thing is not said to be because it is
in potency but because it is in act. Consequently, if the divine
essence were other than its being, there would be a composition
of essence and being in God, and his essence would be potential
to his being. Since God is pure act, he must be pure being, and his
essence must be Being itself.

The sequence of St. Thomas' thought leads us to the notion of
God as the pure act of being or existing. He finds this remarkable
conclusion confirmed by sacred Scripture: the "sublime truth"
that God's essence is his being was revealed to Moses by God himself when he told the patriarch his proper name: *I Am Who Am*
(*Exod.* 3:14). In calling himself "He Who Is," God revealed that

his essence is Being itself, for names are meant to signify essences or natures.[14]

This interpretation of the divine name introduces us to St. Thomas' notion of being, which lies at the very center of his metaphysical view of reality. Its significance can perhaps best be seen when contrasted with St. Augustine's interpretation of the same text of Scripture. For him, the divine name "He Who Is" means that God is unchangeable and eternal. This is because Augustine identified being with immutability. For St. Thomas, on the other hand, being is the act whereby something exists. Hence to say that God's essence is his being is to say that it is the pure act of being or existing. In other words, God is pure existential act or pure existence. Creatures differ from God in that their essences are not the acts by which they exist; they have essences that are other than their acts of being.

The conception of God as pure existence was anticipated by Avicenna, Maimonides, and William of Auvergne, but it finds its fullest expression in the writings of St. Thomas. He was the first to appreciate fully the consequences of the existential view of God and to see the act of being as the central feature of all reality.

We may wonder whether St. Thomas is not demeaning God by saying that he is nothing but the act of being. Are there not other perfections besides being, such as life and intelligence, and is it not more perfect to live and to understand than simply to be? St. Thomas points out, however, that to live and to understand are *ways of being* included in being itself. The life of a living thing, for example, is simply its being: *vivere viventibus est esse.* "Being," indeed, is the richest and most comprehensive of all terms, for it includes all perfections. Hence to say that God is Being itself is to say that he is all-perfect, or that his perfection is without limits.[15]

CREATION

ST. THOMAS' METHOD is to mount up to God from the visible world, then from this vantage point to cast his eyes back upon the world to see what new facts are revealed about it. The first and most important is that it has been created. By this St. Thomas means that God has given it its complete being, producing it, not from pre-existing matter but from non-being (*ex nihilo*).

This is a conclusion from the truth already established, that the being of God is identical with his essence. Now this is necessarily a unique case. There cannot be two beings that are Being itself, because each would be absolutely perfect and hence indistinguishable from the other. In short, there can be only one God.[16] Consequently, everything besides God exists, not by its own essence but by receiving being from him who is Being itself. This precludes the possibility of a pre-existing and non-created subject out of which God fashioned the universe.[17]

If we ask why God created anything at all, St. Thomas assures us that, strictly speaking, this question has no answer. There was no necessity for God to create a universe, for he is all-perfect and in need of nothing. Creation was the result of a free decision of his will to share his perfection with finite beings; and since his will is uncaused, no reason can be assigned for his decision to create or for his choice of the present universe out of the infinite number of possible ones he could have created.[18]

However, it was eminently fitting for God to create because he is the pure act of being. As St. Thomas sees it, everything in act tends by its nature to communicate itself as far as possible. In other words, being is endowed with an intrinsic dynamism to the extent that it is actual. Now it has been shown that the divine nature is supremely in act. It is only to be expected, then, that the divine nature communicates itself to the fullest possible extent. Scripture tells us of the mysterious self-communication taking place within the divine substance through the processions of the Persons of the Trinity. These internal processions witness to the internal fecundity of the divine being. Creation is another example of the impulse within God to communicate himself, this time to beings outside himself.[19]

The origin of creatures is consequently the divine will freely choosing to express itself outward, so to speak, by making finite things participate in the divine being. But the divine intellect also plays a role in creation. Because God's understanding is infinite, he knows himself in every possible way, not only as he is in himself, but also in the numberless ways in which creatures can participate in his being. Consequently, he possesses an infinite number of Ideas, each of which is a model or exemplar according to which something can be created. These Ideas are not distinct from the divine essence. They are the divine essence itself, known as capable of being imitated in a particular way by a creature. And since creatures are individual things, the divine Ideas are primarily of individuals, although they represent them not only in their individuality but also in their genera and species.[20]

Created by a God who is supremely good, the universe itself must be good. Is it the best of all possible worlds? St. Thomas replies: "The universe cannot be better, as things actually exist, because the order God has established among them, and in which the good of the universe consists, most befits them." However, since God is infinite, no finite being is such that God cannot create something better. Hence an absolutely best possible universe is inconceivable.[21]

The finite character of created being also accounts for the deficiencies and physical evils we find in it. Evil is not a being: every being as such is good, for it is a reflection of the divine being, which is the supreme good. Evil is the absence in a being of what it should naturally possess; for example, the lack of an eye in a man. God is not the cause of such evils; he intends only the good of the universe. But he may be said to cause evil *per accidens*, inasmuch as he has willed to create a finite universe in which the interplay of secondary causes can introduce deficiencies and physical defects into creatures. Moral evil results from the free will of man, and it is but another sign of the limitation found in anything created.[22]

To the question: Did the universe always exist or did it begin to exist in time? St. Thomas did not think philosophy can give a decisive answer. His reason is that the temporal duration of the universe depends upon God's will, whose decisions cannot be investigated by reason but are known only by revelation. Now God has revealed that in fact the universe began in time; he has told us in Scripture: *In the beginning God created heaven and earth (Gen.* 1:1). But if God had chosen otherwise, he could have created a universe of eternal duration.

This is contrary to the opinion of St. Bonaventure, who thought it possible to prove the non-eternity of the world by rational arguments. The first of these is that if the world had no beginning in time it has already existed an infinite number of days. But an infinite number cannot be traversed. Since we have in fact reached the present day, it follows that the universe has not always existed. St. Thomas, however, saw no impossibility in an infinite series of beings, one succeeding the other in time. At any given moment this infinite succession would in fact be finite, for it would be closed by the last member in the series. Hence it would be possible to reach that moment in the series. Secondly, St. Bonaventure contended that it is impossible to add to the infinite. But each day adds to the duration of the universe. Hence the universe cannot always have existed. In reply to this, St. Thomas points out that if, as has been shown to be the case, an infinite series is finite at any given moment in it, there is no reason that an addition cannot be made to it. Finally, St. Bonaventure maintained that if the universe always existed, an infinite number of human beings has existed in the past and consequently an infinite number of immortal souls actually exists at the present moment. This he considered an impossibility. St. Thomas retorts that God could have created an eternal universe while reserving the creation of man and human souls for a given moment of time. Besides, he adds, no one has ever proved that God cannot create an infinite number of simultaneously existing beings.

In this way St. Thomas distinguishes the problem of the temporal origin of the universe from that of its origin in being. He considers its ontological origin, or creation, rationally demonstrable, but not its origin in time. The eternity or non-eternity of the universe must remain an open question to the philosopher: only by faith do we know that it had a beginning in time.[23]

This throws considerable light on the Thomistic notion of creation. It is natural to compare God's creation of the universe with an artist's production of a work of art; but there are two fallacies in this analogy. The artist precedes his artifact in time, so that the latter cannot always have existed. God, however, does not exist in time. Hence the universe has no temporal relation with him but only a relation of dependence in being. There is no reason, then, that the universe cannot always have existed, although eternally dependent upon God for its existence. Secondly, an artist does not give his work of art its total being. He simply alters matter, conferring on it a new mode of being. As a result, the artifact continues to exist after the artist has ceased to work upon it. God, on the other hand, gives the universe its complete being. Hence the universe would cease to exist if God withdrew his action from it. Not only has he created the universe, but he constantly conserves it in existence. If God had chosen to create a universe without a beginning or end in time, it would nonetheless have been a created universe, for it would have eternally owed its total being to him.

THE STRUCTURE OF CREATED BEING

THE UNIVERSE CONTAINS a multitude of beings differing not only in number but also in species. According to St. Thomas, the perfection of the universe demands this diversity and the inequality among beings resulting from it. Since no one creature adequately expresses the divine goodness, God produced a vast number of them and arranged them in a hierarchy of perfection, so that together they might form a whole, or a universe, fittingly representative of the divine goodness.[24]

At the peak of this hierarchy are the angels, whom St. Thomas conceives as immaterial substances. Their existence is known not only by revelation but also by reason, for without them there would be an obvious gap in the plan of creation and the continuity of creatures would be broken. Below the angels are human beings, who are partly spiritual and partly material. Animals and plants follow next in order, and in final place we find the four elements: fire, air, water, and earth. The continuity of created being is such that the lowest member of a superior order borders upon the most perfect member of the order just below it. The highest types of plants, for example, are similar to the lowest species of animals.

By the fact of its creation every creature is a finite, limited being. God cannot create simply Being: this would be to create himself. What he creates is an *angelic* being, a *human* being, and so on. There is consequently a limiting factor within each created being which is not being itself. This St. Thomas calls the creature's essence, quiddity, or nature. Unlike God, then, the essence of a creature is not identical with its being but forms a real composition with it.[25]

The nature of this composition has often been misunderstood, even by the disciples of St. Thomas. It has frequently been interpreted to mean that essence and being in a creature are two realities joined together by the creative act of God. This is not the mind of St. Thomas, however, for he teaches that essence in itself is not a reality; it is in fact nothing unless it exists—that is to say, unless it has being. Humanity, for example, has no reality in itself. It is real only inasmuch as it exists in individual men. The only other existence an essence has is in a mind that conceives it; for example, in the divine mind, where it is identical with the divine being.[26]

St. Thomas sometimes describes the relation of essence to being in terms suggesting that essence is a reality in itself. He tells us, for example, that in creatures essence receives being, and consequently that a created essence is potential with respect to being, which is an act. But these statements must be correctly understood. St. Thomas does not mean to attribute any perfection or reality to an essence in itself. It is a perfection to be an angel or to be a man, but the angelic or human nature owes all its perfection to the being by which it exists, for if it did not exist it would be nothing.

The real composition of essence and being follows from the fact that no creature is its own being, but receives its being from God according to the measure of its essence. Essence may be said to "receive" being, not as one being receives another, but as the measure according to which the creature is endowed with being.

A corollary of this is the excellence of being or existence in comparison with essence. St. Thomas has told us that the name "being" signifies an act; namely, the act of existing. Essence is a possible measure or limit of being, but of itself it is nothing. The whole perfection of a being, therefore, comes from the act whereby it exists. For this reason St. Thomas calls the act of being (*esse*) "the actuality of all acts and consequently the perfection of all perfections." [27] Far from being an accident of essence, as Avicenna and his followers claimed, existence is "that which is innermost in each thing and most fundamentally present within all things." [28] This is hardly surprising if, as St. Thomas says, God is the pure act of being. Nothing in a created being could be more important or noble than its existence, in which it reflects most luminously the proper perfection and mystery of God.

Besides the composition of essence and being, there is in all creatures the composition of substance and accident. These latter notions can be understood only in the light of the real composition of essence and being that we have just examined. St. Thomas defines substance as that which has an essence to which it belongs not to exist in a subject. This is in contrast to an accident, which he defines as that to whose essence it belongs to exist in a subject. [29] A substance is not identical with its being, but it has an essence capable of receiving its own act of being. This does not mean that a substance exists by itself, in the sense that it has no cause. Only God is uncaused. A substance is made to be by its causes, but the existence it receives from them is its own. An accident, on the other hand, does not have its own existence; it simply modifies or determines in a particular way the existence of the substance.

An individual existing substance is called a suppositum. This term is derived from the mode of being of a substance, which is subsistence. In the vocabulary of St. Thomas, to subsist means to exist with an existence of one's own (*per se*). If the suppositum is of a rational nature, it is called a person, the name reserved by St. Thomas for the noblest of all beings. [30]

A third composition found in created beings is that of form and matter. In opposition to the majority of his contemporaries, St. Thomas restricted this composition to corporeal substances. The current notion that angels and human souls contain spiritual matter seemed to him both paradoxical and unnecessary. He was too good an Aristotelian to admit the presence of matter in a substance that is not corporeal or extended in space. The partisans of spiritual matter contended that without such matter spiritual substances would contain no potential element but would be pure act—which is a divine prerogative. St. Thomas rejoined that every created essence is potential to its existence. Hence even though the essence of a spiritual substance is a pure form without matter, that form is not pure act, for it is potential to its existence. In this way St. Thomas' doctrine of the real composition of essence and being eliminates the need of the ambiguous notion of spiritual matter.[31]

The essences of corporeal substances, unlike those of spiritual creatures, are composed of matter and substantial form. Of these, the form is the nobler constituent, for it makes the substance to be what it is. For example, the substantial form of a man (which is his soul), determines him to be a human substance. The matter entering into composition with the substantial form has no determination or specification of its own. It is simply a potency determinable by a form, which, when it actualizes matter, makes it to be the matter of a particular substance.

Corporeal substances are subject to change because of the material element in their make-up. The forces acting in nature can deprive matter of one form in favor of another, giving rise to generation and corruption. The absence of matter in spiritual substances is a convincing proof to St. Thomas that they are naturally incorruptible.[32]

St. Thomas ascribes to matter a further role: it accounts for the presence of many individuals in the same species. Because matter is extended in space, it is divisible into parts, each of which may share in the same form and consequently belong to the same species. Matter, with extension, is consequently the "principle of individuation," in the sense that it makes possible the multiplicity of individuals in one species. Matter is well suited to play this passive role in individuation, for in itself it is purely potential. Its passivity, however, prevents it from accounting for any of the positive perfections in an individual being, including its individuality, or in the case of man his personality. The nobility of being an individual or a person does not come from the individual's matter but from its act of being, which is the intrinsic root of all its perfection.[33]

A corollary follows from St. Thomas' denial of matter in the angels: they are not individuals in a species as, for example, men are members of the human species. Each angel is a subsisting form, differing from other angels not only in number but also in species. The difference among the angels is consequently not material or based on a difference of matter, but purely formal. Each angel is, as it were, a single species, comparable to the human species if it were not shared by a multitude of men but were itself an individual being.[34] The angels are therefore arranged in a hierarchy according to their degrees of formal perfection, from the angel nearest God to the angel most akin to the human species.

MAN

MAN IS SITUATED below the angelic world among corporeal substances. In determining his structure, St. Thomas depends heavily upon Aristotle's *De Anima*, although in his usual manner he transforms everything he borrows from it. St. Thomas describes man as a physical substance, distinguished from other bodies by the fact that he is living and rational. Like all physical substances, he is composed of matter and substantial form. His form is also called his soul. Soul in general is the substantial form of a living being and the intrinsic source of its self-motion and self-development. All living beings possess a soul: plants, animals, and men. Men are distinguished from the rest of the animate world by the fact that their souls are rational.

In determining the nature of man, St. Thomas keeps two facts constantly in mind. First, man is capable of intellectual knowledge, which would be impossible unless he possessed an intellect intrinsically independent of matter. Second, it is the entire man, and not his intellect alone, who understands. He understands *by* his intellect, as he walks *by* his legs, but it is the man who understands, just as it is the man who walks. Consequently, the intellect must be united to man in such a way that it makes up one substance with him.

St. Thomas did not think that any of the current notions of man adequately accounted for both of these facts. Most of his contemporaries adopted the Augustinian doctrine of the soul as a spiritual substance, by nature independent of matter. They agreed with Aristotle that the soul is the form of the body but denied that this relationship with the body is essential to the soul. The soul, they contended, is not the form of the body *by its substance*, but only through one of its operations. They also inserted one or more substantial forms between matter and the human soul, the better to insure the latter's independence of the body. They conceived matter as endowed with at least the form of corporeity before the advent of the human soul. Some even held that man is endowed with distinct vegetative and sensitive souls as a preparation for the intellectual soul. Consequently, they viewed man as a composite of matter and several substantial forms.

The weakness of this position, in the opinion of St. Thomas, is that it fails to account for the substantial unity of man. If man is indeed one substance, he has only one substantial form, for substantial form confers substantial being on matter. If there were several substantial forms in man, he would have several substantial beings and he would not be one substance. Since it is obvious that he exists and operates as one substance, an individual man has but one substantial form, and this is his rational soul.[35]

The solution of the problem of man proposed by Averroes and his followers seemed even less reasonable to St. Thomas. They took Aristotle's statement that the agent intellect is "separable, not acted upon and unmixed" (with the body), (*De Anima*, III, 5, 430a17) to mean that the intellect is not the form of the body but a separately existing substance. Men may be said to know by this intellect because it operates in them and uses their sense powers. St. Thomas, however, does not consider this the correct interpretation of Aristotle, nor does he think it explains human knowledge. If Averroes is right, it is not the individual man who knows, but the intellect operating within him.[36]

St. Thomas concludes that the human soul is both an intellectual substance and by its nature the form of the body.[37] This is a bold assertion, for it is not easy to see how an intellectual substance by its nature can be the form of matter, nor indeed why it should inform matter at all. As already explained, a substance has its own act of being and hence it exists by itself. Why should a being of this sort lower itself, so to speak, to inform a body?

St. Thomas finds the answer to this question in the very nature of the human soul. Like the angels it is an intellectual substance, but unlike them it cannot understand without sense powers and sense organs. The angels do not need this bodily equipment because they are given their ideas by God himself. The human soul, as the lowest of all intellectual substances, must gain all its knowledge through the senses. By its very nature, therefore, it requires a body in order to do its work as an intellect.[38]

Man's nature is therefore composite, comprising both soul and body. The human soul, however, is in its own right a spiritual substance with its own being. Incomplete in essence, it is nevertheless complete as far as its being (*esse*) is concerned. That is why, according to St. Thomas, the human soul is by nature incorruptible and immortal.[39] It contains no matter from which its form could be separated; and, possessing its own being, there is no force in nature that can deprive it of its existence. In this respect it is unlike the substantial forms of the elements and the souls of other living things. These are not substances but material forms, thoroughly tied up with matter and without any being of their own. They exist only with the existence of the composites of which they are the forms, and they cease to exist when these composites are destroyed.

The human soul, on the other hand, possesses its own being. When it informs the body, it confers upon it (by way of formal causality) its own being, so that soul and body now share the same being (*esse*).[40] The resultant individual man, although composed of soul and body, is truly one substance with one substantial being. From a metaphysical point of view, therefore, the unity of man rests upon the unity of his act of being.

As the one substantial form of man, the human soul confers on him not only his being but also corporeity, life, sense, and understanding. Through his soul man is also enriched with manifold powers, which are the proximate principles by which he acts: the vegetative powers of nutrition, augmentation, and reproduction; the external and internal senses; and the spiritual powers of intellect and will. The intellect is the noblest power of man, for it constitutes him in his species as a rational animal, and it is the means by which he attains his goal in life, the vision of God.

KNOWLEDGE AND TRUTH

IN HIS TREATISE *On Spiritual Creatures*, St. Thomas gives a short history of the problem of knowledge and points out his own position on the subject.[41] Some ancient (Greek) philosophers, he says, limited man's knowledge to sense perception of the physical universe and denied that we can be certain of anything. They gave two reasons for this: 1] Sensible things offer no fixed object of knowledge, for they are constantly changing.   2] Men judge differently about the same object, and there is no criterion by which we can know whose judgment is true. How can we determine whose perceptions are correct, the man awake or asleep, the healthy man or the sick? Imbued with this skeptical attitude toward our knowledge of the physical universe, Socrates turned his attention to ethics. His disciple Plato inherited this distrust of sense knowledge, but he found a way to escape from skepticism and to establish the certitude of knowledge. He posited the existence of Ideas separated from the material world which are the unchanging objects of intellectual knowledge. He also showed that man has a mind or intellect, which is a power of knowing superior to the senses. Through this intellect we know the truth, but only when we are illumined by a higher intelligible light, as sight is illumined by the visible sun. Augustine, St. Thomas continues, followed Plato as far as the Catholic faith permitted. Where Platonism clashed with the faith, he brought Platonic philosophy into agreement with it. For example, in place of the separated Ideas of Plato, he held that there are Ideas in the divine mind and that we judge the truth through the influence of these Ideas upon our mind illumined by the divine light.

After this exact description of St. Augustine's position, St. Thomas goes on to explain that of Aristotle, which he adopts as his own. Aristotle, he says, established the certitude of knowledge in another way. First, he showed that there is something stable in sensible things. These are not pure change or flux. Wherever there is change, there is a stable reality that changes. Substances change in accidental ways—for example, by decreasing or increasing in size—but they remain constant in their substance. They also undergo substantial change, but there is a stable substance at the beginning and at the end of the change. There is consequently stability in sensible substances along with change, and this stable element serves as a basis for certain knowledge of them.

Secondly, Aristotle showed that the senses judge their proper objects correctly; namely, those perceived directly and primarily, as sight perceives color. The stability in the sensible world insures that even sense knowledge has a measure of truth.[42] Under normal circumstances the senses do not err regarding their proper objects, but they can be deceived regarding objects they have in common; for example, the size or motion of a body. Even more so can the senses err regarding objects perceived *per accidens*, such as existence and substance. These latter objects are not sensed, properly speaking, but understood. They fall under the senses only because the proper objects of the senses are qualities of existing substances.

Thirdly, after correcting the earlier views concerning the sensible world and sense knowledge, Aristotle was able to give a true account of intellectual knowledge. He showed that we know the truth, not by means of Ideas existing outside the sensible world but by the light of the agent intellect—a power whereby we abstract our ideas from sensible things.

Averroes interpreted Aristotle to mean that all men share the same agent intellect, but St. Thomas considers this to be not only a distortion of Aristotle's thought but contrary to experience. We are aware of our ability to abstract universals and to understand them when we wish. Each man, therefore, must have his own agent intellect, just as he has his own knowledge. What is this agent intellect? In St. Thomas' opinion it is simply the intellectual light created by God in our soul as a participated likeness of the uncreated light. St. Thomas is consequently in agreement with St. Augustine that our knowledge is possible only as the result of a divine illumination.[43] Nevertheless, he was convinced that Aristotle had accurately described the nature of our created light of knowing as the agent intellect. This was in contradiction to the Augustinians of his own day, for whom the divine illumination was a special or quasi-special divine influence added to our native intellectual powers.

The angels also participate in the divine light, to such an extent that at their creation they have an innate knowledge of things. St. Thomas compares their intellects to a painted canvas or a mirror reflecting intelligible forms. But the human intellect does not participate so fully in the divine light. When it comes into existence it is like a blank tablet on which nothing is written. It has the power to know, but by itself it is devoid of objects. Hence it must go below itself and seek out its objects in the sensible world.

Sense perception is consequently the necessary starting point of our knowledge. It is not, however, its goal. The senses have for their objects individual sensible things, which are represented by likenesses (called phantasms) in the interior senses. It is the function of the agent intellect to abstract intelligible natures from these likenesses by disengaging the universal from the particular; for example, the nature of man from the particular characteristics of individual men.[44]

In order to receive the universal thus disengaged from the individual, we must have a suitable intellectual faculty. St. Thomas, following Aristotle, calls this the "possible intellect," because it is in potency to receive the forms of all things. This intellect has two functions. First, it enables us to apprehend essences abstracted from sensible things and to form concepts of them. Second, it enables us to make judgments about the objects thus apprehended. These are the two basic intellectual operations of man, and they correspond to the two basic constituents of created being: essence and existence (*esse*). The first operation has to do with the essences of things: it is the act by which we apprehend essences and form concepts of them. There is more in reality, however, than essence; at its very center there is the act of existing. A further operation is therefore required by which we lay hold upon the

existence of things, and this, according to St. Thomas, is judgment.*45*

The existential import of judgment is most apparent in a judgment of the type "Socrates exists," which simply affirms Socrates'
existence in reality. In other judgments the reference to existence,
or to some mode of existence, is less obvious but is nonetheless
present. For example, the affirmation "Socrates is a man" expresses
the actual existence of the form "humanity" in Socrates.*46*

St. Thomas' doctrine of knowledge is consequently in close harmony with his notion of being. The same can be said of his doctrine
of truth. Along with his contemporaries, he defines truth as the
conformity of intellect and thing (*adaequatio intellectus et rei*).
This conformity is brought about by the assimilation of the intellect to its object, which takes place in two phases. In the first phase
the intellect is informed by the essences of things, which it makes its
own by conceiving them within itself. In the second phase the
intellect is more perfectly assimilated to its object by judgment,
which has to do with its very existence. The intellect can be
said to be true when it judges that what is is, and that what is not
is not. Truth is consequently a property of judgment, and it is
founded upon the existence (*esse*) of things more than upon their
essence.*47*

The truth here described is that of speculative judgments about
existing objects. We also make *practical* judgments about acts to be
done or things to be made. We judge that we should pay our bills
or that we should build a certain house. Since these judgments do
not concern existing things but acts and objects to be brought into
existence, their truth does not consist in the conformity of the intellect with being but with right desire.*48* For a practical judgment
to be true, it must be in accord with the human will inclining man to
suitable goals by appropriate means. In the moral order, therefore,
the intellect is not ruled by being but by the will and its native
propensity toward the good.

THE WILL AND MORALITY

ONE OF THE MOST obvious facts about the universe, which
has furnished all philosophers with food for meditation, is its rest-

lessness and ceaseless activity. Even non-living things are dynamic
centers of action, not to speak of the animate world in which self-
movement and development are the law. This dynamism is understandable in the perspective of St. Thomas for whom all creatures
by their activity reflect the pure act of Being who created them.
A creature exercises its most basic act simply by being; but no
sooner does it exist than it begins to expand and perfect its being
by operating. The dynamism of the act of being spontaneously
results in operation: *operatio sequitur esse*. All the activity of a
creature is a striving on its part to imitate as fully as possible its
creator, who is pure act. For a creature, then, *to be* is *to tend* toward God. Having placed creatures outside himself by creation,
God has at the same time endowed them with a spontaneous
tendency to return to him by resembling him as far as possible.[49]

Man's native restlessness and urge to action are, for St. Thomas,
simply one instance of this general law, although the most important of all. The rest of creation tends to God naturally and
instinctively. Only in man does this tendency become conscious of
itself, so that it can be called a rational desire or "appetite."

St. Thomas distinguishes three kinds of "appetites" or inclinations in man. Like all physical substances, man has certain natural
inclinations resulting from his substantial form. For example, like
all heavy bodies, he is inclined to fall downward. Secondly, in
common with the animals, he has sense appetites in conjunction
with his powers of sense knowledge: a concupiscible appetite by
which he is inclined to sensible objects perceived as good, and an
irascible appetite by which he shuns sensible objects perceived as
harmful. The human passions, such as love, pleasure, and fear, are
the acts of these sense appetites. Thirdly, man possesses a rational
appetite or will in conjunction with his power of reason. The
proper object of this faculty is the good in general apprehended by
reason. The will inclines a man toward particular goods only insofar as they share in the universal good. In the absence of the apprehended good, love and desire are engendered in man; when the
good is possessed, he experiences joy.[50]

Now the universal good is identical with the most perfect of all
beings; namely, God. Hence the will is the faculty by which man

tends toward God and enjoys him when possessed. Man reaches God, however, not by his will but by his intellect. That is why St. Thomas insists on the superiority of the intellect over the will: it is the faculty by which we lay hold upon God, our ultimate end and supreme happiness. The will, however, has an essential role to play here, for our happiness would not be complete without the enjoyment accompanying the possession of God.

St. Thomas consequently places man's highest good in the intellectual life and ultimately in the knowledge of God. However, he balances this intellectualism with a deep appreciation of the importance of the will and of love in human life. Indeed, he points out that in the present life it is better to love God than to know him. Of course we cannot love God unless we have some knowledge of him, but our love can outstrip our knowledge. When we know something, we bring it within our minds, where it exists with the mind's own existence. Love, on the other hand, goes outward to the object as it is in itself. As a result, our feeble knowledge of God, attained through creatures by means of concepts, does not unite us as closely to God as does our love, which draws us to him as he is in himself.[51]

Man's present situation also accounts for his wide range of free choice. If we were given a clear vision of God, the universal Good, such as the Blessed in heaven enjoy, we would necessarily will him as the fulfillment of all our desires. In the present life, however, we are offered only particular goods, which never completely satisfy us. Hence we are left free to choose among them: we can choose to act or not to act, to will one good thing rather than another. Freedom of choice is the inevitable result of the gap between the finite goods of this world and the infinite Good that alone will quiet the human heart.[52]

An act is human, according to St. Thomas, insofar as it is free, that is to say to the extent that it issues from knowledge and will. Since the object of the will is the good, every human act is directed to some good. This object, however, may not be really but only apparently good. If it is really good, it is in harmony with human nature and reason; if it is contrary to reason, it is evil. Consequently, the basis of morality is human nature. A good human act is one that perfects a human being, making him more like God and thus bringing him closer to his goal. An evil act, on the contrary, is one opposed to the development of the human being and contrary to his rationality, thus carrying him away from his goal.[53]

St. Thomas describes in detail the two guides to good acts: the virtues directing us from within, and laws directing us from without. The moral virtues are good habits of the will and sense appetites, regulating our conduct in accord with right reason. Chief among these are justice, temperance, and fortitude. These, together with the intellectual virtue of prudence, make up the four cardinal virtues, which are the hinges, so to speak, on which our whole moral life turns.

A law is defined by St. Thomas as "an ordinance of reason for the common good, promulgated by him who has the care of the community." [54] The eternal law is the first of all laws and the source of all others. This law is the divine rule for the government of the whole universe. As expressed in human nature, this law is called the natural law.[55] The prescriptions of the natural law correspond to the basic inclinations of our nature. Since the natural tendency of our will is toward the good, the most general prescription of the natural law is: Do good and avoid evil. There are three fundamental particular precepts of the natural law. Like every being, a man is inclined by nature to preserve his existence. This tendency to self-preservation is expressed by the natural law that every man should conserve his life and protect his health. Secondly, man has in common with the animals the inclination to reproduce himself and raise his children. This leads to the natural laws governing man's relations with his wife and family. Thirdly, because man is rational, he is inclined to live in a civic community, where he can develop his rational life more fully by seeking the truth in common with others and developing the social virtues. Human laws, promulgated by the state, are particular ordinances aimed at insuring the full adhesion to the natural law.

Throughout his moral doctrine St. Thomas is concerned with the natural tendencies of man and the means of liberating them so that he can most fully develop his rational nature. In this sense,

Thomistic ethics can be called a naturalism. St. Thomas was aware, however, of the inadequacy of natural means for the attainment of man's complete happiness. This happiness can be found only in a future life in which man will see God face to face and rejoice in him as the universal Good; and this is beyond the natural powers of man. Consequently, a natural ethics is bound to be incomplete. It must be supplemented by the Good News of Christian revelation, that God has ordained man to the beatific vision and has given him the supernatural means to reach it. Lacking Christian faith, philosophers like Aristotle and Averroes realized that man's happiness consists in the contemplation of God, but they hoped for nothing beyond the pale and fleeting knowledge of him afforded by metaphysics. St. Thomas was stirred to pity at the frustration of these brilliant minds, who saw the goal of man so clearly but did not realize that God has put it within man's grasp. How greatly must these geniuses have suffered from the narrowness of their views, he exclaims.[56] A wider vista is opened to the Christian philosopher. Revelation assures him that the natural desire of man to know God is not doomed to frustration. Man can reach his longed-for goal with the help of God's grace. Here, as elsewhere in the thought of St. Thomas, grace perfects nature and revelation is an indispensable guide to reason.

CONCLUSION

BECAUSE THEY TOWER so far above their contemporaries, great philosophers, like great artists, are apt to be little understood or appreciated in their own day. Their true stature becomes visible only when they are seen from a distance, like peaks rising above a mountain range. So it is with St. Thomas Aquinas. In his own century he was highly esteemed for both his theology and philosophy; but, as we shall see, he was more often misunderstood and criticized. Indeed, some of his doctrines were formally condemned by the ecclesiastical authorities at Paris and Oxford. No one could have foreseen the unique position he would one day hold in the Church as theologian and Christian philosopher; nor could anyone have foretold that among all the works of the schoolmen those of Brother Thomas would be read so widely in the twentieth century. There could be no better proof that, despite his outmoded scientific ideas and scholastic style, he expressed truths of enduring value. Among medieval writers, only St. Augustine rivals him in ability to surmount the accidents of time and to communicate to all ages doctrines of universal appeal because they are eternally true.

One of the reasons that Thomistic philosophy has been so frequently misunderstood is its close alliance with Aristotelianism. It has often been presented as simply the philosophy of Aristotle, baptized and brought into harmony with Christian doctrine. But this fails to do justice to Thomism on two scores. First, it does not take into account the many non-Aristotelian influences that helped to shape it. It is true that he considered Aristotle unequaled as a philosopher and that he learned from him both the method of philosophy and countless doctrines which he incorporated into his own thought. But he drew not only upon the works of Aristotle but upon practically all the philosophical and theological literature known in his day. Not only is Aristotelianism present in the Thomistic synthesis, but also elements of Greek Neoplatonism and of Arabian and Jewish philosophy.

Secondly, the equating of Thomistic philosophy with Aristotelianism fails to do justice to St. Thomas' originality as a philosopher. He was not content simply to take over Aristotle's philosophy as he found it, any more than St. Augustine was content simply to adopt the Neoplatonism of his day. Both profoundly transformed their favorite philosophies in the light of revealed truth and in so doing created Christian philosophies peculiarly their own. This is nowhere more evident than in St. Thomas' transformation of the Aristotelian notion of being. Whereas Aristotle viewed being primarily as form, St. Thomas conceived it primarily as the act of existing. Since being is the first of all our concepts and that on which all others depend, this transformation was bound to have far-reaching consequences. Because of his new notion of being, St. Thomas' doctrines of God, of God's causal relation to the universe, of man and human knowledge, mark a distinct departure from earlier ways of thought. In general, he approached philosophical problems from an existential point of view rather than from the formalist viewpoint common to so many Greek and medieval philosophers. In subsequent chapters we shall see how tenaciously his contemporaries and successors clung to traditional patterns of thought and bitterly resisted the innovation of Thomism.

XIV

Latin Averroism

THE SCHOOLMEN we have met so far were theologians by profession. Their interest in philosophy was keen and their contributions to its development were of great importance, but their primary concern was with theology and not with philosophy. They were for the most part professors in the Faculties of Theology at Paris and Oxford, and even those who on occasion taught philosophy or wrote philosophical treatises did so with a view to their work as theologians. In their own day they were known as "philosophizing theologians" or simply "philosophizers" because of the large part philosophy played in their theological speculation.

The discovery of Aristotle's works in the thirteenth century was responsible for the rise of another group of schoolmen who made no pretension to be theologians but simply philosophers. Inspired by the example of Aristotle and Averroes, they wanted to follow human reason without regard for the teachings of religion. As their leader, Siger of Brabant, put it: "At present we have nothing to do with the miracles of God, since we treat natural things in a natural way." [1] This separatist attitude, which divorced philosophy from religion, was something new in medieval thought, and it was bound to clash with the traditional view of the close connection and harmony of faith and reason.

The schoolmen we shall be concerned with in this chapter were professors of philosophy in the Faculty of Arts at Paris. As such, it was their duty to lecture on the works of Aristotle, who by that time was universally accepted as The Philosopher. So it was natural

* See Addenda, p. 427.

for them to turn to Aristotle as their model in philosophy. And since Averroes was the recognized commentator on Aristotle, it is not surprising to find them frequently interpreting his thought in an Averroistic manner. Because of their affiliation with Averroes, these schoolmen are generally called Latin Averroists. This does not mean that all were equally under the spell of Averroes or that other philosophers had no influence upon them. Neither does it mean that at this early date they formed a strict philosophical school; this will be a development of the next few centuries. But they had in common with Averroes the desire to separate philosophy from faith and to close Aristotelianism to any influence from religion. Moreover, like Averroes, they did not hesitate to teach philosophical doctrines contrary to their faith. For this reason they are sometimes called heterodox Aristotelians.

The authors of this purely philosophical movement claimed allegiance to the Catholic faith, and there is no evidence to doubt their sincerity in this regard. Whenever they taught a doctrine contradicting a tenet of their religion, they were careful not to propose it as true but simply as the conclusion of reason and of philosophy. To their opponents this was tantamount to teaching a double truth, one valid for philosophy and another for religion, and in contradiction to each other. But the Averroists themselves never made this absurd claim. When the theologians rebuked them for their heterodoxy, they did not deny the truth of revelation. They simply explained that they were doing the work of a philosopher, and this, according to Siger of Brabant, is to seek out the teaching of the philosophers rather than the truth.[2] But at the same time the Averroists considered their heterodox teachings to be the inevitable conclusions of philosophy. Sometimes they softened the clash between philosophy and religion by asserting that a rational doctrine contradicting a religious truth was not a necessary conclusion of reason but only a probable one. But this did little to allay the hostility of the theologians, to whom it was inconceivable that reason could lead to propositions contradictory to revealed truth. It was inevitable that the paradoxical position of the Averroists would eventually give way to a more or less open assertion of the supremacy of reason over revelation, and that the latter would be relegated to the realm of myth. This was what actually happened as the Averroist movement developed in the next few centuries.

We shall limit ourselves here to a consideration of some of the leaders of this movement in the thirteenth century. We shall then examine the theological reaction it provoked.

Siger of Brabant

THE ACKNOWLEDGED LEADER of the Averroists in the thirteenth century was Siger of Brabant.[3] A bold and adventuresome spirit, he was fearless of authority and gifted with considerable philosophical acumen. In his own day he was known as Siger the Great, and Dante honored him in his *Divine Comedy* (written about 1300) by putting him in paradise, in the circle of wise men, close to Thomas Aquinas and Albert the Great. Dante even puts Siger's eulogy in the mouth of St. Thomas, who introduces him with the words: "This is the eternal light of Siger, who, when he taught in the Street of Straw, established unwelcome truths." [4] This is an allusion to Siger's lecturing in the Faculty of Arts at Paris on the Rue du Fouarre, where his teaching landed him in a hornets' nest of controversy. The fact that Dante makes St. Thomas eulogize Siger has long puzzled historians, for Aquinas was one of his many critics. Some historians have theorized that Siger eventually abandoned his heterodox views and adopted a position close to Thomism, thus meriting the praise of St. Thomas. But this is not confirmed by his authentic writings. It seems more likely that Dante chose Siger as an outstanding Aristotelian to symbolize philosophical wisdom, which Dante himself loved so dearly. In any case, the differences between St. Thomas and Siger did not prevent their sharing a love of philosophy and an admiration for the great philosophers of the past, and especially for Aristotle. There is also a certain poetic justice in St. Thomas' eulogy of Siger, because Siger himself once praised St. Thomas and St. Albert as "outstanding men in philosophy."

Siger's general views on God and the universe can be gathered from his treatise *On the Necessity and Contingency of Causes*. He describes God as the First Being and Cause of all things. Like Avicenna, however, he restricts God's immediate effect to the first celestial Intelligence, whose whole being issues from God eternally and necessarily. This creature in turn produces the other Intelligences, the heavenly spheres, and the sublunary world in which we live. This creative process is ruled by necessary laws and admits of no chance or accidental happenings. Only in the sublunary world, which is the realm of generation and corruption, do we encounter contingency; that is to say, the possibility of something's either being or not being. Contingency is not due to God's intervention in the universe but simply to matter, which may lack the proper disposition to receive the influence of the celestial causes, whose effects may then fail to take place. Terrestrial causes can stand in the way of the influence of higher forces and can also interfere with each other's effects. As a result, everything does not happen necessarily in the sublunary world. This world is the scene of many contingent events that cannot be predicted with certainty because they are not the outcome of necessary causes. Not even God knows future contingent events, except in the general sense that he knows himself to be the remote cause of all things.

Just as there is chance and contingency in the universe, so too there is freedom in man's will, and for exactly the same reason. The will of man is not an independent and unmotivated power, as some of the thirteenth-century followers of St. Augustine claimed. Its freedom does not consist in an inner spontaneity that gives it complete sovereignty over its acts. It is moved by causes, and especially by the judgment of the intellect. But these causes can be prevented from acting upon the will, and this is what is meant by saying that the will is free. However, if the will is disposed to act and the forces moving it are likewise disposed to act upon it, it cannot then fail to act. This was condemned in 1277 as a denial of the freedom of the will.[5]   *

The theme of Siger's essay *On the Eternity of the World* is consistent with this general view of the universe and man. He portrays the universe, with its various natural species, as without a beginning or end in time. Even the human species is eternal: there

* See Addenda, p. 427.

was no first man, nor will there be a last. Following the Aristotelian view of the universe, Siger presents the course of history as cyclical. Owing to the eternal movement of the spheres around the earth, all terrestrial phenomena, including the ideas and religions of mankind, appear and disappear an infinite number of times in the course of history. Siger hastens to add that he is setting this down as the teaching of Aristotle and not as the truth. Nevertheless, he does not think the eternity of the world can be disproved by reason. Rather, it is the natural conclusion of a philosophical reflection on the world. The Christian view of the world as created in time and progressing toward a definite goal appears to him as an object of belief contrary to reason. In this, as in other matters (to use Siger's own words), "the conclusion reached by human reason must be denied." [6]

Although Siger describes God as the First Cause of the universe, he does not think this entails a real composition of essence and existence in creatures.[7] On this point he resolutely takes his stand with Averroes against Avicenna and St. Thomas. If we are to believe Avicenna, the existence of a creature is an accident added to its essence. In itself, the creature (for example, a man) is a possible being, but in order to exist it must be given existence by the First Cause. Hence its essence (humanity) is not identical with its existence. To this, Siger replies that God is the cause of everything in a creature, its essence as well as its existence. As the first efficient cause, God produces the essence of man as well as his existence. Consequently, these cannot be distinguished on the ground that one is caused by God and the other is not.

Siger was also acquainted with the Thomistic notion of existence and he was frankly puzzled by it. St. Thomas taught the real composition of essence and existence in creatures but denied that existence is an accident of essence. Into what Aristotelian category, then, does existence fall? It is not the essence of a creature, nor is it the matter or form constituting a material essence. Neither is it an accident. Siger concludes that, according to St. Thomas, existence must be a fourth kind of nature unknown to Aristotle. This is a clear indication that Siger appreciates the novelty and unAristotelian character of the Thomistic notion of existence, but it also reveals his inability to understand it. As we have seen, existence (*esse*) for St. Thomas is not an essence or nature but the act whereby a nature exists. St. Thomas did not add a new nature or category to those described by Aristotle. He simply pointed out that in every being there is an act more important than the form constituting the essence of that being—namely, the act of existing —for without this act the form or essence would be nothing.

Siger himself considers the Aristotelian doctrine of being, as interpreted by Averroes, an adequate explanation of reality. In this perspective, existence is not something added to the essence of a creature but is identical with it. For example, it belongs to the very essence of man to exist. This is not surprising, for Siger has already told us that all natural species are eternal and necessary. Only the individual in the species is contingent, because its causes can be prevented from bringing it into existence. The essence of man, however, must always exist in some individual man, for existence is of its very essence.

By an analysis of the terms "thing" and "being," Siger shows that they are simply two different names signifying the same reality in different ways. They do not designate distinct realities or even different concepts. When we speak of something as being or existing, we mean that it enjoys a certain actuality. "Being" signifies a reality in the manner of an act (*per modum actus*). When we call the same reality a thing, we mean that it possesses being in a stable manner. "Thing" signifies a reality in the manner of a habit (*per modum habitus*). Avicenna's mistake, according to Siger, was to translate this grammatical distinction of being and thing into a metaphysical distinction between existence and essence. Because the name "being" adds a new signification to "thing," he thought that it added a new reality; namely, existence.

If there is no composition of essence and existence in creatures, how do they differ from God? Siger points out that there are other kinds of composition by which creatures are clearly distinguished from their First Cause. God is absolutely simple, whereas material things are compounded of form and matter and of substance and accidents. The latter composition is found even in spiritual creatures; for example, they know by means of intelligible species which differ from their substance. What is more, God is pure act, whereas creatures have some measure of potentiality; indeed, the more potentiality they have, the further removed they are from God.

These metaphysical notions can be traced back to the Arabian philosopher Averroes. The same is true of Siger's doctrine of the human soul and intellect. He grants that each man is endowed with a soul that is the substantial form and perfection of his body.[8] This soul, however, is so bound up with the body that it cannot survive its destruction. In short, in the perspective of philosophy there is no personal immortality. Does this mean that God leaves evils unpunished and good deeds unrewarded? Not at all, for the good we do is its own reward, just as our evil acts carry with them their own punishment. There are moral sanctions in this life, if not in the next.[9]

As for the human intellect, Siger reflected for a long time on Aristotle's statements about it and Averroes' commentary on them. He was convinced that both philosophers understood the intellect to be a spiritual substance separated from matter because of the spiritual character of intellectual knowledge. We know by means of spiritual and universal ideas, and hence there must be an intellectual soul, distinct from the sensitive soul that is the substantial form of the body. This intellectual soul is a spiritual substance, separated from the human body in its being though united to it in its operation. It operates within man, making use of his senses and interior faculties (especially his cogitative sense), abstracting concepts from the sense data they provide. Because of its activity within man, the intellect may be said to be his form and perfection; not, however, as a substantial form perfects matter and constitutes one being with it, but as a mover is united to the object it moves and uses.[10]

Siger vigorously opposes the Thomistic doctrine that the intellectual soul and the human body are one in their very being. In his view, this would bind the human intellect too closely to the body and make it a corporeal faculty on the same level as the senses.

The intellectual soul thus described by Siger is the last of the series of Intelligences produced by the First Cause, or God. As such it is eternal and immortal. Individual men are born and die, but it remains, always finding new human beings in which to operate, thus carrying forward its work of knowing. This intellect is possessed in common by all men. It can be said to belong personally to each of them only in the sense that each bears a special relation to it: each man possesses his own sense powers and knowledge that dispose him in a special way for the activity of the intellect within him.

In a treatise *On Happiness,* known only through passages quoted by Agostino Nifo, Siger makes its clear that the intellect operating within man is, in Averroes' terminology, the possible intellect. Siger identifies the agent intellect with God, who illuminates the possible intellect, thereby conferring beatitude upon it. He agrees with Averroes that the human intellect finds its ultimate happiness in the contemplation of God, and that individual men share in this happiness in the present life to the extent that they cooperate with the intellect.[11]

Boetius of Dacia

IN MEDIEVAL DOCUMENTS the name of Boetius of Dacia (sometimes called Boetius of Sweden) is often linked with that of Siger of Brabant as his associate in teaching heretical doctrines condemned in 1277 by the bishop of Paris.[12] Indeed, one of the oldest manuscripts of this condemnation calls him the principal exponent of the proscribed errors. But until recently only a few small treatises of his were known and he was little more than a name to historians. Discoveries of the last few years have added to the number of his known writings, and we can now appreciate better why he was included in the bishop's condemnation.

Among the condemned propositions taught by Boetius of Dacia are the following: 1] There is no state more excellent than the pursuit of philosophy. 2] The philosophers alone are the wise men of the world. 3] The philosopher has the right to raise and to settle all problems that can be handled by human reason. 4] Creation is impossible, although the contrary must be held by faith.   5] There was no first man, nor will there be a last.   6] Once a body has corrupted, it cannot return to life.   7] A future resurrection should not be conceded by the philosopher, because it is not subject to rational investigation.   8] The philosopher of nature should deny that the world began in time, although this contradicts Christian faith.

These propositions indicate a complex attitude toward philosophy and religion. Most striking is Boetius of Dacia's love of philosophy and his insistence on its independence of the teachings of faith. Like Averroes, he respects both, but he keeps them carefully separated, and this for a methodological reason. Philosophy is the work of the human intellect uncovering the natural causes and principles of the universe by rational investigation. Faith, on the other hand, is based upon supernatural revelation and the miracles of God. Because they have different viewpoints and sources, philosophy and faith never meet exactly on the same ground. This can be illustrated by their attitudes toward the eternity of the world—a subject to which Boetius of Dacia devotes a special treatise. The philosopher, he says, goes to nature itself for his information about the origin of the universe. Now all natural events are caused by preceding events. So every event in nature is preceded by another event, and consequently movement and time have no absolute beginning. In short, the world is eternal. The man of faith, on the other hand, knows by revelation that the world did not always exist but was created with a beginning in time. This is the truth of the matter, unknown to the philosopher because he does not rise above the level of nature and rational inquiry.

Through faith, therefore, we have access to truths beyond the ken of the philosopher, but Boetius does not think the latter should on this account deny the conclusions of his own science. Philosophers, he protests, have the right to follow natural principles to their inevitable conclusions, even though they may be opposed to the truths of faith. Like all the sciences, philosophy has its limitations, and not all of its conclusions are necessary; some are only probable. The eternity of the world is a case in point. Human reason cannot demonstrate the eternity of the world, for even though it is the conclusion of the philosopher of nature, the metaphysician knows that the universe depends on the divine will, which is inscrutable to human reason, and that God could have chosen to create the world with a temporal beginning.

A way is thus open for the reconciliation of faith and reason in the mind of Boetius of Dacia. Faith teaches the absolute truth, which must be believed. Reason sometimes comes to conclusions opposed to faith, but these are the result of rational investigation, which often yields only probable knowledge. Hence the Christian should not deny his faith because philosophers come to conclusions contrary to it.

Should not the philosopher, in such instances, simply keep silent and leave the field to faith and to theology? Boetius is not content to capitulate to the theologians in this way. He vehemently defends the right of philosophers to deal with all questions that can be discussed by human reason. The freedom of the philosopher is here at stake, and Boetius has no intention of accepting the restrictions some theologians want to place upon him. St. Bonaventure, for one, denied philosophers the right to take up difficult problems like the eternity of the world, on the ground that such daring inquiries led to errors among the philosophers. In 1272 the Faculty of Arts at Paris forbade philosophers to discuss theological matters or to use textbooks containing anything contrary to the faith. This was a disciplinary measure to keep the teachers of philosophy from venturing into areas in which conflicts might arise between them and the theologians. Boetius, however, looks upon this as a denial of the rights of the philosopher. Does not the philosopher have being for his subject? The whole range of being, therefore, should come within his grasp. He should investigate all being, whether it is natural, mathematical, or divine, insofar as human reason is competent to deal with it. He shows nothing but contempt for those in authority who in their ignorance criticize the philosophers and even try to destroy philosophy itself. "The deeply intelligent Christian," he writes, "is not compelled by his religion to destroy the principles of philosophy, but preserves both his faith and philosophy by attacking neither." [13]

Both faith and philosophy, he would say, have their place and value in human life. The condition of their reconciliation, however, is that they remain separated from each other. They can co-exist, but there can be no harmony or intimate connection between them. Faith does not shed light upon human reason, nor is reason an ally of faith, enabling the Christian to understand better what he believes. Quite the contrary: we must expect tensions and even contradictions between faith and reason. Boetius of Dacia was too intelligent to claim that there is a double truth, one for faith and another for philosophy, and in contradiction to each other. But he thought that philosophy inevitably comes to conclusions contrary to theology, for reason and faith have different routes to travel and different destinations. To the theologians this was tantamount to teaching the possibility of contradictory truths, and they condemned him for upholding this position.

The condemnation of Boetius of Dacia is hardly surprising, for his separation of reason from faith struck at one of the most cherished ideals of medieval theology. Indeed, it amounted to a denial of theology itself as the Fathers of the Church and the schoolmen understood it. All through the Middle Ages, Christians held that the noblest task of human reason is to be the support and defense of the Christian faith. Boetius of Dacia, with the other Latin Averroists, exalted reason as an autonomous instrument of man and set it along its own path without regard for the teachings of revelation. Averroes had done the same thing before him, incurring the condemnation of Moslem theologians. It is no mere coincidence that his Latin followers suffered the same fate at the hands of Christian theologians.

Boetius of Dacia's attitude toward philosophy and faith can be clearly seen in his essay *On the Highest Good, or On the Life of the Philosopher*. The purpose of this short treatise is to define the supreme good accessible to man, insofar as it can be known by human reason. This warns us that Boetius is writing as a philosopher and not as a theologian. He is asking: What can human reason tell us about man's happiness, leaving aside the teachings of faith?

Boetius' answer to this question closely follows the doctrine of Aristotle. Man's supreme happiness consists in the exercise of his noblest power, which is his intellect. Since the human intellect has

both a speculative and practical activity, Boetius distinguishes between man's supreme good in the speculative and practical orders.
The highest good possible to man through his speculative power
is knowledge of the truth and the pleasure accompanying it. Our
intellectual pleasure increases according to the nobility of the object known and the ability of the knowing power. Consequently,
the greatest good possible to man through his speculative intellect
is the most perfect knowledge of all beings, and especially of God,
who is their First Cause.

As for man's supreme good in the practical order, it consists in
acting virtuously; that is to say, in preserving the golden mean in
human actions, with the pleasure found in so doing. In his treatise
On Dreams, Boetius expresses the typical Aristotelian notion that
the highest good possible to man in the practical order is the
happiness found in activity conducive to the welfare of the state.
This he calls "political happiness."

The happy life, accordingly, consists in contemplating truth
and in doing good, and taking pleasure in both. Man's supreme
happiness consists in contemplating the First Cause of the universe
and in loving this noblest Being. And the man who achieves this
supreme knowledge and love, thus reaching the ultimate goal of
life, is the philosopher. "This is the life of the philosopher," Boetius
concludes, "and whoever does not lead it does not live rightly.
Now I call a philosopher any man who, living according to the
right order of nature, has reached the best and ultimate end of
human life." [14]

A more glowing and optimistic description of the life of pure
reason cannot be found in the Middle Ages. A rationalist spirit
permeates the work of Boetius, though it is not a case of pure rationalism, as has been claimed.[15] Boetius makes a passing reference
to faith, which in this case he claims is in continuity with philosophy. After extolling the happiness of the philosophical life, he
adds: "The man who is more advanced in the happiness that we
know by reason is possible in this human life, is also closer to the
happiness that we await through faith in the life to come." [16] This
is clear proof that Boetius believed in a future life and a happiness
beyond that of the philosophers. The happiness he describes is

supreme only from the standpoint of human reason; beyond it lies another made known to us by faith. And yet it is understandable that the theologians at Paris who read his work were shocked by the spirit in which it is written, as well as by some of its statements. We can easily imagine their consternation on reading: "It is easier for the philosopher to be virtuous than anyone else," and "When a man is engaged in [philosophical] activity he is in the best state possible to man." [17] But we have no need to conjecture what their reaction was. It is clear enough in the writings of contemporary theologians and in the condemnation of Averroism by the bishop of Paris.

THE CONDEMNATION OF 1277 [18]

ABOUT THE SAME TIME that Siger of Brabant began to attract attention at Paris (1266), we find the first symptoms of a theological reaction to the Averroists. St. Bonaventure, who from the beginning of his career maintained a cautious attitude toward philosophy, lashed out against the philosophers at Paris who were teaching doctrines contrary to the faith, particularly the eternity of the world, the oneness of the intellect in all men, and the denial of personal immortality. The tone of his criticism became more severe as the battle between the theologians and philosophers became more intense. St. Thomas entered the fray with his treatises *On the Unity of the Intellect against the Averroists* and *On the Eternity of the World*. At the end of the former work St. Thomas abandons his customary impersonal tone and shows his irritation at those who claim that reason necessarily arrives at the oneness of the intellect of all men, yet who hold the opposite by faith. To him, this is an evident contradiction, because the necessary conclusions of reason must be true, and they cannot oppose the truths of faith. He inveighs against philosophers who presume to discuss purely theological matters; for example, whether the soul can suffer from the fires of hell. He is also disturbed by the fact that these men do not teach their errors openly but in secret, and to boys who cannot handle such difficult subjects. The troubled atmosphere of the time is clearly visible in this work of St. Thomas,

as it is in Giles of Rome's treatise *On the Errors of the Philosophers.*[19] Giles lists the errors of Aristotle, Averroes, Avicenna,
Algazel, Alkindi, and Maimonides, in order to caution his contemporaries against putting too much trust in the great philosophers
of the past.

In the same year that Giles of Rome's work appeared (1270),
the dispute between the philosophers and theologians was so bitter and dangerous that Stephen Tempier, the bishop of Paris,
thought it prudent to issue a formal condemnation of thirteen
propositions upheld by the philosophers: 1] All men are endowed with one and the same intellect.   2] It is false to say that
man understands.   3] The will of man is not endowed with freedom of choice.   4] All terrestrial events occur necessarily, through
the influence of the heavenly bodies.   5] The world is eternal.
6] There was no first man.   7] The soul, which is the form of
the body, corrupts with the body.   8] When the soul is separated
from the body at death it cannot suffer from corporeal fire.   9]
Freedom of choice is a passive, not an active power, and it is necessarily determined by the object desired.   10] God has no knowledge of individual things.   11] God knows only himself.   12]
God exercises no providence over human acts.   13] God cannot
make a mortal being to be immortal.

This condemnation, however, did not stem the rising tide of
heterodoxy, and early in 1277 Pope John XXI asked the bishop of
Paris to investigate the situation and to report to him about it. The
bishop rather hastily gathered together a commission of sixteen
theologians who drew up a list of 219 propositions, and these the
bishop condemned on March 7, 1277. On March 18 of the same year
Robert Kilwardby, the archbishop of Canterbury, condemned a
shorter list of thirty propositions. A second and more detailed letter from the pope to the bishop of Paris, dated April 28, again asks
for information concerning the names and writings of those
teaching errors at the university. It is not certain whether he knew
about or endorsed the condemnation of March 7, although he was
gravely concerned with the state of affairs at Paris and wanted
the writings of those suspected of heresy examined and their errors
condemned. As the condemnation actually took place, however, it

was solely on the authority of the bishop of Paris and the arch-bishop of Canterbury.

In the prologue of his decree of condemnation Stephen Tempier condemned those members of the Faculty of Arts who, under the influence of pagan philosophy, taught errors opposed to the Catholic faith and then tried to evade the charge of heresy by dis-tinguishing between the truth of philosophy and that of faith, "as though there were two contrary truths." Among the specific doc-trines condemned were the thirteen already proscribed in 1270, with the addition of many more, traceable to Avicenna, Averroes, and other non-Christian philosophers. The main thrust of the at-tack was against pagan naturalism in all its forms and against a philosophy separated from and opposed to faith. Even some Thomistic theses were listed in the bishop's syllabus of errors, in-cluding the following: That matter is the principle of individua-tion; that each angel constitutes a separate species; that the action of the will naturally follows upon the judgment of reason. Among the theses condemned by Robert Kilwardby was the Thomistic doctrine that man has only one substantial form. These doctrines of St. Thomas were part of his legacy from Aristotle, and their in-clusion in the proscribed list of errors reveals how far-reaching was the assault of the ecclesiastical authorities on all forms of Aristotelianism.

The long drama of the conflict between Greco-Arabian philoso-phy and Christian thought reached its climax with the condemna-tion of 1277. Welcomed with misgivings in Christian circles at the beginning of the century, Aristotelianism gradually won general acceptance and became the core of the philosophy curriculum at Paris and Oxford, the two greatest centers of learning in Christen-dom. The scholastic theologies of the mid-thirteenth century were born of the fruitful union of Christian faith and Aristotelianism. Thomism achieved the finest balance between them, enriching the understanding of faith by philosophical insights gleaned from Aris-totle and his commentators, while creating a new philosophy under the guidance of the light of faith. But this fine balance was not maintained for long. The rise of heterodox philosophies inspired by Averroes and Avicenna convinced conservative theologians (whose hearts always remained loyal to St. Augustine and the Neoplatonism he espoused) that Aristotle and his followers were fundamentally inimical to the faith. The result was the condemnation of the various forms of Aristotelianism in 1277.

The condemnation was of great importance for the future of medieval thought. It did not stop the teaching of Aristotle, nor did it kill the Averroist tradition of philosophy which lasted well into the Renaissance. From 1277 on, however, theologians showed a growing suspicion of philosophers and tended to disengage the findings of philosophy from the tenets of faith. Philosophers, on the other hand, were more inclined to go their own way without regard for the religion they professed as Catholics. In short, we find the progressive separation of faith and reason, which culminated in their divorce in modern times. As for the history of Thomism after the condemnation, this will be the subject of our next chapter.

XV

The Reaction
to Thomism

BECAUSE THOMISM IS SO WELL-KNOWN TODAY and has received such extraordinary approbation from the Church through the centuries, it is easy to fall into the illusion that it was equally successful in the thirteenth century. This is far from the case. It immediately attracted the attention of everyone because of its profound treatment of contemporary problems in theology and philosophy and its masterly organization of Christian doctrine. But at the same time St. Thomas' innovations did not escape notice. As his biographer William of Tocco pointed out,[1] he raised new questions and taught new doctrines, and these novelties aroused the opposition of the theologians of the old school. We have already seen that three years after the death of St. Thomas some of his teachings were condemned by the bishop of Paris and the archbishop of Canterbury. This condemnation was subsequently lifted, but it reflects the opposition that Thomism met almost from the start.

The attack upon Thomism came from two different quarters. It was criticized by the Latin Averroists, who, while praising St. Thomas for his allegiance to Aristotle, refused to accept his novel development of Aristotelianism. Thomism was also opposed by the conservative theologians, who believed that it gave too much ground to the naturalism of Aristotle and his Arabian commentators, to the detriment of the Catholic faith. In short, they saw in it a paganizing of Catholic doctrine. These theologians turned to St. Augustine and took from his writings philosophical notions with which to oppose the novel doctrines of St. Thomas. Their use of St. Augustine resulted in a new Augustinism, which was pitted against Aristotelianism and Thomism. This thirteenth-century Augustinism, however, did not always represent the true doctrine of the bishop of Hippo. It was an adaptation of his ideas with a view to settling new problems of the scholastic age, and it mingled with St. Augustine's own teachings Neoplatonic ideas of Jewish and Arabian origin.

The attitude of the new Augustinians toward Thomism is clearly seen in a letter of John Pecham, a Franciscan theologian and the successor of Robert Kilwardby as archbishop of Canterbury. Writing to the bishop of Lincoln in 1285, Pecham inveighs against the new-fangled language and ideas introduced into theology within the last twenty years, in opposition to the Fathers of the Church and philosophical truth. Pecham advises those seeking the truth to read the Franciscans Alexander of Hales, Bonaventure, and others like them, who rely upon the Fathers and upon sound philosophers and who have composed treatises beyond reproach. The new doctrine (Thomism) is almost entirely opposed to them. It has given rise to wordy disputes and has tried to destroy Augustine's teachings on the eternal Ideas, the divine illumination of the intellect, the powers of the soul, the seminal principles inherent in matter, and countless other subjects.[2]

THE "CORRECTIVES" OF THOMISM

A NEW TYPE OF LITERATURE arose out of this opposition to Thomism, called "Correctives" (*Correctoria*) of the teaching of St. Thomas. The most popular of these was written by the English Franciscan William de La Mare (d. *c.* 1285). William gives St. Thomas' position on a particular point and then corrects it, generally following Alexander of Hales and St. Bonaventure. The official adoption of this *Corrective* by the Franciscan Order in 1282 helped to solidify the Franciscans in their opposition to Thomism.

The Dominicans were not slow in replying to this assault on

their confrere. William de La Mare's *Corrective* was in turn corrected by a number of Dominicans, including Richard of Clapwell (or Thomas of Sutton), John of Paris and Rambert of Bologna. Although loyal to the memory of St. Thomas, these men unfortunately did not always understand his doctrine, with the result that the controversy often degenerated into mere confusion. Thomism was specially recommended by General Chapters of the Dominican Order from 1278 to 1315, but this does not mean that all Dominicans became Thomists or that those professing to follow St. Thomas actually did so. Modern research into the early Thomistic school is far from complete, but it has yet to unearth a member who shows a deep understanding of St. Thomas' thought and a loyal adherence to it.

The controversies aroused by Thomism covered a wide range of subjects, three of the most important of which were the distinction between essence and existence, the oneness of substantial form, and the nature of divine illumination.

ESSENCE AND EXISTENCE

ONE OF THE QUESTIONS made classic in scholastic circles by St. Thomas is whether the essence of a creature differs from its existence. He himself answered that only in God are essence and being (*esse*) identical; everything created is composed of an essence and an act of being by which it exists. Corporeal substances have a twofold composition. They are made up of matter and form, which constitute their essence, and this essence in turn enters into composition with the act whereby it exists. Immaterial substances, on the other hand, have only the composition of essence and act of being.

As conceived by St. Thomas, this is not a composition of two realities or things but of two metaphysical constituents which together make up a created being or reality. In itself, the essence of a creature has no reality, for without existence it is nothing. Neither is the existence of a creature a being or reality, but it is the act that turns a possible essence into an actual being.

This is admittedly difficult to understand, for it is the natural tendency of the human mind to think in terms of *things*. Once we leave the realm of things, which can be pictured or at least defined by precise concepts, we feel out of our depth and struggle to return to surer ground. It was almost inevitable, therefore, that the Thomistic composition of essence and being (*esse*) should soon be changed into a real distinction between essence and existence, both conceived as things (*res*).

This is what happened with Giles of Rome, a member of the Order of the Hermits of St. Augustine, who died in 1316. Giles was the author of the real distinction of essence and existence as it was popularly known and frequently criticized in the later Middle Ages and even in modern times. According to him, essence and existence are two really distinct things, so that God can separate them if he chooses. This real distinction follows from the fact of creation. If the essence of a creature were identical with its existence, it would exist through its essence and hence it would not need to be created. In fact, God gives existence to all things, each of which receives it according to the measure of its essence. The essence itself has a certain amount of actuality, but not enough to make it exist. It is in potency to existence, which supplements the being of the essence and posits it among natural things.[3]

This curious doctrine attributes to essence a being of its own given to it by its form. Over and above this, essence receives existence in the proper sense from its efficient cause, and then it is an actually existing being. There is consequently a twofold being in creatures: one belonging to the essence in itself and another conferred on it from without by God. Giles of Rome pictures God as an infinite ocean of existence which, through creation, fills up finite vessels (that is, created essences) according to their respective capacities. This picture, borrowed from Neoplatonic writers, shows what happens when a metaphysician uses his imagination rather than his understanding.

Henry of Ghent, archdeacon of Bruges (d. 1293), did not allow Giles' doctrine to go unchallenged. If Giles is correct in thinking that existence is a reality distinct from essence, it must be either a substance or an accident, both of which are impossible.

Moreover, as a reality, a creature's existence must have a nature of its own, to which another existence must be added in order that it exist, and so on to infinity. For these reasons Henry of Ghent rejects the real distinction and concludes that there is only a conceptual distinction between a creature's essence and its existence, of the type designated by him as an "intentional" distinction. This is not a real distinction (between things) or a distinction of reason (between two different ways of conceiving the same thing; for example, between "man" and "rational animal"), but a distinction between several concepts of the same thing, one of which is not included in the other. It is clear that we can form the concept of an essence, such as humanity, without including the notion of existence. Existence adds something to the concept of man not included in that concept. It is not, however, a metaphysical or real principle added to the creature's essence.

What exactly does the notion of existence add to the notion of essence? Henry of Ghent replies that it adds a relation of dependence upon God. For a creature to exist means to have been created by God. In God's mind the essence of a creature is a possible being, endowed simply with the being of an essence (*esse essentiae*). When it has been created, it is an actual being endowed with existence (*esse existentiae*). This simply means that it has a new relationship to God: it stands outside him as his effect.[4] This notion of existence enjoyed considerable popularity in the later Middle Ages, and it was sometimes opposed to St. Thomas' doctrine of existence as the act of being.

Throughout the long and often heated controversy over the real distinction it is remarkable how seldom St. Thomas' own doctrine was taken into account by either its defenders or opponents. When Suarez criticized the real distinction in the sixteenth century, it was Giles of Rome's doctrine and not St. Thomas' that he attacked. Suarez hesitates to attribute the doctrine to St. Thomas, although he adds that it is thought to be the Thomist view and almost all the ancient Thomists follow it. But he himself shows no knowledge of the true position of St. Thomas.[5]

We may well ask the reason for this extraordinary situation.

Why did so many scholastics not only refuse to accept St. Thomas' doctrine but even fail to understand it? One of the main reasons seems to have been the influence of Aristotle. Nurtured as they were on his philosophy, it was difficult for them to go beyond his categories and ideas. They could readily understand and accept the compositions of form and matter and of substance and accident. They were also well schooled in the Boethian distinction (also of Aristotelian origin) between an individual (*quod est*) and the essence or form by which it is what it is (*quo est* or *esse*). But it was more difficult to grasp the novel Thomistic notion of the act of being (*esse*) and its unique kind of composition with essence. St. Thomas proposed the un-Aristotelian thesis that there is an act and perfection superior to form—namely, the act whereby a thing exists—and this was extremely difficult for even Thomists to accept, not to speak of those who opposed his philosophy. Writing in the sixteenth century, Bañez, a Dominican commentator on St. Thomas, bears witness to the unwillingness on the part of Thomists to accept the Thomistic notion of the act of being (*esse*). "And this is what St. Thomas so often exclaimed," he writes, "and what Thomists will not hear: that *esse* is the actuality of every form or nature . . ." [6] When Bañez wrote these words he was thinking principally of the Thomists of his own day, but they apply equally well to the immediate successors of St. Thomas. These Thomists generally agreed with their master whenever he spoke the language of Aristotle, but they turned a deaf ear to his novel development of Aristotelianism.

THE PLURALITY OF FORMS

THE PROBLEM of the oneness or plurality of forms is closely linked with that of the nature of being. The question at stake can be stated as follows. Granted that a substance receives its essence and being from an intrinsic principle called a substantial form, is it possible for a single substance to have more than one principle of this kind? This problem concerns all substances, whether non-living or living, but its importance is especially

obvious in the case of man. Has a man more than one substantial
form? In particular, are there other substantial forms in him besides his intellectual soul?

St. Thomas answered these questions quite simply. A single
substance can have only one substantial form, which in the case
of man is his intellectual soul. The reason for this is that a substance receives its essence and being (*esse*) through its substantial form. Consequently, if it has several substantial forms it
has several essences and beings, and it is not strictly one substance. Suppose, for example, a man were a body through a special
substantial form of corporeity, a living being through another
form called the vegetative soul, an animal through another form
called the sensitive soul, and a man through still another form
called the intellectual soul. That man would not be absolutely one
substance or being.[7] But it is obvious that he is one substance, for
it is the same man who is extended in space, lives, senses, and
thinks. Since man *acts* as one substance, he must *be* one substance,
for activity follows upon being and is proportionate to it. "Whence
we must conclude," St. Thomas writes, "that there is no other
substantial form in man besides the intellectual soul; and that
just as the soul contains virtually the sensitive and vegetative
souls, so does it contain virtually all inferior forms, and does alone
whatever the imperfect forms do in other things. The same is to
be said of the sensitive soul in brute animals, of the vegetative soul
in plants, and universally of all more perfect forms in relation to
the imperfect." [8]

No doctrine of St. Thomas provoked more violent controversy
and criticism than this. The reason for the strong reaction to it
is not hard to understand. The issues at stake were important:
the nature and structure of man and the immortality of his soul.
All the schoolmen agreed that man has an intellectual soul which
is a spiritual and immortal substance. But many of them recoiled at
the thought that this soul is the only substantial form of the body,
giving it not only its rationality and life but its very substance
and being. Does this not degrade the human soul and bind it so
closely to the body that it loses its independence of matter and
consequently its immortality? A spiritual substance is intrinsically

independent of a body; how, then, can it be the principle that extends matter in three dimensions, making it to be a body? Is it not more reasonable to suppose that there is at least one other substantial form in man (a form of corporeity) that makes him a bodily substance? Some even envisaged distinct vegetative and sensitive souls informing the body prior to the coming of the intellectual soul in man. In this hypothesis man has several substantial forms arranged in a hierarchy, the lower preparing the way for the higher, and the higher in its turn perfecting and completing the lower.

The opposition to the oneness of substantial form came to a head in 1277, when it was condemned by Robert Kilwardby, the archbishop of Canterbury.[9] Kilwardby forbad the masters at Oxford to teach that the vegetative, sensitive, and intellectual souls are one simple form or that the intellectual soul is united to prime matter in such a way that all preceding forms are destroyed.

The bitterest opponent of St. Thomas on this point was John Pecham. In 1270 he engaged St. Thomas in public debate on the question of the oneness of man's substantial form, and after succeeding Kilwardby as archbishop of Canterbury he stigmatized the Thomistic doctrine as "false and wicked" and the source of many heresies. He also called the doctrine a presumptuous novelty [10]—a charge that does not do justice to the facts. The doctrine comes from Aristotle and was taught in the universities before St. Thomas' day. To mention but two examples: John Blund (d. 1248), a master at Paris and Oxford, maintained that the rational soul is the only substantial form in man, and this was also upheld by St. Albert at Paris. Pecham was right, however, in calling St. Thomas' doctrine a novelty, for his understanding of the oneness of substantial form and his reason for it were new. The fact is that St. Thomas revolutionized the Aristotelian doctrine in the light of his new notion of being. As we have seen, he held that a substance is a composite of an essence and an act of being (*esse*). Now if a substance is one, its act of being must be one; otherwise it is not strictly one being. And since substantial form is the intrinsic principle of being (for a substance receives being through receiving form), one substance can have but one substantial form.

Any subsequent form is an accidental and not a substantial form.

This conclusion is inevitable in St. Thomas' philosophy, which is based upon the notion of the act of being. It was not inevitable, however, in Pecham's, which centers around the notion of form. For Pecham and the other supporters of the pluralist thesis, the unity of a substance is not founded upon the unity of its act of being and hence upon the unity of its substantial form. A substance is composed of many substantial forms, each of which confers upon it a degree of perfection, such as corporeity, life, and rationality. The unity of the substance consists in the hierarchical order of these forms, which dovetail with each other, so to speak, and consequently make up one substance.

Two philosophies were here at grips with each other: the Thomistic philosophy of the act of being and the Neoplatonic philosophy of form, especially as it was known to the schoolmen through the Jewish philosopher Ibn Gabirol. It is interesting to notice that the majority of the schoolmen favored some version of the latter philosophy rather than that of St. Thomas. St. Thomas, however, did have his defenders. Among others, Giles of Rome and Giles of Lessines wrote treatises upholding the oneness of substantial form in all substances, including man.

The stigma left on Thomism by the condemnation of 1277 was partially removed in 1325, when the bishop of Paris, Stephen de Bourret, lifted the censure against the condemned propositions of St. Thomas. In 1914 Pope Pius X made a special point to approve his doctrine of the oneness of substantial form in man. He wrote: "The same rational soul is so united to the body that it is its sole substantial form, and through it man is a man, an animal, a living thing, a body, a substance and a being. Consequently, the soul gives to man every essential degree of perfection; moreover, it imparts to the body the act of being (*actum essendi*), by which it exists." [11] The pope declared this to be one of the fundamental tenets of Thomism and directed it to be taught in the schools as a "safe and sound" doctrine.

DIVINE ILLUMINATION

ST. THOMAS regarded the problem of divine illumination as one aspect of a wider problem concerning created nature in general, which can be stated as follows. When God created the natures of things, did he endow them with sufficient power to do the work which, as natures, they were meant to do, or did he create them deficient in power so that he must supplement it by assisting nature in a special or quasi-special way? The question is not whether nature owes everything it has to God or whether it must be conserved and moved by him once it has been created. It is beyond dispute that God is the creator, conserver, and prime mover of all things. The question has to do rather with the sufficiency of natural powers to achieve their natural results. Can fire, for example, produce the form of fire in combustible material, or does fire simply awaken within matter the form of fire created there by God as a seminal principle? Has the human will the power to acquire natural virtues by performing virtuous actions, or are these virtues created in germ, so to speak, in the will, requiring divine grace to bring them to perfection? Lastly, has the human intellect the power to acquire knowledge by abstracting the intelligible contents from sense data, or must it be assisted to know the truth by a special or quasi-special divine illumination?

St. Thomas' confidence in the perfection of nature is reflected in his answers to these questions.[12] Efficient causes can engender forms similar to their own in subjects disposed to receive them, and man can acquire by his own efforts true moral virtues and intellectual knowledge. St. Thomas defended the efficacy of secondary causes in all domains, in opposition to the Augustinian notions of seminal principles and divine illumination. This reveals the deep-seated naturalism of St. Thomas, which no doubt he owes to Aristotle but which is also in profound harmony with Christian doctrine. Does not sacred Scripture tell us: *The works of God are perfect* (*Deut.* 32:4)? St. Augustine and his thirteenth-century followers wished to exalt the power of God by subtracting from that of his creatures. With surer insight St. Thomas saw that, on the contrary, we honor God by recognizing the perfection of his handiworks.[13]

The Franciscan school did not abandon the doctrine of divine illumination after the death of St. Thomas. We have already seen Matthew of Aquasparta, a disciple of St. Bonaventure, adopt it and bring to light some of its serious implications. He saw clearly that if we cannot know the truth without an additional influx of the divine light, the human intellect is deficient because it fails in the very task which, as a nature, it is meant to do. As a consequence, philosophy, which is a work of that intellect, is also deficient. That is why he turned to theology, and not to philosophy, for the truth. Skepticism in philosophy was the inevitable result of this conception of knowledge.

Roger Marston, an English Franciscan who died in 1303, rejected the Thomistic doctrine that divine illumination consists simply in the intellect's participation in the divine light by creation. He saw clearly that St. Augustine had something more in mind than this when he taught that we know the truth in the light of the divine Ideas. It is true that God has created us with an intellect, Marston held, but by its own nature this intellect does not enable us to know the truth. It must be illumined by a higher agent intellect, who is God. Marston stresses that philosophy belongs to the order of natural knowledge as far as its object is concerned, but he insists that the origin of its truth is not purely natural, for it depends upon a divine illumination.

Another Franciscan, Peter Olivi (d. 1298), is a good witness to the perplexity this doctrine caused in many theologians. How is the truth of natural knowledge to be defended if it depends upon a supernatural source; namely, God? He realized the strength of St. Thomas' position, which accounts for philosophical truth by the nature of the intellect and its object, but out of loyalty to his Order he could not bring himself to adopt it. In the absence of any clear solution of the problem he considered it his duty to cling to the traditional doctrine of the Franciscans.

The influence of the Augustinian doctrine of illumination was not confined to the Franciscans. It was adopted by Henry of Ghent, a secular teacher at Paris and one of the finest minds of the time. The problem of skepticism was becoming so important that Henry of Ghent begins his *Summa* of theology by asking whether anything can be known with certainty. With St. Augustine he replies that we can know the truth. Of course pure truth cannot be expected from sense knowledge, for it often makes things appear to be different than they are, but reason can reach the truth under the illuminating influence of God. In short, we can know the truth about the universe and God, but not by our own efforts or by our own means. For this we need the help of God's illumination. Before original sin this illumination was given to all men. Now it is a special gift of God, given to certain chosen men at particular times.

In the next chapter we shall see Duns Scotus attempt to stem the tide of philosophical skepticism by maintaining, against Henry of Ghent, that we do not need a special influence of God in order to know truths in the natural order. But despite his effort, mistrust of philosophy and of natural knowledge in general became more prevalent in theological circles. The Franciscan John of Rodington (d. *c.* 1348) advised those looking for the truth to go to the theologians rather than to the philosophers, and his contemporary, Hugolin of Malabranca, thought that if the philosophers did say anything true it was due to a special illumination of God. These theologians were not skeptics, because they held fast to the faith. The day was coming, however, when the faith would cease to attract so many of the educated men of Europe. Distrustful of natural knowledge and bereft of the faith, they would content themselves with probable opinions about God and the origin and destiny of man, when they were not outright skeptics in these matters. This was the situation Descartes faced in the seventeenth century and that he attempted to remedy with his reform of philosophy.

XVI

John Duns Scotus

ALTHOUGH DUNS SCOTUS' DEATH at the early age of forty-two prevented him from fully formulating his ideas, the writings he left to posterity place him in the ranks of the greatest Catholic theologians and philosophers.[1] Like St. Thomas, he was a theologian keenly aware of the need of philosophy as a vehicle for his theological work, and the philosophical instrument he developed for this purpose is a creation of genius. St. Thomas and Scotus shared the same Catholic faith, but their understandings of that faith—in other words, their theologies—differed because their philosophical views, and especially their notions of being, were radically different.

Living in the aftermath of the condemnation of rationalist philosophy in 1277, Scotus was more sensitive than St. Thomas to the limitations of the philosophers and to the conflicts between them and the theologians. Not that he despised human reason or philosophy; but he does not let his reader forget the handicap under which the philosophers labored or the deficiencies and errors in their writings. In contrast to the poverty of pure philosophy, he extolled the Christian use of reason. He saw the human mind, enlightened by faith, mounting above the pagan philosophers and easily proving truths beyond their reach.

THE LIMITATIONS OF PHILOSOPHY

IN THE BEGINNING of his greatest work, the *Opus Oxoniense*, Scotus defends the necessity of revelation against the presumptions of rationalist philosophers, who claim that man is perfect and can know everything by reason alone.² He was acutely aware of the inroads being made into Christian circles by the philosophies of Aristotle, Avicenna, and Averroes. These men introduced into the West the new ideal of a purely rational philosophy, sufficient in itself and adequate to satisfy man's desire for knowledge. This undermined the whole Christian conception of life, with its insistence on the fall of man and his need of grace and revelation for salvation.

At first sight the philosophers' case is plausible. They point out, Scotus says, that man has a nature endowed with powers, each of which has an object proportioned to it. For example, the natural object of sight is color; hence everything colored falls within the scope of this sense. Now the proportioned object of the intellect is being. It is only reasonable to conclude that all beings, including the Primary Being, or God, fall within the natural grasp of this power. If the senses, which are inferior faculties, can perceive their objects without supernatural help, surely the intellect is just as capable of knowing the whole range of its object without divine aid. Aristotle sums up the case of naturalism in a nutshell: "Nature is not lacking in what is necessary" (*De Anima*, III, 9).

Scotus grants that the object proportionate to our intellect is being in all its fullness. Its object is just as broad as that of the angelic intellect, for no being lies outside its grasp. It can even behold God, the infinite Being; but this surpasses its power in the present life. In our present state, the object of our intellect is not the full range of being, but only *sensible* being. Aristotle was correct in teaching that we must draw all our knowledge, including our notion of being, from the world of sense. At present, therefore, our knowledge of being is restricted to what the sense world can tell us about it. We enjoy no intellectual intuitions of spiritual beings which would give us a notion of being that is equally comprehensive of the material and spiritual realms.

Like St. Bonaventure, Scotus considers the basic fault of pure philosophers such as Aristotle to be ignorance of original sin. Failing to realize man's fallen state, they take his present way of knowing by means of the senses to be natural to him, and they consider the natural object of his intellect to be the essences of sensible things. Scotus assures us that this is not so: these essences are the object of our intellect only in its present state, which is due to man's fall from grace or to the will of God for man in his present condition. The Christian should not judge the proportioned object of man's intellect from man's present way of knowing, any more than he should judge the object of sight by what sight can perceive in semidarkness. Scotus thought that Avicenna was more correct than Aristotle in describing the proportioned object of man's intellect as being in all its fullness, and not the essences of sensible things. However, Scotus attributes Avicenna's insight to the influence of his Moslem religion and not to philosophical insight alone.[3] Far from being self-sufficient, therefore, philosophy is not even capable of teaching us the true object of our intellect. Much less can it assure us of a direct knowledge of spiritual beings such as God, or point out the means of reaching this goal.

In our present state we abstract the notion of being from sense data. For want of a fuller and richer notion drawn alike from material and spiritual beings, we must use this notion as the object of our metaphysics. For this science concerns being *qua* being, its necessary properties and primary divisions. On this point Scotus agrees with Avicenna against Averroes, who claimed that God was the object of metaphysics.[4] But Scotus points out that Averroes failed to recognize theology as a science superior to metaphysics. Thinking metaphysics to be the highest science, he assigned to it the noblest object; namely, God. In fact, God, known through the concept of infinite Being, is the object of our theology. Below theology, metaphysics has for its object being in general: a notion that, as we shall see, is common and univocal to everything. Only at the end of his inquiry about being does the metaphysician— at least if he accepts the guidance of revelation—touch upon God by proving him to be the primary and infinite being.[5]

THE EXISTENCE OF GOD

SCOTUS' INSISTENCE on the limits of philosophy (whose spokesman he considered to be Aristotle) can be seen in his atti-

tude toward the Aristotelian approach to God. Aristotle proved
the existence of a primary mover by analyzing motion. To Scotus,
the conclusion of this analysis is correct, but as an approach to
God it is inadequate and imperfect. Aristotle's proof belongs to
the order of physics, the science of movement. It demonstrates
the existence of a first cause of movement and not the existence
of a being who is absolutely first, unique, and infinite. Until the
existence of such a being has been demonstrated in metaphysics,
the human mind falls short of its goal, for it has not reached God
in his proper perfection, which is infinite being.

The metaphysical proof of God's existence offered by Scotus
is not an *a priori* demonstration; that is to say, one deducing his
existence from the knowledge of his essence. Scotus thought this
kind of demonstration impossible in the present case, because we
have no proper concept of the divine essence. Accordingly, we
can prove God's existence only *a posteriori;* that is to say, starting from God's effects and mounting up to him as to their cause.
In this regard Scotus agrees with St. Thomas; but he differs from
him in his choice of the effects on which the proof should be
based. St. Thomas selected sensible, empirical facts, such as the
existence of things in motion, whereas Scotus chooses a metaphysical truth: *Some being is producible.* The advantage of this
starting point is its absolute necessity. Although it is learned
through sense experience, in itself it is a truth independent of the
actual existence of creatures. Even if God had not willed to create,
it would be eternally true that some being can be produced.

The starting point of Scotus' proof is thus neither a concept
nor a sensible, empirical fact, but rather a metaphysical truth about
some being; namely, its producibility. The disadvantage of this
starting point is that it is a truth concerning *possible being* (the
possibility of something being produced) and not about actually
existing being. Since the proof must conclude with the actual
existence of God, a transition must be made within it from the
level of possibility to that of actual existence. This transition, as we
shall see, is made in a striking way at the very end of the proof.

The proof itself can be summarized as follows. Some being is
producible.[6] Now it is producible either by itself, or by nothing,

or by something. The first two possibilities must be eliminated, because no being can produce itself, and nothing can be produced by nothing. Hence being is producible by some other being that is productive. Let us designate this efficient cause A. Now if A is the primary efficient cause, we have reached our conclusion: there is a first efficient cause that is not produced by a prior cause and which produces its effects by its own power. If A is not primary in this sense, it is a secondary efficient cause, produced by a prior cause B. We can then reason about B as we did about A. Either it is the primary efficient cause or it is a secondary cause. We shall either continue on in this manner to infinity, or we shall stop at an absolutely primary efficient cause. But it is impossible to regress to infinity in a series of essentially ordered efficient causes. Hence the conclusion: a primary efficient cause exists, and this is God.

An integral part of this proof is the impossibility of an infinite series of essentially ordered causes. Scotus distinguishes in three respects a series of this sort from one accidentally arranged: 1] In an essentially ordered series of causes, a secondary cause depends on the primary cause for its very causality. For example, a pen in the hand of a writer can cause its effect only because it is moved by the hand. In an accidentally ordered series of causes, this is not so. The secondary cause may depend on the primary cause for its existence but not for its causality. For example, a man gives existence to his son, but the son can then beget his own son independently of his father. 2] In essentially ordered causes, the causality of the primary and secondary causes are of a different nature and in a different order, because the causality of the primary cause is more perfect than that of the secondary cause. This is not true of causes accidentally ordered. 3] Unlike accidentally ordered causes, all essentially ordered causes must be present simultaneously to produce their effect.

Scotus does not deny the possibility of an infinite series of accidentally ordered causes; for example, a series of men, without beginning or end, each member of which begets children. However, he offers several proofs for the impossibility of an infinite series of essentially ordered causes. He asks us to consider the sum

total of the effects of essentially ordered causes. That totality has
been caused, because everything in it is an effect. Hence the
cause of that totality must be outside it and not included within
it as an effect. So the cause of the sum total of these effects must
be separated from them; and since it is the cause of the totality
of effects, it must be the first cause. Moreover, essentially ordered
causes are arranged in a hierarchy, the superior cause being more
perfect than the inferior. Now if there were an infinite series of
causes ordered in this way, the cause of that series would be
infinitely superior to it and infinitely more perfect. Indeed, it
would have an infinite causal power, and so it would require no
cause prior to itself in order to produce its effects. In short, it
would be the absolutely first cause, or God.

Even if we grant the possibility of an infinite series of accidentally ordered causes, there must be a first cause among causes
essentially ordered. For in this hypothesis there is an infinite succession of causes spread out in time (for example, a man begetting
another, who in turn begets another, and so on to infinity), but
the whole series and each of its members depend for their existence on a being of infinite duration and not upon any one of the
members of the series, whose temporal span is finite. This being,
which must be outside the temporal sequence of causes and transcend the sequence and time itself, is the first efficient cause.

Up to this point Scotus has proved only the possibility of a
first efficient cause and not its actual existence. He began his proof
with the statement that some being can be produced. He has now
shown that this possibility involves another; namely, a first efficient cause. The next step is to prove that this being is not only
possible but that it actually exists. Scotus does this by showing
that if it did not actually exist it would be in fact an impossible
being. For since by nature it is the first cause, it is incapable of
being caused by a prior being. Hence, if it did not actually exist,
no cause could produce it and it would be impossible for it to
exist. The only way out of this difficulty is to admit that the
first efficient cause is possible because it exists. In short, its actual
existence is the only reason for its possibility.

Using a similar argument, Scotus proves the existence of a

primary end toward which all beings tend, and of a primary being transcending the whole created universe. He then shows that the primary efficient cause is identical with the primary end and the primary being, for primacy in any one of these orders involves primacy in the others.

These are proofs of the existence of God in his attributes relative to creatures. Lofty as this knowledge of God is, Scotus strives to mount still higher by proving the existence of God in an attribute intrinsic to himself; namely, infinity. For Scotus, infinity is the distinctive mode of the divine being, and the notion of "infinite being" is the most perfect we can form of God in the present life. Hence the proof of the divine infinity is the culminating point of our ascent to God.

It has been shown that God is the first and uncaused cause. It follows that his causal power is unlimited. Aristotle demonstrated the infinite motive power of the primary mover by showing that it can move the universe over an infinite period of time. Scotus goes beyond Aristotle by showing that God has in the supreme degree all causal power, so that he can simultaneously produce an infinite number of beings. Moreover, as the supreme being, God conceives an infinite number of intelligible objects, and so his intellect must be infinite. The divine will must also be infinite, because God's love is as unlimited as his knowledge. Furthermore, our will is naturally drawn to a supreme good, which is none other than God.

It follows from this that the notion of an infinite being is wholly reasonable, involving no contradiction. Indeed, the intellect takes the greatest pleasure in thinking about this highest object of thought. Hence such a being is at least possible. Does it actually exist? Yes, for if it did not exist it would be an impossible being, which is contradictory. The only reasonable conclusion is that infinite being exists in reality and that this being is the reason for its own possibility.

In proving the existence of God as infinite being, Scotus appeals to St. Anselm's argument, which he claims simply to have "touched up." The central point of the Anselmian argument is that the highest object of thought, or God, cannot be conceived as non-existent.

Scotus adds that the notion of this being involves no contradiction; hence this being is possible. And if it is possible, it actually exists, for no other reason can be given for its possibility.

HOW WE KNOW GOD

IT SHOULD NOW BE CLEAR that we can have some knowledge about God. Exactly what kind of knowledge can we have of him in this life? [7] Scotus considered negative knowledge of no value unless founded upon positive knowledge. If we know God is not a stone, we cannot distinguish him from nothing, which is also not a stone. All our negative concepts of God presuppose a positive concept of him. Moreover, we cannot know *that* God exists without knowing *what* he is, for how can we know the existence of something if we have no notion of what it is? Neither can we simply know the truth of the proposition "God exists" without knowing the being of God, for we must conceive the terms of this proposition and have a concept of God's being. Moreover, this must be a positive concept of God in himself and not simply as he is represented by creatures. True, our knowledge of God has its origin in creatures, but unless it terminates in God we do not truly know him.

These criticisms of the Dionysian and Thomistic approaches to God by way of negation and analogy clear the way for Scotus' own position, that we have a positive knowledge of God in himself by means of concepts univocal to God and creatures. By a univocal concept he means one that has the same meaning whenever it is used, so that it is contradictory to affirm it and to deny it of the same thing. For example, it is contradictory to say that God is both being and non-being. Hence the concept of being is univocal. The alternative is that the concept of being, applied to God, is analogous to that applied to creatures. But Scotus thought this impossible. The only notion of being we have is the one we abstract from sense data; no other source of information is available from which we could form a concept of being analogous to this concept. If our concepts do not apply univocally to God and creatures, we can have no knowledge of him at all.

The univocal concept of being is thus indispensable for a knowledge of God in this life. This is the concept of the nature of being as such, similar to our concepts of other natures, such as humanity and animality. Of course being is not a genus; unlike a genus, it is predicable of absolutely everything. However, being is like a genus in that it can be conceived apart from all the differences it exhibits in actual existence. When being exists, it is always determined by some mode; it is, for example, either infinite or finite, uncreated or created. The univocal concept of being abstracts from all modes of being and retains only the nature of being as such. If our concept of being includes the modes of being, it is no longer univocal, because then it does not equally apply to all beings. Being is attributed primarily to infinite being and secondarily to finite being. In actual existence, therefore, being is not univocal but analogous, in the sense that it belongs primarily to some beings and secondarily to others, and it is predicated of them *per prius* and *per posterius*.[8]

Besides the univocal notion of being, the metaphysician has at his command univocal notions of goodness, wisdom, and so on, by which he conceives God in his various attributes. Through the notion of being, however, he knows God is his very essence. The most perfect concept of God is that of infinite being, for this is the simplest concept we have of him, and it virtually includes all others. Infinity for Scotus, as for Henry of Ghent, is a positive perfection of the divine being: it is its "proper greatness" (*magnitudo propria*). Scotus also calls infinity the intrinsic mode of the divine being.[9] A mode of being is said to be intrinsic when it adds no formal determination to the essence of the being but simply determines the way the being exists. Color added to white light is an extrinsic and formal addition to the light because it alters its essence. But if the intensity of white light is increased, nothing is added to it but a new modality of being. Similarly, infinity is the mode determining the divine "intensity" of being; creatures, on the other hand, have a finite mode of being.

THE DIVINE ATTRIBUTES

WHILE PROVING GOD'S EXISTENCE Scotus establishes several
of the divine attributes, including power, knowledge, and goodness. Other divine attributes are known only through revelation,
such as God's absolute omnipotence (that is, his power to produce
an infinite number of effects by himself), immensity, omnipresence,
justice, mercy, and providence.[10] What relation have these attributes to each other and to the divine essence? [11] Scotus rejects
the Thomist view that there is simply a distinction of reason between them, and insists that they are distinct in God himself prior
to any act of understanding, human or divine. The intellect does
not make the distinction between them but discovers it already
present in God. In Scotus' eyes the intelligibility of God is here
at stake. If God's attributes are not distinct from each other and
from his essence, he is neither intelligible to himself nor to us.
The theologian's deduction of the attributes would be a useless
play of concepts, for God would be known as perfectly by one
concept as by all of them.

Scotus calls the distinction between the divine attributes a formal
non-identity. This differs from a distinction of reason, even one
with a foundation in reality, in that it is not caused by the mind
but exists in reality (*a parte rei*). Properly speaking, however, it
is not a real distinction. A real distinction exists between things,
one of which can exist without the other, at least by God's absolute power. Two men are really distinct, because they can exist
separately. So, too, matter and form are really distinct, for even
though they are not separable by nature, God can make them
exist apart if he wishes. Formal non-identity does not concern
things in their existence, but the formalities or essences in things,
one of which does not enter into the definition of the other. For
example, goodness does not enter into the definition of truth;
hence goodness and truth are formally non-identical.[12]

Does not formal non-identity in God conflict with his absolute simplicity? Is not God a composite being, made up of an essence with the addition of formally distinct attributes? Not at all, according to Scotus, for both God's essence and attributes are infinite in their mode of being, and through their infinity they are really identical. Considered precisely in itself, each attribute is formally non-identical with every other and with the divine essence. But each is actually infinite in existence. God's goodness is infinite, and so too are his wisdom and love. On the level of essence or quiddity (which is expressed in a definition), the attributes are formally irreducible to each other; but they are really one in their common mode of existence, which is infinity. Infinity confers on them and on the divine essence real identity without suppressing their formal distinction.

Owing to God's infinity, the rules of human logic cannot be perfectly applied to him. We cannot say, "Animality is rationality," because these are finite quiddities that are identical only in a third quiddity that contains them; namely, humanity. However, it is correct to say of God, "Deity is goodness," because despite the formal non-identity of these terms they are really identical. Each term is infinite and thus virtually includes the other and is identical with it. Scotus writes: "Goodness and greatness and other (divine attributes) of this sort are the same as it were by mutual identity, because each is formally infinite, and owing to this infinity each is the same as the other." [13]

The role of infinity in Scotism is thus similar to that played by *esse* in Thomism.[14] For St. Thomas, the most perfect concept of God is the pure Act of Being (*Ipsum Esse*); for Scotus, it is infinite Being (*Ens Infinitum*). And as for St. Thomas, the pure Act of Being embraces eminently, and with perfect unity, all the divine perfections, so for Scotus the infinity of being assures the real identity of all God's attributes.

THE DIVINE IDEAS AND CREATION

SINCE GOD IS A CAUSE with infinite power, he can create an unlimited number of things. And being infinitely intelligent, he must possess an infinity of Ideas, each of which is an eternal model according to which something can be created outside his mind. What is the relation of these Ideas to God, and what kind of being do they have in the divine mind?

Scotus describes the divine Ideas as the essences of possible creatures known by the divine mind. The divine Idea of stone, for example, is simply stone as known by God within his mind. The divine Ideas are therefore objects of God's knowledge, but they are not the same object as the divine essence. Stone and Deity are formally distinct objects of the divine knowledge, even though in God they are really identical.

Not only are the objects of God's knowledge formally distinct, but there is a definite order among them. It is only to be expected that the first object God knows is his own essence. Through his knowledge of this infinite object he conceives an infinite number of other essences, thereby giving them intelligible being within his mind. For example, he conceives the essence of stone and understands it. Having produced this Idea in his mind, a relationship is established between the divine mind and the Idea. The divine mind then reflects, so to speak, upon this relationship and knows it.[15]

As a result, there are several stages in God's knowledge of his Ideas and of their relationship to himself, but these stages are not distinct in time. All God's knowledge is eternal. The sequence in the objects of God's knowledge, as described by Scotus, is not a temporal but a natural one. But this is sufficient for Scotus to deny that a divine Idea is constituted by its relationship to the divine essence. As we have seen, Ideas are produced by God within his mind and are known by him prior (in nature) to the relationship between the Ideas and the divine mind. For this reason Scotus rejects the Thomist definition of a divine Idea as the divine essence itself insofar as it is capable of being imitated by a creature. For him, the divine Ideas are not constituted by a relation to the divine essence; they are absolute objects of God's knowledge, formally non-identical with the divine essence.

Although Scotus speaks of the divine Ideas being produced by the divine intellect, he does not mean that they are created. The divine conception of the Ideas differs from creation in two respects.

First, both the divine intellect and will concur in creation, the intellect knowing the object to be created and the will choosing to give it real being outside God. The production of the divine Ideas, on the other hand, is wholly intellectual. Scotus writes: "The Ideas are in the divine intellect prior to every act of the will." There is consequently no voluntarism in Scotus' doctrine of God's speculative knowledge of his Ideas. Unlike Descartes, he does not submit these Ideas, and the eternal truths they contain, to the divine will. As a consequence, the divine Ideas and God's knowledge of them are not contingent on God's will but are as necessary as God himself.

The second difference between the production of the divine Ideas and creation is that they result in different types of being. Creation terminates in a reality, possessing both essential being (*esse essentiae*) and existential being (*esse existentiae*). The divine Ideas possess neither of these types of real being, but only cognitional being (*esse rationis*). The whole being of the divine Idea is to be an object of God's knowledge; hence its being is *to be an object* (*esse objectivum*). Henry of Ghent attributed essential being to the divine Ideas, but Scotus points out that this is a kind of real being; it is the reality an essence possesses in itself. If the divine Ideas had this kind of being, creation would simply add existence to an already real essence, and so the total reality of creatures would not be created. In order to assure that creation is from nothing (*ex nihilo*), Scotus denies to the divine Ideas all real being, whether essential or existential, attributing to them solely objective being.[16]

God's Ideas perfectly represent to him the essences of possible creatures and all their possible combinations; but by means of them alone God does not have a definite knowledge of the creatures he chooses to create. God knows through his Ideas essences such as humanity, whiteness, and sitting. But these Ideas do not suffice for the knowledge that at a given moment in time there will exist a man who is white and sitting. This is a contingent event, and it cannot be explained by a necessary cause, such as God's intellect and Ideas. God's will must come into play as well as his intellect in order to account for the actual existence of contingent beings and for God's knowledge of them. God freely chooses certain possible creatures and wills them to exist under definite circumstances of time and place. They then become not only possible beings but willed objects. And it is only through recourse to the free decisions of his will that God has a definite knowledge of these willed objects with all the circumstances of their existence.

In this way God's infinite will accounts for the contingency of creatures and the determinate knowledge he has of them. On this point Scotus was conscious of the gulf between his own Christian metaphysics and Greco-Arabian philosophy. As depicted by the latter, the universe is ruled from above by necessary causes. The only contingency in the universe is due to matter, which by its lack of proper disposition may prevent the effects of celestial causes from taking place. These philosophers, Scotus says, did not understand that God's causality is perfect, as Catholics maintain.[17] As a result, they did not recognize that the true explanation of the contingency of creatures is not simply matter but the infinite will of God, which is free to create or not to create, and to create any number of possible universes besides the one in which we live.

THE STRUCTURE OF CREATED BEING

THE UNIVERSE GOD WILLED to create is composed of individuals arranged in a hierarchy of perfection, from the highest angel to the lowliest inanimate thing. Scotus considers two facts about created beings of special importance to the philosopher analyzing their essential structure. First, each creature is an individual being; that is to say, it is endowed with an individuality that makes it unique among beings. Because it is an individual it is separated from every other being and it cannot be divided into parts identical with the whole. Secondly, not only is each creature an individual, but it also has something in common with other individuals in the same genus or species. Socrates, for example, is an individual man and he also shares the nature of humanity with all other men. How can these two facts be explained?

The first point established by Scotus is that an individual substance is not individual by its very nature. This is clear enough, for if the nature of the individual is common to other individuals, by itself it cannot account for the uniqueness of the individual. Of itself, a nature is common to many individuals and not proper to any. Humanity, for example, exists in Socrates, and in him it is his own humanity; but nothing prevents humanity from existing in other men. From this, Scotus concludes that of themselves natures have a real being outside the mind, formally distinct from the individuals in which they exist, although they are really identical with these individuals. Here again, as with the divine attributes and Ideas, formal distinction is compatible with real identity. And because natures of themselves have real being, they also have real unity, distinct from the real unity of the individual. An individual stone has numerical unity; the nature existing in a stone has a unity that is real but less perfect than unity of number. According to Scotus, the real, proper, or sufficient unity of the nature of stone, existing in this stone, is less than numerical unity. Therefore, it is not of itself one with numerical unity.[18]

Scotus' reasons for this position reveal some of his basic philosophical presuppositions. 1] The proper objects of our knowledge are not individuals as such, but the natures existing in them. This is true even of our sense powers.[19] Now these objects are real; hence natures must have a reality of their own and a real unity distinct from the numerical unity of individuals. 2] There are real relations among individuals; for example, some are really equal or similar to others. Now real relations must have a real foundation distinct from the individuals themselves, since no individual is really equal or similar to itself. This foundation is the nature existing in the related individuals with its own real, less-than-numerical unity. 3] There must be some real unity of form between an efficient cause and its univocal effect; for example, between two fires, one of which causes the other. So there must be a form present in the cause and its effect with a real unity which is not numerical.

For these and other reasons Scotus concludes that natures are common in reality, in the sense that, existing in one individual, it is not impossible for them to exist in another. Nevertheless, he does not identify a common nature with a universal. A universal not only exists in many individuals but is predicable of them. Now a common nature is predicable of many subjects only as it exists conceptually in the intellect, abstracted from individuals. It must be released, so to speak, from its bondage to individuals by the abstractive power of the intellect before it fulfills completely the conditions of a universal. In short, universals exist only in the intellect.

In Scotus' terms, therefore, a common nature is not of itself universal, but it must be made universal by the intellect. Similarly, it is not of itself individual, so there must be a cause of individuality. Scotus reviews all the principles of individuation proposed by his predecessors, only to reject them. Among others, the Thomistic solution of this problem comes under his criticism: neither matter nor quantity, he maintains, can be the principle of individuation. Matter is part of the nature of a material substance and, like the nature itself, it is of itself common; hence it cannot account for the individual as such. An appeal to quantity is equally futile, because quantity is an accident of substance and naturally posterior to it. So it cannot account for the individuation of substance, which must be individuated prior to its receiving accidents. Moreover, like other natures, quantity of itself is something common. It cannot, therefore, be the cause rendering substances individual. In fact, it too requires a cause of its individuality.[20]

In order to solve this vexing problem, Scotus points out two requirements for the principle of individuation. First, it must be a positive entity, for individuality adds something positive to the nature as such: there is more perfection in Socrates than in the common nature of man. Second, it must be individual in itself, because if it were common it would not be the ultimate principle of individuation. This positive entity Scotus calls the "individual difference" or "thisness" (*haecceitas*).[21] The former term was obviously coined by analogy with the term "specific difference," and indeed Scotus compares the two in a certain respect. The specific difference "rational" is added to the genus "animal" to form the specific reality "man." The only possible division of the species "man" is into individuals, and this is the function of individual differences. An individual difference, or "haecceity," is thus a positive entity or act, determining and perfecting a specific nature, thereby rendering it individual. Unlike a specific difference, it adds nothing new in the order of essence. It simply seals off a specific essence, so to speak, by causing it to be individual and really distinct from every other individual in the same species. For example, the humanity of Socrates is made to be *his* humanity, really distinct from the humanity of every other man, by his individual difference.

God's essence alone has no need of an individuating principle since it is individual in itself (*de se haec*). All created natures are common of themselves and require to be individualized by an individual difference. We have seen that in God formal non-identity is compatible with real unity owing to the divine infinity. Scotus envisages an individual difference as playing a similar role in a creature. A creature contains many formal non-identical entities, including a genus, a specific difference, and an individual difference. It even contains really distinct entities, such as matter and form in material substances, and real accidents. Over and above all these realities in the essential order, a creature has existence (*esse existentiae*). All of these diverse entities are sealed into real unity by the individual difference, which is consequently the ultimate reality of a being.[22] It is because Socrates has his own individuality, or "individual difference," that everything in him, including his existence, is rendered individual and really his own.

Scotus' conception of created being as composed of formal entities dovetailing with each other and brought into real unity by the perfection of individuality is an original development of the traditional formalism we have met in philosophers such as Boethius and Gilbert of Poitiers. The real composition of essence and *esse* in creatures, as taught by St. Thomas, was foreign to Scotus' outlook, and he criticized it as others before him had done. If *esse* is something added to essence, that *esse* itself must be a being requiring another *esse* for its existence, and so on to infinity.[23] In Scotism, essence and existence are really identical, existence being a mode of essence. Essence and existence are conceptually distinct in creatures, for the essence of any creature can be conceived without existence; the divine essence, however, cannot be thought of as non-existent.[24]

MAN

THE SCOTIST DOCTRINE of man is in line with these metaphysical notions. Man is composed of matter, with its own form of corporeity, and the human soul. Each of these elements in man's constitution has its own partial being (*esse*); together they form a whole with a composite being. Scotus rejects as unintelligible the Thomist doctrine that man's being (*esse*) is simple, whereas his essence is composite, embracing soul and body.[25]

The limits of the philosopher's knowledge of the human soul are strictly drawn by Scotus. Philosophy can demonstrate that it is the substantial form of man by showing that it gives him his nature as a rational animal, but philosophy cannot prove that the soul has been separately created by God or that it is an immaterial and immortal substance. These latter truths are known with certainty only by faith.

The powers of the soul are formally distinct from each other and from the soul's substance, although all these are really identical. Man's highest powers are his intellect and will, to each of which Scotus gives considerable attention.

In common with his contemporaries, Scotus accepts the Aristotelian division of man's intellectual powers into an agent and possible intellect, although his description of their roles in knowledge is his own. Because natures are common in reality and are represented as such by the senses, all the agent intellect has to do is to make them completely universal by abstracting them from sense data. In order to do this, the agent intellect does not have to act upon images in the sense powers and prepare them for the abstraction of universals, as St. Thomas taught. It can read as in an open book the intelligible message presented by the senses and directly form its universal concepts from it.[26]

In our present state all knowledge is gained by abstraction, but Scotus distinguishes between two types of knowledge: intuitive, by which we know something as actually existing and present to us; and abstractive, by which we know something without regard for its existence or non-existence. The object of both kinds of knowledge can be either an individual thing or a common nature; they differ only in that the object of the former is known as existing, whereas the object of the latter is known in abstraction from existence. Scotus points out a similar distinction in sense knowledge. Sight is intuitive, for it reaches its object as present and existing; imagination, on the other hand, is abstractive, disregarding the existence and non-existence of its object.[27] In the fourteenth century the question was widely debated whether under any circumstances there can be intuitive knowledge without the existence of its object. Those who answered in the affirmative opened the way to skepticism by making it impossible to be certain that the objects we perceive really exist. Scotus refuses to ally himself with this skeptical trend and calls the intuitive knowledge of a non-existent object a contradiction in terms.[28]

On still another point Scotus attempts to withstand the growing skepticism in philosophy. In one of his finest philosophical analyses he shows, in opposition to Henry of Ghent and most of the Franciscan school, that a special divine illumination is not required for the truth of natural knowledge.[29]

More specifically, Scotus outlines three areas in which natural certitude is possible without special divine help. First, principles and conclusions drawn from them. Principles are known to be true through a knowledge of their terms. This knowledge comes to us through the senses, which can err; but Scotus insists that the senses are not the causes but only the *occasion* of the knowledge of principles. Through an error of the senses the intellect can wrongly judge that Socrates is white. But no mistake of the senses can lead the intellect into error regarding a principle such as "The whole is greater than its part," because the intellect knows this truth simply by understanding its terms.

Second, we can also be certain of some general empirical facts; for example, that the moon is frequently eclipsed, or that a certain species of herb is "hot." The certainty of these truths does not rest upon our experience of every individual case to which they apply, but upon the regularity with which these effects occur, leading us to the conclusion that they are natural. We are certain of the proposition: The effect regularly produced by a cause that is not free (that is, a natural cause) is the natural effect of that cause. When we regularly observe a species of herb to have the quality of "heat," we can be certain that this is a natural effect of this kind of herb, even though we do not know why this is so, and consequently we know that this quality regularly attends this kind of herb. Scotus adds, however, that perhaps we should formulate a scientific proposition of this kind as follows: a certain species of herb is *apt to be* hot, because under certain circumstances the quality may be lacking in the herb.

Third, we can be certain of our own acts. No proof is necessary to convince me that I am awake or that I know and love: these facts are immediately evident to me. Ocular illusions are possible, but in these cases at least I am certain *that I see*. Despite errors of the senses, we can be certain of the existence of the external world with the qualities we perceive it to have. Once again we can invoke the truth that the effect regularly produced by a cause that is not free is the natural effect of the cause. The sensation regularly produced by a sensible thing is the natural effect of that thing. Hence, if our senses regularly perceive the same object, we can be sure that it is as we perceive it. Sometimes, it is true, our senses disagree in their judgments, as when our eyes perceive a stick in the water as bent and our hands feel it as straight. But in cases such as this our intellect can decide which sense is in error. It knows, for example, that a harder body is not broken by contact with a softer one, and hence that a stick thrust into water is not really broken.

Being formally distinct, the intellect and will each has its own operation: the intellect knows the truth, and the will loves the good. The will is the nobler faculty in man because of its commanding position in human activity. It even commands the intellect, for we know only because we will to do so. In a sense the intellect causes the act of the will; we must know an object before we will it. But Scotus thought the role of the intellect in volition quite accidental. In presenting to the will objects to choose and to love, the intellect, he says, is an *occasional* cause of volition.

But in the last analysis the will is autonomous and accounts for its own act. "The will alone," Scotus writes, "is the total cause of volition in the will." [30]

There is consequently a strain of voluntarism in Scotus' outlook, but this must be seen in its proper perspective. We have already noted that there is no voluntarism in the Scotist conception of God: the divine will is not elevated above the divine intellect, determining the divine Ideas and the eternal truths they contain. The will of God comes into play in his free decision to create and in his selection of the essences to be created, but the essences themselves of creatures are independent of the divine will. They are necessary and unchangeable, as are the eternal truths deducible from them.

There is thus a body of necessary speculative truths that does not come under the sway of the divine will. Similarly, in the moral order there are natural laws, which are not arbitrary commands of God but rooted in the very nature of things. Scotus considers the first three commandments natural laws in the strict sense; so absolute is their binding force that not even God can abolish them or dispense from them. He cannot permit men to practice idolatry or to take his name in vain, for these acts are contrary to man's purpose in life, which is the love of God. Similarly, man's obligation to worship God is strictly based upon natural law, and perhaps even the obligation to worship God on a given day, although Scotus is uncertain about the latter.[31]

The other seven commandments do not concern our relation to God but to our neighbor. These are natural laws, at least in the broad sense of being in harmony with man's nature and well adapted to secure man's happiness. But they cannot necessarily be deduced from the first principles of the moral order, nor are they necessarily connected with our final end. God has willed that they should be observed, and consequently acts performed in accordance with them are good, for whatever God wills is good. But the fact that he sometimes dispenses from them shows that they do not strictly belong to the natural law. For example, God allowed the Israelites to carry off the property of the Egyptians, and he commanded Abraham to kill his son Isaac. Such dispensations would have been impossible if the laws forbidding us to steal and to kill were strictly natural.

Consequently, most of the moral code appeared to Scotus as not strictly necessary but fixed by God's will. This does not mean that God rules man as a despot, imposing on him arbitrary laws. God is infinitely good, and all his laws are good by the very fact that he made them. But because of his infinity and absolute power he is not restricted to a limited set of moral laws. Just as he is capable of creating an infinite variety of universes different from our own, so he has the power to lead man to himself by other moral laws than those he has established.

In his ethics, as in his metaphysics, Scotus keeps in the foreground the infinity of God and the contingent bond between himself and creatures. It was left to Ockham to take the final step and to make the whole moral code dependent upon God's will. But in order to do this, he first had to eliminate those elements in Scotism that introduce some necessity into God and the universe; namely, the divine Ideas and common natures.

THE
4 🌿 MODERN
WAY

WE ARE SO SURE of our own modernity that we cannot fail
to feel some surprise on seeing men of the Middle Ages call
themselves "modern" in comparison with their predecessors. We tend to forget that "modernity" is a relative term,
and that what we call medieval was once thought to be
modern, and that what we now consider to be modern will
one day be called ancient. In the second half of the fourteenth century Thomism and Scotism were already called
the "old way" of philosophizing and theologizing in contrast to the "modern way" (*via moderna*) of William of
Ockham and his followers. These men were called nominalists because they attributed universality only to names,
whether mental, spoken or written, in distinction to the
realists of the old school, who thought that universal terms,
such as genera and species, have a real foundation in things.
In this Part we shall be concerned with the nominalist
movement, in which Ockham is the central figure; but
before taking up this subject we shall describe some of the
new developments in logic that helped to prepare the way
for it. Then, broadening our perspective, we shall examine
the new trends in medieval physics and philosophy that
herald the coming of what we call today the modern age.

XVII

The New Logic
and Physics

NEW DEVELOPMENTS IN LOGIC

THE DISCOVERY of the works of Aristotle in the twelfth and thirteenth centuries gave an impetus to the development of all the branches of philosophy, including logic, their common instrument.[1] Most of the logical treatises of the thirteenth and fourteenth centuries were commentaries on the logical works of Aristotle. In them, as we might expect, Aristotelian ideas predominate, although even here the schoolmen found room for originality. St. Albert, for example, thought it necessary to complete Aristotle's doctrine of science in the *Posterior Analytics* by recourse to the Platonic theory of Ideas, and St. Thomas introduced his new notion of being into his Commentary on the *Perihermenias*. Of greater significance, however, for the progress of logic were the independent treatises of logicians such as William of Sherwood, Lambert of Auxerre, Peter of Spain, William of Ockham, and Walter of Burleigh. These contain tracts on the properties of terms, new types of consequences, and other aspects of logic hitherto completely neglected or inadequately treated. Among these we shall consider only two: the supposition of terms and syncategorematic terms. After that we shall examine speculative grammar, a new type of scientific grammar developed in the thirteenth century in close connection with logic.

Supposition of Terms

The notion of the supposition of terms can be traced back as far as Abelard, but only in the mid-thirteenth century do we find well-developed tracts on the subject in the books of logic. The *Summulae Logicales* of Peter of Spain (*c.* 1210–1277) was one of the first to contain a detailed treatment of supposition and its various kinds.[2]

Peter of Spain distinguishes between complex and incomplex utterances. Examples of the former are "Man runs" and "white man," of the latter, "man" and "white." The latter are also called incomplex terms. A term is defined as a word (*vox*) that signifies something; and since things are either universal or singular, all words with signification fall into one of these two classes. The word "man," for example, is universal because it signifies a universal reality, while the word "Socrates" is singular because it signifies a singular reality. By signification Peter of Spain means the property of a term whereby it conventionally represents something. If the term is a substantive, such as "man," the signification is also substantive. If the term is adjectival (*adiectivum*), such as "white" or "runs," the signification is also adjectival; that is to say, it adds something to what is signified by a substantive term. For this reason the function of an adjective or a verb is "to connect with" (*copulare*), whereas the function of a substantive name is "to stand for" (*supponere*).

As defined by Peter of Spain, supposition is different from signification. Signification results from the arbitrary imposition of a name in order to signify something; supposition is the use of the name, already endowed with its signification, to stand for things. For example, in the proposition "Man runs," the term "man," which signifies human nature, stands for individual men, for it is they, and not human nature as such, who run.

The most general division of supposition is between discrete and common. Discrete supposition obtains when a term in a proposition stands for only one individual; for example, "Socrates" in the statement "Socrates is a man." Common supposition obtains when a term stands for more than one individual. This kind of supposition is twofold: natural and accidental. Natural supposition is the natural capacity of a word, once it has been given a meaning, to stand for everything of which it can be predicated. For example, the word "man," arbitrarily chosen to signify human nature, by its very nature is capable of standing for all men who are, have been, and will be. However, in any proposition in which the word "man" appears, the verb limits its supposition. When we say "Man is," the subject stands only for present men; when we say "Man was," the subject stands only for past men; when we say "Man will be," the subject stands only for future men. Because the supposition of the subject-term in a given statement is determined by the verb that happens to be joined to it, Peter of Spain calls this accidental supposition.

Peter of Spain's notion of natural supposition is ambiguous because it is not clearly differentiated from signification. The function of supposition, unlike that of signification, is related to the use made of a term in a proposition; but in natural supposition a term is considered in abstraction from any given proposition. As soon as a term enters into a proposition it takes on one of the functions of what Peter of Spain calls accidental supposition. The notion of natural supposition is therefore superfluous, and it was dropped by later logicians.

Peter of Spain subdivides accidental supposition into simple and personal. In simple supposition a common term stands for the universal reality signified by it. For example, when we say "Man is a species," the term "man" stands for the universal nature signified by it; it stands for man in general and not for any particular man. The predicate of a universal‑affirmative proposition always has simple supposition. For example, in the proposition "Every man is an animal," "animal" has simple supposition because it stands for the nature of the genus "animal." [3]

The exact definition of simple supposition was a matter of dispute between the realists and nominalists. Peter of Spain is obviously a realist, for his definition assumes that there are in reality common natures that terms can signify and stand for. In the next chapter we shall see William of Ockham redefine this type of supposition to fit his own nominalist philosophy, which denies the reality of common natures. For Ockham, a term with simple supposition does not stand for a common nature, but only for a concept in the mind. In reaction to Ockham's nominalism, logicians like Richard of Campsall (d. 1350–1360) returned to a realist interpretation of simple supposition.[4]

The second type of accidental supposition described by Peter of Spain is called personal. This is the use of a common term in a proposition to stand for individual beings. For example, when we say "Man is running," the term "man" stands for individual men, for it is not man in general but persons who run. This proposition is true if only one man is actually running. Hence Peter of Spain calls it an example of determinate personal supposition. Another example of the same type of supposition is "Some man is running." But if the universal sign "every" or "all" is added to the term, the supposition is indeterminate or confused. Examples of indeterminate personal supposition are: "Every man runs" and "All men are running." In these propositions the term "man" is taken for each human being, so that the propositions are not true unless every man is actually running.

Further subdivisions of supposition were added by Peter of Spain, and the theory of supposition grew to great complexity in the hands of later logicians. One detail in Peter of Spain merits attention. He tells us that in the proposition "Every man is an animal" the verb "is" stands for as many essences as the term "man" stands for men; in short, that the copula stands for the same individual essences that the subject of the proposition does.[5] We could not wish for a more clearly essentialist interpretation of the role of the copula. In comparison, St. Thomas' doctrine of the function of "is" as signifying the act of being is plainly existentialist.[6]

Later logicians added material supposition to the kinds described by Peter of Spain. According to Ockham, for example, a term with material supposition stands for the material sound or written word; for example, the term "man" in the proposition " 'Man' is composed of three letters."

Syncategorematic Terms

The scholastic logicians distinguished between the primary and secondary words in a sentence. The primary words are the noun and verb, which together form a complete sentence. Secondary words are adjectives, adverbs, conjunctions, prepositions, and the like. These do not signify anything by themselves but only in conjunction with the subject and predicate of a sentence. For this reason they are called *syncategoremata*, a Latin word made up from two Greek words whose literal meaning is "co-predicates." The term *syncategoremata* goes back to the Latin grammarian Priscian (*c*. A.D. 515), who attributes it to certain Dialecticians, probably the Stoics.

From this description of syncategorematic terms it would seem that they are the business of grammarians and not of logicians. The reason they interest logicians is that some of them have a definite bearing on the truth or falsity of propositions. By adding or omitting them a true proposition may become false, or vice versa. A good example is the syncategorematic term "not." Obviously its addition or omission alters the truth-value of a proposition.

Medieval logicians distinguished between syncategorematic terms that modify the subject, the predicate, and the sentence as a whole. In the sentence "Every man is running," the term "every" affects the subject. In the sentence "Socrates is only human," the term "only" affects the predicate. In the sentence "If Socrates runs, he moves," the term "if" affects the whole sentence by making it conditional.

Modifiers of the principal parts of sentences are syncategorematic terms only if they affect these parts in their role as subject or predicate, and not insofar as they point out what something is. For example, the adjective "white" joined to "man" is not syncategorematic, for it points out that man, as a reality, possesses a certain quality. *Syncategoremata* affect terms only in their role as parts of a sentence. For example, when we say "Every man is running," "every" modifies man as subject of the sentence. It does not signify that man as a reality is universal, but that the term "man" is a universal subject because the predicate applies to every individual in the human species.

Unlike categorematic terms, such as "man" and "animal," syncategorematic terms do not signify objects by themselves; they simply modify the meaning of other terms. For this reason they cannot function as the subject or predicate of a proposition, at least insofar as they are meaningful terms. It is true that we can form sentences in which they appear as the subject or predicate; for example, " 'If' is a syncategorematic term." But the term "if" here does not have the role of a sign. It simply stands for itself, with simple supposition, as defined above.

William of Sherwood, who wrote one of the most influential treatises on syncategorematic terms about the middle of the thirteenth century, raises the interesting question whether the verb "is" is syncategorematic.[7] Some are of the opinion, he says, that this verb does not point out any reality but is only a copula, consignifying the composition of subject and predicate. Since it is a cosignifying word, it appears to be syncategorematic. This view, which seems to be that of Boethius and Abelard, is not correct according to William of Sherwood. Like all verbs, he explains, "is" is a predicate, whose main function is to signify what is said of the subject. If the verb "is" is not qualified in any way, as in the sentence "Man is," it signifies the actual existence of man. On the other hand, if the verb "is" is determined or specified by the addition of another word, as in the sentence "Man is an animal," it serves as a copula, but its main function is to be a predicate along with the specifying word. That is to say, both "is" and "animal" are predicated of man, the reality signified by "is" being specified by the added word "animal." In this sentence the verb "is" does not signify the actual existence of man, since man is an animal even though no man actually exists; it attributes to him the permanent being (*esse habituale*) that belongs to the nature of animal in itself. When we say "Man is an animal," we attribute to him animal being or the nature of animality, which can exist in every individual man, past, present, or future.

William of Sherwood's analysis of the verb "is" shows that he accepts the Avicennian notion of essence or nature as possessing in itself an essential being quite apart from actual existence. This is a good illustration of the close bond between logic and philosophy in medieval logical treatises. No one of the medieval logicians tried to divorce logic from philosophical presuppositions, nor did he think it possible to do so. The result was a variety of logics, each dependent upon the philosophical views of the logician.

SPECULATIVE GRAMMAR

MEDIEVAL LOGIC also maintained a close relationship with grammar. Throughout the early Middle Ages the Latin grammars of Donatus (*c.* A.D. 350) and Priscian (*c.* A.D. 515) were used as the textbooks in this subject, and even in the thirteenth and early fourteenth centuries these books had to be studied in the arts course at the universities.[8] But in the twelfth century the rise of scholasticism led to the development of a new type of grammar that gradually replaced the old. The works of Donatus and Priscian were banished from the University of Toulouse in 1328 and from Paris in 1366 in favor of what was then called "speculative grammar."

Speculative grammar differs from the older types of grammar in several important respects. The grammar of Priscian is a descriptive analysis of the Latin language in linguistic terms. It defines the parts of speech and gives the rules of composition that must be followed if one is to speak or write Latin correctly. Speculative grammar, on the other hand, is a philosophical analysis of language. Its aim is to make grammar a science by making it universal and applicable to all languages, and by making it deductive and capable of assigning the causes of language. In short, it is a philosophy of language.

The complaint of the new grammarians against the old is well summed up in a comment in one of the new textbooks in grammar: "Since Priscian did not teach grammar by every possible means, the value of his books is greatly diminished. Thus he explains many constructions without assigning reasons for them, relying solely on the authority of the ancient grammarians. Therefore he does not teach, because only those teach who give reasons for what they say."[9] The scholastic who wrote these lines obviously learned from Aristotle that science is knowledge of the causes of things, and that teaching consists in showing these causes to the student. Since Priscian's grammar does not do this, it is not scientific and it cannot be said to teach the science of grammar.

One of the results of the rise of speculative grammar was to crowd out of the universities the reading of the Latin classics, which formed an integral part of the teaching of grammar in the earlier Middle Ages. The arts course came to be centered around logic and philosophy, to the neglect of literary studies. Incidentally, this was one of the main reasons for the decline in good Latin style in the later Middle Ages. The allegorical poem of Henry of Andelys entitled *The Battle of the Seven Arts*, written about 1250, describes the defeat of Dame Grammar, the champion of the University of Orléans, supported by the humanists and the classical authors, by Dame Logic of the University of Paris. The Muse of Poetry goes into hiding after this defeat, but Henry of Andelys is not discouraged. He foretells the return to the study of classical literature in the next generation.[10] In fact, classical grammar seems to have declined at the University of Orléans as well as at Paris in the late thirteenth century. Henry of Andelys' prophecy came true only in the fourteenth century, when Petrarch began to revive classical humanism.

The purpose of grammar, as stated by the speculative grammarian Siger of Courtrai (d. 1341), is to enable us to express our thoughts aptly and correctly, whether it is a question of a simple concept or of a composite thought expressed in a sentence.[11] Grammar is therefore different from logic, for the logician is not concerned with the expression of thought but with the distinction between truth and falsity in thought. Moreover, grammar differs from logic in its subject matter. Logic deals with concepts and the modes of knowing, whereas grammar has to do with words, either spoken or written, and their various modes of signifying concepts. There is, however, a close connection between grammar and logic, because the modes of signification studied by the grammarian correspond to the modes of knowing studied by the logician. And since the modes of knowing in turn are based upon the modes of being, which are the concern of the metaphysician, it is clear that grammar is ultimately grounded upon reality and upon metaphysics. That is why a universal grammar, common to all languages, is possible. That is why, too, the speculative grammarians introduce so many philosophical notions into their grammar. For them, the science of grammar must be based upon philosophy, for the grammatical modes of signifying can be explained only by recourse to the ways in which the mind thinks and ultimately to the ways in which things are.

In order to illustrate the type of analysis made by the speculative grammarian, we shall consider his explanation of the two principal parts of speech; namely, the noun and verb.

The function of the noun is to signify what is stable and permanent in reality. Now this is substance. The noun, therefore, primarily signifies substance, although secondarily it can signify any being, substantial or accidental, real or notional, as long as it is conceived after the manner of a substance and in abstraction from movement and change. Even movement itself can be thought of as possessing a stable nature, capable of definition, and hence it can be signified by a noun. Accidents, too, such as qualities and quantities, can be conceived in the manner of substance (for example, "whiteness" and "thirty"), and therefore they can be signified by a noun. A noun differs from a pronoun in that a noun signifies an object distinctly and determinately, whereas a pronoun does so indeterminately. The speculative grammarians liken the pronoun to primary matter in substances: as primary matter can receive any substantial form, so the pronoun is capable of any formal determination. For example, the pronoun "he" can signify any individual man. The case, number, gender of nouns and pronouns are accidental modalities that affect them. They do not belong to the nature of the noun or pronoun, but flow from them somewhat as accidents flow from substance.

Unlike the noun and pronoun, the verb signifies movement, becoming, and the act of being (*esse*).[12] The verb signifies an act or movement as a mode of being predicable of a subject; for example, "Socrates runs," or "Socrates grows." A participle, on the other hand, signifies an act or movement as a mode of being accidentally informing a being; for example, "running Socrates," or "growing Socrates." The verb, like the noun, has its accidental modalities;

namely, mode, conjugation, genus, number, figure, time, and person. These receive extensive treatment at the hands of the speculative grammarians. Finally, they deal with the modes of signifying that are proper to the non-essential parts of speech; for example, adverbs, conjunctions, prepositions, interjections, and so on, all of which are syncategorematic terms.

THE NEW PHYSICS

UP TO FAIRLY RECENT TIMES it was customary to date the beginnings of science in western Europe from the Renaissance. Modern research has made it necessary to revise this notion and to recognize the existence of a scientific renaissance in the Middle Ages that prepared the way for the great achievements in science at the beginning of the modern era.[13] It is now clear that men were engaged in scientific activity at least from the thirteenth century, and that these men are, in the words of Christopher Dawson, "the humble and half-forgotten founders of the long and glorious line of Western scientists." [14]

The rebirth of science in the Middle Ages is all the more remarkable in that the early medieval period was so completely cut off from the ancient scientific world and was so neglectful of scientific studies. Greek philosophical ideas survived in the West, thanks to men such as St. Augustine, Boethius, Dionysius, and Scotus Erigena. The tradition of Latin humanism and classical scholarship, handed down by Cicero and Quintilian, also survived in the Middle Ages; while suffering an eclipse in the Age of the Schoolmen, it never completely died out. But the break between the ancient science of Greece and the early Middle Ages was almost complete. The state of affairs in science is well summed up by Plato of Tivoli, a twelfth-century translator of Arabian scientific literature, who complained that in astronomy the Latin world had nothing but "follies, dreams and old wives' fables." In order to remedy the situation, translators put into Latin the works of Aristotle, Euclid, Ptolemy, Galen, and the Arabian mathematicians and astronomers who continued the scientific work of the Greeks. The result was an awakening of interest among Latin scholars in physical science and in the methods of inquiry that would most effectively unfold the secrets of the universe.

In the thirteenth century Aristotle dominated the world of science as he did that of philosophy. Science during this period remained in general within the framework of his theory of nature. The notions of science itself and of its methods were taken from his *Posterior Analytics*. Natural science was thought to be demonstrative knowledge revealing the reasons for observed phenomena. These "reasons" were summed up in the four causes: material, formal, efficient, and final. A natural being or event was explained when its four causes were assigned to it. Aristotle also taught the Middle Ages the basic methods of science: induction, which proceeds from observed effects to causes; and deduction, which proceeds inversely from causes to effects. In short, he gave the Middle Ages not only a systematic view of the universe far superior to any it knew in accounting for observable phenomena, but also a scientific method for making further discoveries in nature.

As early as the twelfth century the Aristotelian method was put into practice by scientists such as Adelard of Bath. In the thirteenth century Albert the Great used it in his investigations in biology and zoology. At the same time the writings of the Arabians turned the attention of medieval scientists to the importance of mathematics in the study of nature. While recognizing the value of mathematics in astronomy, Aristotle himself did not put the mathematical method into use. His own physics is an investigation of nature through its qualities rather than through the measurement of its quantity. This is a reflection of his predominate interest in science, which was biology rather than the study of the inanimate world. He carried over into the latter the qualitative, descriptive method he used in the investigation of the living world. The result was a qualitative rather than a quantitative physics. Moreover, although Aristotle made simple observations of nature, he knew nothing of controlled experiments to prove or disprove a hypothesis. Once again, it was the Arabs who introduced medieval scientists to this essential feature of the new physics.

In the thirteenth century, therefore, scientists were already in possession of the two methods that eventually transformed natural science and brought about the downfall of Aristotelian physics; namely, the use of mathematics and experimentation. We have already seen Robert Grosseteste and Roger Bacon insist on the necessity of mathematics for a knowledge of nature. We have also seen that Peter of Maricourt conducted experiments in magnetism and that Bacon used the experimental method in his study of the rainbow and other phenomena of light. The German scholar Dietrich of Freiberg (d. *c.* 1311) continued the tradition of Bacon and improved on his theory of the rainbow. As a result of his experiments with water in spherical glass vessels he concluded correctly that the rainbow is caused by a double refraction and a single reflection of light in each raindrop. He also investigated experimentally the shape and colors of the rainbow. These were but simple beginnings that took place within an essentially Aristotelian framework of natural science, but the day would come when the developing use of mathematics and the experimental method would lead to the downfall of Aristotle's physics.

Physics at Oxford

In point of time the Oxford physicists took the lead in using mathematics to study nature. This is hardly surprising, because Oxford was less under the spell of Aristotelianism than Paris. Platonism, which had the special approval of St. Augustine, always remained strong at Oxford, and it favored the study of mathematics and the mathematical approach to physics.

The pioneering work in this field by Grosseteste and Bacon was carried on and extended at Oxford in the fourteenth century by Thomas Bradwardine and the so-called Merton School of physicists. Bradwardine (*c.* 1295–1349) is best known for his theological treatise *De Causa Dei*,[15] but he was also a remarkable mathematician, considering the age in which he lived, and his mathematical study of motion was destined to have far-reaching effects. Like Grosseteste and Bacon, Bradwardine had unlimited confidence in the power of mathematics to unlock the secrets of nature. He writes: ". . . whoever then has the effrontery to study physics while neglecting mathematics should know from the start that he will never make his entry through the portals of wisdom." [16]

That Bradwardine was serious in this contention is clear from his analysis of motion in his treatise on the proportion of velocities.[17] Aristotle and his medieval followers conceived of local motion, as well as all kinds of change, as a process by which the potentiality of a body to movement is made actual by a motive agent. According to Aristotle's definition, motion is "the act of a being in potency insofar as it is in potency." Although valid from a philosophical point of view, this conception of motion hardly interests the mathematician, for, as such, motion does not lend itself to mathematical treatment. Velocity, however, which Aristotle conceived as a property of motion, can be measured. Bradwardine's innovation was to identify motion with velocity, thus making motion itself directly capable of measurement. Velocity, in his view, is a qualitative ratio admitting of degrees, like heat, color, and density, and capable of being stated in a mathematical law. In working out this law Bradwardine found it necessary to correct the dynamics of Aristotle. In his treatment of motion in the *Physics*, Book VII, Aristotle proposed that the velocity of a moving body is doubled if the moving power is doubled or the resistance is halved. Bradwardine considered this law both inadequate and based on a false assumption. It is inadequate because it takes into account only cases in which the ratio of motive power to resistance is 2:1. It is based on a false assumption because, according to the law, a body should move with a given velocity as long as there is a motive power and some resistance. But in fact there is no motion unless the power of the mover is greater than the resistance. Aristotle himself recognized that there are exceptions to his law; for example, the case of a man trying unsuccessfully to move a heavy weight.

Bradwardine worked out a mathematical formula that would be valid for every variation of ratio of motive power to resistance and that covers cases in which no motion results from the application of force to an object. He argued on mathematical grounds that in order to double the velocity of a moving body the ratio of power to resistance must not be doubled but squared, and in order to triple the velocity the ratio must be raised to the third power. Conversely, half the velocity follows from the square root of the ratio, and one-third the velocity from the cube root, and so on. In modern terms this can be expressed by the function: $v = \log (p/r)$. This formula corrects both of the weaknesses in Aristotle's statement. Since the logarithm of $1/1$ is zero, if the ratio between power and resistance is equal, the velocity is zero. Furthermore, this formula holds good for every variation of velocity.

Bradwardine also showed that circular motion (for example, that of the celestial spheres) can be compared to rectilinear motion. This was denied by Aristotle, who considered these two types of motion to be specifically different and incommensurable. Bradwardine was thus on the way toward a unified mathematical explanation of both terrestrial and celestial motion.

In his use of mathematical analysis and in his development of mathematical formulae to express the laws of motion, Bradwardine made a significant advance over his predecessors. His treatment of motion, however, suffers from the serious defect of failing to test his law by empirical observations. We shall have to wait until Galileo for a fruitful union of mathematical analysis and experimental observation in the study of motion.

Bradwardine's treatise on the measurement of velocities was immediately acclaimed by his contemporaries. Its method was adopted and developed not only at Oxford but also at Paris and Padua. At Oxford a group at Merton College followed Bradwardine's example and wrote treatises that used and extended his approach to problems of kinetics. These writers were called "calculators" because of their use of mathematics in measuring local motion and other kinds of change. The most important of these scientists were William Heytesbury (*c.* 1313–1372),[18] John Dumbleton (*fl. c.* 1331–1349), and Richard Swineshead (*fl. c.* 1344–1354). Swineshead wrote a treatise entitled *Liber Calculationum* that earned for him the name "The Calculator." In the seventeenth century Leibniz admired his work and ascribed to him the introduction of mathematics into scholastic philosophy. In fact, Swineshead was simply following in the footsteps of the earlier Oxford mathematicians.

The followers of Bradwardine extended his quantitative expression of local motion to qualitative changes; for example, to increase and decrease in heat, light, and color. The increase and decrease in intensity of these qualities were known as the "intension" and "remission" of forms. Local motion itself was thought to admit of "intension" and "remission" according to the increase and decrease in acceleration. The intensity of local motion or of a quality was identified with a numerical value, and this was related to another number expressing distance, time, or quantity of matter. Changes could thus be classified as uniform or "difform." Local motion, for example, was said to be uniform if equal distances were traversed in equal successive intervals of time. As early as the fourteenth century, graphs were used to indicate the relationship between the intensity of a form and other factors such as time and distance.

William of Ockham, who was Bradwardine's contemporary at Oxford, did not share the mathematical interests of his fellow Oxonians, but his own views on motion were important for the new physics. As we shall see in the next chapter, Ockham's basic principle is that only individual, absolute realities exist; everything else is a name or term standing for these realities or describing them in a concise and convenient way. Now, for Ockham, there are only two kinds of realities: substances and qualities such as color, heat, and weight. Quantity, time, relation, place, motion, velocity, causality are nothing but terms signifying individual substances and their qualities in their varying conditions. Quantity, for example, is not a real accident inhering in a substance and extending it in space. It is a term signifying an existing body with distinct parts and capable of occupying space.[19] Neither is motion a reality distinct from the moving body; it is simply a name signifying a body that is not at rest. According to Ockham's interpretation, Aristotle's definition of motion as "the act of a being in potency" has two parts: one positive (the act of a being), which refers to the individual body; the other negative (in potency), which means the negation of rest. Hence there is no positive reality in a moving body besides the body itself.[20] Motion is not a real process that the body undergoes, nor is it caused by an impulse or impetus given to the body by its mover. Ockham rejects both of these explanations of motion as violating the principle of economy of thought, sometimes called "Ockham's Razor." [21] As we shall see, Ockham insists that explanations should be as simple as possible; no entities should be postulated unless they are absolutely necessary to explain observed phenomena. In the case of motion, all that is required is a body that is not at rest in a place. The term "local motion" is simply a convenient way of expressing the complex phrase: "a body that was in one place, and later will be in another place, in such a way that at no time does it rest in any place." [22] Ockham is here practicing the method of linguistic analysis so popular today among Oxford philosophers. As he sees it, the problem of motion is really one of grammar. As a result, he passes over the philosophical and even the mathematical aspects of the problems involved in motion. Since motion is only a term, there is no need to explain how it starts, continues, or is accelerated. Neither is there any reason for assuming the existence of a mover distinct from the moving body. Ockham thus denies the Aristotelian principle that whatever is moved is moved by another, thereby opening the way to the principle of inertia, although he himself did not formulate it.

Physics at Paris

While these developments in physics were taking place at Oxford, Parisian physicists were also busy trying to solve the problems connected with motion. Outstanding among them was John Buridan, who was twice rector of the University of Paris between 1328 and 1340. One of the problems that engaged his attention was the motion of projectiles. Aristotle was convinced that action at a distance is impossible and consequently that a projectile must have a mover in contact with it all the while it is moving. He theorized that the air plays the role of this mover. When a hand throws a stone, for example, it moves not only the stone but also the surrounding air. This air moves the adjacent air, which keeps the stone in motion until the motive power of the air is exhausted. In other words, Aristotle imagined a continuous air wave closing in behind the projectile and moving it throughout the course of its journey.

As early as the sixth century A.D. this theory of the motion of projectiles was attacked by John Philoponus, a Greek commentator on Aristotle. Philoponus showed by simple observations that air cannot be the cause of the continued motion of projectiles. We can beat the air violently without moving a stone. Bodies passing close to one another are not deflected from their courses by air, but only by colliding with each other. If Aristotle is correct, why can a heavy stone be thrown farther than a light one? For these reasons Philoponus conjectured that the mover imparts directly to the projectile a motive power or energy by which the projectile is moved when no longer in contact with its original source of motion.

The scholastics knew Philoponus' theory of projectile motion through Avicenna and Avempace, and it won considerable support from them in the fourteenth century. At Paris, Buridan accepted it in preference to Aristotle's. To Philoponus' criticism of the Aristotelian theory he added that the air cannot account for the spinning of a disk or grindstone, for their motion continues even when the surrounding air is cut off by a covering. He concluded that the mover must impress on the body it moves an impetus by which the body continues to move until adverse forces bring it to a stop. The impetus given to projectiles is gradually weakened by the resistance of the air and the natural tendency of the body to fall. The impetus of falling bodies, on the other hand, is strengthened by natural gravity, resulting in acceleration. Buridan describes this impetus as a quality added to the substance of the moving body. Like all qualities, it admits of degrees. Its intensity is proportionate to the velocity with which the mover moves the body and to the body's own density or "quantity of matter." In formulating the relation between velocity on the one hand and power and resistance on the other, Buridan used Bradwardine's mathematical law.

Buridan thought that the impetus theory alone fits all the phenomena of moving bodies. It explains why we can throw a stone farther than a feather: because a stone has a greater density, it receives an impetus of greater intensity and it takes longer for the impetus to weaken. For the same reason a big mill wheel is harder to stop than a small one; other things being equal, there is a greater impetus in the former than in the latter. So, too, a man can jump farther by running a longer distance and acquiring a greater impetus. Moreover, when he runs and jumps he does not feel the air moving him but rather resisting him.

A further advantage of this theory is that it permitted Buridan to explain terrestrial and celestial movements by the same principles. It was customary at the time to ascribe the circular motion of the celestial spheres to Intelligences, but Buridan points out that this is an unnecessary supposition. We only have to assume that when God created the universe he set the spheres in motion by impressing on them an impetus which, because the spheres meet no resistance, has moved them ever since. This theory, which Robert Kilwardby anticipated at Oxford in the thirteenth century, greatly simplified medieval astronomy, and it foreshadowed Galileo's notion of *"impeto"* and Descartes' "quantity of movement." It should be pointed out, however, that Buridan, like other late medieval physicists, made his innovations within a basically Aristotelian cosmology. Although these men tried new hypotheses and used mathematics in the study of nature, their physics was dominated by the Aristotelian notions of substance, form, and quality. Only in the seventeenth century was Aristotle's qualitative physics seriously attacked by Descartes, opening the way for a truly quantitative physics.

Buridan's ideas were developed by his pupil Albert of Saxony (*c.* 1316–1390). Albert worked out the theory of a compound impetus to account for the trajectory of a projectile. He argues that the impetus impressed on a projectile at first nullifies the natural force of gravity, but in later stages the impetus is joined to gravitational force until the latter, together with the resistance of the air, overcomes the impetus and the body falls to the ground. Like his master Buridan, he opposes the current notion that the natural place of an element exerts an attractive force (*vis trahens*) upon it. He reasons that if it did, a heavier body would offer a greater resistance to this force than a lighter body, with the result that it would fall more slowly, which, he says, is contrary to experience. Nevertheless, he did not abandon the concepts of natural movement and natural place. Heavy bodies, he claimed, have a natural tendency to move to the gravitational center of the earth, which is the absolute center of the universe.

The speculations of Nicholas Oresme (*c.* 1320–1382) were more daring. While agreeing that our universe has a fixed center, he questions whether the universe itself is fixed in space and whether there cannot be other universes besides our own. He imagines our universe surrounded by an infinite space, which, like Newton, he identifies with the immensity of God. Nothing prevents God from creating many universes within this space, or from moving our universe in a straight line while its spheres remain at rest. Oresme points out that the contrary opinion was condemned by the bishop of Paris in 1277, indicating the theological inspiration of these speculations.[23] As in the case of Nicholas of Cusa, the theological doctrine of the omnipotence of God had a liberating effect on the mind of Oresme, prompting him to entertain theories of the universe different from the Aristotelian.

One of these theories, known to Oresme through the Greek astronomer Heraclides of Pontus, was that the earth revolves daily while the heavens are at rest. Oresme did not think that observation proves the contrary Aristotelian theory that the earth is at rest while the heavens rotate around it. He points out that, although the heavens appear to revolve around the earth, the observation of local motion is always relative to the observer. If a man were situated in the sky and moving about the earth, it would seem to him that the earth were moving, just as to us on earth the sky seems to move. The objection was raised that if the earth revolved from west to east there would be a continuous wind blowing from the east. To this Oresme replies that the air would rotate with the earth, so that there would be no such wind. It was also objected that if the earth were turning, an arrow thrown vertically into the air would not fall to the ground at the spot from which it was thrown. But Oresme explains that on the supposition of the rotation of the earth the arrow would in fact have a twofold motion. It would move upward and also sideward with the motion of the air. So the movement of the arrow would appear the same to an observer on earth whether the earth were moving or not.

Oresme concludes "that it is impossible to show by any observation that the heavens are moving with daily motion and that the earth is not moving in this way." [24]

As a positive argument in favor of the earth's rotation, Oresme contends that all the appearances are explained more simply by the daily motion of the earth than by that of the heavens. God and nature do nothing in vain; but they would if, instead of the simple motion of the earth, they moved the great, complex mechanism of the heavens to gain the same effect. Even before Oresme the supposition of the earth's motion was entertained by a certain master mentioned by Francis of Meyronnes in the early fourteenth century but unfortunately unnamed by him. This master also held that "if the earth were in movement and the heavens at rest, that arrangement would be better."

Oresme was aware that certain texts of Scripture seem to imply the movement of the heavens, but he did not think these had to be interpreted literally. Scripture tells us that God stopped the sun to help Joshua win his battle, but Oresme points out that Scripture often uses everyday language, as when it says that God became angry and repented. Oresme (who was the bishop of Lisieux) saw no insurmountable difficulty in reconciling Scripture with the motion of the earth, unlike some theologians at the time of Galileo. Oresme's attitude was that neither experience, reason, nor Scripture definitely settles the question whether or not the earth moves. In the end, the weight of tradition prevailed in his mind and he adopted the geostatic view of the universe; but his arguments in favor of the hypothesis of the earth's motion were not forgotten during the next few centuries.

XVIII

William of Ockham
and Fourteenth-Century
Nominalism

IN COMPARISON with the thirteenth century, the fourteenth was a period of disunion and disintegration. This can be seen in almost every department of life. The papacy, having reached its apogee in the thirteenth century, began to decline in prestige and power. Among other humiliations, it suffered the so-called Babylonian captivity. In 1305 the pope was forced to leave Rome and to reside at Avignon, largely under the domination of the French king. At the end of the century the Great Schism gave the Church several pretenders to the throne of St. Peter, dividing the allegiance of Christians. The Church was also torn by the heresies of Wyclif and Huss and weakened by a general slackening of the religious spirit. On the political scene, the fourteenth century saw the rise of powerful national kings, shattering the dream of an empire that would embrace all Christians. The Black Death, which probably carried off William of Ockham in the middle of the century, decimated Christendom and contributed in no small measure to the economic and social upheaval of the late Middle Ages.

It is only to be expected that fourteenth-century thought would reflect this tendency toward division and decline. We observe the hardening of scholasticism into several different schools, the chief of which were the Thomist, Scotist, and Ockhamist, whose rivalry was often bitter and uncompromising. Skepticism in philosophy permeated the atmosphere. Human reason, which soared to such heights in the previous century, began to grow weary and to distrust itself. Many of the truths considered demonstrable by human reason in the thirteenth century were now held only on faith, with reason giving simply probable arguments in their support.

William of Ockham

THIS DISENGAGING of faith from reason, already noticeable at the end of the thirteenth century, was one of the characteristics of the late Middle Ages. We have already observed signs of it in Scotism, but it is even more plainly evident in Ockhamism.[1]

THEOLOGY AND PHILOSOPHY

THE NOTIONS OF THEOLOGY and of its relation to philosophy underwent a drastic revision in Ockhamism. One of the chief aims of St. Thomas was to defend the scientific character of theology and to show that it is in fact the noblest of all the sciences. Ockham, on the other hand, refuses to grant it the status of a science in the proper sense of the term because it rests upon faith and authority rather than upon evidence. Science in the proper sense he defines as evident knowledge, whether the evidence comes from experience, from principles, or from conclusions drawn from evident principles. The beliefs held on divine faith are true, but because they lack evidence they are not, strictly speaking, knowledge or science.[2]

Ockham also denies to theology the universality attributed to it by St. Thomas. As we have seen, St. Thomas considered the scope of theology to be unlimited, for it embraces all truths, whether actually revealed by God or known by reason and used by the theologian to understand revelation. This means that all philosophical and scientific truths can enter into theology, because the theologian can use all of them to elucidate, to explain, and to defend the faith. Their relation to revelation brings them under the formal object of theology, which is "the divinely revealable." For St. Thomas this does not entail the elimination of the various philosophical disciplines, each of which has its own formal object and method, distinct from those of theology. Ockham, however, sees this as the denial of any other knowledge besides theology, for he rejects the distinction of sciences by their formal objects. In his view, each science is a rather loose collection of related habits and propositions, so that no other science is possible, or indeed necessary, if all propositions belong to theology. Theology would be the sole body of knowledge, and the other sciences would lose their independence.[3]

The scope of theology is limited by its purpose, which is to lead man to eternal happiness. Hence only those truths are theological that are conducive to salvation.[4] For each of these truths there is a distinct habit of belief in the mind; for example, each of the articles of the Creed has its corresponding mental disposition of belief. At the basis of all these theological habits lies the divinely infused habit of faith. Theology is consequently not a single habit of the soul capable of unlimited development, as St. Thomas taught, but a collection of habits united by their common purpose of leading man to salvation.

Similarly, each of the branches of philosophy is a collection of related mental habits. Metaphysics or logic, for example, is not one habit of the mind but an ordered group of habits. Since these habits are expressed outwardly by written propositions, a science can also be called an ordered collection of propositions. In this latter sense Ockham speaks of Aristotle's book of *Metaphysics* as the science of metaphysics. The unity of a science is consequently that of an ordered whole, similar to the unity of an army or city. And just as a man is not by nature a member of an army or city, neither is a certain truth by nature theological or metaphysical. It can become theological or metaphysical, or both, by being incorporated into theology or metaphysics. Of course the theologian considers some subjects that are not the concern of the metaphysician; for example, the Trinity and Incarnation. Since these are known only through divine revelation, we should not expect to

find propositions about them in metaphysics. But there is a wide
range of truths about God that are, so to speak, neutral, and these
can be incorporated into both theology and metaphysics; for example, the wisdom and goodness of God.[5]

Because a science is a collection of many truths or propositions,
it is not limited to one subject. The propositions in a science may
have different subjects. For example, some propositions in metaphysics have being for their subject, while God is the subject of
others. So we cannot say that metaphysics has one subject. It is as
meaningless to ask: "What is the subject of logic or mathematics?"
as it is to ask: "Who is the king of the world?" Each kingdom
has its own ruler, and so, too, each part of a science has its own
subject.[6]

The unity of a science, therefore, is not based upon the unity
of its subject. Neither is it based on the unity of its object, for
each science has many objects. The objects of a science are the
propositions it contains. This is true of both logic (rational science)
and the sciences of reality (real sciences). "Every science," Ockham writes, "whether it be real or rational, is concerned only with
propositions as with objects known, for only propositions are
known." [7] This does not mean that science has nothing to do with
reality. The propositions of "real science," such as natural science
and metaphysics, are composed of terms that stand for individual
things existing outside the mind. The terms of logical propositions, on the other hand, stand for concepts in the mind. So the
sciences of reality do treat of the real world, but only indirectly
and improperly; their proper objects are the terms and propositions that substitute for realities when we think and write about
them.

In conceiving theology and the branches of philosophy as collections of mental habits or of propositions arranged according to
some principle, Ockham was one of the initiators of the modern
notion of science as an ordered body of knowledge or a collection
of propositions. His reason for making this radical departure from
earlier notions of science will become evident when we examine
his nominalistic doctrine of knowledge.

GOD

OCKHAM'S SKEPTICAL ATTITUDE toward human reason is nowhere more evident than in his criticism of the Scotistic proof of the existence of God. As we have seen, Scotus offered a proof of the existence of the Christian God; that is to say, of a Being who is absolutely supreme and perfect, unique and infinite, the efficient and final cause of all things. Ockham did not think natural reason capable of demonstrating the existence of such a being. At best it can give probable arguments in favor of his existence; faith alone convinces us of it.

The main weakness in Scotus' proof of the existence of God, in Ockham's opinion, is the distinction between an accidentally and an essentially ordered series of causes. That Ockham casts doubt upon this central element in the proof is not surprising, for, as we shall see, he denies the reality of essences and consequently an essential order among beings. He asks us to consider a series of efficient causes of the same kind; for example, a series of men each of whom begets a son. It is difficult, if not impossible, he says, to prove that there cannot be an infinite regress in causes of this sort, so that the series has no primary efficient cause. If someone maintains (as Scotus did) that in this case the whole infinite series depends on an eternal Being extrinsic to the series, Ockham retorts that it would be difficult to prove this. How can we prove that each man in the series is not the cause of the total being of his son? In that case the series is self-sufficient and needs no extrinsic cause to explain it.

Ockham finds the proof more convincing if it is stated in terms of conserving causes instead of producing or efficient causes. An effect produced is conserved in existence as long as it endures, so that its conserving cause must be simultaneous with it. Now this conserving cause is either the primary conserver or it is itself conserved in existence by something else. In this case we cannot proceed to infinity but must arrive at a primary conserver, for it is "reasonable enough" to suppose that there cannot be an infinite number of actually existing conserving causes.[8]

Reasonable arguments can therefore be given for the existence of a primary conserver of the world. But it cannot be proved that there is only one such being. Other worlds are possible besides our own and consequently other primary conserving causes. No demonstration is possible of an absolutely primary cause or of a Being than which none greater can be conceived. Many primary causes are possible, each of which is uncaused and independent of the others. In short, human reason cannot satisfactorily prove that there is only one God.[9]

Indeed, from the point of view of human reason, it is possible that the primary efficient cause of our world is simply the heavenly bodies, in which case we need not suppose the existence of God in the Christian sense of the term. How in fact can natural reason prove that God is the efficient cause of any effect? The only way we know that one thing is the efficient cause of something else is by experiencing that the latter follows upon the presence of the former. "An efficient cause," Ockham writes, "is defined as that whose existence or presence is followed by something." [10] The relation of an efficient cause to its effect is simply one of sequence, and this sequence can be known only by experience. Now we experience the effects of the heavenly bodies upon our world, but not God's. The heavenly bodies adequately account for the coming into being and passing away of things in this world, and it cannot be proven that these bodies have been produced by an efficient cause. Ockham adds that for the same reason we cannot demonstrate the existence of an intellectual soul in man or that if there is such a soul it has been produced by an efficient cause.[11]

Just as there is no adequate proof that God is the efficient cause of the universe, so there is none that he is its final cause. The term "final cause" in this context means that God foreordains and wills creatures to act as they do. But neither experience nor any evident proposition convinces us that the heavenly Intelligences or natural agents act in view of an end intended by God. True, natural agents act uniformly, but they would act in this way whether God intended it or not; they act by natural necessity and not for an end.[12]

THE DIVINE ATTRIBUTES

MOST OF THE ATTRIBUTES of the Christian God are consequently beyond the reach of human reason. In this respect Ockham goes farther than Scotus, adding to the Scotistic list of un-
demonstrable attributes the infinity and oneness of God. Some
divine attributes are knowable by reason, according to Ockham,
such as God's wisdom and goodness, but most are known only by
faith.

What relation have these attributes to God himself? In solving
this problem Ockham asks us to keep in mind the nature of an
attribute: it is something "said" or predicated of a subject. Now
realities are not "said" or predicated, but only terms. So the divine
attributes are, properly speaking, terms. Now when we use terms
in propositions, whether as subjects or predicates, they stand for
something. The property of terms standing for something is
called *supposition*. Following the current logic, Ockham distinguishes between three kinds of supposition: material, simple, and
personal. Material supposition is the standing of a term for itself;
for example, the term "man" in the proposition "Man is a noun."
Here the term stands for itself as a written or spoken word. Simple supposition is the standing of a term for a concept in the mind.
For example, in the proposition "Man is a species" the word
"man" stands for the species "man," which, according to Ockham,
is not a reality but a concept in the mind. Personal supposition is
the standing of a term for individual things. For example, in the
proposition "man runs" the word "man" stands for individual persons who run. In personal supposition the term not only stands
for something but it also *signifies* it. No signification is involved in
the other types of supposition. For Ockham, signification is present
only when a term points out or refers to individual things.[13]

The problem of the divine attributes is quite easy to solve if we
keep in mind this doctrine of supposition and signification. In the
proposition "God is good" the term "good" has personal supposition because it stands for God himself and by the same token signifies him. Obviously, the term "good" is not identical with God,

for God is a reality and not a term. The term simply substitutes for and signifies God when we speak about him. The same is true of all terms attributed to God. They differ as terms, but the reality they stand for is identical; namely, God himself.

It should now be clear that the question whether there is any distinction between the divine attributes admits of two replies. If the question concerns the attributes themselves, they differ from each other as distinct concepts or words. But if the question concerns the reality they stand for, they are in every sense identical. The goodness of God is identical with his wisdom, and both are identical with his essence (that is, his deity). If this were not so, God would be composed of many perfections and he would not be an absolutely simple being. The divine simplicity excludes any distinction between the divine attributes in God himself.[14]

In Ockham's view, both the Scotist and Thomist doctrines of the divine attributes contradict the simplicity of God. As we have seen, Scotus posited a formal distinction between the divine attributes. By this he meant a distinction between the essences of these attributes in God himself and not simply a distinction between our concepts of them. The divine goodness, for example, is formally non-identical with the divine wisdom on the part of God himself. Ockham, however, denies any philosophical validity to the formal distinction.[15] His criticism of Scotus on this point is a good illustration of his logicism; that is to say, his use of a logical principle to settle a philosophical problem. The only method he admits of proving a distinction between beings is the application of the logical principle of non-contradiction. If we can say: A is in every respect the same as A, but B is not in every respect the same as A, then it follows that A and B are distinct. Now when we apply this rule to beings, we discover only three kinds of distinction between them: 1] a real distinction between things,   2] a distinction of reason between concepts,   3] an unnamed distinction between things and concepts. The Scotists add to these a formal distinction between quiddities existing in things. They point out that the principle of non-contradiction applies to quiddities as well as to things and concepts. The divine wisdom, for example, is a quiddity that is not in every respect the same as the divine goodness. Hence these

attributes are formally or quidditatively distinct in God while being really identical.

To this, Ockham replies that the principle of non-contradiction
admits of no degrees. When applied to reality it proves but one
type of distinction; namely, a distinction between things (*res*), one
of which can exist without the other. For example, it is true to
say that a man is rational and that an ass is irrational. And, since
these are realities, we can infer that a man is really distinct from
an ass. The Scotists urge that contradictories can likewise be attributed to the divine goodness and wisdom, from which they
deduce that these divine perfections are formally distinct. Ockham
retorts that he can just as easily say that a man and an ass are
formally, and not really, distinct. In short, there is no criterion to
differentiate between a formal and a real distinction. By introducing the formal distinction, the Scotists destroy the only method
we have of proving a real distinction; namely, the principle of
non-contradiction. Ockham prefers to keep the method and to
eliminate the formal distinction.

Ockham concludes that if the distinction between the divine
attributes is not real or formal it must be a distinction of reason
(*distinctio rationis*).[16] On this point he agrees with St. Thomas,
but he does not think the latter correctly understood the nature
of this kind of distinction. According to St. Thomas, a distinction
of reason is a distinction between concepts, but it can have a foundation in reality. The divine attributes are a case in point. The
divine being is too immense for us to conceive it adequately by
means of one concept, so we attempt to make up for this deficiency
by conceiving it by many concepts. The fullness of the divine
being is consequently the foundation of the distinction of our
concepts of God, and because of this foundation St. Thomas does
not hesitate to say that the *ratio* (that is, meaning) of wisdom and
goodness *differ in God*.[17] That is why, according to St. Thomas,
every added concept of God increases our knowledge of him. Ockham denies this, however, for he rejects any foundation in God
for the diversity of concepts we form of him. He insists that one
reality can never be the basis for several concepts: a diversity of
concepts always points to a diversity of realities. Hence the

diversity of our concepts of God is meaningful only when they include a reference to other realities besides God. If we conceive God as wise and good, the concepts of wisdom and goodness have exactly the same meaning as far as God is concerned; they both signify the one, simple, divine reality. They differ in meaning only inasmuch as they connote a reference to created wisdom and goodness, which are really distinct qualities in creatures.

We attribute to God both a will and an intellect, but there is no distinction in him between these two powers. The concepts "will" and "intellect," when applied to God, have exactly the same meaning; namely, God himself. So it is not absurd to say that God wills through his intellect and knows through his will, for in him, intellect and will are one reality. Ockham acknowledges that this is not the usual way of speaking and that he is establishing a new use of terms in saying that God knows through his will. Ordinarily when theologians speak of the divine intellect and will they do not use these terms precisely to signify God. Rather, they use them connotatively; that is to say, the terms principally signify God but secondarily something created. When used in this way the terms differ in meaning because of the different created perfections connoted, and it is impossible to say that God knows through his will and wills through his intellect.[18]

Ockham is consequently in verbal agreement with the great theologians of the thirteenth century, but in reality his doctrine of the divine attributes is a denial of the science of theology as they conceived it. These theologians, each in his own way, thought that their knowledge of God increased in proportion to the necessary attributes they demonstrated of him. Each attribute demonstrated of God added something to the theologian's knowledge of him not given by the other attributes, because the diversity of attributes is in some way based upon God himself. Ockham denies this foundation and with it the significance of the diversity of our concepts of God, as far as God himself is concerned. As Scotus warned, the deduction of the divine attributes becomes a useless play of concepts, for God is known as well by one concept as by all of them. It is hardly surprising that interest in scholastic theology declined as the influence of Ockhamism pervaded the schools, and that theologians turned to a more patristic type of theology, emphasizing the reading of Scripture and the linguistic study of it.

THE DIVINE IDEAS

WE HAVE ALREADY NOTED that for Ockham the creation of the world is a tenet of faith and not a matter of philosophical demonstration. The same is true of God's knowledge of other things besides himself. Only probable arguments can be given in favor of these religious beliefs.

Granted, however, that God has created the world and that he knows the beings he has created, can he be said to have Ideas of them, and if so what are these Ideas? It was the current opinion that the divine Ideas were the models according to which God produced his creatures. We have seen Duns Scotus call them the essences of possible creatures, existing in the divine mind with their own special cognitional or objective being. We have also seen St. Thomas identify the divine Ideas with God himself insofar as he is capable of being participated by creatures. But neither the Scotist nor the Thomist solution of this problem was acceptable to Ockham. If, as Scotus thought, the divine Ideas have their own being distinct from that of the divine essence, there are many beings in God and he is not absolutely simple. On the other hand, if St. Thomas is correct and the being of God is identical with his Ideas, there can be only one divine Idea.

Ockham finds his way out of this impasse by denying that the divine Ideas have any being at all in God. They are neither identical with God nor realities eternally existing in the divine mind. Since they are not God, they must be creatures—the infinity of creatures God can create. But before creation they have no positive being; rather, they must be classified among non-beings or "nothings." In terms of modern logic they belong to the null-class; that is to say, the class without any real members. Each of the divine Ideas is a "nothing" (*nihil*), but not in the sense in which this term is applied to an impossible being like a chimera. A chimera cannot exist, whereas a creature can if God produces it. A "nothing" prior to creation, a creature begins to be at the moment God creates it.

Before this, it had no positive being or status in the divine mind.[19]

The motives behind this remarkable doctrine of the divine Ideas are not difficult to discover. Ockham has no intention to deny that God creates intelligently and by means of Ideas. However, his conception of the divine simplicity as impervious to all distinction prevents him from ascribing any being to these Ideas. God cannot contain a multitude of Ideas and at the same time be absolutely one. Ockham's conclusion is surprising but consistent with his principles: a creature is a "nothing" which God knows from all eternity as capable of being created. With this negative status, the divine Ideas do not conflict with the absolute simplicity of God, yet they guarantee that God knows things other than himself.

Several important consequences follow from this doctrine. First, since the divine Ideas have no being of their own, they have not existed from all eternity, but they began *to be* at creation. Prior to creation they were simply an infinity of "nothings." Second, God did not know creatures as positive beings before his act of creation. Man or stone, for example, did not always exist; at creation they began to exist and to be positive objects of knowledge. Third, creatures are entirely dependent upon God's will both for their actual existence and for their intelligibility. Contrary to Duns Scotus, God does not necessarily produce within his mind the intelligible essences of creatures. These essences are nothing but creatures themselves, and they are the result of a free decision on God's part to create. In this way Ockham escapes the necessitarianism of Greek and Arabian philosophy even more completely than Duns Scotus, because not only is the actual existence of creatures dependent on the free will of God but also their intelligible natures. Fourth, since creatures are individual beings, there are divine Ideas of individuals but not of universals, such as genera and species. God has no need of universal ideas in order to create; ideas of individuals suffice. A created artist makes use of general ideas, but this is an inferior mode of knowing that is unworthy of God, who has a distinct and particular knowledge of every thing he can create.[20] The far-reaching consequences of this latter point will be obvious if we consider Ockham's notion of reality and universals.

REALITY AND UNIVERSALS

ONE OF OCKHAM's cardinal principles—indeed, the foundation of his metaphysics—is that universals exist only in the mind; everything outside the mind is by that very fact individual. Others before him said the same thing, but he thought all his predecessors compromised this principle by admitting that in some way universal natures exist in reality. "All those whom I have seen," he writes, "agree that there is really in the individual a nature that is in some way universal, at least potentially and incompletely, although some say that it is really distinguished [from the individual], some that it is distinguished only formally, some that the distinction is in no way in reality but only according to reason and the consideration of the intellect." [21]

Ockham here lists in decreasing order of realism the three main positions on universals known to him. The first, which he calls Platonic, is the most extreme form of realism, because it posits a real distinction between the individual and its nature; for example, between Socrates and humanity. The second, which he ascribes to Duns Scotus, is a lesser form of realism, because it grants only a formal distinction between the individual and its nature. The third, which is that of St. Thomas, is the least realistic of all, positing only a distinction of reason between the two. After examining each of these positions and stating his objections to them, Ockham presents his own, which in the Middle Ages was called nominalist or terminist, because it identifies universals with names or terms, either mental, spoken, or written.

Ockham dismisses the first type of realism as absolutely false and absurd. A universal cannot be really distinct from the individuals in which it exists, because if two beings are really distinct they can exist separately, at least through the power of God. But it is absurd to think that God could create man-in-general without creating individual men, or that he could create individual men without at the same time creating man. Furthermore, if man were really distinct from individual men, it could not be predicated of them. We could not say that Socrates is a man, because man would be only a part of Socrates, really distinct from the other elements in him. But we cannot predicate a part of a whole; we cannot, for example, say that Socrates is his body or hand. The fact that we can predicate man of Socrates shows that human nature is not really distinct from him as an individual. In fact, as we have already seen, "man" is simply a term standing for individual men in propositions.

More attention is given by Ockham to the second position, which posits a formal distinction between individuals and the natures they have in common. He identifies its author as "the Subtle Doctor, who surpassed the others in keenness of judgment." [22] After this word of praise for Scotus, Ockham gives an extended criticism of his doctrine of the common nature and its formal distinction from the individuals in which it exists. The main point of his attack is that Scotus confused logic with metaphysics, or concepts with reality. Scotus was impressed by Avicenna's statement that an essence, such as animality, can be conceived in three different ways: as universal in the mind, as individual in reality, and simply in itself as animality. From this, Scotus concluded that an essence has a reality in itself and that it is really indifferent to being individual or universal. But Ockham points out that Avicenna merely claimed that an essence can be *conceived* in three different ways, not that it has three different modes of being. It is true that an essence can be conceived in itself, in abstraction from individuality and universality, but it does not follow that it has a reality in itself or that it has a real indifference to various modes of being. Animality is simply an abstract concept, and its indifference to individuality and universality is not in the real order but in the logical order. We can predicate indifferently "individual" and "universal" of the concept "animality" by saying: "Animality is individual," and "Animality is universal." In the first proposition the supposition of the term "animality" is personal, because the term stands for individual animals; in the second the supposition is simple, because the term stands for the concept "animal." There are consequently universal concepts in the mind and individual things in reality, but there is no need to suppose that there exist in reality essences or quiddities formally distinct from individual things.[23]

In thus eliminating from reality the Scotist common natures, Ockham makes use of his logical notion of simple supposition, which he defines as the standing of a term for a concept in the mind. We have already seen Peter of Spain, in the thirteenth century, define this type of supposition as "the taking of a universal term for a universal reality signified by that term." [24] Peter of Spain's definition is geared to a realist doctrine of universals, since it presupposes the existence of universal realities which common terms stand for and signify. Ockham redefined simple supposition to fit his own nominalism. According to him, there are no universal realities for common terms to stand for; there are only universal concepts in the mind. Furthermore, universal terms do not signify the concepts they take the place of in discourse; they signify individual things. This is but one instance of the innovations Ockham made in logic in order to bring it into line with his metaphysical conception of reality as radically individual.

Ockham's rejection of the Scotist common nature entailed the elimination of a host of Scotist doctrines dependent upon it. 1] Since every reality is individual by itself, there is no need of an added principle of individuation, or haecceity, to render it individual. 2] For the same reason, the only real unity is the numerical unity of individual things; there is no real unity that is less than numerical. 3] The primary object of our knowledge is not a common nature but an individual thing. We shall presently return to this point. 4] Two individuals are really related to each other *by themselves* and not by a real relation distinct from them. Moreover, there is no common nature serving as a real foundation for the relation. 5] There is no communication in form or being between an efficient cause and its effect. Efficient causality is simply a term designating the fact that one thing is observed to follow another.

After this critique of Scotism, Ockham turns his attention to the position that there is simply a distinction of reason between the individual and universal.[25] Those upholding this thesis (among whom Ockham appears to include St. Thomas) maintain that something individual in reality can be universal when it is understood by the intellect. The intellect confers universality upon it by giving it a new mode of being within itself. But to Ockham this appears to contradict the basic principle that everything outside the intellect is individual. If we take this principle seriously, it is contrary to the very nature of an individual to be common to several things, or universal. Consequently, an individual can never be made universal by being understood or by receiving a new mode of being in the intellect.

Ockham makes his point clear in his criticism of Henry of Harclay, a contemporary at Oxford. According to Harclay, an individual thing can be conceived either distinctly or indistinctly. When distinctly conceived, the intellect forms a particular concept of it; when indistinctly conceived, the intellect forms a universal concept of it. For example, we can form a distinct concept of Socrates representing him alone, but we can also form a vague concept of him representing Plato as well. Harclay concludes that an individual is universal when indistinctly conceived.[26] But even this slight trace of realism is abhorrent to Ockham. If Harclay is correct, he says, Plato is Socrates indistinctly conceived, and God is a creature vaguely understood. But this is absurd, for one individual reality can never be another. Under no circumstances, then, is an individual common or universal.[27]

This leaves open the question of the nature of a universal. Ockham tells us that a universal is a sign of many things. And since there are two kinds of signs, conventional and natural, there are two corresponding types of universals. Spoken and written words are examples of conventional signs; they have been arbitrarily instituted to signify certain objects. The proof of this is the plurality of languages in the world. Some signs, however, are natural. Groaning, for example, is a natural sign of pain, and smoke is a natural sign of fire. Natural signs are facts of nature and consequently they do not differ from one country or people to another. Concepts are natural signs of individual things.[28] If the concept is the sign of only one thing it is an individual concept; if it is the sign of many things it is a universal concept.

In itself every sign is an individual thing. This is true whether the sign is a word or a concept. Its universality lies in the fact that it signifies many things. Universality is therefore a matter of signification; it is not itself a thing or reality. This leaves Ockham's principle intact, that every *thing* is individual; there are no universal things or realities.

What kind of being or reality does a concept have? In his early writings [29] Ockham presents three theories, all of which he considers defensible: 1] A concept is a mental fiction (*fictum*) or resemblance, made by the intellect as a representation of the thing known. According to this theory, a concept has only objective being; that is to say, its being consists in being-an-object-of-knowledge (its *esse* is its *cognosci*). This is not a type of real being, nor does it fall under Aristotle's ten categories. 2] A concept is a real quality existing in the soul as in a subject, so that it is said to have subjective being. According to this theory, the concept is a likeness of the object known, distinct from the act of knowing and posterior to it. 3] A concept is a real quality of the soul, as the second theory maintains, but it is identical with the act of knowing. A particular concept is a distinct act of knowing, while a universal concept is a confused and indistinct act. This theory allows for no mental representation or likeness of the object known prior or posterior to the act of knowing. The act of knowing, in short, is the sole intellectual instrument of knowledge.

In his later writings [30] Ockham discards the first two theories of the concept in favor of the third. The reason for his choice was his love of simple explanations and his desire to remove from philosophy all unnecessary suppositions; but deeper than this was his growing realization of the harmony of the third theory with his metaphysical and epistemological principles.

KNOWLEDGE

OCKHAM DIVIDES KNOWLEDGE into two kinds: incomplex and complex. Incomplex knowledge is the knowledge of terms and the simple objects for which they stand; for example, "Socrates," "man," "white." Complex knowledge is the knowledge of propositions formed from terms; for example, "Socrates is a white man." Incomplex knowledge is divided in turn into two kinds: intuitive and abstractive. By intuitive knowledge we can judge that something exists or does not exist. For example, if we see Socrates, we can judge that he exists. Abstractive knowledge, on the other hand, does not provide the evidence enabling us to judge that something exists or not. For example, if we form the image of Socrates in our imagination, this does not permit us to judge that he exists or does not exist.[31]

Our knowledge of the external world begins with sense intuition or perception. This is immediately followed by an intellectual intuition of the same object. There is only one case in which intellectual intuition is not preceded by sense knowledge; namely, knowledge of our own acts of understanding and willing, and of our states of soul like pleasure and sadness. Ockham is in the tradition of St. Augustine in claiming that we have a direct intellectual experience of these intelligible objects without any previous sense perception.[32]

Intuitive knowledge is experimental knowledge of individual things. The object of simple abstractive knowledge, on the other hand, is not primarily an individual but a universal. Nevertheless, an individual can be known abstractively (that is, in abstraction from existence) as well as a universal. Thus intuitive and abstractive knowledge do not differ because of their objects. In themselves they are two radically different kinds of cognition; they do not differ by their objects or causes but simply by themselves.[33]

Scotus based the distinction between intuitive and abstractive knowledge on their objects: the object of intuitive knowledge is something existing and present to the knower, whereas the object of abstractive knowledge need not exist or be present. Ockham rejects this distinction because he thinks there can be an intuition of a non-existent thing. This doctrine, which has been the object of much controversy among historians, is deeply rooted in Ockham's conception of the universe as composed of radically distinct individuals. He points out that an intuition is an absolute reality (a quality of the mind) really distinct in place and subject from its object. When I see a star in the sky, for example, my vision of the star is a reality distinct from the star itself. Now in the ordinary course of nature God causes the sight of the star by means of the star. But, absolutely speaking, he does not need to use secondary causes to produce his effects. We hold on faith that he is omnipotent and that he can cause directly what he ordinarily causes by means of creatures. Hence there is nothing to prevent him from performing a miracle and causing the sight of a star even though it does not exist.[34]

The question here at stake is what God can do, absolutely speaking, because he is omnipotent. Ockham never doubted that in the normal course of events the object perceived is really the cause of our perception; in short, that the material world really exists and is the immediate cause of our knowledge. Two other qualifications must be added. It would be impossible for God to give us an intuition of something that neither actually nor possibly exists; for example, an intuition of a chimera. This mythical animal cannot possibly exist, and so it would be contradictory for God to give us an intuition of it by which we would judge that it exists. In other words, the objects of intuitive knowledge must be either actually or possibly existing things.[35] In this respect they resemble the divine Ideas, which are non-beings eternally seen by God, some of which he creates, but all of which are at least possible beings. If God gave us an intuition of a non-existent thing, it would be an intuition of a "nothing" in the sense in which God's Ideas are "nothings."

The final qualification is that if the intuition of a non-existing thing were perfect, through this intuition we would clearly know that the thing does not exist. We would mistakenly judge that it exists only if the intuition were imperfect. Because God is omnipotent he can cause us to assent to the proposition "This white thing exists" even though it does not; but our assent would lack the evidence furnished by true intuitive knowledge. The assent would be of the same kind as that caused by a true intuition, but because it would not be based on evidence it would more properly be an act of belief.[36]

Ockham, as a Christian, is concerned above all with upholding the omnipotence of God; but at the same time, as a philosopher, he is preoccupied with the problem of evidence as the basis of assent. His doctrine of the intuition of non-existing things blends together an empiricism according to which every evident assent must be based on the experience of individual existents, and a theology according to which God is all-powerful and knows no law except that of non-contradiction.

"OCKHAM'S RAZOR"

OCKHAM'S LOVE of simple explanations has already been noted. It was axiomatic for him that "a plurality is not to be posited without necessity." This principle of economy of thought, sometimes called "Ockham's Razor," was not original with him. It was a common dictum of the scholastics and it can be traced back to Aristotle. But Ockham's use of it was new because of his empiricism and nominalism.

One instance of his use of the principle is to eliminate representative likenesses (called "species") as means by which we know reality. Ockham considers both sensible and intelligible species to be superfluous for intuitive knowledge, and after some hesitation he extends this to abstractive knowledge. Objects of knowledge need not acquire within the mind an intelligible or phenomenal being as a medium by which they are known. All that is required to explain knowledge is an act of knowing and individual realities as its object.[37] As for our knowledge of unrealities, such as a chimera or non-being, we need not suppose that these are objects with an intelligible being in the mind. In their case all that is in the mind is an act of knowing to which nothing corresponds in reality. In short, they are acts of knowing without an object.[38]

Not only are sensible and intelligible likenesses superfluous to explain knowledge; if they existed they would stand in the way of our knowing reality. They are supposed to represent reality and to make it present to our intellect, but how can we recognize them as likenesses unless we first know the realities they resemble? How can we know that a statue is a likeness of a man if we do not first know the man? Now the defenders of representative likenesses claim that these likenesses come before every act of knowledge. But if this were true, our knowledge would stop at them and we would never know reality itself.[39] The validity of this argument rests upon Ockham's assumption (denied by St. Thomas and Duns Scotus) that sensible and intelligible species are likenesses of reality in the same way that a statue represents a man. Ockham presupposes that all signs must be known prior to the things they signify; there are no signs or likenesses whose whole function is to lead to a knowledge of something else, and which are not themselves direct objects of knowledge.

Ockham also uses the principle of economy of thought to eliminate the distinction between the agent and possible intellects. According to him, these intellects are identical in reality; they differ only as terms with different connotations. The agent intellect designates the soul as actively producing knowledge; the possible intellect designates the same soul as passively receiving knowledge.[40]

Ockham can find no compelling reason to hold that man is endowed with an agent intellect in the traditional sense of the term.[41] Philosophers, he says, were of the opinion that this intellect illuminates phantasms and the possible intellect, thereby abstracting intelligible natures from things. But there are no essences or natures in individual things to be abstracted from them. Abstraction, for Ockham, is simply the act whereby the intellect produces a general or universal concept. This it does through the intuitive knowledge of one or more things alike in some respect. For example, a person seeing one or more particular white things abstracts from them whiteness in general. This does not mean that whiteness is an essence in some way present in white things which the intellect disengages from them. It simply means that on seeing one or more white objects the intellect can elicit so indistinct an act of knowing that its object is any white thing whatsoever. As we have already noted, this indistinct act of knowing is the universal concept of whiteness. As for the manner in which the intellect elicits this act, Ockham has not much to say. He simply observes that universals are produced by nature in a mysterious way, without attempting to probe this secret of nature.[42]

ETHICS

OCKHAM'S ETHICAL NOTIONS follow consistently from his nominalistic views of man and reality in general.[43] The fundamental ethical problem is the nature of goodness, or more exactly the nature of moral goodness. The scholastics prior to Ockham looked upon goodness as a property of being. St. Thomas, for example, speaks of goodness as the perfection of being that renders it desirable. Because God is all-perfect and supremely desirable, he is supremely good. A creature is good to the extent that it achieves the perfection demanded by its nature. Moral goodness consists in man's acting in accordance with his nature, with a view to attaining his final end (happiness), which is identical with the perfection of his being. For St. Thomas, therefore, morality has a metaphysical foundation, and it links man with God, giving him a share in the divine goodness and perfection.

Ockham, on the other hand, severs the bond between metaphysics and ethics and bases morality not upon the perfection of human nature (whose reality he denies), nor upon the teleological relation between man and God, but upon man's obligation to follow the laws freely laid down for him by God.[44]

Goodness, in Ockham's opinion, is not a property of being but a term signifying that something is as it ought to be. A knife is good, for example, if it is made as it should be in view of the function for which it has been designed. Now the will determines what a thing or action should be. The notion of goodness is therefore tied up with that of will: something is good if it is in conformity with a will exterior to itself. We can say, therefore, that all creatures are good, for they have been created by God in conformity with his will. But it is meaningless to speak of God as good, for there is no will external to himself determining what he should be or do. God is a law unto himself; he is absolute master of himself and of his actions. Goodness, therefore, is not an essential property of God.[45]

Because God is omnipotent and absolutely free, he is not bound to impose a given set of laws upon men. We should not imagine him as ruled by an eternal or divine law, from which human laws flow as necessary conclusions from premises. The laws he imposes on men are completely arbitrary, so that he can change or annul them at will. In order to make this point as clear as possible, Ockham chooses the most extreme examples. God has commanded us to love him, but nothing prevents him from changing this order and commanding us to hate him. If God decided to change the first commandment in this way, we would be obliged to hate him just as we are now obliged to love him. Indeed, it would then be meritorious for us to hate God because we would be carrying out his will. Similarly, adultery is wrong in the present moral order, but God can change this order and make adultery good and meritorious.[46] This makes it clear that a human act is good simply because God wills it and not because it is in accord with human nature preconceived by God or because it is conducive to man's perfection or happiness. The only law binding God as a legislator is that of non-contradiction. He cannot order a man to love and hate him at the same time. However, he can impose these contradictory orders on a man at different times or on two different men at the same time.

Although God is free to legislate as he wills, he has in fact laid down a particular moral code that all men are obliged to respect and obey. We should not think of God as an absolute ruler who is constantly changing his laws for men. In creating them, he has established a moral code which they must freely obey, just as in creating the universe he has established physical laws which inanimate things naturally follow. For example, he has ordained that fire heats, although he could have decreed that fire cools. Hence there is a natural morality and a natural law which even the pagans can discover and which they are obliged to follow. The consciences of men prompt them to perform some acts as good and to avoid others as bad, and they are obliged to follow the dictates of their conscience or right reason.[47] These dictates, however, are not rooted in human nature, nor are they necessary consequences of that nature. They are simply expressions in men of God's free decision that they should act according to given norms.

Nominalism after Ockham

DESPITE the censures of Ockhamism at the Papal Court at Avignon and subsequent prohibitions against teaching it at Paris, it spread rapidly through the universities and began to rival Thomism and

Scotism in popularity. Ockham's influence is easy to detect in the anonymous treatise *De Principiis Theologiae*,[48] written about 1350, which deduces the main tenets of Ockhamism from two principles: that God is omnipotent, and that a plurality is not to be posited without necessity. The *Collectorium* of Gabriel Biel (d. 1495) summarizes Ockham's doctrines but at the same time fills in gaps left by the master. The influence of Biel was considerable, especially in the German universities, where he was read by Luther, who claimed to belong to the Ockhamist sect.[49]

Beyond the circle of commentators and systematizers of Ockhamism, many in the fourteenth century shared its basic principles but developed them in a more or less original way. Two of the most important were John of Mirecourt and Nicholas of Autrecourt, both of whom taught at the University of Paris.

John of Mirecourt (*fl. c.* 1345) agreed with Ockham that, outside of faith, there are only two avenues of certainty: the principle of non-contradiction and experience. By the former we are sure that if God exists, he exists, and that if man exists, animal exists (for man is an animal). Propositions of this sort, which affirm that something is identical with itself, are absolutely certain and must be admitted by everyone. As for experience, its object is either the external world or our own selves. We are absolutely certain that we exist, for, as St. Augustine pointed out, we cannot doubt our existence without affirming it. By means of the principle of non-contradiction, therefore, I am absolutely certain that I exist. Our experience of the external world is not equally infallible, because God can perform a miracle and cause the appearance of something that does not really exist. The evidence of experience is natural and sufficient for science, but, strictly speaking, it is always open to question.

In emphasizing the absolute power of God and in exalting the divine will, Mirecourt is but following the lead of Ockham. Like Ockham, he portrays God as an authoritarian ruler who imposes the moral law on man by force of his will. God cannot sin, no matter what he does or causes man to do. Since the moral law depends on the divine will and not upon reason, God can even cause us to hate him or our neighbor. The divine will extends to everything that happens, including sin. God is the efficacious cause that sin is committed and that a particular man is a sinner. These extreme conclusions of Mirecourt's voluntarism were condemned in 1347.

The tendency toward skepticism in philosophy, already apparent in Ockham and Mirecourt, is even more marked in Nicholas of Autrecourt (*fl. c.* 1347).[50] In Nicholas it takes the form of a bias against Aristotle, whose popularity was on the wane among the theologians ever since the condemnation of 1277. Replying to a correspondent who claimed that Aristotle demonstrated a thousand truths, Nicholas assures him that these are only attempted demonstrations and that contrary opinions are just as probable, if not more so. Nicholas was one of the growing number of theologians who looked upon the lifelong study of Aristotle and the other philosophers as a waste of time. It is far better, he asserts, to devote oneself to the study of Scripture and to the pursuit of a good life. This was a return to the tradition of Tertullian and St. Peter Damian and a denial of scholasticism.

Nicholas of Autrecourt was not a complete skeptic in philosophical matters. With Ockham and Mirecourt he accepts the principle of non-contradiction and experience as bases of certainty. The primary law upon which all truth is founded is that contradictory propositions cannot be true at the same time. Nicholas uses this law not only to prove the truth of what are today called analytic judgments, in which the predicate is contained in the notion of the subject (for example, The whole is greater than the part), but also to establish the truth of judgments of experience (for example, that I see redness). If I see redness, it is contradictory to affirm that I do not see redness. Empirical judgments are consequently certain, although only as long as the experience on which they are based lasts. As soon as the experience is past and is only a memory, the judgment founded upon it is only probable.

Nicholas draws important conclusions concerning causality and substance from these principles. We cannot prove by the principle of non-contradiction that one thing is certainly the cause of another. This principle assures us that A is A and not B, and hence that it is not contradictory to say that A is and B is not. From the existence of A, therefore, we cannot infer the existence of B or that there is any necessary causal connection between them. However, we have a direct experience that one thing is the cause of another; for example, that fire heats an object close to it. The certainty of this relationship lasts as long as the sensible experience; after that it is only probable that the same effect will follow upon the cause. This empirical doctrine of causality earned for its author the title of the medieval Hume.

One of the conclusions Nicholas of Autrecourt draws from his doctrine of causality is that we cannot prove the existence of God by natural reason. Because the existence of one thing cannot be deduced from the existence of another, we cannot demonstrate God's existence from that of the world. Moreover, we do not experience God's causal effect upon the world. The certainty of the existence of God, therefore, is based on faith and not on reason.

A further conclusion is that we cannot be certain of the reality of substance. We experience qualities, such as heat and color, and our acts of understanding and willing, but we cannot be certain that there are substances underlying them. We do not see substances, and we cannot infer their existence from the objects we do see, because it has been shown that the existence of one thing cannot lead to the evident knowledge of something else. For example, we cannot conclude with certainty that we have an intellect from the fact that we understand, or that we have a will from the fact that we exercise the act of willing. At best, these inferences are probable and not certain.

By his skeptical attitude toward the reality of substance Nicholas casts doubt upon the whole of Aristotle's physics, in which the notions of substance and accident play a central role. In its place he suggests a return to the atomism of ancient Greek philosophy. According to atomism, the universe is composed of an infinite number of eternal atoms or indivisible particles in constant motion. Generation and corruption are not accounted for by the succession of different forms in the same subject but by the coming together and separating of atoms. All change is consequently the result of local motion. Since Nicholas, like Ockham, identifies material substance with quantity, the two basic factors to be considered by the physicist are quantity and local motion.

Atomism appealed to Nicholas of Autrecourt as a plausible sub-stitute for the philosophy of Aristotle, which he considered harmful to the Christian religion. Atomism also fits in well with his anti-metaphysical frame of mind. Besides offering easy solutions of the problems of philosophical physics, such as change, the continuum, and the void, it does not require the supposition of forms or sub-stances lying outside our immediate experience. It is also easy to reconcile with the freedom of God, because a universe of atoms without necessary ties between them cannot offer an obstacle to the divine will; God can do with it what he chooses. Above all, if atomism is adopted as the most reasonable philosophy, it will put an end to the vain disputes of the Aristotelians, and Christians will be free to devote themselves to the more important things of life, such as moral problems and the commonweal. This critical atti-tude toward scholasticism and this desire to return to a simple re-ligious life were prevalent features of the late Middle Ages and Renaissance. We shall meet them again when we study the pro-ponents of "modern devotion."

XIX

Master Eckhart and
Speculative Mysticism

Master Eckhart

A LTHOUGH a pupil of St. Albert, St. Thomas was too independent in his thinking to be called a disciple. The true
disciples of St. Albert were the German Dominicans Hugh and
Ulrich of Strasbourg, Dietrich of Freiberg, and Master John Eckhart. These men took up and developed—often in an original way
—some of the central themes of St. Albert. From a philosophical
point of view their adherence to Neoplatonism is of primary importance. St. Albert himself was strongly under its influence, although his good Christian sense kept him from following out some
of its more extreme consequences. His disciples did not always
show the same restraint, as we shall see in the case of Master Eckhart.[1]

GOD

ECKHART'S FAVORITE and almost exclusive theme is God. This
is only to be expected because, as we shall see, he thought that God
is the only being or reality; in themselves creatures are simply
nothing. He liked to quote the ancient saying: "God is an infinite
sphere whose center is everywhere and whose circumference is
nowhere." [2] This is but another way of saying that God is without

limits or boundaries, so that nothing exists outside him. Creatures exist only within God and have meaning only in relation to him. If Eckhart's mind was filled with God it was because, in his opinion, there was nothing else to fill it or, more exactly, there was nothing else in which it could be absorbed.

Eckhart describes God so differently in his various writings that some historians conjecture that he radically changed his notion of God in later life.³ In some works he identifies God with being and denies being of anything else; in these works God is said to be the only being. In others he denies being of God on the ground that he is an intellect, and an intellect is superior to being.

The latter description of God is to be found in Eckhart's *Parisian Questions*, written about 1302–1303, during his first period of teaching at Paris. One of the questions he debated at this time was whether God is more properly called Intelligence or Being. He certainly knew the answer of St. Thomas and Duns Scotus, that Being is the proper name of God and the basis of all the other divine perfections: because God is Being, he is also intelligent, good, and so on. Eckhart, on the contrary, teaches that God is more properly called Intelligence. Surely, he argues, it is more perfect to understand than only to live or to be. Understanding is the noblest of all perfections, and therefore Intelligence is the most fitting name of God.

Eckhart was well aware that when Moses asked God his name, he replied, *I Am Who Am* (*Exodus* 3:14); but in Eckhart's interpretation this was not a revelation of the divine name but a concealment of it.⁴ Suppose you meet someone at night and ask him: Who are you? If the person wants to hide his identity, he will reply: I am who I am. That is exactly what God meant to do in his reply to Moses. But if God hid his name from the Jews, he deigned to reveal it to Christians. We read in the beginning of St. John's Gospel: *In the beginning was the Word*. Eckhart points out that the Evangelist does not say: "In the beginning was Being, and God was Being," but: *In the beginning was the Word, and the Word was God*. Now a word is connected with intelligence, for it expresses thought. God also said: "I am the Truth." This is a clear indication that God's proper name is Intelligence and not Being.

From this it is obvious that God is superior to being, so much so that Eckhart refuses to call him a being in the proper sense of the term. Properly speaking, a being is something created. As the *Book of Causes* says: "The first of created things is being." Now if this is so, God must be higher than being, for a cause is always greater than its effect. Eckhart has no objection if someone calls God a being, so long as he understands what he is saying. What he means is that God is the cause of being, not that he is being itself. In the same way we call a diet healthy because it is the cause of health. But health exists formally only in an animal and not in a diet. So, too, being is formally present only in creatures; it is attributed to God only by analogy, because he is its cause. As Eckhart puts it: "Since being belongs to creatures, it is not in God except as in its cause. Consequently, there is no being in God, but purity from being *(puritas essendi)*." 5

In locating God above being, Eckhart follows the Neoplatonic tradition whose influence we have already seen at work in the philosophy of Scotus Erigena. Both Erigena and Eckhart call God "super-being" and even "non-being" or "nothing," because in their view a being is something limited and circumscribed and hence capable of definition and description in finite terms. God, on the other hand, is beyond all the names we can apply to him. He is so rich and full that he cannot be confined within our human categories and concepts. He is even beyond knowledge as we understand it. Like all mystics, Eckhart resorts to imagery to express the mystery of God: he is "darkness," a "wilderness," and a "desert." These images are meant to remind us that the union of the mind with God is a plunge into the unknown, where all our human ideas and categories must be put aside.

Like all Neoplatonists, Eckhart finds the term "unity" especially applicable to the First Principle of all things. In contrast to the multiplicity of creatures, their primal source is One. Eckhart was fully aware of the agreement between Scripture and the Neoplatonists on this point. He writes: "God is one; this is confirmed by the fact that Proclus, too, and the *Book of Causes* frequently call God the One or Unity." 6 The divine unity is even at the basis of the Trinity of Persons. Deeper and more hidden than the Father,

Son, and Holy Spirit is the Godhead, which Eckhart describes as "motionless unity and balanced stillness" and "the source of all emanations."

In his Scriptural commentaries, which seem to postdate the *Parisian Questions*, Eckhart is less hesitant to call God being. Commenting on the divine name *I Am Who Am* in the *Book of Exodus*, he explains that being is the very essence of God. This distinguishes him from all his creatures, whose essences are not being but "man," "angel," and so on.[7] In his Prologue to the *Opus Tripartitum*, Eckhart identifies God with Being (*esse est Deus*), and he goes on to say that God alone is properly being, one, true, and good. Creatures are called being, not because they truly are, but because they are related to God, who alone truly is. Through creation, creatures participate in the divine Being, but in such a way that they do not possess it as their own. Of themselves, creatures are pure nothingness. They exist through creation, not with their own existence but with the existence of God. Hence Parmenides was right in saying that there is only one Being, and that Being is God.[8]

The identification of being with God makes it easy for Eckhart to prove God's existence. Since the existence of all things is God's existence, it is as absurd to doubt his existence as it would be to doubt that of any creature. We can no more question his existence than we can our own, for basically they are the same. Existence belongs to the essence and definition of God, so that it is as certain that God exists as it is that man is man.[9] Eckhart bases the certainty of God's existence on an intimate experience of him and not on a complicated reasoning from the existence of creatures to the existence of God, as in the philosophy of St. Thomas. Eckhart's approach to God is more akin to that of St. Anselm and St. Bonaventure, who found the evidence of God's existence in the very nature of God as revealed by faith in the depths of the soul.

But does not the identification of God with being contradict Eckhart's statement in the *Parisian Questions* that God is above being because he is Intelligence? Are not these views contradictory, and do they not represent two phases of Eckhart's doctrinal development? It is impossible to give a definite solution of this problem until the chronology of his works is better established. It is probable, however, that the contradiction is more verbal than real. Eckhart seems to consider God from two points of view: in himself and in his causal relation to creatures. In himself, in his ineffable mystery, he is above being; and from this point of view the *I Am Who Am* of *Exodus* conceals the divine name. But in relation to creatures, he contains all the perfections that he creates in them, and especially the most universal of all or being; from this point of view Eckhart follows the Augustinian tradition in interpreting *I Am Who Am* as a revelation of the divine name.[10]

Eckhart expresses both these points of view in a Sermon dating from the period of the *Parisian Questions*. "Ignorant masters," he writes, "say that God is pure being; He is as high above being as the highest angel is above a midge. If I called God a being it would be just as wrong as to call the sun pale or black. God is neither this nor that [i.e., He is not limited or finite]. . . . But if I said that God is not a being and that He is above being, I did not by so doing deny being to God. On the contrary, I enhanced it in Him. If I take copper alloyed with gold, it is still there, but in a higher manner than it is in itself. . . . When we apprehend God as being, we apprehend Him in His antechamber, for being is the antechamber in which He dwells. Where is He then in His temple, in which He, the Holy One, shines? Reason is the temple of God. God dwells nowhere more properly than in His temple, in reason, as the second master said: 'God is an intellect which lives in the knowledge of itself alone.' He dwells in Himself alone, where nothing has ever troubled Him, because He is there alone in His stillness. In His knowledge of Himself God knows Himself in Himself." [11]

CREATION

CREATION IS THE ACT by which God gives existence to creatures. There is nothing unusual in this statement of Eckhart's, but we should carefully note its meaning in his philosophy. Since God is existence, and since there is no other existence than that of God, creation is the act whereby God in some way confers himself upon creatures. We should not imagine that God creates beings with existences of their own, distinct from his existence. If this were so, Eckhart argues, there would be something outside God, existing side by side with him, so to speak, and he could not claim to be existence itself.[12] In short, he would have rivals to the claim of being. In fact, all things exist in God and with the divine existence, not outside him with their own existences.

It goes without saying, therefore, that God created the universe out of nothing (*ex nihilo*).[13] He did not organize pre-existing matter as a workman does when he builds a house, but he conferred on the universe its total existence. Neither did the universe emanate from God as a part of himself, for the creature is not its creator or a part of him. In itself a creature is nothing. Man, for example, is nothing in himself, because in himself he has no being or existence. But by creation God gives him existence, and since he had no existence before creation he must have been created from non-being or nothing.

Eckhart's startling statements that creatures are absolutely nothing and that existence is identical with God expose him to the charge of pantheism. If all things exist with God's existence, are they not identical with the divine being and consequently with God himself? In defending himself against this charge Eckhart distinguishes between two meanings of the term "existence." There is absolute existence (*esse absolutum*) and existence formally inhering in creatures (*esse formaliter inhaerens*).[14] These are not really distinct; they are the same existence considered from two different points of view. Absolute existence is God himself in his inner solitude and isolation from creatures. Inherent existence is that same existence diffusing itself and penetrating creatures by a kind of formal causality, thereby making them exist. Again, absolute existence is the inner face of God; inherent existence is his outer face, with which he looks toward creatures and draws them out of nothingness. This distinction enables Eckhart to deny that inherent existence is, strictly speaking, God. It is not God himself but the divine existence exercising the secondary function of informing and actualizing creatures in order to make them exist.

Some light is thrown on this difficult doctrine by Eckhart's analogy (borrowed from St. Albert and earlier Neoplatonists) between God and the soul. God is in the world, Eckhart says, as the soul is in the body.[15] Now the soul can be considered in two different ways: in itself as an independent spiritual substance, and in its function of informing and vivifying the body. So, too, Eckhart says, God can be considered either in himself as independent Being, or in his role as creator of the universe. In himself God is one and undivided, but he contains within himself (that is to say, in his power) the manifold beings he creates. So, too, the soul is undivided in itself and yet it contains in a unified way all the parts of the body it informs and vivifies. The soul is immediately and totally present to all the parts of the body, conferring upon them their existence, life, and powers. Similarly, God is intimately present to all his creatures, giving them existence and all their other perfections.

This analogy helps us to understand how Eckhart avoids pantheism, or the identification of creatures with God. As the body is not the soul, so the universe is not God. And yet the universe is contained in God and exists through his presence to it, as the body is contained in the soul and exists with its existence.

Another difficult problem taken up by Eckhart is: When did God create the universe? [16] He considers this an ambiguous question because its answer differs according to one's point of view. From the divine viewpoint, the creation of the world did not take place in time but in eternity. The reason for this is the fact that God does not live and act in time but in eternity. "It would be foolish," Eckhart writes, "to say that God created the world yesterday or tomorrow. He created the world and all things in a present Now, and the time a thousand years ago is the same to God as the present moment." This is why Eckhart can say: "As soon as God was, he created the world." Although he was condemned for this statement, its meaning is orthodox when it is understood in its context. Eckhart does not deny that from our point of view the world has not always existed. He is simply pointing out that creation is an eternal act on the part of God and that consequently creation is eternal from his point of view. That is why he considers it meaningless to ask why God chose one moment rather than another in which to create the world. Since there was no time before the world was created, it is an illusion to think that God waited for some future time in which he would create it.

MAN

AS WE HAVE SEEN, Eckhart teaches that man is a composite of soul and body. Like St. Albert and St. Thomas, he maintains that the intellectual soul is the only substantial form of the body; there are no lower substantial forms or souls in man besides his human or intellectual soul. Eckhart warns us against imagining that the soul is in the body: it would be truer to say that the body is in the soul. We are apt to think of the body as a receptacle containing the soul, but in reality the soul as a spiritual substance contains the body by sustaining it in existence and imparting life to it. This is in accordance with the general law ruling the relationship between superior and inferior beings: the inferior is contained in the superior and is one with it. Consequently, the body is contained in the soul and the soul is contained in God. There is a sense, however, in which we may say that the soul is in the body. The body is the prison in which the soul resides until it purifies itself by turning away from creatures to their creator.[17]

Like Avicenna and St. Albert, Eckhart distinguishes between the nature of the soul and its function of informing the body. By its nature the soul is a spiritual substance, flowing directly from God and destined to be united with him in mystical ecstasy in this life and in beatific vision in the life to come. This spiritual substance is called a "soul" (*anima*), not because of its nature, but because in the present life it animates the body and operates by means of its organs. Eckhart writes: "If anyone were to name the soul in terms of its simplicity, its clarity and its purity, as it is in itself, he would not be able to find a name for it. They call it 'soul,' just as one would call someone 'the carpenter.' This is not like calling him 'the man' or 'Henry,' or really calling him according to his nature, but it is calling him according to his occupation."[18]

As a consequence, the soul has two aspects, or, as St. Augustine says, two faces. One of these is turned toward matter and the body, the other is turned toward God, who continually bathes it with his own light. God is immediately present to the whole soul and vivifies it, just as the soul in its turn vivifies the body. But he is most intimately present to the soul in its innermost sanctuary, which Eckhart calls its "citadel" or "spark." This lies more deeply in the soul than its powers, even than reason and will. The powers of the soul enable it to communicate with the outer world; they are the gates by which creatures penetrate the soul. But nothing created has access to its inner sanctuary or citadel. This is open to God alone, and it is the means by which the soul enters into union with God.[19]

THE CITADEL OF THE SOUL

ECKHART'S NOTION OF THE CITADEL of the soul is difficult to grasp. He sometimes speaks of it as the intellect, which he describes as a spark of the divine intelligence. Since he has told us that God is pure Intellect, it is easy to see why the deepest part of the soul, which has been made in his image, should likewise receive the name of intellect. If by intellect, however, we mean a power of the soul, residing in the brain, then there is something deeper in the soul, namely, the soul's essence or nature. The powers of the soul are but outward manifestations of that nature and they operate in the body. Beyond them lies the soul's essence and from it they spring like branches from the trunk of a tree. That is why Eckhart sometimes calls the essence of the soul its citadel; the intellect is simply its highest power and most perfect manifestation.

The citadel of the soul is comparable to the essence of God or to the Godhead. As the Godhead is one and simple and the source of the three Persons of the Trinity, so the citadel of the soul is one and simple and the source of the soul's manifold powers. Consequently, the soul bears the image of God in its citadel or essence, and it is through this citadel that the soul is one with God.[20]

In order to be united with God we must lock ourselves up in the citadel of our soul, where God dwells. We must put aside all material things and even the use of our powers of intellect and will. These powers grasp God only in his various properties and not in his very essence. The intellect apprehends him as the truth, and the will apprehends him as the good, but these properties are, so to speak, the veils or garments of God; they are not the Godhead itself, which is one and simple, and consequently beyond all names and properties. Only in the citadel of the soul do we penetrate beyond these veils and grasp God as he is in himself, divested of being and all names.

No one reaches this lofty, mystical union with God unless he has been purified of the desire of created things, and even of his own salvation, and has given himself completely to God. The mystic then passes beyond sensory knowledge, which is limited to material, tangible objects, beyond rational knowledge, which reaches intelligible objects by means of abstract concepts, until he arrives at a pure knowledge of God as he is in himself. This knowledge is identical with the indwelling of the soul in God. Eckhart makes it clear that we cannot achieve this supernatural state by our own powers, but only by the illumination and grace of God.

Like all Christian mystics, Eckhart falters in describing his intimate experience of God, and no wonder, since it takes place in a realm beyond human concepts and language. He naturally avails himself of scriptural terms, but of greater interest to the student of philosophy is the use he makes of Neoplatonism to depict the ascent of the soul to God. Eckhart finds the language of Plotinus and Proclus especially apt to describe that journey, as Dionysius the Pseudo-Areopagite and Scotus Erigena did before him. The presence of the soul in the body as in a prison, the gradual purification of the soul from contact with matter by its turning toward God, its final liberation by union with him in a region beyond knowledge and being—all this reminds us of Plotinus' flight of the soul to the One and its absorption in it. We must remember, however, that Eckhart was first and foremost a Christian mystic and not a Neoplatonist philosopher. He uses Neoplatonic ideas, but only to express in intellectual terms the Christian experience of supernatural contemplation, made possible through divine grace won for us by the Redemption of Jesus Christ.

THE CONDEMNATION OF ECKHART

ECKHART'S LANGUAGE, even more than his thought, was a scandal to his contemporaries, and it led to his condemnation shortly after his death.[21] We can imagine their shock on reading: "There is something in the soul that is uncreated and uncreatable. If the whole soul were of such a nature, it would be uncreated and uncreatable. And this is the intellect." Taken at their face value, these statements imply the division of the soul into two parts, one created and the other (the intellect) uncreated. In his defense Eckhart agrees that the whole soul and all its powers are created. But he insists that the soul is spiritual and made in the image of God. Indeed, if it were pure intelligence, like God, it would be uncreated and not a soul. Whatever we may think of this explanation, it is difficult to dissociate Eckhart's statement that the intellect is uncreated from the Neoplatonic doctrine of the divinity of the intellect. Wherever we meet Neoplatonism in the Middle Ages, we find the conviction that intelligence in men is something more than human, since it involves the divine and the uncreated. This conviction is at the basis of the Augustinian doctrine of divine illumination, and it also appears in Eckhart's statement that the intellect in man is uncreated. In the deepest recess of the soul, which Eckhart calls its citadel or intellect, the soul is one with God, so much so that divine properties can be attributed to it.

The identity of the soul with God through mystical experience accounts for other sayings of Eckhart that were scandalous to his readers. For example, he says: "We are transformed totally into God and are converted into him in a similar manner as in the Sacrament the bread is converted into the Body of Christ. I am converted into him in such a way that he makes me one being with himself—not a similar being. By the living God, it is true that here there is no distinction." Again, "Whatever the Holy Scriptures say of Christ is wholly true of every good and divine man." And again, "Whatever is proper to the divine nature is entirely proper to the just and divine man. For this reason such a man brings about whatever God brings about, and he created heaven and earth together with God. He is the begetter of the eternal Word, and without such a man God would not be able to do anything."

These bold and paradoxical statements are typical of Eckhart's use of figurative and imaginative language to express the intimate union of the soul with God. In his defense he explains that they are not to be taken literally, and he makes it clear that he intends his doctrine to be orthodox. He wishes to drive home the fact that Christ is born within the soul by grace, so that the soul becomes one with Christ, the Head of the Mystical Body of which we are the members. Just as many hosts on many altars are changed into the Body of Christ while the accidents of the hosts remain, so we are united to the Son of God and are made members of the Church of which he is the Head.

Certain statements of Eckhart's, although perfectly orthodox in their context, seem to deny all value to external acts. He tells us that God loves souls, not external works, and that an external work is not, properly speaking, good or divine. At first sight this appears to anticipate Luther's rejection of good works as an aid to salvation, but in reality Eckhart does not deny the utility of good works. He simply wishes to emphasize the essential importance of sanctifying grace, which alone gives human actions a supernatural value. The external act, he says in his defense, has no moral goodness without the goodness of the interior act. Hence God prefers the latter. When seen in proper perspective, therefore, these rather shocking and daring assertions of Eckhart lose their heretical appearance and become expressions of a deep faith in the Catholic religion.

Disciples of Eckhart

THE EXTRAORDINARY FLOWERING of mysticism in the Rhineland after Eckhart's death can be directly traced to his influence. His dynamic personality and deep spirituality could not fail to attract those who read his works or listened to his sermons, even though they did not always follow his lofty speculations. The condemnation of twenty-eight of his sayings by Pope John XXII in 1329 cast a pall over his name and doctrine, but he kept a loyal band of followers among the pious laity and religious. They understood that it was not so much his doctrine as some of his paradoxical and exaggerated sayings that came under the papal censure. They simply avoided these sayings while retaining the essentials of his speculative mysticism.

One of Eckhart's earliest and most faithful disciples was John Tauler. Born at Strasbourg about 1300, he entered the Dominican Order at an early age and studied at Cologne around 1325. There he became acquainted with Eckhart's thought, either through the master himself or from other teachers. Whether he studied at Paris is doubtful, but it is certain that he knew the works of the Parisian masters and occasionally cited them in his sermons. St. Thomas was a revered name to him, as it was to Eckhart. But his own heart lay in the mystical life so movingly described by Eckhart rather than in the metaphysical and theological speculations of the schoolmen. "The masters of Paris," he writes, "read big books and turn over the leaves. It is well, but these [that is, the mystics] read the living book wherein everything lives." [22] To Tauler, the choice was between a scholasticism busied with books and no longer in vital contact with reality, and a mysticism that opened to man the living splendors of his soul and the God in whose image it has been made. It is no wonder that he, like so many of his contemporaries, chose the latter.

Many of Eckhart's themes reappear in Tauler's sermons, the only certainly authentic works that have come down to us. Like his master, he describes three births: the eternal generation of the Son in the divine essence, the birth of Jesus in the world, and the birth of God in the soul. This latter birth takes place in a holy soul which turns to God with attention and love. The soul must leave aside worldly cares, summon all its forces, and turn inward upon itself where God is dwelling. A mutual embrace then takes place, God giving himself to the soul, which in turn receives him as its closest possession.

Adopting a typical Neoplatonic theme, Tauler describes the soul as on the borderline between time and eternity. By its higher part it belongs to eternity; by its lower part—that is to say, by its sensory and animal powers—it belongs to time. However, owing to the close connection between its higher and lower parts, the whole soul is dispersed in time and in the world. Even its most sublime faculties of memory, intelligence, and will, by which it is an image of the Trinity, are so closely engaged in time that they easily disperse their energies in the sensible world and thus sever their ties with eternity. In order to remedy this condition the soul must turn inward and concentrate all its powers, both sensory and intellectual, upon itself. Then the sensory, affective, and active powers are reunited in the superior powers, and they in turn are reunited in the citadel or "ground" of the soul, from which they spread outward like branches from the trunk of a tree.

After this inward movement of concentration on the part of the soul, it passes outward and above itself by renouncing its every will and desire and action. There remains only a pure and simple attention to God: the soul seeks only to be and to receive God in the most intimate way so that he may be born in the soul and accomplish his work there. In order for the eye to see, it must be void of all colors and images; for the ear to hear, it must be empty of all sounds. Similarly, if the soul is to receive God it must be empty of all created things. When the ground of the soul has been prepared in this way, God will surely enter in and take possession of it. As Tauler puts it: "If, then, you wholly go out, God will no doubt wholly enter in, neither more nor less, for as much as you go out, so much will he enter." [23]

When a man is practiced in turning the powers of his soul inward upon its center or "ground," he is said to have a good character or *Gemüt*. This is a permanent disposition to use his powers as he should. If, on the other hand, he constantly misuses his powers by turning them away from God's dwelling place in the soul and centering them upon creatures, he acquires a contrary disposition or *Gemüt*. In other words, each man has a permanent disposition or attitude toward his soul's center and toward God, and this basically determines whether his character is good or evil.

Another follower of Eckhart, Blessed Henry Suso, was born at Constance about 1300 and died at Ulm in 1366. His *Little Book of Truth, Little Book of Eternal Wisdom, Letters,* and autobiographical *Life of the Servant* reveal him to be one of the most delightful and readable of the Rhineland mystics.[24] He made Eckhart's acquaintance at Cologne and became one of his most loyal followers. When Eckhart was accused of failing to distinguish clearly between God and creatures, Suso came to his defense. He explains that creatures have eternally existed in God and are identical with him, but only in the sense that their Ideas are eternally in him. When creatures issue forth from God they receive their own being, as well as their own essence and form. Creatures as such exist only through being created; they do not possess "creatureliness" as they exist in God. Moreover, their creatureliness is nobler and more useful to them than the being they have in God. This language is far different from that of Eckhart. Suso was less under the spell of Neoplatonism and more careful than his master to harmonize his teaching with traditional Catholic formulae.

The same effort to express the mystical union of the soul with God in intelligible terms, within the limits of orthodoxy, was made by Blessed John Ruysbroeck (1293–1381).[25] Ruysbroeck was not born in the Rhineland but in the Flemish village of Ruysbroeck, just south of Brussels. In 1343 he retired to Groenendael with a group of friends, where they formed a monastic community and gave themselves over to a life of contemplation. In 1350 they took the habit of the Canons Regular of St. Augustine.

Ruysbroeck's doctrine is centered around the drama of the human soul: its origin in God, its exile in the material world, its longing to return to its divine abode, and its final beatitude in the vision of God. The main stages of this drama were laid down for him by the Christian Neoplatonists, especially St. Augustine, Dionysius the Pseudo-Areopagite, and Scotus Erigena.

Ruysbroeck describes God as above eternity, being, and all other human concepts. He is, Ruysbroeck says, "a simple unity, without any mode, without time or space, without before or after, without desire or possession, without light or darkness. He is a perpetual now, the bottomless abyss, the darkness of silence, the desert wilderness." [26]

The universe pre-exists in God in an ideal state and issues forth from him by creation. The angels were created first; men were created to take the place of the fallen angels. In his original state man was free and happy, but through original sin human nature fell and became separated from God. Man freely separated himself from his maker, but he cannot be reunited to him by his own efforts. Man's will must be assisted by divine grace won from him by Christ.

In his treatise *The Spiritual Marriage*, Ruysbroeck describes the three lives by which man, liberated by grace, returns to God: the active life, whose beginning is marked by a moral conversion to God; the interior life, in which Christ enters into the soul, first in its lower and higher powers and finally in its very essence; and the contemplative life, which raises man above reason and intelligence and unites him with God in one single life and spirit.

Ruysbroeck was criticized by John Gerson (1363–1429), the chancellor of the University of Paris, for using pantheistic language in describing the oneness of the contemplative soul with God. The Flemish mystic, he says, claimed that in contemplation the soul beholds God in a brightness identical with the divine essence, and that the soul is this divine brightness; moreover, that the soul is changed, transformed, and absorbed into the divine being. But in justice to Ruysbroeck we must remember that when the mystic expresses his intimate experience with God he speaks his own language, which is not the same as that of the speculative theologian or philosopher. There is no doubt that Ruysbroeck himself did not intend his statements to be understood in a pantheistic sense. In 1909 the Church set her seal on the orthodoxy of his thought, as well as on the saintliness of his life, by declaring him Blessed.

Modern Devotion

THE MYSTICS we have just met were the heirs of the great spiritual masters of the Middle Ages, especially St. Augustine, Dionysius, St. Bernard, and the Victorines. They knew and admired the leading schoolmen of the thirteenth century (especially St. Bonaventure, with whom they had much in common), but they had little sympathy with the scholasticism of their own day. When they used philosophical ideas they tended to take them from the Neoplatonists, as the Fathers of the Church had done, rather than from Aristotle. Scholasticism no longer seemed a living force, and men were returning to the literary study of the Bible and to direct religious experience, both of which were characteristics of the Patristic Age.

The religious movement we have been describing began in Germany and soon spread into what is now Belgium and Holland. In the low countries much of its success was due to the work of Gerard Groot (1340–1384). Groot had been a student at Paris, but, like Tauler, he became disgusted with its arid scholasticism. He considered philosophy to be the ruin of the university and a source of heresy in the Church. After giving all his possessions to the poor, he spent some time with Ruysbroeck at Groenendael and then went into monastic retreat in his home town of Deventer. His ideal was to imitate the life of Christ. A good scholar himself, he was not opposed to study, but he did not think one should take university courses to earn money or to obtain degrees. He recommended above all the reading of sacred Scripture, St. Augustine, and St. Bernard; in short, those Christian authors who, like Socrates and Plato (whom he considered the wisest philosophers), stressed the moral formation of man rather than the abstract speculations of physics or metaphysics.

At Deventer, Groot laid the foundation for the Brethren of the Common Life, an institution devoted to the monastic life and the education of youth. Its course of studies centered around Scripture, the Fathers of the Church, and the languages needed to read them. The importance of this school can be appreciated from the fact that its pupils included Nicholas of Cusa and Erasmus, both leaders in the cultural and religious life of their day. But perhaps the best-known pupil of Groot's school was Thomas à Kempis, who is generally believed to be the author of *The Imitation of Christ*.[27] Whether Groot or Thomas à Kempis was its author, it is a perfect expression of the spirituality of the Brethren of the Common Life and of what has come to be called "modern devotion" (*devotio moderna*). Without altogether condemning the intellectual life, *The Imitation of Christ* gives scant place to it in the Christian scheme of things. It is not difficult to detect the author's antipathy to scholasticism in the following remarks: "What have we to do with genera and species? He to whom the Eternal Word speaks is delivered from many questionings"; and "I had rather feel compunction than know how to define it." These statements recall the attitude of the anti-dialecticians of the eleventh century toward philosophy. After several centuries of scholasticism and the dominance of Aristotelian logic, Gerard Groot and his followers were urging Christians to forsake the subtleties of dialectics and to return to the monastic ideals of the Age of the Fathers.

XX

Nicholas of Cusa

NICHOLAS OF CUSA attended the school at Deventer, where
he imbibed the solid religious training of the Brethren
of the Common Life.[1] Later, at the University of Cologne, he came
into contact with the Christian Neoplatonism of Master Eckhart,
and this left an indelible impression upon him. A prodigious scholar,
he knew Latin, Greek, as well as Hebrew, besides mastering all
the scientific, philosophical, and theological knowledge of his time.
One can still visit his library at Kues, on the Moselle River, and see
his collection of more than three hundred manuscripts, with his
own comments in the margins. In this collection writers of Neoplatonic inspiration occupy a prominent place; for example, St.
Augustine, Proclus, Dionysius, Avicenna, and Eckhart. Besides his
academic interests, he was a great administrator and conciliator between warring princes and conflicting religious groups. He played
an important role at the Council of Basle, where the supremacy of
the pope or General Council of the Church was in dispute. Later
he was the pope's legate to Greece and Constantinople to prepare
for the union of the Greek and Latin churches, which was brought
about for a short time at the Council of Florence. The unity of dis-
cordant parties was his chief aim in practical affairs. We shall see
that his speculative thought is governed by a similar ideal of the
harmony of opposite views.

LEARNED IGNORANCE

TO ONE LIVING in the fifteenth century the rival sects of philosophy, all claiming allegiance to Aristotle, presented a bewildering spectacle. After surveying the scene, Nicholas of Cusa came to the conclusion that the lesson his contemporaries most needed to learn was their own ignorance. Ignorance as the greatest wisdom is the theme of his most important treatise, entitled *On Learned Ignorance*. In the beginning of this work he observes that God has implanted in us the desire to know but that our judgments only approximate the truth without completely comprehending it. He commends Socrates for realizing that he knew nothing except his own ignorance, and Solomon for saying that we cannot explain everything. Aristotle also showed his wisdom by affirming that we are like owls looking at the sun when we try to uncover the deepest mysteries of nature. In this situation, the first thing we should know is our own ignorance, and when we have fully realized it we have acquired "learned ignorance" (*docta ignorantia*). The more learned a man is, the more he will appreciate how much he does not know.

The inadequacy of human knowledge is particularly clear when its object is the infinite. Every rational inquiry begins with a premise presupposed as certain and ends with a conclusion. When there is comparatively little distance between premise and conclusion, it is easy to make the inference; but when many steps are needed the task is more difficult. We see this to be true in mathematics. The mathematician begins with axioms and draws conclusions from them. It is easy to draw the first conclusions, but those more remote from the axioms give rise to greater difficulty, because it is only by means of the first conclusions that we reach those more remote. Now, no matter how many steps we take in an inquiry, we will never arrive at the infinite, because it is infinitely distant from our starting point. Indeed, there is no relation at all between the finite and the infinite: the infinite is out of all proportion to the finite, so that no comparison or analogy can be established between them. The infinite is an absolute, and hence no inquiry based upon a relation or proportion will reveal the infinite to us as it is in itself.[2]

Rational inquiry not only fails to lead us to the infinite; it is inadequate to reveal the whole truth about anything. Nicholas' reason for this is that truth, like the infinite, is something absolute. Truth does not admit of more or less; by nature it is indivisible and without degrees. But rational inquiry proceeds by steps, relating conclusions to premises. Since it is based upon relations, it never arrives at absolute truth. We can never grasp the truth with such precision that it cannot be comprehended with infinitely greater precision. Nicholas of Cusa compares the mind's knowledge of truth to a polygon inscribed in a circle. No matter how many sides are added to the polygon, it will never be identical with the circle. So, too, our mind approaches ever closer to the truth but never coincides with it.

This is obvious when it is a question of knowing God, for we cannot expect our finite mind to comprehend the infinite. But Nicholas points out that it is equally true of our knowledge of the essences of creatures. He observes that all philosophers desire to know the essences of things, but no one has discovered these essences. They draw near to them in varying degrees, but in their entirety they always remain beyond their grasp.[3]

These limitations of human knowledge result not only from the finite nature of our mind but also, as we have seen, from the method of human reasoning. Reason is a discursive power. It moves from object to object, comparing and relating them to each other. Hence it is at home with the relative, the multiple, and the finite, not with the absolute, the one, and the infinite. It discerns the difference between things and judges that one is not the other. Its primary rule is the principle of non-contradiction, which states that two contradictories cannot be true at the same time. When applied to God, this principle allows us to affirm certain attributes while denying the contrary attributes. But it does not enable us to grasp the unity of all perfections in God. For this we are endowed with a higher power than reason; namely, intellect. Intellect does not employ the method of comparison and relation. It is a power of insight or intuition which sees unity where reason sees difference and opposition. Through the power of intellect we attain our most perfect knowledge of God. If we follow the method of reason, we first affirm attributes of God and then deny them of him. For example, we say that God is one; but since he is not one in the sense that a creature is one, we then deny his unity. This is the "affirmative" and "negative" theology which we have already met in Dionysius and Scotus Erigena and which Nicholas of Cusa claims is the work of reason. Through the power of intellect, however, we rise to "copulative" theology, which apprehends God as transcending all perfections in a perfect unity and "coincidence of opposites."

Nicholas of Cusa considered the prevalence of Aristotelianism a great obstacle to the mind's ascent from reason to intellect. The principle of non-contradiction governs Aristotle's philosophy, and consequently it cannot admit the identity of opposites. Aristotelianism is the perfect embodiment of the work of discursive reason. Its failure is to remain on this level and not to ascend to the higher point of view of intellect. Nicholas complains that the partisans of Aristotelianism are so rooted in their conviction that contradictories are incompatible that it takes almost a miracle to get them to admit the "coincidence of opposites." And yet, he goes on to say, the ascent to mystical theology is impossible without this admission.[4] Nicholas himself prefers the Neoplatonists to the Aristotelians because they know how to lead the philosopher in his search for truth beyond the realm of the finite and contradictory to the Infinite Being who transcends all distinctions and oppositions.

GOD, THE COINCIDENCE OF OPPOSITES

THE CENTRAL IDEA of Nicholas of Cusa's treatise *On Learned Ignorance* is the notion of the maximum or the greatest. Book I concerns the absolute maximum, or God; Book II concerns the relative maximum, or the universe; Book III concerns the union of the absolute and relative maximum, or Christ.

By the greatest or maximum, Nicholas means a being than which nothing greater can exist. The absolute maximum is infinite being; that is to say, the being so rich in perfection that nothing restricts it or stands in opposition to it. It is at once absolute unity and absolute fullness of being, for unity is really identical with being. Nothing can be added to it or taken away from it. Because it is the absolute maximum, it contains all things, so that it can be called the all. And since it is the all, there is nothing to oppose or limit it. It limits all things without receiving any limitation from them. It is not difficult for Christians to recognize in this infinite being the God in whom they believe. He embodies an intellectual mystery which, Nicholas of Cusa warns us, surpasses human comprehension but upon which he hopes to throw some light by means of suitable symbols and analogies.[5]

This description of God is noteworthy on several scores. To begin with, it reminds us of the Anselmian definition of God as the being than which none greater can be conceived. Like St. Anselm, Nicholas of Cusa describes God in terms of the maximum; with this difference, that for him God is the greatest being, while for St. Anselm he is the greatest object of thought. Secondly, Nicholas of Cusa identifies the infinite with positive fullness of being. This marks a radical departure from the Greek Neoplatonists, who considered infinity to be a negative notion, signifying the absence of limitation. Nicholas of Cusa adopts the positive notion of infinity developed by Henry of Ghent and Duns Scotus under the influence of Christian doctrine.

It is natural for us to think of the maximum as the supreme degree in a series containing other members which are less in relation to it. But Nicholas warns us that this is not true of the absolute maximum or God. "More" and "less" are applicable only to finite, relative beings, not to the infinite and absolute being. The nature of the absolute excludes degrees of more and less.

It is also natural for us to think of the maximum as in opposition to the minimum. We conceive it as one extreme set over against another. But once again Nicholas cautions us that this is not true of the absolute maximum. The absolute maximum is everything, so that nothing stands outside it in opposition to it. It is in fact all extremes; it is the minimum as well as the maximum. And since there is no diversity or difference in the absolute maximum, the minimum and the maximum are identical in it. The absolute maximum or God is the "coincidence of opposites."

Nicholas of Cusa admits that this is far beyond the comprehension of our finite minds, which are not accustomed to know the infinite. We cannot see how contradictories that are infinitely distant from each other can be identical, and yet we are sure that they are identical in the infinite or absolute maximum. Since the absolute maximum is absolutely perfect, it is all that it can be. Hence it is equally true to say that it is as great as it can be and that it is as small as it can be. The maximum and minimum are two extremes or "superlatives," equally applicable, of a being that is infinite.

In order to throw some light on this paradox Nicholas asks us to consider the maximum and minimum in quantity. The maximum quantity is infinitely great, while the minimum is infinitely small. Now if we mentally lay aside the notions of greatness and smallness, we are left with nothing but the maximum and minimum quantity, both of which are infinite, and as such they are identical. In other words, if we consider quantity as an absolute, in abstraction from the relative qualities of greatness and smallness, it is infinite, and the maximum and minimum are identified in it.[6] Similarly, if we consider being as an absolute, it is infinite, and the maximum and minimum coincide in it.

Nicholas of Cusa liked to employ mathematical symbols to illustrate the coincidence of the maximum and minimum in infinity. He was conscious that in this use of mathematics to gain some insight into spiritual realities he was continuing the Platonic tradition as handed down by Christian thinkers, whom he calls "our philosophers," particularly St. Augustine, Boethius, and St. Anselm.[7] Anselm, he says, compared absolute truth to infinite straightness. Now infinite straightness can be symbolized by an infinite straight line. This infinite straight line is the absolute of straightness and it is identical with the absolute minimum of curve. This can be shown as follows. Imagine a circle of a particular size. As you increase the size of the circle, the curvature of the circumference decreases. The circumference of the absolutely greatest possible circle will have the smallest possible curvature, so that if the circle is infinite in size its circumference will be absolutely straight. In infinity, therefore, the maximum of straightness is identical with the minimum of curve; or, to put it another way, an infinite circle is identical with a straight line.[8]

Nicholas also shows that an infinite straight line is a triangle. The angles of a triangle are equal to two right angles. If one angle increases in size, the other two become proportionally smaller. Of course, in any triangle we can imagine, the expansion of one angle is always less than 180 degrees. But if we suppose that the angle is expanded to the maximum, or 180 degrees, without the triangle's ceasing to be a triangle, then it is evident that the triangle is a line. It is a triangle of one angle that is three, and of three angles that are one.

Nicholas grants that the imagination cannot grasp the coincidence of the straight line and the triangle, but he does not think mathematics is limited to what can be imagined. The mathematician must use his intellect, and it is not difficult for the intellect to understand that a line can be a triangle.[9]

These mathematical speculations are meant to give us some insight into the more profound truth of the coincidence of opposites in infinite being or God. But even if this coincidence is granted, it still remains to be proved that God really exists. Nicholas of Cusa has pointed out that we believe in the existence of God as the absolute maximum, but he has not yet demonstrated his existence. This he does by showing that the finite is inconceivable without the infinite. What is finite and limited has a beginning and end, so that there must be a being to which it owes its existence and in which it will have its end. This being is either finite or infinite. If it is finite, it has its beginning and end in another being. This leads either to an infinite series of actually existing finite beings, which is impossible, or to an infinite being which is the beginning and end of all finite things. Consequently, it is absolutely necessary that there be an infinite being or absolute maximum.

Moreover, the absolute truth about the absolute maximum can be stated in these three propositions: It is or it is not; it is and it is not; it neither is nor is it not. Now no matter which of these is taken to be the absolute truth, Nicholas insists that he has proved his point. There is an absolute truth and consequently an absolute maximum, since these two are identical.[10]

These proofs suffice to show Nicholas of Cusa's method of demonstrating God's existence. He does not begin with sensible data and show that God must exist as their cause. Rather, like St. Anselm, he starts with an object of thought and shows that it is not intelligible unless God exists. The finite has no meaning without the infinite; the relative is incomprehensible without the absolute. Infinite being and the absolute maximum force themselves upon our thought as absolutely necessary in order to account for the intelligibility of anything else.

THE UNIVERSE, OR RELATIVE MAXIMUM

IN BOOK II OF HIS TREATISE *On Learned Ignorance*, Nicholas of Cusa turns his attention to the universe. His first question is whether it is finite or infinite. He replies that only God is infinite in the full sense of the term, since he alone contains all things. The universe contains everything else, but it does not contain God, and so it is finite or limited. However, it can be said to be relatively infinite. By his infinite power God could make the universe greater than it is, but in fact he has fixed matter with a limited extension beyond which it cannot expand. Since there is no possibility of the universe increasing in extension, it is a maximum; not of course the absolute maximum which is God, but the relative maximum.[11]

In a sense the universe is also infinite in respect to time. Before the creation of the universe there was no time, so that it is not bounded by time any more than it is by space. Nicholas adopts the Platonic theme that time is an image of eternity.[12] Time proceeds from eternity and consequently participates in it. So we can say that the universe itself is eternal. However, this must be qualified by saying that, unlike God, the universe is only relatively, and not absolutely, eternal.[13]

In describing the relation between God and the universe, Nicholas uses expressions reminiscent of the philosophy of Scotus Erigena. God, he says, is invisible in himself, for he is hidden in infinity, which no creature can comprehend. He is visible, however, through creation. In his innermost depths God is neither a creator nor creatable; he is the absolute infinite transcending the relations implied by these terms. At a level more accessible to our understanding, God is the coincidence of creating creator and creatable creator; in short, he is both creator and creature.[14] In calling God a creature, Nicholas does not mean to impute limitations to God; he means that God contains within himself all the perfection found in created things. The creature is, as it were, God created and manifested to the world. This is but another way of saying with Scotus Erigena that the universe is a theophany, or appearance of God.

As appearances of God, creatures have no being in themselves; rather, their whole reality consists in their dependence upon the God they manifest. In this respect they are unlike accidents of a substance. Accidents depend upon substance for their being, so that they cease to exist when the substance in which they inhere is destroyed. But it cannot be said that an accident is nothing, for it confers something on substance. For example, it is by quantity that a substance is extended in space. In short, an accident gives something to a substance; but a creature contributes nothing to God. How could it add anything to God if he is the absolute maximum and as such cannot be added to or increased? Consequently, a creature does not even have as much reality as an accident; in itself it is strictly nothing.

This is not to deny that creatures have a positive status or being, given to them by their creator. Nicholas' point is that this status or being is not something absolute but relative, since creatures exist only as appearances of God. Imagine a face whose image is reproduced more or less perfectly in a number of mirrors. It is the same face that appears in many different ways in the images. As images, they have no reality of their own: their whole reality is to mirror more or less exactly the original face. This analogy, with some adjustments, will enable us to understand better the relation of creatures to God. Of course, in this case there are no mirrors in which God projects his appearances. There is nothing but God and his appearances, each of which is a more or less exact resemblance of him.

Nicholas of Cusa expresses this truth in more abstract language by saying that God is both the "enfolding" (*complicatio*) and "unfolding" (*explicatio*) of all things. He is their enfolding because he contains all of them in his simple unity, and he is their unfolding because they issue forth from him while he remains in them. Hence God is both transcendent to his creatures and immanent in them.

He is above them, for he is infinite and they are finite. He is also in them because they are multiple images of him, and reality is present in its appearance.[15]

But if God is in everything, it follows that "everything is in everything else." [16] Nicholas quotes this saying of Anaxagoras, with the remark that perhaps we can understand it even better than he could. Christians know better than pagan philosophers that God is infinite and that all things are in him, while he in turn is in them. And because God is present in all things, it is not difficult to see that each thing is present in every other. The mutual implication of everything in everything becomes clear if we remember Nicholas' illustration of the face reflected in a number of mirrors. The face is present in each image; and since all of them are images of the same face, each image is present in every other. Similarly, God exists in all his creatures and each creature exists in every other. There is consequently a basic unity in all things—a unity which is their reality and which is nothing else than God himself.

When Nicholas says that God is in his creatures, he does not mean that God is limited to what they are. This would be the same as saying that a face is nothing but the reflection it casts on a mirror. As we have seen, God is infinite, and as such he is not identical with anything finite. And yet it is true to say that God is everything that his creatures are, although he is of course infinitely more. In relation to God the universe is finite or limited; or, to use a favorite expression of Nicholas of Cusa, it is a "contraction" of the infinite. By "contraction" he means "the restriction of being in a particular thing." The universe is the maximum contraction of the infinite because it contains all creatures. Individual creatures in turn are lesser contractions of the universe.[17]

This latter statement is in need of explanation. In what sense are the parts of the universe contractions of it? Nicholas of Cusa explains that the term "universe" means universality, or the unity of distinct things. The universe, in short, is the underlying unity of all its distinct parts. The relationship of the universe to all things can be compared to that of universal humanity to individual men. An individual man is a contraction or limitation of universal humanity. Similarly, any particular part of the universe is a contraction or limitation of it. And because the part is not the whole, we cannot say that the universe is identical with any of its parts. The universe, for example, is not the sun or the moon; and yet it is the sun in the sun and the moon in the moon. In somewhat the same fashion humanity is neither Socrates nor Plato, but in Socrates it is Socrates and in Plato it is Plato. The universe, too, exists in a contracted way in all the particular beings that go to make it up. Through contraction, therefore, the universe is in all things, as God is in the universe. Conversely, its parts exist in the universe and the universe itself exists in God. Anaxagoras' dictum is thus verified: everything is in everything. God is in all things through the intermediary of the universe, and all things are in God through the intermediary of the universe.

This line of argument shows that Nicholas of Cusa attributes reality to universals. The universe itself, he tells us, is a universal: it is the universal form embracing all lower forms. This form of the universe is called the Soul of the World.[18] This first and most universal form does not exist apart from individual things; it exists only as contracted in them, just as universal humanity has no separate existence, but exists only as it is contracted in individual men. The form of the universe contains in a unified manner the forms of the ten most general genera (Aristotle's categories), and these in turn contain the forms of all species. Hence a natural genus (for example, substance) is a contraction of the form of the universe, and a species (for example, humanity) is a contraction of the genus of substance. The final contraction is that of the individual in the species (for example, Socrates in the human species). Nicholas agrees with Aristotle that universals have no actual existence apart from individual things, but he does attribute to universals a distinct reality of essence or nature. The form of the universe is not by nature substance, substance is not by nature humanity, nor is humanity by nature Socrates. Universals are distinct in the order of essence or nature but they have no distinct existence, for they exist only in the individuals in which they receive their final contraction or limitation.[19]

From the absolute infinite, therefore, to the lowest of finite beings we observe a progressive contraction. The first contraction results in the form of the universe, which contains the entire universe in a unified manner. This form is further contracted to the most general genera; genera are contracted to species, and species to individual beings. This throws into clearer light the analogy between God and the universe in which he is reflected. Just as God contains the whole universe in a unified manner, so the universe contains in its unity the manifold forms and individuals which go to make it up. And just as God reconciles in his unity all contradictories, so the universe in its unity reconciles all the contradictions within it.

MAN, THE MICROCOSM

MAN OCCUPIES A UNIQUE PLACE in the universe because he is situated between the angels and material beings. And because of this advantageous position he is able to be a link between the spiritual and material worlds, embracing the perfections of both. Man combines within himself matter, organic life, animal life, and rationality. He is consequently the world in miniature or the microcosm. The maximum perfections of the spiritual world are united in him with the minimal perfections of the material world. So the universe, though mirrored in each of its parts, is most perfectly mirrored in man. Indeed, man in himself is a perfect world, though he is also part of the universe. He is also in a special way the image of God, for he unites within himself opposite perfections such as spirituality and materiality.[20]

Because human nature combines within itself the greatest possible number of created perfections, it is eminently suited for union with the absolute maximum or God. This union is found in the Person of Christ, who possesses both the divine and human nature. Christ is therefore the ultimate perfection of the universe and the most perfect union of God and man, of the uncreated and the created. For this reason Nicholas calls Christ the "absolute intermediary" (*medium absolutum*). He is the most perfect link between God and man and the necessary means by which men are united to God to achieve supreme happiness.[21]

The system of Nicholas of Cusa is well designed to achieve its purpose of showing the basic unity of all things and the ultimate reconciliation of opposites. As we have seen, this involves the rejection of the Aristotelian principle of non-contradiction and with it much of his philosophy. It also involves the destruction of Aristotelian physics, which presupposes the existence of opposites in the physical universe. According to Aristotle, the universe is a finite sphere whose center is the earth and whose circumference is the sphere of the fixed stars. This sphere and the others it contains move with a uniform circular movement, while the earth remains at rest. Since the universe has a fixed center, the motion of bodies can be calculated absolutely in reference to it. Bodies move in opposite directions from this absolute center, and there is an absolute "up" and "down."

Nicholas of Cusa's thesis of the coincidence of opposites completely changes the picture of the universe. As we have seen, there is nothing outside the universe which limits it, so that it cannot be said to have a circumference. It is not enclosed within limits, and yet it is not absolutely infinite. It is at once finite and infinite. And because the universe has no circumference, it has no center. Nicholas refuses to give the earth a privileged position in the universe: it is not at its center, nor is it absolutely at rest. Like everything else, it moves, and its motion is relative to other moving bodies. In reply to the objection that the earth does not appear to move, he explains that we detect movement only by reference to something fixed. If a man in a boat on a river did not see the banks and know that the water is moving, he would think that he was standing still. That is the reason why a man on the earth, the sun, or any other planet always has the impression that everything else is moving while he himself is stationary. In short, motion and place are not absolute but relative to the observer.[22]

The main point Nicholas of Cusa wants to make is that the universe is not the scene of unreconcilable oppositions. There is no center in opposition to a circumference; no maximum movement of the spheres in opposition to the minimum movement (or rest) of the earth; no absolute opposition of the directions of moving bodies. We observe oppositions in the universe, but they are relative and not absolute, and they are reconciled in reality. In this respect the universe is a true image of its creator, who is the "coincidence of opposites."

A consequence of this view of the universe is that our knowledge of it is always partial and incomplete. Looking at reality from several points of view, we form various images of it and then merge them together. The result is a "conjecture" but not the entire truth. By a conjecture Nicholas of Cusa does not mean a mere guess, which may be either true or false. Rather, he means a conclusion that is true as far as it goes, though it does not go the whole way and completely measure up to its object.[23] Our knowledge of the universe is in this sense conjectural, just like our knowledge of God, and for exactly the same reason. The truth of the universe is basically one, just like that of God. But we gain knowledge piecemeal, and no synthesis of our bits of knowledge will ever equal the one truth at which they aim. We must rest content with approximate knowledge of the truth and not expect knowledge that is total and absolute. The attitude of learned ignorance is just as necessary in regard to the universe as it is in regard to God.

CONCLUSION

THE COMPLEX PHILOSOPHY of Nicholas of Cusa is not easy to assess. From one point of view it marks a return to the Neoplatonism of the Age of the Fathers. Nicholas did not think that Aristotelianism, which dominated philosophy in the thirteenth and fourteenth centuries, was of much help to the Christian philosopher or theologian. Of what use is Aristotelian logic in solving problems arising in the Christian universe, in which God, the first principle of all things, is infinite and creatures are his finite reflections? Following the example of Eckhart, Nicholas abandoned Aristotelianism in favor of the Neoplatonism espoused by Christian thinkers from St. Augustine to the school of Chartres.

From another point of view Nicholas of Cusa prepared the way for important developments in modern philosophy and science. Echoes of his philosophical ideas can be found in Leibniz' *Monadology*, particularly the notions that every created thing is qualitatively different from every other and that each thing is a mirror of the whole universe. Hegel makes an effort similar to that of Nicholas of Cusa to surmount the principle of non-contradiction and to reach the absolute in which all differences disappear. The interest shown by the nineteenth-century German idealists in Nicholas of Cusa is indicative of the affinity they felt between his thought and their own.

Although Nicholas was interested in mathematics primarily as a help to mystical theology, his speculations concerning mathematical infinity opened up new avenues for the mathematician. Like modern mathematicians, Nicholas does not restrict the field of mathematics to what is directly imaginable, but extends it to the purely intelligible. This marks a great advance over the mathematics of the Middle Ages.

His interest in the infinite is also at the root of his new conception of the physical universe. Although he owned and used astronomical instruments, his cosmology was not inferred from observable data but suggested to him by his notion of the infinite. It was his theological speculation about the infinite that led him to discard the Aristotelian conception of the universe and to propose a new one, in some respects similar to that of modern science. Far from shackling science to Aristotelianism, medieval theology was here liberating the mind and opening up a new vista on the universe.

5 THE MIDDLE AGES AND RENAISSANCE PHILOSOPHY

XXI

Marsilio Ficino and
Pietro Pomponazzi

E VER SINCE THE PUBLICATION in 1860 of Jacob Burckhardt's
The Civilization of the Renaissance in Italy it has been
customary to distinguish between the Middle Ages and the Renaissance as two well-defined periods of history, each animated by its
own spirit and in contradiction to the other. In contrast to the Middle Ages, the Renaissance is said to be characterized by the love of
antiquity, the exaltation of the individual, the cultivation of the
sciences, and naturalism in art and literature. More recent studies,
however, have shown that the popular antithesis between the Middle Ages and the Renaissance is an oversimplification.[1] It is undeniable that in the fifteenth and sixteenth centuries (the period generally assigned to the Renaissance) there were important changes
in Christian culture in western Europe, but it is becoming increasingly clear that there was more continuity between these centuries
and the Middle Ages than was previously suspected. The Renaissance has been described as the period of the rebirth of pagan classical literature, but if we are to believe a recent historian the classical humanism of the Renaissance was fundamentally medieval
and fundamentally Christian.[2] It is true that the Renaissance humanists reacted against Aristotelianism, the dominant philosophy
since the thirteenth century, but they were not opposed to the
Patristic culture of the early Middle Ages, especially as it was
represented by St. Augustine.[3] Not only did they discover the
Latin classics in the manuscripts lovingly copied and preserved by

the monks of the early Middle Ages, but they found among the writers of this period kindred spirits whom they admired and emulated. It is not exact, therefore, to say that the humanists of the Renaissance opposed the Middle Ages. What they generally disliked was but one phase of medieval culture, and indeed its latest; namely, Aristotelianism. They continued and developed, often in brilliant fashion, the Christian culture of the Age of the Fathers.[4]

In the field of philosophy this is most obvious in the cultivation of Platonism by the Renaissance humanists. Throughout the early Middle Ages, Platonism—or more exactly Neoplatonism—was the ruling philosophy. It had been christianized by St. Augustine and had reigned unchallenged until the advent of Aristotelianism in the thirteenth century. With the decline of Aristotle's prestige at the end of the Middle Ages, Christian thinkers once more began to turn to the Neoplatonism of the Fathers for philosophical inspiration. We have seen this happen with Master Eckhart and Nicholas of Cusa. The sources of their knowledge of Platonism, however, were limited to those handed down by the Middle Ages. With minor exceptions they were ignorant of the *Dialogues* of Plato and they had only indirect knowledge of the philosophy of Plotinus. In short, they had practically no firsthand acquaintance with the main source of either Platonism or Neoplatonism. Ficino's translations of Plato and Plotinus in the second half of the fifteenth century filled up this lacuna and opened up a new era in the history of Platonism.

Marsilio Ficino and the Platonic Academy

FICINO'S MEETING with Cosimo de' Medici in Florence in 1452 was a turning point in his life and in the advancement of Platonic studies.[5] Under Cosimo's patronage he founded the Platonic Academy and dedicated the rest of his life to translating, interpreting, and teaching the Platonic philosophy. The idea of a Platonic Academy had been inspired in Cosimo by the Byzantine Platonist Pletho, who lectured in Florence in 1438. With the capture of Constantinople by the Turks in 1453, Greek scholars came to Italy in great numbers, affording a new contact between the Latin world and Greek learning. Ficino mastered the Greek language and translated into Latin the *Dialogues* and *Letters* of Plato, the *Enneads* of Plotinus, and some of the works of Porphyry, Proclus, and other pagan Neoplatonists. He also translated the works of Dionysius the Pseudo-Areopagite, as Scotus Erigena had done in the ninth century. Besides this, he wrote commentaries on Plato's *Parmenides*, *Timaeus, Phaedrus, Sophist, Philebus*, and *Symposium*, and on Plotinus' *Enneads*. His most important work is the *Platonic Theology*, written between 1469 and 1474.

Ficino's attachment to Plato was religious in its fervor. He describes himself as born of his father but reborn of Cosimo de' Medici, who consecrated him to the "divine" Plato.[6] In his opinion Plato ranks above Aristotle, for the latter deals with the world of nature while the former reveals divine realities. Through Platonism the soul rises from lower to higher things and from darkness to light—light that has its source in the divine mind. The Platonism extolled by Ficino, however, is not simply that of Plato himself but the Platonism of living Christian tradition. Indeed, he tells us that Platonism reached its peak in Dionysius, whom he thought to be a disciple of St. Paul. This Platonism lived through the Middle Ages up to the time of Ficino, although it had grown dim and needed to be restored. Among medieval authors he recommends for their Platonism not only Dionysius but also St. Augustine, Boethius, Apuleius, Chalcidius, Macrobius, Avicebron, Alfarabi, Avicenna, Henry of Ghent, Duns Scotus, and in his own time Nicholas of Cusa.[7] The name of St. Thomas Aquinas is noticeably absent from this list; but if Ficino does not recommend him for continuing the Platonic tradition, he does have high praise for him as a theologian. He calls St. Thomas "the splendor of theology" and incorporates passages from his *Summa Contra Gentiles* into his own *Platonic Theology*. As a youth, Ficino was persuaded to read this work of St. Thomas by a Dominican named St. Antoninus, and it exercised a considerable influence upon him. As we shall see, however, he uses St. Thomas within the framework of his own Platonic philosophy.

Throughout the works of Ficino there is no condemnation of the scholastic theologians. He sincerely admires them and freely draws upon them when their ideas are useful for his purpose. The chief objects of his criticism are the Aristotelian philosophers of his day. These philosophers, he says, are divided into two sects: the followers of Alexander of Aphrodisias and the followers of Averroes. They have the whole world in their hands, Ficino laments, and they lead men away from religion by their false doctrines. Both sects undermine Christianity: the Alexandrists by denying the immortality of man's soul, the Averroists by claiming that there is only one intellectual soul for all men. Ficino did not think this danger to Christianity could be averted simply by preaching the Gospel; irreligion was too widely diffused and defended by too clever arguments for that to be effective. In the absence of widespread miracles that would convince everybody of the truth of the Catholic faith, there was needed a "philosophical religion" or "pious philosophy" that would appeal to the philosophers' reason and win them over to Christianity.[8] Ficino thought he had found this philosophy in Platonism. His revival of Platonic studies, therefore, was not the work of an antiquarian interested in Platonism for its own sake. It was the work of a Christian theologian who, like St. Augustine, saw in Platonism the philosophy closest to Christian doctrine and the most effective means of leading philosophers to Christ.

GOD AS UNITY

IN THE SYSTEM OF PLOTINUS the multitude of beings that make up the universe emanate from a First Principle called the One or the Good. It is called the One because it contains no division or multiplicity of parts; it is called the Good because it bestows on all things whatever perfections they have. The One itself is not a thing or being, for every being is but one of a number of other beings. In other words, a being is a part of the whole that we call the universe, whereas the One is the source of the whole universe and of all its parts. Because it is the source of beings, it is superior to them.

Ficino christianizes the Plotinian system, as St. Augustine, Dionysius, and Scotus Erigena did in the early Middle Ages. In his philosophy the One of Plotinus becomes the Christian God, and the beings emanating from it become the universe created by God out of nothing. The mark of Neoplatonism, however, remains stamped upon Ficino's philosophy, for he agrees with Plotinus that the First Principle is most properly called Unity and not Being. The proper name of God, he tells us, is Unity. The reason for this is that the concept of unity is more simple and universal than that of being, and so it is more suitably attributed to God, who is most simple in himself and most universal in his causality. We speak of privations and primary matter as one, although we do not call them beings. Hence oneness or unity is a broader concept than that of being and it is more fittingly applied to God.⁹

A contemporary of Ficino's named Pico della Mirandola wrote a small treatise, *On Being and Unity*, in which he takes the opposite position; namely, that God is more properly called Being than Unity. He points out that Aristotle shows that being and unity are convertible terms, and hence one is not more universal than the other. Moreover, God revealed his name to Moses as "I Am Who Am," indicating that his proper name is Being and not Unity.¹⁰

Ficino takes issue with the position of Pico, which we shall recognize as that of St. Thomas Aquinas. He points out that this opinion is contrary to the Platonists and to the "divine" Parmenides. Because of its simplicity, unity is superior to all being. A being is not simple but is composed of several parts. The union of these parts is the cause of the being. In short, unity is the cause of being and consequently it is more excellent than being.¹¹

The most basic composition in beings is that of essence and existence (*esse*). In describing this composition Ficino obviously draws upon the works of St. Thomas. The essence of a being, Ficino tells us, is not the same as its existence. Its essence is that which is contained in its definition, while its existence is the actuality of the essence and its presence in nature. For example, the essence of a comet is "a dry vapor in the upper air, set on fire and bearing an orderly course through the sky." This definition is always true because the essence it signifies is always the same. No matter where or when comets appear in the sky, they have the same essence. So, too, the essence "humanity" is the same no matter when or where it is found; it is the same today as it was in past centuries, and it is the same in the East and in the West. When God creates essences, however, he gives them existence in nature. If they are the essences of natural bodies, they are restricted in place and time; and they come into being gradually, change, and then go out of existence. Accordingly, the essence of a natural body is immortal in itself, but it is mortal in the individual body in which it exists.[12]

This shows that the presence in nature, or the existence, of a being is not the same as its essence, since the former is changeable, whereas the latter is not. In describing the relation of essence to existence, Ficino agrees with St. Thomas that essence is potential to existence, which in turn is the act of essence. Since the essence is in potentiality to existence, an external agent is needed to make it actually exist, and this is the Being who is pure act; namely, God.[13]

At this point Ficino is in a position to conclude with St. Thomas that God is the pure act of Being, and he does not hesitate to do so. But he immediately qualifies this conclusion by noting that, according to the Platonists, this does not mean that God is, properly speaking, being, but rather that he is the source of being. God is properly unity and goodness.[14] Ficino's Thomism is consequently short-lived. He follows St. Thomas up to the point where the Angelic Doctor proves that God is pure act, but then abandons him for the Platonists. And his reason is clear. In his view, act is relative to potency, and existence is relative to essence. Hence existence is found only in a being composed of parts, one of which is potential to the other. Now it is clear that God is simple and not composed of parts. Consequently, we cannot properly attribute existence or being to him. Rather, we must call him the One or the Good.

THE IMMORTALITY OF THE SOUL

THE IMMORTALITY of the human soul was one of the central problems of Renaissance philosophy. It looms large in the works of Ficino; indeed, the subtitle of his *Platonic Theology* is *On the Im-*

mortality of Souls. The reason for his preoccupation with this subject has already been suggested. The majority of contemporary philosophers adopted either the Alexandrist or Averroist interpretation of Aristotle, both of which denied personal immortality. The result was a widespread falling away from the Christian religion in educated circles. Alarmed by this growing irreligion, Ficino set out to give a philosophical defense of the immortality of the soul to win men back to Christianity.

Most of the arguments in favor of immortality amassed by Ficino in Books 5–14 of his *Platonic Theology* are inspired by Plato and St. Augustine, although, surprisingly enough, St. Thomas' preferred proof is also among them. Among the Platonic-Augustinian arguments is that based upon the affinity between the human soul and the immaterial and eternal. In its search for truth the intellect leaves matter entirely behind and ascends to the realm of the eternal and incorporeal. This is clear from the fact that, just as the body is nourished by bread, the mind feeds and waxes strong on truth. Now truth is not found in bodies, for they are changeable, while truth is unchangeable. It may be thought that truth is present in the forms of bodies, but this is an illusion. A bodily form is not a true form. This is obvious to the mathematician, who knows that the true figures he studies are not those perceived by the senses. The mathematical circle, for example, touches a tangent at only one point, but this is not true of a material circle. Nor are there any true points, lines, or surfaces in bodies. What we perceive in them are only images of true mathematical forms. But truth must reside somewhere, and if it is not in the senses or in bodies it must exist in spiritual beings. Hence truth is incorporeal, and the soul that feeds upon it is also incorporeal and immortal.[15]

Ficino also argues that the natural desire of the human soul would be frustrated if it died with the body. The intellect desires to know the truth, and the will longs for goodness, and these powers of the soul are not satisfied with finite truth and goodness but want to press on to the infinite. The longing itself of the soul for the infinite reveals its kinship with eternity and infinity. But in its present life the soul cannot satisfy its desire for the infinite. It must live its life among finite things, which are bound to leave it unsatisfied.

The very thought of dying leaves the soul miserable. If there were no future life, its state would be one of unhappiness and frustration. Men would be even less happy than brute animals, which can fulfill their natural desires in this world. Certainly men are more perfect than they and as capable of gaining possession of their desired end, which is nothing short of infinite truth and goodness. Consequently, the human soul must be immortal.[16]

Ficino offers a more abstract metaphysical argument for the immortality of the soul based upon its essence as a spiritual substance and its relation to existence. The source of this argument is neither Plato nor St. Augustine but St. Thomas Aquinas. Ficino read St. Thomas' *Summa Contra Gentiles* with great care and insight, including Book II, Chapter 55, in which intellectual substances are proved to be incorruptible. Whole passages from this chapter reappear in the *Platonic Theology,* couched in more elegant Latin, according to Renaissance standards, but with the thought essentially unchanged.

Ficino observes with St. Thomas that a thing begins to exist by receiving form, and it ceases to exist by losing form. For example, a bronze statue comes into existence when it is formed by the artist, and it loses existence by losing its form. Now the human soul is not composed of matter and form. It is a simple, spiritual essence or form. So it cannot be separated from its form. If it could, it would have to be separated from itself. The soul receives a spiritual mode of existence from God, and it possesses that existence in its own right (*per se*), as a circle possesses roundness. It cannot lose its existence, therefore, any more than a circle can lose roundness. Once it has been given existence, it can never lose it by itself or by the action of an external agent. It cannot lose it by itself, because existence belongs to it through its very essence (that is to say, through its form, which is identical with its essence). Neither will it be deprived of existence by God, because it was he who determined the soul to be what it is and he will not go contrary to his own law. Ficino concludes with St. Thomas that the human soul will never go out of existence, because it has no potentiality to non-existence. It has no tendency in itself to cease to exist, and

God will not destroy it, because he has willed it to be indestructible, and his will is unchangeable.[17]

It is all the more remarkable to find this Thomistic demonstration of the immortality of the soul in Ficino's *Platonic Theology* in view of the fact that Thomists themselves during the Renaissance (and much later) did not avail themselves of it. Even Cajetan (1469–1534), one of the leading commentators on St. Thomas, does not use it. In his later life Cajetan says that he knows of no philosophical or demonstrative argument in favor of immortality, and he rests the certainty of life after death upon faith.[18] It was to combat this attitude, so widespread in Ficino's day, that he drew upon all the philosophical sources at his command, including St. Thomas, to demonstrate the immortality of the soul.

PLATONIC LOVE

A REMARKABLE EVENT took place at Careggio on November 7, 1474. At the invitation of Lorenzo de' Medici a group of nine Platonists gathered at the Platonic Academy to attend a banquet in honor of Plato's birthday. Up to the time of Plotinus and Porphyry this memorial feast was held each year on the traditional date of Plato's birth. After a lapse of twelve hundred years Ficino and his friends were reviving this ancient custom. When the banquet was over, one of the group read Plato's *Banquet* and the others were then invited to comment on the speeches on love which it contains. Afterward Ficino incorporated these comments in a commentary on Plato's *Banquet*, which enjoyed great popularity and exercised a deep influence on both the philosophy and literature of the Renaissance.

Love plays a central role in Ficino's thought, for he conceives it as the bond uniting all the parts of the universe to each other and the whole universe to God. By the unitive power of love the universe most closely resembles its creator, who is Unity itself. As we can see, Ficino uses the term "love" in a broad sense. It is the bond uniting any two things as a result of their similarity to each other. Love is universal, therefore, because everything bears some resemblance to everything else. "Consequently all the parts of the universe," Ficino writes, "are bound to each other by a mutual love because they are the works of one artist and parts of one structure similar to each other in their being and life, so that love may well be called the perpetual bond and connecting link of the universe, the immovable support of its parts and the solid foundation of the whole structure." [19]

Because all men are members of the same species, there is a special bond between them and a special love which Ficino calls "humanity" (*humanitas*). This love impels us to regard all men as our brothers, born in a long series from the same father. The greater love we have for our fellow men, the more humane we are and the more perfectly we measure up to the essence of humanity. Boys and stupid persons are crueler than intelligent adults because the former fall short of the perfect nature of man.[20]

Love in souls is the desire to enjoy beauty. It is at the same time the desire for goodness, for, according to Ficino, the good is the same as the beautiful. More precisely, beauty is the effulgence or splendor of goodness, attracting souls and leading them to pursue the good. Beauty ordinarily consists in the harmony or proportion of the parts of some whole. In bodies, for example, beauty is the harmony between several colors and lines, and in sounds it is the consonance of several voices.[21] Pure beauty, like pure goodness, however, does not consist in a relation of parts but in pure Unity, which is identical with God. The beauty and goodness of the universe are but faint reflections of the divine beauty and goodness—reflections that are meant to attract us to their source in God.

Human souls are attracted first of all by the beauty of bodies, but here a snare is lying in wait. No body is completely beautiful, nor is it beautiful forever. Its beauty is but a passing reflection of the beauty of the soul that animates it. So the lover should raise himself to admire the beauty of souls rather than that of bodies. He abuses love if he concentrates his gaze on bodily beauty and lusts for it to the forgetfulness of the nobler beauty of souls. This latter beauty consists in the harmony of knowledge and virtue, and it is but a reflection of the beauty of the angels. Their beauty in turn is an image of the pure and infinite beauty of God.

The true lover, therefore, is he who loves God. Wherever he encounters beauty, whether in bodies or in souls, he is drawn to the divine beauty, which is the real center of the universe and the true inspiration of all love.[22]

By his translations of the Platonists, his writings and his lectures, Ficino (to use his own expression) "restored the Platonic doctrine from darkness to light." His Platonic Academy became the mecca of Platonist scholars and the center of diffusion of the Platonic philosophy throughout Europe. In particular, Ficino's doctrine of love had a deep influence on the literature of the Renaissance. Traces of it can be found in Italy in the works of Pico della Mirandola, Bembo, and Castiglione; in France in the writings of Lefèvre d'Etaples, Symphorien Champier, and Marguerite de Navarre; and in England in the poetry of Spenser and the works of the Cambridge Platonists.

Pietro Pomponazzi

WHILE PLATONISM GREW in popularity through the efforts of Nicholas of Cusa and Ficino, Aristotelianism still ruled supreme in the universities. The success of Aristotle's philosophy since its discovery in the thirteenth century was due not only to its intrinsic merits but also in no small measure to its adaptability for classroom purposes. The division of Aristotle's works into logic, physics, metaphysics, ethics, and politics, and the orderly arrangement of their contents, made them almost ideal instruments for teaching philosophy. As a result, it was difficult to displace them in the universities despite the growth of anti-Aristotelian forces at the end of the Middle Ages. As late as the seventeenth century Descartes tried in vain to win the schools away from Aristotelianism to his own philosophy.

We know from the testimony of Ficino that Aristotelianism in the fifteenth century was divided into two sects, the Alexandrists and the Averroists. The Averroists traced their origin to Siger of Brabant. The Averroist movement he began did not die out with its condemnation in 1277, but continued to hold its ground at the

University of Paris, whence it spread to the universities of northern Italy. In the fourteenth century the outstanding Averroist at Paris was John of Jandun (d. *c.* 1328), who called himself the "ape of Averroes." Associated with him was Marsilius of Padua (d. between 1336 and 1343). Marsilius' strict separation of Church and state and subordination of the former to the latter reflect Averroes' views on the relation between religion and philosophy. By the end of the fifteenth century the majority of Aristotelians in northern Italy accepted Averroism, especially the doctrine of the oneness of the intellect in all men.

The origin of the Alexandrist sect is more obscure. Alexander's doctrine of the intellect was known in the thirteenth century through Averroes' account of it and through Gerard of Cremona's translation of a fragment of Alexander's *De Anima* entitled *On the Intellect*. But there is no evidence of the existence of an Alexandrist school at that time. The sect seems to have arisen in the fifteenth century as a result of renewed contact with the Greek text of Aristotle and of his ancient commentators. The revival of Greek learning in Italy prompted scholars to read the works of Aristotle in their original language, and in 1497 the Faculty of Arts at Padua erected a chair for the teaching of Aristotle in Greek. A greater effort was thus made to understand the thought of Aristotle as expressed in his own language. Interest was also aroused in Aristotle's Greek commentators, one of the most important of whom was Alexander of Aphrodisias. In the 1480's his treatise *On the Intellect* was printed in Venice, popularizing his opinion that, according to Aristotle, each man is endowed with his own intellect, which dies with the body. A growing number of Aristotelian scholars began to prefer Alexander's interpretation of Aristotle to that of Averroes, the most famous of whom was Pietro Pomponazzi.[23]

THE PROBLEM OF THE SOUL

THE AVERROISTIC DOCTRINE of the soul appeared to Pomponazzi as absurd and completely foreign to Aristotle. Averroes' notion that all men share the same intellect was especially repugnant to him, as it was to St. Thomas Aquinas. Pomponazzi does not bother to refute it but simply refers his readers to the works of St. Thomas, "the glory of the Latins," who, he says, has so completely destroyed the Averroist doctrine of the soul that the Averroists could do nothing in rebuttal but rail and curse him. As for Averroes' claim to teach the true Aristotelian doctrine, Pomponazzi points out that in fact Averroes contradicts the words of Aristotle. According to Averroes, the human intellect is so separated from matter that it does not have to gather its knowledge through the sense powers. But Aristotle clearly states in his *De Anima* that there is no human knowledge without images—a fact, Pomponazzi adds, confirmed by experience. Contrary to Averroes, therefore, the intellect does not have an operation entirely independent of the body. It necessarily depends upon the body and its sense organs to furnish it with objects of knowledge.[24]

While accepting St. Thomas' criticism of Averroes, Pomponazzi considers the Thomistic solution of the problem of the soul equally unacceptable to the philosopher. St. Thomas tries to prove that the intellectual soul is a spiritual and immortal substance, directly created by God as the form of the human body. Pomponazzi does not deny that this is true, but he doubts whether it can be rationally demonstrated and if it is in agreement with Aristotle. "I do not doubt at all," he writes, "the truth of this position, since the canonical Scripture, which must be preferred to any human reasoning and experience because it was given by God, sanctions it. But what I do question is whether [the Thomistic propositions concerning the soul] go beyond the limits of nature, so that they presuppose faith or revelation, and whether they conform to the statements of Aristotle as St. Thomas himself declares." [25]

Following his usual practice, Pomponazzi here professes to be a loyal Catholic and to accept the teachings of sacred Scripture. He does not call into question the truths of revelation, but he does have serious doubts whether human reason can demonstrate revealed truths such as the immortality of the soul. On the contrary, he is quite convinced that reason, left to itself, concludes that the human soul dies with the body. Moreover, he is quite convinced that this is what Aristotle taught. We shall have to return to

Pomponazzi's attitude toward faith and reason. From what we have seen, however, it is clear that he does not think they agree on the subject of the immortality of the soul.

Pomponazzi objects to St. Thomas' doctrine of the soul on two main scores. First, he does not see how the intellectual soul can be both a subsistent reality in itself and also the substantial form of the body. A substantial form, he argues, is the actuality of matter, and as such it is inseparable from matter. A soul is simply the substantial form of a living being or, more exactly, according to Aristotle's definition, the actuality of a physical and organic body. But if this is true, a soul cannot be something existing in its own right and separable from the body.

We have already seen St. Thomas' solution of this apparent contradiction. According to him, the intellectual soul is a unique kind of form in that it possesses its own being (*esse*), which it communicates to the body by informing it. The souls of plants and brute animals, on the other hand, have no being besides that of the composite of which they are a part. Hence they cannot survive the dissolution of the composite. Intellectual souls, however, being endowed with their own existences, do not cease to exist when the bodies they inform are destroyed.

A correct understanding of St. Thomas' doctrine of the human soul and of man presupposes a knowledge of his metaphysical notions of essence and being, which Pomponazzi, like so many of his contemporaries, lacked. He so far misunderstands St. Thomas as to ascribe to him the notion that the Aristotelian definition of the soul applies univocally (that is to say, in the same sense) to all souls.[26] But it is just on this point that Pomponazzi differs from St. Thomas, who emphasizes that the intellectual soul informs the human body in a manner unlike that of any other substantial form.

The second objection Pomponazzi directs against St. Thomas is that the immortality of the soul contradicts the evident fact that the intellect depends upon the senses for its knowledge. If the soul is the actuality of an organic body, this is because the soul needs the body in order to know. Indeed, in all its knowledge it must use the imagination. But if this is so, the intellectual soul is material and inseparable from the body.

Pomponazzi qualifies this conclusion by distinguishing between subjective and objective dependence of the intellect upon the body.[27] The intellect, he says, is *objectively* dependent upon the body and its sense organs, for without them it would have no objects to know. But the intellect is not *subjectively* dependent upon the body, because it does not reside in an organ. In this respect it is unlike the power of sight, which is in the eyes, or the power of hearing, which is in the ears. If the intellect resided in an organ, it would be quantitative and extended with the organ, and then it could not reflect upon itself, think discursively, or understand universals, for no organic and extended power can perform these operations. Pomponazzi is willing to grant that self-reflection and the understanding of universals are beyond the power of mere matter. Properly speaking, they are operations of the separated Intelligences, which are truly spiritual and immortal beings. The fact that the human intellect is capable of an obscure knowledge of self and of universals proves that it touches upon the immaterial order even though it does not strictly belong to it. Pomponazzi expresses this by saying that the intellect participates in immateriality and immortality without properly possessing these characteristics. The notion of participation that he invokes at this point is the Platonic one, according to which the participant in a perfection does not strictly possess that perfection but simply bears a resemblance to it. The participated quality is but a shadow of the true quality. So it is with human understanding. It has but a shadow or trace of immateriality and immortality; strictly speaking, it is material and mortal. The same is true of the human soul. It is a material and mortal form, and it owes its existence not to an act of creation but to an act of natural generation; moreover, it ceases to exist when the body is destroyed.

Pomponazzi defended this conception of the human soul against Alexander Achillini (1463–1512), who taught the Averroist doctrine at the Universities of Padua and Bologna. He also upheld it against Agostino Nifo (1469/70–1539/46), who was an Averroist in his youth but soon turned from Averroism to a distorted form of Thomism.[28] But Pomponazzi always qualified his stand by the admission that even though Alexandrism is the most acceptable philosophical doctrine of the soul and most in conformity with Aristotle, it is but a probable opinion, which must give way to the revealed truth that the human soul is immortal.[29] Hence he was able to accept the decree of the Fifth Lateran Council (1512–1517), which condemned both the Averroist and the Alexandrist doctrines of the soul.

ETHICAL NOTIONS

SOME OF THE OBJECTIONS leveled against Pomponazzi's doctrine of the soul involve moral issues. It was claimed that if the human soul is mortal, happiness lies beyond the grasp of man and he has no final goal in life. It will be remembered that one of Ficino's arguments for immortality rests upon man's desire for infinite truth and goodness, which can be found only in a future life. Pomponazzi agrees that man has a goal in life, but he points out that this goal must be suitable to man's nature. Since man is mortal, his goal is not eternal and immortal, but something that he can attain in this life. Immortal and eternal happiness is suitable to a divine being but hardly to man. A man who desires eternal happiness is not temperate, for he desires the impossible. "For it is characteristic of a temperate appetite," Pomponazzi writes, "to desire only as much as it can digest. So it is characteristic of a temperate man to be content with what is suitable to him and what he can have." The fact that he cannot know everything or live eternally will not disturb such a man, nor does it put him on a lower level than brute animals. Anticipating John Stuart Mill, Pomponazzi asks: "Who would prefer to be a stone or a deer of long life rather than a man of however miserable condition? The wise man would much prefer to be in extreme necessity and the greatest troubles than to be stupid, cowardly and vicious under the opposite conditions." [30]

What, then, is the fitting goal of human life? In answering this question Pomponazzi compares the whole human race to a single man. A man has many members, each with its own function and proximate end, but all contribute to the one final end of the man, and in so doing they are brought into unity and have something in common with each other. So, too, the members of the human race have different and unequal tasks to perform in society, yet they all contribute to the common good of mankind. And in doing this they share in three intellects: the speculative, the productive, and the practical. All men share in the speculative intellect, for they know at least some primary principles and notions, such as being, the good, and so on. They also have some share in the productive intellect because every man, to some extent, has to be a builder and maker. Finally, all men participate in the practical intellect, which Pomponazzi conceives as man's moral faculty, concerned with virtue both public and private. The perfection of the practical intellect is the common goal of all men and it most befits man as man because it is in everyone's power and it makes man good without qualification. Not everyone can be a perfect metaphysician, mathematician, or builder, nor is it desirable that he be. The good of society demands that perfection in these pursuits be divided among its members. But it is within everyone's power to be perfectly virtuous, and he is blamed if he falls short of this goal. "So the universal goal of the human race," Pomponazzi concludes, "is to participate relatively in the speculative and productive intellects, but perfectly in the practical." [31]

Since moral virtue is the ultimate goal of mankind, it should not be valued because of external rewards. Following the ancient Stoics, Pomponazzi claims that virtue is its own reward, so much so that if a person seeks virtue for some other reason his virtue is thereby lessened. No good action goes unrewarded and no bad action unpunished, since virtue carries with it its own reward and vice its own punishment. Hence divine justice is fulfilled in the present life; we do not have to wait for a life beyond the grave to receive the reward for our good deeds or the punishment for our evil ones. [32] Pomponazzi's ethics consequently does not look beyond the horizon of the present life. Man can attain his goal in this world through his own efforts by cultivating virtue and avoiding vice.

This naturalistic attitude is also found in Pomponazzi's *De Incantationibus,* which concerns miracles, magic, and in general extraordinary occurrences in nature. At the outset he proclaims his belief in the teachings of the Church. He believes that God can cause miracles by directly intervening in nature and that demons can influence matter and bring about preternatural phenomena, but he is convinced that this is contrary to Aristotle and to sound philosophy. Like Siger of Brabant, he proposes a natural explanation of magic and the marvelous in nature.[33] Nature, he says, contains hidden powers capable of extraordinary effects, and man himself has a great influence upon his own body and those of others through his ideas and imagination. What these powers cannot account for can be explained by the influence of the heavenly bodies, which have a visible effect upon the world. The cures worked through the relics of the saints can be explained by the secret powers of nature and also by the faith and imagination of the one healed. There is no necessity to think that these cures are brought about by spiritual beings acting through the power of God.[34]

The popular conceptions of God moved by our prayers, and of angels and demons interfering in human affairs are poetic fictions, useful for inducing the uneducated crowd to do good and to avoid evil, but without a place in philosophy. Pomponazzi, like Averroes, grants that religion has an important role to play in society by stimulating men to virtue,[35] but he insists that philosophers, whom he calls "the only gods of this earth," do not need the incentive of rewards to lead a virtuous life. They know that virtue is its own reward, just as vice is its own punishment.

RELIGION AND PHILOSOPHY

BECAUSE OF THE DIFFERENCE of their viewpoints and the opposition between their teachings it is inevitable that conflicts arise between the devotees of religion and the philosophers. In order to avoid trouble Pomponazzi gives the philosophers of his day the same advice Averroes gave the philosophers of Islam: Keep philosophy out of the hands of the common people and of uneducated priests. They are incapable of learning it, and because it goes counter to their accustomed ideas they will drive philosophers from their cities and even kill them.[36] Pomponazzi obviously had in mind

Socrates' death at the hands of the Athenians, and he was careful to avoid a similar fate at the hands of his countrymen. Although he wrote the *De Incantationibus* in 1520, he did not allow its publication within his lifetime. The first edition appeared in 1556. He also took the precaution in his published works (as in the *De Incantationibus*) to retract as false whatever he wrote contrary to the Catholic faith. Like Siger of Brabant and Boetius of Dacia, he never professed a double truth. He was careful to place truth on the side of faith and to present his opposing philosophical ideas as the conclusions of fallible human reason or simply as the opinions of past philosophers.

Was he a sincere Christian or simply giving lip-service to the faith to avoid persecution? From the available evidence it is impossible to be sure of the answer.[37] We cannot probe his innermost thoughts, any more than we can those of the thirteenth-century Latin Averroists. There are, however, some disquieting statements in his works. In the *De Incantationibus*, for example, he detects the decline of the Christian religion in his own day and predicts its impending end. "In our faith," he writes, "everything is growing cold, miracles are ceasing except fictitious ones; for the end seems to be near." [38]

When Pomponazzi writes in this manner he reveals a spirit foreign to Siger of Brabant and Boetius of Dacia. We find nothing in their works comparable to the Italian philosopher's anti-clerical and anti-religious sentiments. But he was writing in a different century, when the rift between reason and faith had widened and minds inclined to rationalism expressed themselves more freely and boldly. He was also writing in a different milieu—northern Italy, where the declining years of the Middle Ages saw the growth of a lay and anti-clerical spirit. It was there in the fourteenth century that Marsilius of Padua drew up the program of a lay state to which the Church was subordinate [39] and John of Jandun philosophized as an Averroist, with an independent and apparently mocking attitude toward the faith.[40] Pomponazzi carried on in his own way the rationalist movement begun by these philosophers.

The influence of Pomponazzi's rationalist tendencies was felt in both Italian and French intellectual circles in the sixteenth century. Jerome Cardan (1501–1576) and Lucilio Vanini (1585–1619) popularized his doctrines in Italy. The latter was not as prudent in his teaching as Pomponazzi and he was burned as a heretic at Toulouse. The Italian philosophy of this period was characterized by freedom of thought and liberation from traditional religious ideas. It was the age of Niccolò Machiavelli (1469–1527), whose political philosophy is a cynical analysis of the state without regard for the moral law, and of Giordano Bruno (1548–1600), whose philosophy shows a tendency toward pantheistic monism, anticipating in some respects the philosophy of Spinoza. Like Vanini, Bruno suffered death at the hands of the Inquisition. It will be noticed, incidentally, that philosophers were treated more harshly for their unorthodoxy in this period than in the Middle Ages.

From Italy free-thought and skepticism spread to France. The Renaissance, which began with the conviction of the dignity of man and the greatness of his powers, was rapidly coming to the conclusion that he is incapable of reaching truth in philosophy. Reviving the skepticism of Pyrrho, Michel de Montaigne (1533–1592) doubted that we can be certain of anything, owing to the fallibility of our senses and the weakness of our reason. He even conjectured that some animals might be more intelligent and prudent than men because they have keener senses. In the absence of any demonstrative proof for the existence of God, the freedom of the will, and the immortality of the soul, Montaigne advised a Stoical attitude toward life and a reliance upon the customs and accepted ideas of the society in which we live. Having reached this nadir, philosophy was awaiting a genius who would reconstruct it by setting it upon a new foundation. This genius appeared in the person of René Descartes; but with him a new era in philosophy begins.

XXII

Renaissance
Scholasticism.
Francis Suarez

SCHOLASTICISM OUTLIVED THE MIDDLE AGES and remained an important intellectual force throughout the Renaissance and early modern times. Although the scholasticism of this period takes us beyond the chronological limits of the Middle Ages, it is perhaps most suitably treated in a volume on medieval philosophy because it lived largely on the medieval scholastic heritage and continued its ideas and methods. For the most part it was untouched by the upheavals of the Renaissance, and it failed to keep pace with the advances of contemporary science. It is significant that one of the chief centers of the revival of scholasticism in the sixteenth century was Spain, a country relatively sheltered from the new winds of doctrine that were transforming Europe. This helps to account for the lack of fecundity and originality of this latter-day scholasticism and for its failure to take the lead in the intellectual life of the day. It preserved many scholastic notions and passed them on to modern philosophers, but with the exception of legal and political theory it contributed little to the advancement of learning.[1] It did not even grasp with exactness and profundity the most personal doctrines of St. Thomas Aquinas. When the Renaissance scholastics commented on or defended Thomism, it was too often the distorted Thomism of the later Middle Ages rather than that of St. Thomas himself.

John Capreolus

THIS IS WELL ILLUSTRATED by John Capreolus, a French Dominican who was born about 1380, taught at Paris and Toulouse, and died at Rodez in 1444. His most important work, a defense of St. Thomas entitled *Defensiones Theologiae Divi Thomae Aquinatis*, won him the title "Prince of the Thomists." [2] Capreolus shows a wide acquaintance with all the great medieval scholastics. His avowed purpose was to advance nothing new but simply to explain and to defend St. Thomas in his master's own words; but this did not prevent his occasionally speaking the language of St. Thomas' opponents and proposing doctrines little in harmony with authentic Thomism. For example, he defends the real distinction of essence and existence in creatures as a distinction between two beings, the "being of essence" and the "being of existence," and not, as St. Thomas does, as a distinction between essence and being (*esse*), conceived as principles within a created being.[3] Capreolus suggests that the being that belongs to an essence in itself is uncreated and eternal, for an essence is what it is without any creative activity of God. A rose, for instance, is eternally a rose, and a man is eternally a man, whether or not God actually created roses or men. God, therefore, is not the efficient cause of an essence; he is only its formal cause by eternally conceiving it within his mind. The existence of creatures, on the other hand, is created; for unless he wills to create them they do not actually exist.[4] There is no doubt, then, that the essence and existence of a creature are really distinct: the former is an eternal, uncreated being, whereas the latter is non-eternal and created.

Capreolus presents this as the teaching of St. Albert and many other scholastics, including St. Thomas. He is aware, however, that St. Thomas expresses himself differently in his own writings. In his *De Potentia*, St. Thomas asserts that both the essence and being (*esse*) of a creature are created by God. An essence is nothing before it is created, except in the mind of the creator, where it is not a creature but the creative essence of God. Capreolus thought this manner of putting the matter safer than the former, but he did not consider the Albertinian doctrine wrong, nor did he consider it altogether at variance with Thomism.⁵ We shall see how vulnerable to the criticism of Suarez this manner of distinguishing essence and existence is.

The two chief centers of Renaissance scholasticism were Italy and Spain. We shall consider each of these in turn.

Italian Dominicans

THE OUTSTANDING ITALIAN SCHOLASTICS belonged to the Dominican Order and made their explicit aim the explanation and defense of St. Thomas. Among them, mention should be made of Barbus Paulus Soncinas (d. 1494), the author of *Quaestiones Metaphysicales* and a summary of Capreolus entitled *Epitome Capreoli.* Chrysostom Javelli (*c.* 1470–*c.* 1538) taught at Bologna and wrote many commentaries on Aristotle and treatises in defense of Thomism. Among the latter is a treatise against Pomponazzi, upholding the capacity of natural reason to prove the immortality of the soul. Francis de Sylvestris (*c.* 1474–1528), called "Ferrariensis" from his native city of Ferrara, lectured at Bologna and wrote a commentary on St. Thomas' *Summa Contra Gentiles* that has been printed in the Leonine edition of the works of St. Thomas.

The most influential Italian Dominican commentator on St. Thomas was Cardinal Thomas de Vio (1469–1534), popularly known as Cajetan. The revival of scholasticism at the end of the nineteenth century, initiated by Pope Leo XIII, brought Cajetan into prominence, and he has exercised a deep influence on modern Thomism. He is best known for his commentary on St. Thomas' *Summa Theologiae* (printed in the Leonine edition of the works of St. Thomas), his commentary on St. Thomas' *De Ente et Essentia*, and his treatise *De Nominum Analogia.*⁶

After studying at Naples, Bologna, and Padua, he lectured at the latter university from 1493 to 1494. At Padua he enjoyed the title of Public Metaphysician, and in this role he defended Thomism against its rivals, Scotism and Averroism. He was the first to use

St. Thomas' *Summa Theologiae* as a theological textbook instead of the *Sentences* of Peter Lombard.

Despite his reputation as a commentator on St. Thomas, recent studies have cast doubt upon his reliability as a guide to the thought of the Angelic Doctor.[7] Cajetan has been revealed as a man of the sixteenth century, preoccupied with the theological and philosophical problems of his own day, and speaking its own language, which is not always that of St. Thomas. This is not said in disparagement of Cajetan, but simply as a warning not to identify his thought with that of St. Thomas. The modern reader who goes to Cajetan for an explanation of St. Thomas will often return to St. Thomas as the best commentator on his own text.

Cajetan defended the real distinction of essence and existence in creatures against the Scotists of his day, especially Trombetta, and in so doing he sometimes adopts their own terminology, which is different from that of St. Thomas. Like Capreolus, he identifies the Thomistic *esse* or *actus essendi* with *existentia* or *esse actualis existentiae*, conceived as a reality distinct from the real essence of a creature. A creature, accordingly, is said to be composed of "two things really distinct"; namely, essence and existence.[8] This reification of existence, and attribution of a reality to essence in itself, is a distortion of the Thomist doctrine traceable to Giles of Rome. Cajetan shows little appreciation of St. Thomas' notion of *esse*. He tends to regard existence as the last actuality a being obtains as a result of its production by an efficient cause, rather than the existential act whereby a substance is a being.[9]

It is no wonder that Cajetan, having lost sight of the Thomistic doctrine of being, does not use St. Thomas' profound metaphysical proof of the immortality of the soul, and that toward the end of his life he denied the ability of human reason to prove beyond all doubt that the soul is immortal. As we have seen, St. Thomas maintained that once a spiritual substance, like an angel or a human soul, has been given being by God, it possesses it necessarily and by its very nature, so that it is naturally immortal. Although Cajetan recommends to his reader the chapter of the *Summa Contra Gentiles* (II, 55) containing this remarkable proof, he himself does not include the proof among his arguments for immortality.[10] Toward the end of his life, while commenting on Scripture, he asserts that no philosopher up to the present has demonstrated the immortality of the soul and that he himself knows of no demonstrative argument in favor of it. At best, probable arguments can be given for it. Like the mysteries of the Trinity and Incarnation, it is held with certainty only by faith.[11] At the Fifth Lateran Council (1513) Cajetan was one of the two members who objected to the proposed decree inviting philosophers to offer rational demonstrations for the immortality of the soul.

Cajetan's treatise *On the Analogy of Names* is an attempt to put order into the Thomistic notion of analogy. Whereas in St. Thomas' writings analogy is used with great suppleness and flexibility as a means of approaching God, who is unknown in his essence, Cajetan proposes a rigid classification of the types of analogy that excludes all but the analogy of proper (or non-metaphorical) proportionality as the true metaphysical analogy. Throughout his treatment of analogy he tends to leave out of consideration the central notion of *esse* and to conceive analogy in terms of concepts rather than of judgment.[12] In both regards he resembles the Scotists against whom he argued.[13]

Other doctrines for which Cajetan is well known among modern Thomists is his notion of subsistence as a substantial mode of essence, really distinct from both essence and existence,[14] and his classification of the speculative sciences according to three grades of formal abstraction.[15]

Franciscan Followers of Duns Scotus

FRANCISCANS CULTIVATED the thought of Duns Scotus from the very beginning. Antonius Andreas (d. *c.* 1320), the secretary of Scotus, expounded and synthesized the chief metaphysical doctrines of his master in his *De Tribus Principiis Rerum Naturalium.* Antonius was probably the editor of the *Quaestiones de Anima*, which faithfully reflect Scotus' thought and are printed among his works.

A more important and original pupil of Scotus was Francis of Meyronnes (d. after 1328), known as "The Prince of Scotists." [16]

He was the author of treatises incorporating Scotus' main metaphysical notions; for example, the univocity of the concept of being, the formal distinction, and intrinsic modes of being. Francis
of Meyronnes preferred Plato and Avicenna to Aristotle. Aristotle,
he says, was the best philosopher of nature but the worst metaphysician because he did not know how to abstract.[17] His basic
error was to attack the Platonic doctrine of Ideas and to claim that
ideas do not exist in reality but only in the mind. Aristotle held
that the real world contains only particular beings endowed with
essences. The function of the intellect is to abstract these essences
from their individual conditions and thus to form ideas of them.

While not denying the abstractive function of the intellect, Francis of Meyronnes is at pains to point out that this is only an accidental abstraction that presupposes a basic "abstractability" and
"quidditative abstraction" already present in reality.[18] In other
words, before the intellect sets to work to form ideas, essences are
already abstract in reality. These abstract essences are what Plato
called "Ideas." Aristotle charged Plato with teaching that the
Ideas are separate entities, existing somewhere in the air, but this
was a malicious fabrication. The Platonic Ideas are nothing but
the essences of things, quidditatively and not existentially distinct
from them. Meyronnes was simply stating in his own words the
Scotist formal distinction between essences and the individual things
in which they exist.

As for the status of Ideas in God, Meyronnes parts company
with Scotus in denying that they are secondary objects of the
divine knowledge with only cognitional being (*esse cognitum*).
Like Henry of Ghent, he preferred to attribute an essential being
(*esse essentiae*) to them. William of Vaurouillon (d. 1463) up-
braided Meyronnes for his infidelity to Scotus on this point.[19]
Vaurouillon is a good witness to the loyalty of the Franciscans
to their theological and philosophical traditions. He draws heavily
upon Alexander of Hales, John of Rupella, St. Bonaventure, and
Duns Scotus, and sees in their teachings an organic unity to be
preserved intact for future generations of Franciscans.[20]

Among the sixteenth-century commentators on Duns Scotus,
mention should be made of Francis Lychetus (d. 1520), who com-

mented on Scotus' *Opus Oxoniense* and *Quodlibeta*. The Irishman Mauritius de Portu (O'Fihely) (1460–1513) edited some of Scotus' works, including the *Opus Oxoniense,* and he annotated the *Quaestiones Metaphysicales.*

Spanish and Portuguese Dominicans

FRANCIS OF VITORIA (*c.* 1483–1546) was one of the first outstanding Dominican scholastics of Spanish birth. Vitoria, who taught at Salamanca, is known as the founder of the doctrine of international law.[21] He regarded the whole human race as constituting a single republic and as subject to the "law of nations" (*ius gentium*), a code of prescriptions for the common good, agreed upon by society at large and derivable from natural law. Two of his most famous pupils were Melchior Cano (1509–1560), the author of *De Locis Theologicis,* a systematic account of the sources of theology, and Dominic Soto (1494–1560), who taught at Salamanca and commented on Aristotle and Peter Lombard.

Dominic Bañez (1528–1604) studied under Melchior Cano at Salamanca and taught there and at Alcalá and Valladolid. He was the adviser and confessor of St. Theresa. His commentary on St. Thomas' *Summa Theologiae* is perhaps the most profound and exact written in the sixteenth century. No one of his contemporaries grasped better than he the meaning and implications of St. Thomas' doctrine of being. Provoked by the misunderstandings of his confreres, he complained, "And this is what St. Thomas so often exclaimed, and what Thomists will not hear, that being (*esse*) is the actuality of every form or nature." [22] Both Capreolus and Cajetan come under his criticism for failing to understand this essential point of Thomism. Cajetan, he says, reduced the *esse* of a substance to the substance itself and failed to see that it is the act whereby a substance is a being; moreover, he identified *esse* with the actual being acquired by a substance at the end of its production and not with the primary and most perfect actuality within a being.

Although statements like these give the impression that Bañez had a deep understanding of the Thomistic notion of being, other remarks of his give the reader pause. For example, he considers it only more probable that St. Thomas taught the real distinction between essence and being (*esse*), both of which he describes as "things" (*res*). Furthermore, although he concedes that *esse* is, absolutely speaking, more perfect than essence, he asserts that in a sense the opposite is true, for essence limits the *esse* of a being to a definite species.[23]

Better known to modern Thomists than Bañez is John of St. Thomas, who was born in Lisbon in 1589 of an Austrian father and Portuguese mother, and died in 1644. He wrote both in Latin and Spanish. After studying philosophy at Coimbra and theology at Louvain, he taught at Alcalá. He is best known for his *Cursus Philosophicus Thomisticus* and *Cursus Theologicus*.[24] John of St. Thomas had no other ambition as a writer than to adhere faithfully to the doctrine of St. Thomas and to develop it with all his powers. He was especially critical of Suarez for deviating from the teachings of St. Thomas. He himself is inclined to interpret St. Thomas through the eyes of Cajetan.

Spanish Carmelites

THE DISCALCED CARMELITES sided with the Dominicans in promoting the thought of St. Thomas. Their theological school at Salamanca offered courses in Thomistic theology which were published in twenty volumes in the seventeenth century. The authors of this corporate work are known as the *Salmanticenses*. Antonio de la Madre de Dios (1588–1640) laid the foundation of the section in dogmatic theology, and Francisco de Jesus-Maria (d. 1677) began the section in moral theology.

At the town of Alcalá de Henares (formerly called Complutum), the Carmelite college of philosophy was incorporated in the university, and the scholastics there received the name of *Complutenses*. Their courses in scholastic philosophy were published at the end of the sixteenth and the beginning of the seventeenth century. Noteworthy is the logic of Liego de Jesus (1570–1621).

Antonio de la Madre de Dios composed most of the remaining volumes.

Spanish and Portuguese Jesuits

THE SOCIETY OF JESUS, founded in 1540, made an important contribution to the scholastic revival of the sixteenth century.[25] The Council of Trent, which began in 1545, promoted scholastic studies as an essential part of the Counter Reformation, and it found in the Jesuits willing instruments of its policy. While St. Ignatius, the founder of the Society of Jesus, was studying at Paris, he acquired a great admiration for Thomism, and he later made St. Thomas the official doctor of his new Order. From the very start, therefore, the theology and philosophy of the Jesuits were oriented toward Thomism. The Jesuit *Ratio Studiorum* of 1586 enjoined members of the Order always to hold St. Thomas in honor and to speak reverently of him even when differing from him.

The first Jesuit theologian and philosopher of note was Cardinal Francis Toletus, who was born at Cordova about 1533 and died at Rome in 1596. After studying under Dominic Soto at Salamanca, the center of the scholastic revival begun by Vitoria, he taught metaphysics and theology at Rome. Peter de Fonseca (1528–1599) was the main figure in a group of Jesuit professors at the University of Coimbra in Portugal known as the *Conimbricenses*. Their writings include commentaries on many of the works of Aristotle. Fonseca was called the Aristotle of Portugal. Of greater fame is Louis de Molina (1535–1600), who may have studied under Fonseca. A Spaniard, Molina is best known for his doctrine of grace and free will, which he upheld against the criticism of Bañez.

Another outstanding Spanish Jesuit was Gabriel Vasquez (*c.* 1551–1604), who taught principally at Alcalá and Rome and published a commentary on St. Thomas' *Summa Theologiae*. Vasquez was one of the most important links between medieval scholasticism and Cartesianism. He denied that the Blessed in heaven see possible creatures in God by seeing the divine essence. His reason was that if possible creatures could be seen simply by seeing God, there would be a necessary connection between them and God, and creatures would be as necessary as God himself. God, the primary Truth, would depend upon creatures and upon created truths.[26] Descartes echoes this doctrine when he denies a necessary connection between God and created truths and makes them dependent upon God. The Cartesian notion of ideas as the direct objects of knowledge can be traced to Vasquez' doctrine of the objective concept. Vasquez distinguishes between the formal and objective concept. The former is a real quality inhering in the soul; it is the operation of knowing, by means of which things are presented to the mind. The latter (namely, the objective concept) is the objective presence of the known thing to the mind. As objectified in knowledge, the known thing acquires an "objective being" in thought—a being that is simply its status of being-known: *esse* is here identical with *cognosci*.[27]

The notion of an objective concept, with objective being, which can be traced back at least to Peter Auriol and Duns Scotus, is also found in Francis Suarez, a contemporary of Vasquez. Suarez' philosophy, however, merits a more detailed treatment because of its importance in the history of scholasticism.

Francis Suarez

SUAREZ IS SIGNIFICANT in the history of philosophy as the main channel by which scholasticism came to be known by modern classical philosophers.[28] Descartes was introduced to him by his Jesuit professors of philosophy at La Flèche, and later he acquired a firsthand knowledge of Suarez' most important philosophical work, the *Disputationes Metaphysicae*. Leibniz boasted that he could read Suarez as easily as most people read novels.[29] Schopenhauer shows a good acquaintance with the *Disputationes*, which he valued as "a true compendium of scholasticism" and "an authentic compendium of the whole scholastic wisdom." [30] Christian Wolff's *Ontologia*, which Kant considered to be the finest treatise in metaphysics, is highly indebted to Suarez. To Wolff, Suarez was the metaphysician "who among the scholastics pondered metaphysical realities with particular penetration," [31] and he identified Suarez' teaching with that of St. Thomas himself.

METAPHYSICS AND THE CONCEPT OF BEING

SUAREZ' PURPOSE in writing the *Disputationes* is typically medieval. In the Preface he tells the reader that he is interrupting his work in theology for a short time in order to set down in an orderly way the fundamental notions of metaphysics required for an understanding of sacred theology. Thus the aim of the book is theological, being designed for the use of students in theology who need to know metaphysics to advance in their subject. Suarez' method is also medieval: he first states the opposing opinions of his predecessors before giving his own views on the point at issue. The book, however, has a modern ring in that it is purely philosophical, making no appeal to revelation. The Middle Ages produced a few small purely metaphysical treatises, such as St. Thomas' *De Ente et Essentia*, but Suarez' *Disputationes Metaphysicae* is the first complete and systematic treatise in scholastic metaphysics.

Suarez describes metaphysics in the traditional scholastic manner as the science whose object is being *qua* being. This does not mean that the adequate and direct object of metaphysics embraces all being, but only real being, whether uncreated or created, substantial or accidental. Conceptual being (*ens rationis*) falls under metaphysics only indirectly and by analogy with real being. This is because there is no one concept of being that extends to real and conceptual being; they have only the name "being" in common.[32] Among real beings, the metaphysician studies material as well as immaterial being, but the former is considered only as a means to arrive at a knowledge of the latter, and especially at a knowledge of God.

If this is true, metaphysics requires one formal concept of being, common to everything real, including God and creatures. This concept of being is the simplest of all concepts and the easiest for the mind to grasp. Like the concept of man or animal, "the proper and adequate formal concept of being as such is one, both in reality and in meaning (*ratio*), prescinding from all other formal concepts of other things and objects." [33] Although we can abstract from things one concept of being, as being really exists it is always different. It is either created or uncreated, substantial or accidental being. The concept of being, as applied to things or as realized in them, is intrinsically different, and therefore it is not univocal but analogous.[34] Suarez is aware that he is following Duns Scotus in teaching the unity of the formal concept of being, but he does not think that he is thereby deviating from St. Thomas; on this point, as on others, he finds a basic agreement between the two schoolmen.

Suarez distinguishes between two meanings of the word "being." [35] In the first sense it is used as a present participle to signify something actually existing or possessing a real act of existing. In its second sense it is used as a noun to mean something with a real essence. By a real essence Suarez means an object of thought that is not a pure construction of the mind (a fictional or chimerical being), but one that is true because it can exist in the real world.

"Being" taken as a participle and as a noun is equivalent to actual and possible being. The only difference between the two uses of the term is that "being" as a noun prescinds from actual existence; that is to say, it neither excludes actual existence nor denies it, but merely leaves it out of account. On the other hand, "being" as a participle signifies being with both a real essence and actual existence. There is only one concept of being common to both actual and possible being. Actual being is but a limited case of possible being (it is actualized possible being), as man is but a limited case of animal (he is rational animal).

Although Suarez calls a real essence anything that can really exist, he makes it clear that such an essence is not real in the proper sense unless it actually exists. Two meanings of the term "real" must accordingly be distinguished.[36] First, it means something capable of existing in the real world. Second, it means something actually existing in that world. The second sense is the usual one, and Suarez calls it the proper meaning. In the first sense something is said to be real only because it can really be produced by a cause. It is an object of thought able to be realized in nature and therefore it has "objective potential being." This is the kind of being creatures have in the mind of God before they are created. But before creation, creatures are not real; they are only conceptual beings in the mind of God.

DISTINCTION OF ESSENCE AND EXISTENCE

AFTER THIS EXPLANATION OF TERMS Suarez is ready to take up the much-controverted problem of the distinction between essence and existence in creatures.[37] There is no doubt that in God essence and existence are really the same, because it is his essence to exist. He exists necessarily and by himself (*a se*). Creatures, on the other hand, do not exist by their essence; they exist only because God wills them. They are not necessary but contingent beings. They do not exist by themselves but by another; namely, God. Since it is not their essence to exist, it seems that their essence and existence are not really the same.

Before settling the question Suarez gives a report of the various answers proposed by his predecessors. The first answer is that existence is really distinct from the essence of a creature. Suarez describes this opinion as follows: Existence is a reality (*quandam rem*) really distinct in the fullest sense from the entity of a creature's essence. "This," Suarez says, "seems to be St. Thomas' opinion, and, understood in this sense, it has been followed by almost all the early Thomists." [38] He cites in its favor Capreolus, Cajetan, Francis de Sylvestris, Soncinas, Javelli, Giles of Rome, St. Albert, and Avicenna. Suarez is aware that not all the early Thomists held the real distinction as defined above. Harvey of Nedellec (d. 1323), for one, denied it. Suarez also hesitates to ascribe it to St. Thomas, saying that it seems to be his opinion. And indeed Suarez has good reason to be cautious. St. Thomas does not teach the real distinction as described by Suarez; for him, existence is not a thing or reality (*res*) really distinct in the fullest sense from essence conceived as having a reality or entity of its own. In St. Thomas' view, essence and being (*esse*) really differ, but not as two entities or realities. The definition of the real distinction proposed by Suarez is that of Giles of Rome and followed by most of the Thomist school. Suarez shows no awareness of the authentic doctrine of St. Thomas.

The second opinion places a modal distinction between essence and existence in creatures. Suarez ascribes this doctrine to Duns Scotus, Henry of Ghent, and "some moderns." According to this opinion, existence is not a reality entirely distinct from essence but only a mode of the essence. If it were a distinct reality, it would be separable from the essence, so that it would be possible for the existence of a man to exist without the man—an eventuality, Suarez adds, that is not likely to occur. The essence of a creature, however, is separable from its mode of existing, because it need not really exist. Hence there is a distinction in reality (*ex natura rei*) between the essence of a creature and its existence, but not a fully real distinction; the distinction is modal or formal.[39]

The third opinion posits only a distinction of reason between the essence of a creature and its existence. This was the view, Suarez says, of Alexander of Alexandria and many others, including Godfrey of Fontaines, Harvey of Nedellec, Gabriel Biel, and other nominalists. These men held that existence and essence are not distinct in a really existing thing but only in thought. Suarez insists that the terms of this distinction be correctly understood. The problem under consideration is the type of distinction between a creature's actual existence and actually existing essence. It is not a question of the distinction between the essence as conceived by the mind and actual existence. These are distinct as non-being and being; for the essence abstractly conceived is not a real being but only a possible being. In short, it is not a being. The problem is rather: What kind of distinction is there between essence and existence as they are actualized in the real world? To this question Suarez answers without hesitation: only a distinction of reason. "And this opinion, so explained," he writes, "I think is absolutely true." His reason is that a reality cannot be intrinsically and formally constituted as a real and actual being by something distinct from itself. Now if a creature's actual existence were distinct from its real essence, either really or modally, the real essence would receive its reality from something extrinsic to itself, which is impossible.[40]

The problem, as Suarez sees it, is: What makes a created essence actual or real? His answer is that nothing really distinct from that essence can account for its actuality. If it were real by an extrinsic reality, such as a really distinct actual existence, what would account for the reality of this actual existence? Either itself or some added extrinsic entity, and in the latter case the process goes on to infinity. In order to avoid an infinite regress in created entities, no one of which accounts intrinsically for its own reality, Suarez concludes that a created essence is intrinsically and formally actual and real.[41] Now that which formally constitutes a created essence as an actual essence is actual existence. The conclusion is obvious: the actual existence of a creature is not really distinct from its actual essence; consequently, there can be only a distinction of reason between them.

What kind of distinction of reason is this? Suarez distinguishes between two kinds: a distinction of reason with no foundation in reality and one with a foundation in reality. In both cases the distinction has its origin in the mind; it is not present actually or formally in reality. But reality may offer an occasion for the mind to make a distinction, so that the distinction is not entirely the work of reason. Such is the distinction of reason with a foundation in reality.[42]

According to Suarez, between a created essence and its existence there is a distinction of reason founded upon reality. To prove this, he points out that we can conceive the essence of any creature without including actual existence in its concept. For example, we can define man without saying whether or not he actually exists. And there is an objective foundation for this distinction in the fact that the creature does not exist necessarily or independently of causes. As a caused being, it can be conceived as standing outside its causes and outside nothingness, and then it is thought of as existing. So a created reality offers an occasion for the mind to conceive it in two ways; first, as definable and therefore as located in a particular genus and species; second, as standing outside its causes. Conceived in the first way, the creature is thought of as an essence; conceived in the second, it is thought of as having existence.[43]

In Suarez' view, this distinction of reason adequately safeguards the contingent and dependent character of creatures and marks them off from God. The real distinction, in the sense defined above, is set aside as not only superfluous to explain created being but also as unintelligible in itself. As for the Suarezian distinction of reason between essence and existence, it has been pointed out that it does not obtain between the *actual* essence and actual existence of a creature, as Suarez himself maintains, but between the essence of a creature, conceived in abstraction from actual being, and actual existence.[44]

THE PROBLEM OF UNIVERSALS

SUAREZ FOLLOWS DUNS SCOTUS in raising the problem of universals in terms of real unity. The problem, as he sees it, can be stated as follows: Everything in the world is an individual, so that all real being is individual or singular. It seems, therefore, that the only kind of real unity is the numerical unity of individual beings. But things differing in number possess the same essence or nature. For example, men differ from each other numerically and materially, but they are formally the same because they have the same nature. Hence there appears to be formal unity in things besides numerical unity.

Suarez finds the Thomists and Scotists agreeing on this point but differing in their explanations of formal unity. The Scotists claim that the formal unity of a nature or essence is formally distinct in reality from the unity of the individual, whereas the Thomists maintain that there is only a distinction of reason between these two kinds of unity. The Scotists also assert that a nature with its formal unity is not multiplied numerically in the individuals in which it exists, so that all the individuals of the same nature have the same real formal unity; whereas the Thomists say that the nature is multiplied in individuals, so that there is no real unity of nature in individuals but only agreement or likeness between them.

According to some interpreters, Suarez observes, these positions are only verbally different: what the Thomists call a distinction of reason the Scotists call a formal distinction, and what the Thomists call an agreement or likeness the Scotists call unity. Suarez himself does not presume to know the real mind of St. Thomas and Duns Scotus, but he definitely opts for the Thomistic explanation of universals as formulated above. He denies that there is any distinction in reality, prior to the operation of the mind, between the formal unity of a nature or essence and the numerical unity of an individual being, and that natures with their formal unities are not multiplied numerically in individuals.[45]

In reality, then, there are no common natures but only individual beings. And since common natures are multiplied numerically in individuals, Suarez concludes that there are as many natures and essences in reality as there are individuals. We speak of several individuals as having the same nature, but they are not one essence with true, real unity; they are one only in thought or definition. Strictly speaking, there is no universality in things; there is only likeness between individuals. And this likeness is not a real unity: it does not entail the absence of division in the beings that are alike but only their agreement or co-existence. But because individuals bear resemblances to each other, they offer a foundation for the universal concepts of the mind.[46]

In asserting that each individual has its own essence, Suarez comes close to Ockham, who multiplied essences according to the number of individuals and placed an essential difference between them. Suarez recognizes the affinity of his thought to that of Ockham. Perhaps, he says, Ockham and the nominalists do not disagree with his own doctrine of universals. Once their language has been corrected, they can be brought into harmony with the truth. They should not say that universals are only words and concepts, or that they, and not reality, are the immediate objects of definition and science. The nominalists are correct, however, in teaching that things are not universal in themselves but only as they exist objectively in the mind.[47]

Despite this gesture of conciliation, Suarez is at loggerheads with nominalism on an essential point.[48] He firmly maintains that natures exist in things, and that the mind does not fabricate them but apprehends them in reality. But these natures are not really distinct from the individuals in which they exist; they have no real entity of their own distinct from that of individuals. Man, for example, is not a reality distinct from Peter and Paul; otherwise there would exist a man different from individual men, and an animal distinct from all the animal species.

Since natures are really identical with the individual beings possessing them, they are not actually but only potentially universal. By this Suarez means that reality offers the mind a foundation for the abstraction of universal concepts. The nature of this foundation, he says, is the crux of the problem. As Suarez sees it, this foundation is not a real, actual universality or community belonging to a nature in itself, but only the likeness beween things. This likeness need not be actual; potential likeness suffices.[49] A nature is potentially universal even if only one individual exists with that nature; for example, the heavens or the archangel Gabriel. The foundation of a universal concept is the communicability of a nature existing in reality or its aptitude to be in many individuals. On the basis of a nature endowed with such an aptitude, or the actual agreement or likeness of individuals of the same nature, the intellect can form an objective universal concept that is predicable of those individuals. Between this objective concept and the individuals there is not a real distinction but only a distinction of reason.[50]

The Suarezian doctrine of universals is an attempt to harmonize, as far as possible, the views of St. Thomas, Duns Scotus, and William of Ockham. Suarez takes from Scotus the notion of a universal as a formal or essential unity with at least a potential reality outside the mind. He hesitates as to Scotus' authentic position on universals, complaining that it is expressed in equivocal terms. But if Scotus meant that universals have a real, true entity of their own, formally distinct from individuals (which is true if by "universal" is meant "common nature"), Suarez will have none of it. He agrees with St. Thomas that the essences of individuals differ from these individuals only by a distinction of reason.

Suarez' notion of being, however, stands between himself and St. Thomas and prevents his fully agreeing with him. For St. Thomas, an essence in itself has no being, although it can exist in two different ways: in the mind as a universal and in reality as an individual. For Suarez, an essence is endowed with an essential being distinct from the existential being by which it actually exists. This essential being is individuated, or made to be individual, by its own entity or being, so that no added individual difference is needed to render it individual. It is individual in its own right and by itself. Consequently, Suarez rejects the Thomistic doctrine of individuation by matter. In his view, the adequate principle of individuation is both matter and form taken together, although form is the chief principle by which an individual being in a species is numerically one.[51]

Suarez recognizes his kinship with the nominalists in holding that individuals differ from each other not only materially and numerically but also formally. He agrees with Ockham that there are as many natures and essences in reality as there are individuals; [52] in short, that each individual being is an individual essence. But Suarez dissociates himself from Ockhamism by his insistence that universals are at least potentially in reality, and that our universal concepts are based upon natures existing in the real world.

If this is true, the true name for Suarez' doctrine of universals is not Scotist, Thomist, or Ockhamist, but Suarezian.

THE EXISTENCE OF GOD

LIKE DUNS SCOTUS, Suarez prefers a metaphysical proof for the existence of God to a "physical" proof. He does not think that God's existence can be demonstrated in the philosophy of nature by means of an analysis of motion. This was the way Aristotle proved the existence of a primary unmoved mover, but in Suarez' opinion Aristotle's proof cannot demonstrate the existence of an immaterial substance or a primary, uncreated substance. The weakness of the proof lies in its presumption that whatever is moved is moved by another. This has not been adequately demonstrated for all types of motion or action. Many things appear to move themselves; for example, men moving themselves voluntarily and bodies falling downward. The heavens, too, appear to move themselves by an intrinsic power. A true demonstration of God's existence cannot rest upon such an uncertain principle.[53]

More evident than this principle of physics is the metaphysical principle: Everything produced is produced by another. It is clearly impossible for a being to produce itself. If it is produced, it acquires being, and nothing can be the author of its own being. Starting from this principle, we can reason as follows: Every being is either produced or unproduced. Now, all beings in the universe cannot be produced. Therefore, there must be some unproduced or un-created being. Suarez proves the minor premise of this syllogism as follows: Every produced being is produced by something else, which is either produced or unproduced. If produced, it must in turn be produced by something else. This series cannot go on to infinity, nor can it form a circle, because then a producer would be produced by its own effect. We must therefore stop at a being that is unproduced and uncreated.[54]

That an infinite series of causes, whether essentially or acciden-tally ordered, is impossible, is clear enough. The whole collection of beings or efficient causes cannot be dependent in its being and operation. For if it were, it would depend on something else, ac-cording to the principle that whatever is produced is produced by another. But this is impossible, because there is nothing outside the totality of beings. And if it depended on a being within the totality, this being would produce itself, since it is the author of the totality of beings. Therefore, the whole collection of beings cannot be pro-duced; there must be one being in it that is unproduced and un-created.[55]

It must still be proved that there is only one such uncreated being. Until this has been done we have not demonstrated the exist-ence of God. For the name "God," in its customary meaning, does not signify one or more uncreated and necessary beings. It means "the most excellent being, who transcends all others and on whom all others depend as on their first cause; who accordingly must be worshipped and adored as the highest power." [56] In short, a proof of the existence of the Christian God must include a proof of his oneness.

Suarez offers two proofs that there is only one God. The first begins with God's effects and is therefore *a posteriori*. The mar-velous connection and order of everything in the universe show clearly enough that there is one primary being by whom every-thing is governed and from whom everything has its origin. But may there not be another universe besides our own with its creator and governor? Aristotle tried to show that another universe is im-possible, but his arguments carry no weight for the Christian phi-losopher, who knows that God can create many worlds. No philosopher can demonstrate that all corporeal matter is located in the present universe. But Suarez concludes that there is no reason or even suspicion that there are in fact several universes, so that it would be bold for a philosopher to deny that there is only one universe and one God.[57]

Lest any doubt remain on this point, Suarez adds an *a priori* demonstration that concludes necessarily to the oneness of God. It has been proved that God is a necessary being and that he exists by himself. Now there can be only one such being. Hence there is only one God. The difficulty lies in proving the minor of this syllogism. After rejecting several arguments of St. Thomas as inconclusive, Suarez finally hits upon a convincing proof. He argues that if several individuals share a common nature, their individuality must in some way be outside that nature; otherwise the nature would not be communicable. In other words, if the individuality of a being were identical with its nature, that nature could not belong to another individual. For example, if Peter's individuality were identical with human nature, there could be no other man. Now the essence of uncreated being is identical with its existence because it exists through its essence. And since existence is always individual, the nature of uncreated being must also be essentially individual and incommunicable. Consequently, there can be only one God.[58]

THE NATURE OF LAW

THE SUBTLE SHIFT from Thomism through the influence of Scotus and Ockham that we have observed in Suarez' metaphysics is likewise visible in his doctrine of law.[59] In the beginning of his monumental treatise on law, entitled *De Legibus et Legislatore Deo*, he quotes St. Thomas' definition of law: "Law is a rule and measure of acts, whereby man is induced to act or is restrained from acting." [60] But he finds this description too broad. It applies not only to men but to everything; there is nothing without its rule and measure of action. Moreover, St. Thomas' description does not distinguish between law and counsel, both of which are rules inducing to act or restraining from doing what is less good. The difference between a law and a counsel is that the former obliges one to carry it out, whereas the latter does not. Hence the notion of obligation is essential to law. It is characteristic of law to bind one morally and to impose upon him the moral necessity of acting or not acting.[61]

Consequently, the central feature of law is obligation; and since obligation arises from the will of the legislator, law is essentially an act of the will. Reason no doubt plays a part in law; the will of the legislator must be just and right in order that his rule of action be truly a law. But law in itself is the work of a will and not of an intellect. Suarez proposes as the true definition of law: "An act of a just and right will by which a superior wills to oblige his inferior to do this or that." [62]

Suarez is well aware that St. Thomas defined law as the work of reason. The most complete Thomistic definition of law is: "Law is nothing else than an ordinance of reason for the common good, promulgated by him who has the care of the community." After quoting this definition, Suarez explains that the expression "an ordinance of reason" does not refer exclusively to an act of the intellect; it can also refer to an act of the will. There can be an ordinance of both intellect and will, and the ordinance of will can be said to be of reason either because the will itself is a rational power or because it ought to be directed by right reason, especially in enacting a law.[63]

But this is hardly compatible with the Thomistic doctrine of law as a work of reason. St. Thomas expressly denies that law pertains to the will, except in the sense that the lawmaker must will the end to be gained by the law before his reason issues its commands about means to the end.[64] For St. Thomas, law is essentially the ordering and directing of means to an end; it is a rule or measure of what must be done in order that an end may be attained. Hence it is an act of command; and according to St. Thomas, command is an act of the intellect. Consequently, law is essentially an act of the intellect and not of the will.

In opposition to St. Thomas, Suarez attributes the act of command to the will and not to the intellect.[65] The intellect judges, but its judgments lack moral binding force and moral motivation, both of which are required for law. It is the will of the legislator that lays down the law and obliges his subjects to obey him. Hence the

principal feature in law is will and not reason. It is the business of
the will to command, to ordain means to an end, and to see to it
that the means are taken to reach the end. The will, therefore, is
the rule and measure of human actions. This is most true of the
divine will, which is the primary rule of action. By participating in
the divine will, the wills of human superiors are secondary rules of
man's acts.[66]

The primary law is the eternal law, by which God governs the
universe. More exactly, it is the rule and measure of the actions of
intellectual beings, who alone can be obligated to act. Divine providence extends to all creatures; the eternal law is that part of providence by which God governs intellectual creatures.[67]

Is eternal law an act of God's will or intellect? In agreement
with his general definition of law Suarez answers that, properly
speaking, it is a free act of God's will. The eternal law may appear
to consist in an act of the divine intellect, for the dictates of the
natural law are contained in that intellect; for example, you ought
not to lie, a promise ought to be kept, evil ought to be punished,
and so on. So it seems that the eternal law is present in God's intellect before the free decision of God's will to oblige man to carry
it out; but this is not true. These dictates do not have the nature of
law insofar as they are in the divine intellect; there they are simply
objects of speculative knowledge and not practical commands moving men effectively to obey them. They receive the nature of law
from the free act of God's will to oblige men to carry them out. So
the eternal law can be defined as "the free decision of God's will,
laying down the order to be observed, either generally by all parts
of the universe with respect to the common good . . . or specifically by intellectual creatures with respect to their free actions." [68]
Commenting on St. Thomas' definition of the eternal law as the
"eternal concept" by which God governs the universe, Suarez
observes that this is true only in the sense that God's knowledge
follows upon the decree of his will. Suarez insists that the heart and
force of the law lie in the free decree of God's will binding creatures to obey it.[69]

All other laws are derived from the eternal law and participate
in it. Human laws are made by human legislators, and they obtain
their binding force from the will of these legislators. The obliga-

tion to follow the divine law comes immediately from God; the obligation to obey human laws is proximately from the will of the superior, although ultimately it comes totally from the will of God.[70]

Suarez treats at length of natural law. Following St. Thomas, he defines it as the participation of the eternal law in a rational creature. It is called "natural" not only to distinguish it from supernatural law but also to signify that it is not freely constituted by man. Of course, it is not natural in the sense that man carries it out naturally and necessarily, as brute animals and inanimate things follow the laws of their nature. Rather, it is natural in that it belongs, as if were, to man's nature, inserted in it by God. Consequently, it is also a divine law, inasmuch as God is its immediate source.[71]

It was the opinion of Suarez' fellow Jesuit, Gabriel Vasquez, that the natural law is identical with human nature. Vasquez taught that human acts are good when they conform to human nature and evil when they are at variance with it. The nature of man is consequently the objective foundation of morality; and more than this, the natural law receives its obligatory character from man's rational nature. While agreeing that rational nature is the standard or measure of the goodness of human acts, Suarez protests that it cannot be called a law. "Law" is a broader term than "standard." Besides rational nature, the natural law requires right reason, and even the actual judgment of reason, dictating what should be done or avoided. The natural law is consequently constituted in reason as the proximate intrinsic rule of human acts. It does not depend on man's will, nor is it located in his will. Nevertheless, man is bound to obey it and to follow his conscience. The reason for this is not found in man but in God, who is the legislator of the natural law. Natural law, as inscribed in man, resides in him as in a subject. It resides in God as in a legislator, and in him it is the same as the eternal law, which, as we have seen, is a work of God's will.[72] Consequently, in describing natural law as right reason in man, Suarez is not denying his original assertion that law is, properly speaking, the work of will and not of reason.

In locating law, in the proper sense of the term, in the will rather than in the intellect, Suarez joins the long tradition of voluntarists represented in the Middle Ages by St. Bonaventure, Henry of Ghent, Scotus, Ockham, and Gabriel Biel, all of whom he mentions with approval in his *De Legibus.*[73] Although he shows sympathy with the nominalists' viewpoint on law, as he does with their doctrine of universals, he himself cannot be called a nominalist. He rejects Ockham's contention that human actions are good or evil simply because they have been commanded or prohibited by God. Ockham wished to make the divine will the sole basis of moral good and evil, but Suarez does not follow him all the way. He argues that this would destroy the difference between positive and natural law. Natural law has an objective foundation in the natures of things. Some acts, Suarez contends, are intrinsically good or evil because they are in accord with, or contrary to the natures of things. For example, adultery, theft, and murder are bad acts, not simply because God has willed to legislate against them, but also because they are contrary to nature. The metaphysical principle of the immutability of natures in their essential being is thus the foundation for the objective goodness or evil of human acts.[74] Consequently, Suarez' theory of law is in strict accord with his doctrine of universals and fundamental metaphysical principles.

CONCLUSION

AS WE COME to the end of our journey it may be well to pause for a moment and look back over the ground we have covered in order to make a general assessment of philosophy in the Middle Ages.

We cannot help but be struck by the vitality and persistence of the influence of Neoplatonism in the centuries between St. Augustine and Marsilio Ficino. Neoplatonism, christianized by the Fathers of the Church, was the ruling philosophy up to the thirteenth century. With the entrance of Aristotle, natural philosopher and metaphysician, onto the Western scene, a new era in philosophy began; but even then Neoplatonism did not lose its vitality, and it mingled freely with Aristotelianism in the minds of many of the schoolmen. Even St. Thomas, whose philosophy owes so much to Aristotle, borrowed important notions from Neoplatonism, such as the divine Ideas, illumination, and participation. It is true that these Neoplatonic doctrines were transformed in the hands of St. Thomas, but it is equally true that Aristotelianism took on a new meaning when incorporated into Thomism. Without attempting to settle the still debated question whether St. Thomas can in any sense be called a Neoplatonist, it seems beyond dispute that Thomism would not be what it is without the influence of the Christian Neoplatonists St. Augustine and Dionysius.

The scholastic age, which saw the triumph of Aristotelianism, was the most creative in the Middle Ages; with the exception of St. Augustine it produced the greatest medieval philosophers and theologians. But as a creative period it was relatively short, extending roughly from 1250 to 1350. In the later Middle Ages Aristotelianism began to lose its hold and the best minds turned once again to Neoplatonism for philosophical inspiration. The scholastic age, therefore, appears as a relatively brief, although prodigiously fruitful, episode in the thousand years of medieval thought. Our first conclusion, then, is that Neoplatonism played at least an equal part with Aristotelianism in shaping the philosophy of the Middle Ages; both must be taken into account if we are to understand medieval philosophy.

Our second conclusion is closely related to the first. It should now be clear that, like the term "modern philosophy," "medieval philosophy" does not designate one particular type of philosophy. It is simply a name for the philosophizing that took place within the historical period called the Middle Ages, and this philosophizing exhibits great variety and diversity. There is no one philosophical system called medieval philosophy.

But even granting the diversity of philosophical outlooks in the Middle Ages, can we not at least say that medieval thinkers were striving for a common goal and that they shared certain fundamental philosophical principles? Undoubtedly they were impelled by a common desire to discover the truth, but in this they do not differ from ancient and modern philosophers. It may be said that the majority of medieval thinkers were primarily theologians and that the truth they pursued was not in the first place rational but one transcending reason; in their hands rational speculation was an instrument used to gain a better understanding of faith. This is indeed the case, but we must not forget the Latin Averroists, who made no pretension to be theologians but simply philosophers.

It is equally futile to look for common fundamental philosophical principles among medieval philosophers. A principle by definition is a starting point, and one can find a diversity of starting points among them. Some agreed with Aristotle that sense experience is the beginning of all our knowledge; others adopted the Neoplatonic view that at least some of our knowledge originates within the mind itself. But do not at least all the scholastics agree that being is our first concept and consequently that it is the principle of all intellectual knowledge? It is indeed remarkable how frequently they quote the famous statement of Avicenna, that being is the first concept formed by the intellect; but it is equally remarkable how widely they differ in explaining the meaning of being. To cite but three examples: for St. Thomas Aquinas being is the act of existing; for Duns Scotus it is entity, one of whose modalities is actual existence; for William of Ockham it is simply a name. Three radically different philosophies are based on these different conceptions of being: Thomism, Scotism, and Ockhamism. It has been said that when Scotus criticized St. Thomas' philosophy he was simply correcting or supplementing it in certain points while leaving intact its metaphysical foundations.[1] But being is the metaphysical foundation of Thomism, so that the rejection of St. Thomas' doctrine of being necessarily entailed the rejection of Thomism as a whole. So too, when Ockham criticized the Scotistic notion of being and substituted his own for it, he was laying the foundation for a new philosophy. There is no philosophical common denominator, therefore, uniting these three leading medieval philosophies. If we go farther afield and take into account Neoplatonists like Master Eckhart, Nicholas of Cusa, and Ficino, we find them holding that unity and not being is the first of all concepts. We have even seen Nicholas of Cusa reject the principle of non-contradiction as inapplicable to the infinite or God.

It is futile, therefore, to look for any doctrinal unity on the philosophical level among medieval thinkers. As Catholics, they shared a common faith, but even their understanding of this faith, in other words their theologies, differ because of the different philosophies they brought to bear upon it. We can mark out common lines of interest and even philosophical schools and types, but we cannot find among them a common philosophy or theology or commonly accepted philosophical principles. Each of the great medieval thinkers produced his own philosophical and theological synthesis which must be studied for its own sake because it is an original creation of its author.

If we look for extra-philosophical principles that might give unity to medieval philosophy, we shall be equally disappointed. The most obvious area in which to look for such principles is religion, but medieval thinkers were far from agreeing on the relation between philosophy and the Catholic faith. Opinions varied from the Latin Averroists, who cultivated philosophy as though they had no religious beliefs, to theologians like St. Bernard and St. Peter Damian, who, in order to preserve the integrity of faith wanted to keep it as free of philosophy as possible. St. Augustine and all the great scholastics saw the need of philosophy for gaining a better understanding of faith, but they were far from agreeing on the value of rational thought and the place it should occupy in theology. St. Bonaventure, for example, was less optimistic than St. Thomas in the ability of philosophers to arrive at truth, with the result that he placed less reliance upon them.

The fact remains, however, that with the exception of the Averroists all Christian medieval thinkers philosophized in close dependence upon their religion. Our third conclusion, then, is that on the whole the creative part of Western philosophy in the Middle Ages can be described as Christian philosophy. We do not simply mean that this philosophy was generally in agreement with the teachings of the Christian faith, but more important still that the Christian faith exercised a positive influence upon it, guiding and directing it to truths unknown to the ancient pagan philosophers. The legacy of medieval philosophy to the modern era includes the notions of one God who is the infinite being and creator of the universe, the dependence of this universe upon the divine will, the existence of a spiritual and immortal soul, and the freedom and dignity of the human person. Ancient philosophers were groping toward these truths but never grasped them clearly; thanks to medieval philosophers they became objects not only of Christian belief but of philosophical demonstration.

To many modern writers, both Christian and non-Christian, medieval thought cannot claim to be philosophical because it was open to the influence of Christian revelation. They insist that philosophy is a work of human reason, depending solely upon man's natural light of knowing. But it is arbitrary to close philosophy to the influence of the higher light of revelation. All that can be demanded in order that a revealed doctrine become philosophical is that it be understood and rationally demonstrated. There were many such revealed doctrines according to most medieval thinkers, although they did not agree on the exact number. St. Anselm thought more of them demonstrable than St. Thomas, while Duns Scotus thought fewer demonstrable. They agreed, however, that through revelation the human mind comes into possession of truths surpassing the philosophy of the ancients, and that at least some of these truths, once believed, can be demonstrated by human reason and thus enter into the body of rational knowledge.

To the medieval mind, therefore, revelation does not destroy the rationality of philosophy but enhances and increases it. The Christian is not prevented from philosophizing because he is a believer; rather, because he possesses the light of faith he is better equipped to do the work of a philosopher than one who depends on human reason alone.

When we call medieval philosophy "Christian" we are describing the state in which Western philosophy existed in the Middle Ages; we are saying that it developed and flourished under the influence of Christian revelation. There was still another condition in which philosophy existed during this period of history; namely, as the instrument and handmaid of theology. These two conditions of medieval philosophy must be distinguished, because a philosophy can be Christian without being by that very fact the handmaid of theology. In our own day there are men who philosophize under the influence of Christian revelation, and who are thus entitled to be called Christian philosophers, but their purpose in philosophizing is philosophical and not theological.[2] Paradoxical as it seems, in the Middle Ages the most creative and fruitful philosophizing was done by theologians in view of their own science of theology. As a result we find the richest treasures of medieval philosophy, not in the commentaries on Aristotle or independent philosophical treatises of the Middle Ages, but in the theological writings of men like St. Augustine, St. Thomas, Duns Scotus, and William of Ockham.

Our fourth and final conclusion, then, is that philosophy in the Middle Ages was creative not only because it was Christian but also because it was associated with the work of theology. As such, it was caught up in the higher life of theology, so that it developed, not according to its own order and in view of its own ends, but according to the theological order and with a view to theology. As the medieval state tended to be absorbed into the life of the Church whose ends it served, so philosophy tended to be incorporated into the science of theology of which it was the handmaid. No doubt other conceptions of Christian philosophy, as well as of the Christian state, are possible. There is no contradiction in the notion of a Christian philosophy, open to the light of revelation and accepting its guidance, but directed to the rational ends of philosophy and developed according to the philosophical order. As we have said, there are philosophers today who are attempting to formulate a Christian philosophy of this sort. It will be the task of future historians to estimate the success of this undertaking. The historian today, looking back over the history of Christian philosophy, finds that it produced its finest flower in the Middle Ages.

NOTES AND REFERENCES

ADDENDA

AND BIBLIOGRAPHIC SUPPLEMENT

ABBREVIATIONS

PL   J. P. Migne, *Patrologiae Cursus Completus, Series Latina*, 221 volumes, Paris, 1844-1864. *Supplementum*, ed. A. Hamman, vol. 1, Paris: Editions Garnier Frères, 1958.

PG   J. P. Migne, *Patrologiae Cursus Completus, Series Graeca*, 162 volumes, Paris, 1857-1866.

CCCM   *Corpus Christianorum, Continuatio Mediaevalis*, vol. 1 – , Turnholt: Brepols, 1971 – .

CCSL   *Corpus Christianorum, Series Latina*, vol. 1 – , Turnholt: Brepols, 1954 – .

CSEL   *Corpus Scriptorum Ecclesiasticorum Latinorum*, vol. 1 – , Vienna: Tempsky, 1866 – .

Archives   *Archives d'histoire doctrinale et littéraire du moyen âge*, vol. 1 – , Paris: J. Vrin, 1926 – .

Beiträge   *Beiträge zur Geschichte der Philosophie des Mittelalters*, 43 volumes, Münster i. W.: Aschendorff, 1891-1980; new series vol. 1 – , 1970 – .

History   E. Gilson, *History of Christian Philosophy in the Middle Ages*, New York: Random House, 1955.

Selections   R. McKeon, *Selections from Medieval Philosophers*, 2 vols., New York: Scribner's, 1929.

GENERAL BIBLIOGRAPHY

See also the Bibliographic Supplement, pp. 428-445

Works of Reference

DeWulf, M. *Histoire de la philosophie médiévale*, 3 vols. 6th edition, Louvain: Institut Supérieur, 1934–1947. English translation of the first two vols.: *History of Medieval Philosophy*, 3rd edition, trans. by E. C. Messenger, London: Longmans, Green & Co., 1935, 1937.

Forest, A., Van Steenberghen, F., de Gandillac, M. *Le Mouvement doctrinal du IXᵉ au XIVᵉ siècle. Histoire de l'Eglise depuis les origines jusqu'à nos jours*, vol. 13; ed. A. Fliche and V. Martin, Paris: Bloud & Gay, 1951.

Gilson, E. *History of Christian Philosophy in the Middle Ages*, New York: Random House, 1955.

Glorieux, P. *La littérature quodlibétique*, 2 vols., Paris: J. Vrin, 1925, 1935.

—— *Répertoire des maîtres en théologie de Paris au XIIIᵉ siècle*, 2 vols., Paris: J. Vrin, 1933, 1934.

Grabmann, M. *Die Geschichte der scholastischen Methode*, 2 vols., Freiburg im Breisgau: Herder, 1909, 1911.

—— *Mittelalterliches Geistesleben; Abhandlungen zur Geschichte der Scholastik und Mystik*, 3 vols., Munich: M. Hueber, 1926–1956.

Lottin, O. *Psychologie et morale aux XIIᵉ et XIIIᵉ siècles*, 4 vols., Louvain: Abbaye du Mont César, 1942-1954; vol. 5, Gembloux: J. Duculot, 1959.

Mandonnet, P. *Siger de Brabant et l'averroïsme latin au XIIIᵉ siècle, Les philosophes belges*, VI, VII, 2nd ed., 2 vols., Louvain: Institut Supérieur, 1911–1908.

Manitius, M. *Geschichte der lateinischen Literatur des Mittelalters*, 3 vols., Munich: C. H. Beck, 1911–1931.

Stegmüller, F. *Repertorium Commentariorum in Sententias Petri Lombardi*, 2 vols., Herbipoli (Würzburg): F. Schöningh, 1947.

Ueberweg, F. *Grundriss der Geschichte der Philosophie*, vol. 2: Die patristische und scholastische Philosophie; 11th ed. by B. Geyer, Berlin: E. S. Mittler & Sohn, 1928.

Van Steenberghen, F. *Siger de Brabant d'après ses oeuvres inédites, Les philosophes belges*, XII, XIII, Louvain: Institut Supérieur, 1931, 1942.

—— *Introduction à l'étude de la philosophie médiévale*, Louvain: Publications Universitaires, 1974.

—— *La bibliothèque du philosophe médiéviste*, Louvain: Publications Universitaires, 1974.

Surveys and Textbooks

Bréhier, E. *La philosophie au moyen âge*, 2nd ed., Paris: A. Michel, 1949.

The Cambridge History of Later Greek and Early Medieval Philosophy, ed. A. H. Armstrong, Cambridge: University Press, 1967. (This volume ends with Anselm and early Islamic philosophers.)

Chevalier, J. *Histoire de la pensée*, vol. 2, *La pensée chrétienne, des origines à la fin du XVIe siècle*, Paris: Flammarion, 1956.

Copleston, F. *A History of Philosophy*, vol. 2: Augustine to Scotus; vol. 3: Ockham to Suarez, Westminster: Newman Press, 1950, 1953.

—— *A History of Medieval Philosophy*, London: Methuen, 1972.

—— *Medieval Philosophy*, London: Methuen & Co., 1952.

Gilson, E. *La philosophie au moyen âge, des origines patristiques à la fin du XIVe siècle*, 2nd ed., Paris: Payot, 1944.

—— *The Spirit of Mediaeval Philosophy*, trans. by A. H. C. Downes, New York: Scribner's, 1936.

—— *Reason and Revelation in the Middle Ages*, New York: Scribner's, 1938.

—— *The Unity of Philosophical Experience*, Part I: The Mediaeval Experiment, New York: Scribner's, 1947.

—— *Being and Some Philosophers*, 2nd ed., Toronto: Pontifical Institute of Mediaeval Studies, 1952.

Hawkins, D. J. B. *A Sketch of Mediaeval Philosophy*, London: Sheed & Ward, 1946.

Jeauneau, E. *La philosophie médiévale*, 3rd ed., Paris: Presses Universitaires de France, 1975.

Knowles, D. *The Evolution of Medieval Thought*, London: Longmans, Green, 1962.

Leff, G. *Medieval Thought. St. Augustine to Ockham*, London: Penguin Books, 1958.

Pieper, J. *Scholasticism, Personalities and Problems of Medieval Philosophy*, New York: Pantheon Books, 1960.

Poole, R. L. *Illustrations of the History of Medieval Thought and Learning*, 2nd ed., New York: Macmillan, 1920. (Paperback reprint: Dover Publications, 1960.)

Vignaux, P. *Philosophy in the Middle Ages*, trans. by E. C. Hall, New York: Meridian Books, 1959.

Translated Sources and Readings

Collins, J. *Readings in Ancient and Medieval Philosophy*, Westminster, Md.: The Newman Press, 1960.

Fairweather, E. R. *A Scholastic Miscellany: Anselm to Ockham* (The Library of Christian Classics, X), Philadelphia: The Westminster Press, 1956.

Fathers of the Church, a New Translation, ed. R. J. Deferrari, New York: Fathers of the Church, Inc., 1947 ff.

Hyman, A. and J. J. Walsh, eds. *Philosophy in the Middle Ages. The Christian, Islamic and Jewish Tradition*, Indianapolis: Hackett Publishing Co., 1973.

Lerner, R. and M. Mahdi, eds. *Medieval Political Philosophy: A Sourcebook*, Ithaca: Cornell University Press, 1963. (Translations of selections from Islamic, Jewish and Christian political writings.)

McKeon, R. *Selections from Medieval Philosophers*, 2 vols., New York: Scribner's, 1929. (Paperback reprint.)

Pegis, A. C. *The Wisdom of Catholicism*, New York: Random House, 1949.

Wippel, J. F. and A. B. Wolter, eds. *Medieval Philosophy from St. Augustine to Nicholas of Cusa*, New York: The Free Press, 1969.

Bibliographical information on medieval philosophy will be found in:

Bulletin de théologie ancienne et médiévale, Abbaye du Mont César, Louvain, Belgium.

Bulletin thomiste, Le Saulchoir, Etiolles (Seine-et-Oise), France. (No longer published.)

Rassegna di Letteratura Tomistica, Rome: Herder; Naples: Edizioni Domenicane. (This review, begun in 1966, continues the *Bulletin Thomiste*.)

Répertoire bibliographique de la philosophie, Louvain: Institut Supérieur, 5 vols. to date, 1949-1953.

F. Van Steenberghen, *Philosophie des Mittelalters*, Bern: A. Franke, 1950 (*Bibliographische Einführungen in das Studium der Philosophie*, 17). (Complements the extensive bibliography in De Wulf's *History*.)

Progress of Medieval and Renaissance Studies in the United States and Canada, ed. S. Harrison Thomson, Boulder, Colorado.

NOTES

Foreword

1. O. Hamelin, *Le système de Descartes*, Paris: Felix Alcan, 1921,
p. 15. By "the physicists" Hamelin meant men like Galileo and
Copernicus. See pp. 7, 8.
2. See E. Gilson, *Études sur le rôle*

de la pensée médiévale dans la
formation du système cartésien,
Paris. J. Vrin, 1930.
3. See E. Gilson, *The Spirit of
Mediaeval Philosophy*, pp. 13–18.

PART 1 THE AGE OF THE FATHERS

1. St. Augustine

1. LIFE. ST. AUGUSTINE was born in
Tagaste (modern Souk-Ahras, Al-
geria), Nov. 13, 354. His mother
was St. Monica; his father Patri-
cius, a pagan, converted in later
life. He attended school at Tagaste
and Madaura, and in 370 was sent
to Carthage for higher studies.
There he fell in with evil com-
panions, and, as he puts it, he
became ashamed not to be shame-
less. In 373 he read Cicero's
Hortensius, now lost. This work,
an exhortation to philosophy, inspired him with an intense love
of wisdom. From 373 to 382 he
was a follower of the Manichaean
religion. In 383 he was won over
to the moderate skepticism of the
New Academy. While teaching
rhetoric at Milan in 384, he heard
St. Ambrose preach, and the same

year he read some works of the
Neoplatonists. He was converted
to Christianity in 386, and after
a year's retreat and study at Cas-
siciacum, outside Milan, he was
baptized by St. Ambrose. After
St. Monica's death at Ostia in 387
he went to Rome and the following year returned to Africa. At
Tagaste he sold his property and
lived a monastic life. He was ordained a priest in Hippo in 391
and became co-bishop of Hippo
in 395, sole bishop in 396. He died
Aug. 28, 430.
WORKS. Augustine's works are
available in Migne, PL, vols. 38–47.
Critical editions of part of his
works in CSEL. For Augustine's
philosophy the following works
are most important: *De Ordine,
Contra Academicos, De Beata*

Vita (all written in 386); *Solilo-quia, De Immortalitate Animae* (387); *De Musica* (387–391); *De Quantitate Animae* (387–388); *De Libero Arbitrio* (388–395); *De Magistro* (389); *De Doctrina Christiana* (397); *Confessions* (*c.* 400); *De Trinitate* (400–416); *De Genesi ad Litteram* (401–415); *De Civitate Dei* (413–426); *Retracta-tiones* (426–427). In the *Retracta-tiones* he reviews his former writings, correcting himself occasionally. It is always to be consulted when using any work of St. Augustine.

TRANSLATIONS. M. Dods, *The Works of Aurelius Augustinus*, 15 vols., Edinburgh, 1871–1876. R. McKeon, *St. Augustine on Free Will*, II, 1–17 in *Selections*, I, pp. 11–64. W. J. Oates, *Basic Writings of St. Augustine*, 2 vols., New York: Random House, 1948. Sister Mary Patricia Garvey, *Against the Academicians*, Milwaukee: Marquette University Press, 1948. *Writings of Saint Augustine* (*The Fathers of the Church*), 14 vols., New York: CIMA Pub. Co., 1948–1952. J. H. S. Burleigh, *Augustine: Earlier Writings* (*The Library of Christian Classics*, VI), Philadelphia: Westminster Press, 1953. A. C. Outler, *Augustine: Confessions and Enchiridion* (*The Library of Christian Classics*, VII), Philadelphia: Westminster Press, 1955. J. Burnaby, *Augustine: Later Works* (*The Library of Christian Classics*, VIII), Philadelphia: Westminster Press, 1955. STUDIES. J. N. Figgis, *The Political Aspects of Saint Augustine's City of God*, London: Longmans, 1921. M. J. McKeough, *The Meaning of the Rationes Seminales in St. Augustine*, Washington, D.C.: Catho-lic University, 1926. *A Monument to Saint Augustine*, by various authors, London: Sheed & Ward, 1930. Sister Mary Patricia Garvey, *Saint Augustine: Christian or Neo-Platonist*, Milwaukee: Marquette University Press, 1939. A. C. Pegis, "The Mind of St. Augustine," *Mediaeval Studies*, 6 (1944), 1–61. V. J. Bourke, *Augustine's Quest of Wisdom. Life and Philosophy of the Bishop of Hippo*, Milwaukee: Bruce, 1945. J. J. O'Meara, *The Young Augustine. The Growth of St. Augustine's Mind up to his Conversion*, London: Longmans, 1954. H. Marrou, *Saint Augustine and his Influence through the Ages*, trans. P. Hepburne-Scott, New York: Harper Torchbooks, 1957. E. Gilson, *The Christian Philosophy of St. Augustine*, trans. L. Lynch, New York: Random House, 1960 (translation of E. Gilson, *Introduction à l'étude de saint Augustin*, 2nd ed., Paris: J. Vrin, 1943). P. Courcelle, *Recherches sur les Confessions de Saint Augustin*, Paris: E. de Boc-card, 1950. E. Portalié, *A Guide to the Thought of Saint Augustine*, trans. J. Bastian, Chicago: H. Regnery, 1960.

2. The religion of Mani (born A.D. 216 in Persia) taught the existence of two independent first principles, one good and the other evil. The good principle is the author of spirits, like the human soul; the evil principle is the author of matter, which is intrinsically evil. The conflict of soul and body in man reflects the eternal warfare of the principles of good and evil. The Manichees did not rise to the notion of a purely spiritual sub-stance: spirit for them was tenu-

ous matter. See S. Runciman, *The Medieval Manichee, a Study of the Christian Dualist Heresy*, Cambridge: University Press, 1947.

3. De Vera Religione, V, 8; PL 34, 126.

4. Contra Academicos, III, 20, 43; PL 32, 952.

5. Isaias 7: 9. This is the reading of the Septuagint version.

6. St. Thomas Aquinas, *Summa Theologiae*, I, 84, 5.

7. De Diversis Quaestionibus 83, q. 9; PL 40, 13, 14. Augustine did not doubt that the external world exists or that we can learn truth through the senses. He writes: "Yet we are by no means to doubt the truth of what the bodily senses have taught us, for through them we have come to know heaven and earth and all that therein is known to us." *De Trinitate*, XV, 12, 21; PL 42, 1075. His point is that the intellect, not the senses, judges the truth.

8. De Civitate Dei, XI, 26; PL 41, 339, 340.

9. De Vera Religione, XXXIX, 72; PL 34, 154. E. Husserl used this quotation as a fitting conclusion to his *Cartesian Meditations*.

10. De Libero Arbitrio, II, 1–15; PL 32, 1239–1263.

11. Ennaratio in Psalmum 145, 5; PL 37, 1887.

12. Soliloquia, I, 2, 7; PL 32, 872.

13. Ibid., II, 1, 1; PL 32, 885.

14. De Moribus Ecclesiae, I, 27, 52; PL 32, 1332.

15. De Quantitate Animae, XIII, 22; PL 32, 1048.

16. De Anima et ejus Origine, IV, 2, 3; PL 44, 525.

17. De Immortalitate Animae, XVI, 25; PL 32, 1034.

18. De Genesi ad Litteram, XII, 16, 33; PL 34, 467.

19. De Trinitate, XII, 15, 24; PL 42, 1011.

20. St. James 1:17; *St. John* 1:9.

21. Retractationes, I, 4, 4; PL 32, 590.

22. De Trinitate, IX, 3, 3; PL 42, 963; XV, 12, 21; PL 42, 1075.

23. De Libero Arbitrio, II, 6, 14; PL 32, 1248; *De Doctrina Christiana*, I, 7, 7; PL 33, 22.

24. Sermo VII, 7; PL 38, 66; *De Trinitate*, V, 2, 3; PL 42, 912; *De Civitate Dei*, XII, 2; PL 41, 350.

25. Confessions, IX, 10, 25; PL 32, 774.

26. Ibid., XII, 15, 22; PL 32, 834.

27. De Genesi ad Litteram, VI, 6, 10; PL 34, 343; IX, 17, 32; PL 34, 406.

28. St. Paul, *1 Corinth.* 3:7.

29. Confessions, XIII, 9, 10; PL 32, 849.

30. Contra Faustum Manich., XXII, 27; PL 42, 418.

31. Ennaratio in Psalmum 57, 1; PL 36, 673, 674.

32. De Libero Arbitrio, II, 19, 52; PL 32, 1268.

33. De Civitate Dei, XIV, 28; PL 41, 436.

34. E. Gilson, Foreword to *The City of God*, in *Writings of St. Augustine*, New York, 1950, vol. 8, pp. lxxxii–xcviii.

35. See J. Maritain, "St. Augustine and St. Thomas Aquinas," *A Monument to St. Augustine*, London, 1930, p. 211.

II. Boethius

* *1.* LIFE. BOETHIUS was born in Rome about 480. As a youth he was sent to study at Athens, the center of Greek culture and philosophy

* See Addenda. p. 427.

since the time of Socrates. There he came into contact with the various types of Greek philosophy: Aristotelianism, Neoplatonism, and Stoicism, all of which influenced his own philosophy. At Athens he also learned Greek—a fact of great importance, for it enabled him to translate Greek philosophical works into Latin and thus become one of the most important channels by which Greek philosophical ideas were passed over to the Latin-speaking world. On his return to Italy he became a consul at the court of Theodoric, King of the Ostrogoths, who showed him favor and honor. Accused of treason by Theodoric, he was imprisoned and put to death at Pavia, in northern Italy, in 524 or 525. During his imprisonment he wrote the *Consolation of Philosophy*. There are over 400 extant manuscripts of this work, attesting its great popularity in the Middle Ages. Boethius is honored as a martyr, and his cult as a *Beatus* was confirmed by the Church in 1883.

WORKS. Works in PL 63–64; *Commentaries on Porphyry*, ed. Schepss & Brandt, CSEL 48, Leipzig, 1906. *Commentary on De Interpretatione*, 2 vols., ed. C. Meiser, Leipzig, 1877, 1880. *De Consolatione Philosophiae*, ed. A. Fortescue, London, 1925; also ed. L. Bieler, *Corpus Christianorum, Series Latina*, XCIV, Turnholti: Brepols, 1957.

Logical works: Translation of Porphyry's *Isagoge* with two commentaries. Translation of Aristotle's *Categories* with a commentary, of the *Perihermeneias* (*De Interpretatione*) with two commentaries, of the *Prior* and *Posterior Analytics, Sophistic Refutations* and *Topics*. (The last four translations seem to have been lost. These works were not known in the Latin West until the middle of the twelfth century.) A commentary on Cicero's *Topics* is preserved in part. Boethius also wrote independent logical works, as well as treatises on rhetoric, mathematics, and music.

Consolation of Philosophy.

Theological Tractates. The most important for philosophy are the *De Trinitate* and *De Hebdomadibus*. The *De Fide Catholica* is of doubtful authenticity. These tractates are generally accepted as authentic since the discovery of a fragment of Cassiodorus, a pupil of Boethius, which attributes four of them to his teacher. Yet the difference in style between them and the other works of Boethius is striking.

TRANSLATIONS. *Consolation of Philosophy*, New York: Modern Library, 1943. Bks. IV–V, trans. A. C. Pegis, *The Wisdom of Catholicism*, New York, 1949. *Theological Tractates and Consolation of Philosophy*, Latin text and trans. by H. F. Stewart and E. K. Rand, London, New York, 1918. *The Second Edition of the Commentaries on the Isagoge of Porphyry*, Bk. 1, trans. R. McKeon, *Selections*, I, pp. 70–99.

STUDIES. H. J. Brosch, *Der Seinsbegriff bei Boethius*, Innsbruck, 1931. H. R. Patch, *The Tradition of Boethius. A Study of his Importance in Mediaeval Culture*, New York: Oxford University Press, 1935. Helen Barrett, *Boethius, Some Aspects of his Times and Work*, Cambridge, 1940. P. Courcelle, *Les lettres grecques en occident de Macrobe à Cassiodore*, 2nd ed., Paris: E. de Boccard, 1948, pp. 257–312. K. Dürr, *The Propositional Logic of Boethius*, Amsterdam: North Holland Pub. Co., 1951. Gerald Vann, *The Wisdom of Boethius* (Aquinas Paper n. 20), Blackfriars, Oxford, 1952.

2. In his commentary on Porphyry's *Isagoge* Boethius distinguishes between three kinds of being: intellectibles (*intellectibilia*), which exist outside matter and are studied in theology; intelligibles (*intelligibilia*), which are souls descended into bodies; and natural beings (*naturalia*), whose natures and properties are studied in "physiology" (corresponding to the Aristotelian physics). Boethius does not give a name to the branch of philosophy that studies souls in bodies, but it more or less corresponds to Aristotle's psychology. See *In Isagogen Porphyrii*, editio prima, I, 3; CSEL 48, pp. 8–9. For Boethius' classification of the sciences, see J. Mariétan, *Problème de la classification des sciences d'Aristote à S. Thomas*, Paris: Felix Alcan, 1901, pp. 63–71.

3. Boethius says that mathematics proceeds *disciplinabiliter*, a word derived from *discere* (to learn). The word "mathematics" has the same root in the Greek infinitive *mathein* (to learn). St. Thomas interprets Boethius to mean that mathematics is the easiest science to learn, for it is most exact and certain. See St. Thomas, *Expositio super Librum Boethii De Trinitate*, Q. 6, a. 1, ed. B. Decker, p. 208.

4. *In Isagogen Porphyrii, ibid.*, p. 9.

5. *In Isagogen Porphyrii*, editio secunda, I, 3; CSEL 48, pp. 140–143.

6. *De Arithmetica*, I; PL 63, 1079.

7. See Cassiodorus, *De Artibus ac Disciplinis Liberalium Litterarum*; PL 70, 1149–1218; also *An Introduction to Divine and Human Readings*, trans. by L. W. Jones, New York: Columbia University Press, 1946.

8. *De Nuptiis Mercurii et Philologiae*, ed. A. Dick, Leipzig: Teubner, 1925.

9. *Etymologiae*, ed. W. M. Lindsay, 2 vols., Oxford, 1911.

10. *Consolation of Philosophy*, III, prose 10.

11. *De Hebdomadibus*; PL 64, 1311.

12. For the identification of being (*esse*) with the form expressed by the definition, see *In Isag. Por.*, IV, 14, editio secunda; CSEL 48, p. 273, lines 13–15.

13. *Contra Eutychen et Nestorium*, 3; PL 64, 1344–1345.

14. *De Trinitate*, 1; PL 64, 1249.

15. *Ibid.*, 2; PL 64, 1250.

III. John Scotus Erigena

1. LIFE. JOHN SCOTUS ERIGENA was born in Ireland about 810. His name indicates his birthplace: the Irish in the ninth century were called "Scots," and "Erigena" means "born of the people of Erin." He went to France about 845, where he became master of the Palace School of Emperor Charles the Bald. After 870 we lose track of him. He seems to have returned to England and died there about 877, stabbed, according to legend, by the pens of his pupils!

WORKS. His works are found in PL 122. They include *De Divisione Naturae; De Praedestinatione.* Translations of the works of Dionysius the Pseudo-Areopagite: *De Divinis Nominibus, De Mystica Theologia, De Caelesti Hierarchia, De Ecclesiastica Hierarchia,* and ten letters. Translations of the *De Hominis Opificio* of Gregory of Nyssa, and the *Ambigua* of Maximus the Confessor. A commentary on Dionysius' *De Caelesti Hierarchia* (the missing part has been edited by H. F. Dondaine, *Archives,* 26–27 [1950–51], 245–302). An incomplete commentary on St. John's Gospel, and *Annotationes in Marcianum,* ed. C. Lutz, Cambridge, Mass.: Medieval Academy, 1939. TRANSLATIONS. *De Divisione Naturae,* IV, 7–9, in McKeon, *Selections,* I, pp. 106–141. Dionysius' *De Divinis Nominibus* and *De Mystica Theologia* have been translated by C. E. Rolt: *Dionysius the Areopagite on the Divine Names and the Mystical Theology,* New York: Macmillan, 1920. STUDIES. H. Bett, *Johannes Scotus Erigena, A Study in Mediaeval Philosophy,* Cambridge: University Press, 1925. M. Cappuyns, *Jean Scot Erigène, sa vie, son oeuvre, sa pensée,* Paris: Desclée de Brouwer, 1933.

2. On Alcuin, see E. S. Duckett, *Alcuin, Friend of Charlemagne,* New York: Macmillan, 1951.

3. *De Divisione Naturae,* V, 38; PL 122, 1010 BC.

4. *De Praedestinatione,* I, 1; PL 122, 357 D–358 A.

5. *Annotationes in Marcianum,* ed. C. Lutz, p. 64, lines 23–24.

6. *In Prologum S. Evangelii secundum Joannem;* PL 122, 284 C–285 A.

7. *De Divisione Naturae,* I, 1; PL 122, 441–442; II, 2, 526 CD.

8. *Ibid.,* I, 1; PL 122, 441 A.

9. For the meanings of non-being, see *ibid.,* I, 3–7; PL 122, 443–446.

10. *Ibid.,* III, 23; PL 122, 689 B.

11. *Ibid.,* II, 28; PL 122, 589 BC.

12. Erigena's disciple points out that there is a sense in which God may be said to know himself. Speaking to Erigena, he says: "You do not prove that God does not know himself, but only that he does not know what he is. And rightly, for he is not a what." *Ibid.,* II, 28; PL 122, 590 CD.

13. *Super Hierarchiam Caelestem,* II, 3; PL 122, 154–156. *De Divisione Naturae,* I, 14–15; PL 122, 459–464.

14. *De Divisione Naturae,* III, 23; PL 122, 689 AB.

15. *Ibid.,* III, 1; PL 122, 622 B–624 B.

16. *Ibid.,* II, 21; PL 122, 561 D–562 A.

17. On this point, see E. Gilson, *Being and Some Philosophers,* Toronto: Pontifical Institute of Mediaeval Studies, 1952, pp. 18–38.

18. *De Divisione Naturae,* I, 72; PL 122, 516 C; 518 A.

19. *Ibid.,* II, 1; PL 122, 523 D.

20. *Ibid.,* IV, 7; PL 122, 768 B.

21. *Ibid.,* II, 6; PL 122, 532 D–533 A; IV, 12, 788 B.

22. *Ibid.,* II, 7; PL 122, 533 AB.

23. *Ibid.,* IV, 8; PL 122, 773 D–774 B.

24. *Ibid.,* I, 56; PL 122, 498 C–499 A.

25. *Ibid.*, I, 34; PL 122, 479 B. Cf. I, 53; 497 A; I, 60; 503 B.

26. *Ibid.*, I, 58; PL 122, 501 BC.

27. *Ibid.*, V, 3; PL 122, 866 CD.

28. *Ibid.*, V, 25; PL 122, 913 AD. For the need of grace, see V, 23; PL 122, 899 B; V, 36; 977 D–979 D.

29. *Ibid.*, V, 8; PL 122, 876 B.

30. *Ibid.*, V, 8; PL 122, 879 AB.

31. *Ibid.*, V, 37; PL 122, 989 A.

IV. St. Anselm

1. For the attitude of the "Tertullian family" toward philosophy, see E. Gilson, *Reason and Revelation in the Middle Ages*, New York: Scribner's, 1948, pp. 3–33.

2. St. Peter Damian, *De Sancta Simplicitate Scientiae Inflanti Anteponenda*, I; PL 145, 695. See E. Gilson, *History*, p. 616, n. 41; J. Gonsette, *Pierre Damien et la culture profane*, Louvain: Publications universitaires, 1956.

3. Berengar of Tours, *De Sacra Coena Adversus Lanfrancum*, ed. A. F. and F. Th. Vischer, *Berengarii Turonensis Opera*, Berlin, 1834, p. 100.

Dialectics, in the Aristotelian sense, is that part of logic which teaches the rules of probable, as opposed to necessary, reasoning. See Aristotle, *Topics*, I, 1, 100a 30. In the Middle Ages dialectics was considered one of the seven liberal arts, and it was often identified with logic in general. Augustine calls dialectics the "discipline of disciplines" because it teaches the nature, purpose, and value of reasoning. See *De Ordine*, II, 13, 38; PL 32, 1013. For Erigena, dialectics is the mother of the arts, teaching us how to dispute well. See *De Divisione Naturae*, V, 4; PL 122, 870.

4. Berengar argued that accidents cannot exist without substance; and since the accidents of bread remain after consecration, the substance of bread also remains. There is simply the addition of another form—that of the Body of Christ. See E. Gilson, *History*, p. 615, n. 41. St. Thomas Aquinas replies to Berengar in his *Summa Theologiae*, III, 75, 1.

5. Lanfranc, *Liber de Corpore et Sanguine Domini*, VII; PL 150, 416.

6. LIFE. ST. ANSELM was born in 1033 in Aosta, northern Italy. Educated by the Benedictines at Aosta, he left home and arrived in 1059 at the Norman Abbey of Bec, where his fellow countryman Lanfranc was famous as a teacher. He wrote most of his works at Bec, where he became Abbot in 1078. He succeeded Lanfranc as Archbishop of Canterbury in 1093. As Archbishop, he staunchly opposed the encroachments on the freedom of the Church by William II and Henry I. He died in 1109. Anselm's prudence and gentleness as a teacher are illustrated by a passage from his friend and biographer, Eadmer, "On the upbringing of boys," quoted in J. Broderick, *A Procession of Saints*, New York: Longmans, 1949, p. 48.

WORKS. PL 158–159. Critical edition by F. S. Schmitt, *Sancti Anselmi Opera Omnia*, I, Seckau, 1938, Edinburgh, 1946; II, Rome, 1940; III, IV, Edinburgh, 1946, 1949; V, London, 1951.

His most important works for philosophy are: *Monologion, Proslogion, Liber Apologeticus contra Insipientem* (written in reply to Gaunilon's *Liber pro Insipiente*), *De Veritate, De Libertate Arbitrii, De Incarnatione Verbi, Cur Deus Homo*.

TRANSLATIONS. Sidney Deane, *St. Anselm: Proslogium; Monologium, an Appendix on Behalf of the Fool by Gaunilon; and Cur Deus Homo*, Chicago: Open Court Co., 1903. This translation is sometimes inaccurate. *Proslogion*, trans. by A. C. Pegis, *The Wisdom of Catholicism*, New York: Random House, 1949, pp. 203–228. *Proslogion* and *Why God Became Man*, trans. by E. Fairweather, *A Scholastic Miscellany: Anselm to Ockham (The Library of Christian Classics*, X [Philadelphia: Westminster Press, 1956]), pp. 69–183. *Dialogue on Truth*, trans. by R. McKeon, *Selections*, I, pp. 150–184.

STUDIES. J. Clayton, *Saint Anselm; a Critical Biography*, Milwaukee: Bruce, 1933. E. Gilson, "Sens et nature de l'argument de saint Anselme," *Archives*, 9 (1934), 5–51. G. B. Phelan, *The Wisdom of Saint Anselm*, Latrobe, Pa.: The Archabbey Press, 1960.

7. *Proslogion*, 1; PL 158, 227 BC.
8. Kant gave the name of "ontological" to Descartes' version of Anselm's proof because he saw it as trying to establish the existence of God from an analysis of the mere idea of God. See I. Kant, *Critique of Pure Reason*, trans. by F. Max Müller, New York, 1896, p. 483. As we shall see, however, Anselm did not consider this to be the method of his own proof.

9. *Monologion*, 1; PL 158, 144–146. In his *De Hebdomadibus*, Boethius argued that there is but one being who is good by his very essence; all others are called good in reference to this supreme good.
10. *Monologion*, 3–4; PL 158, 147–150.
11. *Proslogion*, 1; PL 158, 225 B.
12. Anselm is here remembering Augustine's doctrine that the mind is the image of God in its triple faculties of memory, intelligence, and love. See St. Augustine, *De Trinitate*, XIV, 8; PL 42, 1044.
13. *Proslogion*, 1; PL 158, 227 B.
14. *Ibid.*, 2; PL 158, 227–228.
15. *Ibid.*, 4; PL 158, 229 B.
16. *Liber pro Insipiente*, 4; PL 158, 244–245.
17. *Ibid.*, 5, 6; PL 158, 245–247.
18. St. Anselm, *Liber Apologeticus contra Gaunilonem Respondentem pro Insipiente*, 8; PL 158, 257, 258.
19. *Ibid.*, 3, 4; PL 158, 252, 253.
20. *Proslogion*, 4; PL 158, 229.
21. *De Fide Trinitatis*, 2; PL 158, 265 A–C.
22. *De Veritate*, 2, 3; PL 158, 469–471.
23. *Ibid.*, 4–7; PL 158, 471–475.
24. *Ibid.*, 11; PL 158, 480.
25. *Ibid.*, 13; PL 158, 486 A–C.
26. *De Voluntate;* PL 158, 487.
27. *De Concordia*, 6; PL 158, 516–517.
28. *De Libertate Arbitrii*, 8; PL 158, 501.

v. Peter Abelard

1. LIFE. ABELARD was born in 1079 in Brittany, France. He studied logic under Roscelin, both logic and rhetoric under William of

Champeaux, and theology under Anselm of Laon. By his critical questioning he forced William of Champeaux to change his opinion on universals and finally to retire from teaching. He opened several schools of his own, first at Melun, then at Corbeil, finally on Mount St. Geneviève on the left bank of the Seine, the site of the future University of Paris. In 1113 he became head of the cathedral school of Notre Dame in Paris. There he achieved fame as a teacher and met Héloïse, whom he married. After his mutilation by the servants of Héloïse's uncle, Héloïse entered a convent and Abelard became a monk. In 1121, at the Council of Soissons, his treatise on the Trinity was condemned. He continued his teaching but was again condemned at the Council of Sens in 1141. While on his way to Rome to appeal to the Pope he fell sick and was given hospitality by Peter the Venerable, Abbot of Cluny. He died in 1142.

works. Uncritical edition in PL 178. *Logical works:* critical editions by B. Geyer, *Peter Abaelards philosophische Schriften, Beiträge,* XXI, 1–4, Münster, 1919–1933, I: *Logica "ingredientibus"* (commentaries on Porphyry's *Isagoge* and Aristotle's *Categories* and *De Interpretatione*), II: *Logica "nostrorum petitioni sociorum"* (second commentary on Porphyry). *Introductiones Parvulorum,* ed. Mario Dal Pra, *Pietro Abelardo Scritti Filosofici, Editio super Porphyrium, Glossae in Categorias, Editio super Aristotelem De Interpretatione, De Divisionibus, Super Topica Glossae,* Rome-Milan, Fratelli Bocca, 1954. *Dialectica,* ed. L. M. De Rijk, Assen: Van Gor-

cum & Co., 1956. Among his theological works are: *Sic et Non, Theologia Christiana, Ethica seu Scito Teipsum,* all in PL 178. On the life of Abelard and Héloïse: *Historia Calamitatum,* critical edition by J. T. Muckle, *Mediaeval Studies,* 12 (1950), 175–211.

translations. *The Glosses of Peter Abelard on Porphyry* (selection), R. McKeon, *Selections,* I, pp. 208–258. *Abailard's Ethics,* J. Ramsay McCallum, Oxford: Blackwell, 1935. *Abailard's Christian Theology,* J. R. McCallum, Oxford: Blackwell, 1948. *The Story of Abelard's Adversities (Historia calamitatum),* J. T. Muckle, Toronto: Pontifical Institute of Mediaeval Studies, 1954.

studies. J. G. Sikes, *Peter Abailard,* Cambridge: University Press, 1932. J. Cottiaux, "La conception de la théologie chez Abélard," *Revue d'histoire ecclésiastique* (1932), 247–295, 523–612, 789–828. Helen Waddell, *Peter Abailard,* London: Constable & Co., 1933. E. Gilson, *Héloïse and Abélard,* trans. by L. K. Shook, Chicago: Regnery, 1951.

2. Peter Abelard, *Epistola 17;* PL 178, 375.

3. On the method of Abelard and its influence, see M. Grabmann, *Die Geschichte der scholastischen Methode,* II, Freiburg im Breisgau, 1911, pp. 199–221. Abelard's influence on the scholastic method of disputation was not decisive, but preparatory and indirect. That method has its origin in the *Topics* of Aristotle, which was unknown to Abelard.

4. See St. Anselm, *De Fide Trinitatis,* 2; PL 158, 265 A.

5. See John of Salisbury, *Metalogicon,* II, 17; trans. by D. McGarry,

Berkeley & Los Angeles: University of California Press, 1955, p. 112; *Polycraticus*, VII, 12; trans. by J. B. Pike, *Frivolities of Courtiers and Footprints of Philosophers*, Minneapolis: University of Minnesota Press, 1938, p. 262.

6. For Roscelin, see F. Picavet, *Roscelin, philosophe et théologien*, Paris: F. Alcan, 1911. The extant medieval texts on Roscelin are conveniently gathered, pp. 112–143.

7. See "Guillemi Campellensis Sententiae vel Quaestiones XLVII," in G. Lefèvre, *Les variations de Guillaume de Champeaux et la question des universaux*, Lille, 1898; E. Michaud, *Guillaume de Champeaux et les écoles de Paris au XIIe siècle d'après des documents inédits*, Paris, 1867.

8. Abelard, *Glosses on Porphyry*, trans. by R. McKeon, *Selections*, I, pp. 222–232; *The Story of Abelard's Adversities*, trans. by J. T. Muckle, pp. 16–17.

9. *Glosses on Porphyry*, p. 228. See John of Salisbury, *Metalogicon*, II, 17, pp. 115–116.

10. Abelard, *op. cit.*, p. 232.

11. *Ibid.*, p. 238. On this point, see E. Gilson, *The Unity of Philosophical Experience*, New York: Scribner's, 1947, pp. 23, 24.

12. Abelard, *Logica "ingredientibus,"* 3; *Beiträge*, XXI, p. 316. For the distinction between sense, imagination, and understanding, see p. 317.

13. Abelard, *Glosses on Porphyry*, p. 250.

14. *Ibid.*, pp. 250–254.

15. *Ethics*, III; trans. by J. R. McCallum, p. 19.

16. *Ibid.*, pp. 31–33.

17. *Ibid.*, XI, p. 46.

18. *Ibid.*, XII, p. 48.

19. *Ibid.*, XIV, p. 55. For the condemnation, see Denzinger, *Enchiridion Symbolorum*, n. 377; ed. 31, Fribourg im Breisgau: Herder, 1957.

20. See J. Rohmer, *La finalité morale chez les théologiens de S. Augustin à Duns Scot*, Paris: J. Vrin, 1939, ch. 2: La crise du subjectivisme moral chez Abélard.

VI. The School of Chartres

1. The *Didascalion* of HUGH OF ST. VICTOR was an influential introduction to the arts and philosophy; ed. C. H. Buttimer, Washington, D.C.: The Catholic University, 1939.

2. *Chalcidius* translated the first part of Plato's *Timaeus* (up to 53D) and wrote a commentary on it probably at the beginning of the 5th century. This was one of the main sources of Plato's philosophy during the Middle Ages. See *Timaeus a Calcidio translatus commentarioque instructus*, ed. J. H. Waszink, London: Warburg Institute, 1962. *Macrobius* wrote in the late 4th century under the influence of Plato and the Neoplatonists. See his *Commentarium in Somnium Scipionis*, ed. F. Eyssenhardt, Leipzig: Teubner, 1893; trans. by W. H. Stahl, *Macrobius, Commentary on the Dream of Scipio*, New York: Columbia University Press, 1952. *Apuleius*, born c. 125, was a Pla-

tonic philosopher and rhetorician. *Apulei Opera*, Leipzig: Teubner, 1905.

On twelfth-century humanism, see C. H. Haskins, *The Renaissance of the Twelfth Century*, Cambridge: Harvard University Press, 1927; G. Paré, A. Brunet, P. Tremblay, *La renaissance du xiie siècle*, Paris: J. Vrin, 1933.

3. WORKS AND STUDIES.

a) *Gilbert of Poitiers*. PL 64. Critical editions by N. Haring: *Commentary on Boethius' De Hebdomadibus*, *Traditio*, 9 (1953), 177–211; *Commentary on Boethius' Contra Eutychen et Nestorium*, *Archives*, 21 (1954), 241–357; *Expositio in Boethii libros De Trinitate*, *Studies and Texts*, I, Toronto: Pontifical Institute of Mediaeval Studies, 1955, 23–98.

De Sex Principiis was attributed to Gilbert during the Middle Ages, but it is likely not by him. Ed. A. Heysse, *Opuscula et Textus*, Münster i. W., VII, 1929.

N. Haring, "The Case of Gilbert de la Porrée, Bishop of Poitiers (1142–1154)," *Mediaeval Studies*, 13 (1951), 1–40.

b) *William of Conches. De Philosophia Mundi*, PL 90, 1127–1178; fragments of a commentary on the *Timaeus*, ed. J. M. Parent, *La doctrine de la création dans l'école de Chartres*, Paris, Ottawa: J. Vrin, 1938, pp. 142–177; Glosses on the *Consolation of Philosophy*, *ibid.*, pp. 124–136; *Moralium Dogma Philosophorum* (authenticity doubtful), ed. J. Holnberg, Upsala, 1929; *Dragmaticon Philosophiae*, Strasbourg, 1567, with fragments in

V. Cousin, *Ouvrages inédits d'Abélard*, Paris, 1836, pp. 669–677; also in *Fragments philosophiques*, Paris, 1865, pp. 340–351.

H. Flatten, *Die Philosophie des Wilhelm von Conches*, Koblenz, 1929.

c) *Thierry of Chartres. Heptateuchon*, an unedited treatise on the seven liberal arts. *De Sex Dierum Operibus*, ed. W. Jansen, *Der Commentar des Clarenbaldus von Arras zu Boethius de Trinitate*, Breslau, 1926, pp. 106*–112*. A better edition of the same work by N. Haring, *Archives*, 22 (1955), 184–200. *Commentary on Boethius' De Trinitate (Anonymous Berliniensis)*, ed. N. Haring, *Archives*, 23 (1956), 257–325. *Librum Hunc,* ed. W. Jansen, *op. cit.*, pp. 1*–25*.

d) *Bernard Silvester. De Mundi Universitate*, ed. C. S. Barach and J. Wrobel, Innsbruck, 1876.

E. Gilson, "La Cosmogonie de Bernardus Silvestris," *Archives*, 3 (1928), 5–24.

e) *Clarenbaud of Arras. Commentary on De Trinitate of Boethius*, ed. W. Jansen, *op. cit.*, pp. 26*–105*; *A Hitherto Unknown Commentary on Boethius' De Hebdomadibus*. N. Haring, *Studies and Texts*, I, Toronto, 1955, 1–21; *Short Treatise on Genesis*, ed. N. Haring, *Archives*, 22 (1955), 200–216.

f) *John of Salisbury, Policraticus*, ed. C. Webb, 2 vols., Oxford: Clarendon Press, 1909; *Metalogicon*, ed. C. Webb, Oxford: Clarendon Press, 1929. *The Metalogicon*, trans. by D. Mc-

Garry, Berkeley: University of California Press, 1955. Selections from the *Policraticus*, trans. by J. Pike, *Frivolities of Courtiers and Footprints of Philosophers*, Minneapolis: University of Minnesota Press, 1938.

C. Schaarschmidt, *Joannes Saresberiensis nach Leben und Studien, Schriften und Philosophie*, Leipzig, 1862.

4. John of Salisbury, *Metalogicon*, IV, 35; trans. D. McGarry, p. 259.

5. See J. M. Parent, *La doctrine de la création dans l'école de Chartres*, Paris, Ottawa: J. Vrin, 1938; N. Haring, "The Creation and the Creator of the World according to Thierry of Chartres and Clarenbaldus of Arras," *Archives*, 22 (1955), 137–216.

6. For Bernard's doctrine of the divine Ideas, see John of Salisbury, *Metalogicon*, II, 17, p. 113; IV, 35, pp. 259–260.

7. Ibid., II, 17, p. 115.

8. In Librum de Duabus Naturis, PL 64, 1372 D.

9. Polycraticus, I, Introduction, trans. J. Pike, p. 10.

10. Metalogicon, II, 20.

11. Ibid., II, 10, p. 100. See E. Gilson, *The Unity of Philosophical Experience*, pp. 29–30.

PART 2   THE COMING OF THE SCHOOLMEN

VII. Introduction to Scholasticism

1. For a more complete list of the new translations, see M. de Wulf, *Histoire de la philosophie médiévale*, II, 6th ed., Louvain: Institut supérieur de philosophie, 1936, pp. 25–58. For the introduction of Aristotle in the West, see F. Van Steenberghen, *Aristotle in the West*, trans. by L. Johnston, Louvain: E. Nauwelaerts, 1955; D. A. Callus, *Introduction of Aristotelian Learning to Oxford*, London: H. Milford, 1944.

2. See M. Grabmann, *Guglielmo di Moerbeke O.P. il traduttore delle opere di Aristoteles*, Rome: Pontificia Università Gregoriana, 1946.

3. See F. Van Steenberghen, *op. cit.*, pp. 66–88; M. Grabmann, *I divieti ecclesiastici di Aristotele sotto Innocenzo III e Gregorio IX*, Rome: Herder, 1941.

4. St. Bonaventure, *Collationes de Decem Praeceptis*, II, 28, Quaracchi, 1891, vol. 5, p. 515. Cited by E. Gilson, *History*, p. 402.

5. For the meaning of scholasticism, see M.-D. Chenu, *Introduction à l'étude de saint Thomas d'Aquin*, Paris: J. Vrin, 1950, pp. 51–60.

6. See H. Rashdall, *The Universities of Europe in the Middle Ages*, ed. F. M. Powicke and A. B. Emden, 3 vols., Oxford: The Clarendon Press, 1936.

7. For the teaching methods of the scholastics, see M.-D. Chenu, *op. cit.*, pp. 66–81. For the technique of disputation, see P. Glorieux, *La littérature quodlibétique de 1260 à 1320*, Le Saulchoir: Kain, 1925, pp. 11–58.

VIII. Arabian and Jewish Philosophy

1. On Arabian philosophy, see T. J. de Boer, *The History of Philosophy in Islam,* trans. by E. R. Jones, London: Luzac & Co., 1903, reissued 1933; M. Horten, *Die Philosophie des Islam in ihren Beziehungen zu den philosophischen Weltanschauungen des westlichen Orients,* Munich: E. Reinhardt, 1924; same author, *Islamische Philosophie,* Tübingen, 1930; G. Quadri, *La philosophie arabe dans l'Europe médiévale,* Paris: Payot, 1947. M. Fakhry, *Islamic Occasionalism and Its Critique by Averroës and Aquinas,* London: George Allen & Unwin, 1958. For a concise history of Arabian and Jewish philosophy, see I. Brady, *A History of Ancient Philosophy,* Milwaukee: Bruce, 1959, pp. 193–226.

2. For the life of AVICENNA, see his autobiography and biography in A. J. Arberry, *Avicenna on Theology,* London: John Murray, 1951, pp. 9–24. The medieval Latin translations of his works were edited in Venice, 1508. Recent reprints: Avicenna, *Opera Philosophica* (Venice, 1508), Louvain: Edition de la bibliothèque S.J., 1961; Avicenna, *Metaphysica sive Prima Philosophia* (Venice, 1495), Louvain: Edition de la bibliothèque S.J., 1961. For his philosophy, see M.-A. Goichon, *La distinction de l'essence et de l'existence d'après Ibn Sina (Avicenne),* Paris: Desclée de Brouwer, 1937; same author, *La philosophie d'Avicenne et son influence en Europe médiévale,* Paris: Adrien-Maisonneuve, 1944; G. Smith, "Avicenna and the Pos-

sibles," *The New Scholasticism,* 17 (1943), 340–357; B. H. Zedler, "Saint Thomas and Avicenna in the 'De Potentia Dei,'" *Traditio,* 6 (1948), 105–159; L. Gardet, *La pensée religieuse d'Avicenne (Ibn Sina),* Paris: J. Vrin, 1951; F. Rahman, *Avicenna's Psychology,* London: Oxford University Press, 1952; S. M. Afnan, *Avicenna, His Life and Works,* London: George Allen & Unwin, 1958.

3. *Metaph.,* IX, 4, Venice, 1508, fols. 104, 105. For the number of the Intelligences, see L. Gardet, *op. cit.,* pp. 52, 53.

4. See E. Gilson, *Being and Some Philosophers,* Toronto: Pontifical Institute of Mediaeval Studies, 1952, p. 76.

5. See E. Gilson, "Les sources gréco-arabes de l'augustinisme avicennisant," *Archives,* 4 (1929), 5–149.

6. The *Opera Omnia* of Averroes will be found in the Venice edition of 1574. A new edition is being prepared, called *Averroes Latinus.* To date the following works have been edited: *Parva Naturalia,* ed. H. L. Shields and H. Blumberg, Cambridge, Mass., 1949; *Commentarium Magnum in Aristotelis De Anima Libros,* ed. F. S. Crawford, Cambridge, Mass., 1953; *Commentarium Medium in Aristotelis De Generatione et Corruptione Libros,* ed. F. H. Fobes, Cambridge, Mass., 1956; *Averroes on Aristotle's De Generatione et Corruptione, Middle Commentary and Epitome,* trans. by S. Kurland, Cambridge, Mass., 1958. *Averroes' Destructio Destruc-*

tionum Philosophiae Algazelis, ed. B. Zedler, Milwaukee: Marquette University Press, 1961. For Averroes' philosophy, see E. Renan, *Averroès et l'averroïsme*, Paris, 1852; L. Gauthier, *Le théorie d'Ibn Rochd sur les rapports de la religion et de la philosophie*, Paris, 1909; M. Horten, *Die Metaphysik des Averroes*, Halle, 1912; B. Zedler, "Averroes on the Possible Intellect," *Proceedings of the American Catholic Philosophical Association*, 25 (1951), 164–178.

7. Averroes, *In Libros de Anima*, III, t.c. 14, Venice, 1574, vol. 6, fol. 159v.

8. The scholastics thought Algazel a follower of Avicenna because they knew him as the author of the *Metaphysics*, in which he summarizes Avicenna's philosophy. Algazel's *Metaphysics* has been edited by J. T. Muckle, Toronto: St. Michael's College, 1933.

See Averroes' *Tahafut Al-Tahafut* (*The Incoherence of the Incoherence*), trans. by S. Van den Bergh, 2 vols., Oxford: University Press, 1954. Algazel's work is sometimes called "The Destruction of the Philosophers," and Averroes' "The Destruction of the Destruction." For these titles, see *op. cit.*, p. xiii.

9. Averroes' treatise on the relation between philosophy and theology has been translated by Mohammed Jamil-ur-Rehman, *The Philosophy and Theology of Averroes*, Baroda, 1921. On this subject, see E. Gilson, *Reason and Revelation in the Middle Ages*, New York: Scribner's, 1948, pp. 37–53.

10. B. Zedler argues from certain statements of Averroes that he may have held for personal immortality. See "Averroes and Immortality," *The New Scholasticism*, 28 (1954), 436–453. However, this is hardly in agreement with his philosophy. The statements in question can better be understood as a concession to religion, or that a man is immortal through the immortality of the Agent Intellect, which alone is eternal and incorruptible.

11. On Jewish philosophy, see J. Husik, *A History of Mediaeval Jewish Philosophy*, New York: Macmillan, 1916; G. Vajda, *Introduction à la pensée juive du moyen âge*, Paris: J. Vrin, 1947.

12. Ed. C. Baeumker, *Beiträge*, vol. 1.

13. *The Guide for the Perplexed*, trans. by M. Friedländer, London: G. Routledge & Sons, 1936.

IX. Early Philosophy at Paris and Oxford

1. See H. Rashdall, *The Universities of Europe in the Middle Ages*, ed. F. M. Powicke and A. B. Emden, 3 vols., Oxford: Clarendon Press, 1936.

2. LIFE. WILLIAM OF AUVERGNE, also called William of Paris, was born about 1180 at Aurillac, in Auvergne, France. He studied and taught at Paris and was consecrated Bishop of Paris in 1228. He died in 1249.

WORKS. His principal work is entitled *Magisterium Divinale*, which includes the following parts: *De Trinitate* (or *De Primo Principio*), *De Universo*, *De Anima*, and *De Immortalitate Ani-*

mae, published in *Opera Omnia*, 2 vols., Paris, 1674. J. R. O'Donnell, "Tractatus magistri Guillelmi Alvernensis *De Bono et Malo*," *Mediaeval Studies*, 8 (1946), 245–299; "Tractatus Secundus Guillelmi Alvernensis *De Bono et Malo*," *Mediaeval Studies*, 16 (1954), 219–271.

STUDIES. A. Masnovo, *Da Guglielmo d'Auvergne a san Tommaso d'Aquino*, 2nd ed., 3 vols., Milan: Società editrice "Vita e Pensiero," 1945, 1946. E. Gilson, "Pourquoi saint Thomas a critiqué saint Augustin," *Archives*, 1 (1926), 46–80. M. D. Roland-Gosselin, *Le "De Ente et Essentia" de saint Thomas d'Aquin*, Paris: J. Vrin, 1926, pp. 72–74, 160–166. E. Gilson, "La notion d'existence chez Guillaume d'Auvergne," *Archives*, 15 (1946), 55–91.

3. De Universo, I–I, 26; vol. 1, pp. 619–620.

4. De Trinitate, II; vol. 2, p. 2.

5. Ibid., VII; vol. 2, p. 9.

6. De Universo, I–II, 30; vol. 1, p. 625.

7. De Trinitate, VII; vol. 2, pp. 8, 9.

8. Summa Theologiae, I–II, 110, 1, ad 2^{m}.

9. De Trinitate, VI; vol. 2, p. 7.

10. Ibid., XI, p. 16.

11. De Anima, III, 11; vol. 2 supp., pp. 100–102. This does not prevent him from agreeing with Aristotle that the soul is the form of the body. See *ibid.*, I, 1.

12. Ibid., VI, 39; p. 199 B.

13. De Universo, I–III, 29; vol. 1, p. 802 A.

14. De Anima, VII, 9; vol. 2, pp. 215, 216.

15. Ibid., VII, 6; vol. 2, p. 211.

16. LIFE. GROSSETESTE was born in Suffolk, England, about 1168. He studied at Oxford and probably also at Paris. After obtaining his degree of Master of Theology he taught at Oxford and became the first chancellor of the university about 1221. When the Franciscans arrived at Oxford in 1224 he undertook their instruction, leaving a deep and lasting mark upon their philosophy. In 1235 he was made bishop of Lincoln, where he distinguished himself as a great ecclesiastical statesman. His death occurred in 1253.

WORKS. For the writings of Grosseteste, see S. H. Thomson, *The Writings of Robert Grosseteste, Bishop of Lincoln, 1235–1253*, Cambridge: University Press, 1940; *Robert Grosseteste, Scholar and Bishop*, ed. D. A. Callus, Oxford: Clarendon Press, 1955, pp. 11–69. His shorter philosophical treatises are edited by L. Baur, *Die philosophischen Werke des Robert Grosseteste, Beiträge*, IX, Münster i. W., 1912. The *Summa Philosophiae*, previously attributed to Grosseteste, is now recognized as spurious. See C. K. McKeon, *A Study of the 'Summa philosophiae' of the Pseudo Grosseteste*, New York: Columbia University Press, 1948.

TRANSLATIONS. *On Truth, On the Truth of Propositions, On the Knowledge of God*, trans. by R. McKeon, *Selections*, I, pp. 263–287. *On Light or the Beginning of Forms*, trans. by C. Riedl, Milwaukee: Marquette University Press, 1942.

STUDIES. D. E. Sharp, *Franciscan Philosophy at Oxford in the Thirteenth Century*, Oxford University Press, 1930, pp. 9–46. L. E.

Lynch, "The Doctrine of Divine Ideas and Illumination in Robert Grosseteste," *Mediaeval Studies*, 3 (1941), 161–173. A. C. Crombie, *Robert Grosseteste and the Origins of Experimental Science 1100–1700*, Oxford: Clarendon Press, 1953. *Robert Grosseteste, Scholar and Bishop*, ed. D. A. Callus, Oxford: Clarendon Press, 1955.

17. Roger Bacon, *Compendium Studii Philosophiae*, 8; ed. J. S. Brewer, London, 1859, p. 469.

18. Commentary on Posterior Analytics, I, 14; Venice, 1494, fols. 13–14.

19. Ibid., I, 11, fol. 10ᵛ.

20. De Lineis, Angulis et Figuris, ed. L. Baur, pp. 59, 60.

21. Comm. on Post. Anal., I, 19, fol. 19ᵛ.

22. On Light; Riedl trans., pp. 11–13.

23. Ibid., pp. 13–15.

24. Ibn Gabirol, *Fons Vitae*, V, 4, p. 263. Neither Gabirol nor Grosseteste speaks of a "form of corporeity"; they call the first form simply "corporeity." The expression "form of corporeity" is found in Avicenna. See E. Gilson, *History*, p. 648, note 30.

25. De Statu Causarum; ed. L. Baur, pp. 124–125.

26. On Light, p. 10.

PART 3   THE AGE OF THE SCHOOLMEN

x. Roger Bacon

1. LIFE. According to tradition, BACON was born in Ilchester, England, about 1214. He studied first at Oxford and then at Paris. He was one of the first to lecture on Aristotle's natural philosophy at Paris. On his return to Oxford between 1247 and 1250 he came under the influence of Grosseteste and turned to scientific studies. He joined the Franciscans about 1257. By 1267 he had finished his *Opus Majus* and sent it to Pope Clement IV, who he hoped would carry out its plan for reforming Christian education. The *Opus Minus* and *Opus Tertium*, shorter works with the same purpose, were sent later when the Pope was not aroused to action by the *Opus Majus*. In 1277 he was condemned by his Franciscan superiors for teaching dangerous novelties—possibly a reference to his views in astrology. He was in prison until 1292, when he wrote his last work, *The Compendium of Theological Studies*. He died the same year or shortly afterward.

WORKS. *Opus Majus*, ed. J. H. Bridges, 3 vols., Oxford: Clarendon Press, 1897–1900. *Opus Minus, Opus Tertium*, and *Compendium Philosophiae*, ed. J. S. Brewer, *Opera quaedam hactenus inedita* (*Rerum Britannicarum Medii Aevi Scriptores*), London: Longmans, Green, 1859. *Compendium Studii Theologiae*, ed. H. Rashdall, Aberdeen, 1911. Philosophical commentaries, ed. R. Steele, *Opera hactenus inedita Fratris Rogeri Baconis*, 16 vols., Oxford: Clarendon Press, 1905–1940. *Moralis Philosophia*, ed. E. Massa,

Turin: In Aedibus Thesauri Mundi, 1953.

TRANSLATIONS. *The Opus Majus of Roger Bacon*, trans. by R. B. Burke, 2 vols., Philadelphia: University of Pennsylvania, 1928. Selections from the *Opus Majus*, in R. McKeon, *Selections*, II, pp. 7–110.

STUDIES. R. Carton, *L'expérience physique chez Roger Bacon*, Paris: J. Vrin, 1924; *L'expérience mystique de l'illumination intérieure chez Roger Bacon*, Paris: J. Vrin, 1924; *La synthèse doctrinale de Roger Bacon*, Paris: J. Vrin, 1924. D. E. Sharp, *Franciscan Philosophy at Oxford in the Thirteenth Century*, Oxford: University Press, 1930, pp. 115–171. T. Crowley, *Roger Bacon, The Problem of the Soul in his Philosophical Commentaries*, Louvain: Institut Supérieur de Philosophie, 1950. S. C. Easton, *Roger Bacon and His Search for a Universal Science*, Oxford: Blackwell, 1952.

2. *Opus Majus*, I, 1.

3. *Compendium Studii Theologiae*, p. 52. Richard of Cornwall was a Master of Theology and teacher of the Franciscans at Oxford after 1256.

4. *Opus Minus*, pp. 325–327; *Compendium Studii Philosophiae*, pp. 425, 426.

5. *Opus Majus*, I, 6.

6. *Ibid.*, I, 8.

7. *Ibid.*, II, 1.

8. *Ibid.*, II, 19.

9. *Ibid.*, II, 6.

10. *Ibid.*, IV, 1, 3.

11. *Ibid.*, V, 1.

12. *Ibid.*, VI, 1.

13. Gloss on *Secretum Secretorum*, V; ed. Steele, vol. 5, p. 9.

14. G. Sarton, *Introduction to the History of Science*, II, 2, Baltimore: The Williams and Wilkins Co., 1931, p. 1031.

15. *Opus Majus*, V, 2–12.

16. *Epistola de Secretis Operibus Artis et Naturae*, IV, ed. Brewer, pp. 532, 533.

17. *Opus Majus*, VII, 1.

18. For Bacon's notion of *respublica fidelium* and its historical setting, see E. Gilson, Introduction to St. Augustine's *City of God* (*The Fathers of the Church* [New York, 1950]), pp. xci, xcii. Same author, *Les métamorphoses de la Cité de Dieu*, Louvain: Publications Universitaires de Louvain, 1952, pp. 75–109.

19. *Communia Naturalia*, ed. R. Steele, vol. 2, p. 105.

20. *Ibid.*, vol. 3, p. 291.

21. *Ibid.*, pp. 294–297.

22. *Quaestiones supra undecimum Primae Philosophiae*, ed. R. Steele, vol. 7, pp. 15, 16; 109, 110.

23. *Quaestiones supra libros quatuor Physicorum*, vol. 8, p. 31.

24. *Opus Majus*, II, 5.

XI. St. Bonaventure

1. ALEXANDER OF HALES, *Summa Theologica*, 4 vols., Quaracchi, 1924–1948. On the problem of authenticity, see V. Doucet, *Prolegomena ad Summam Halensianam*, Quaracchi, 1948, pp. lix–lxxxi; same author, "The History of the Problem of the Authenticity of the Summa," *Franciscan Studies*, 7 (1947), 26–41, 274–312.

2. LIFE. ST. BONAVENTURE (John Fidanza) was born in 1221 at Bagnorea, near Viterbo, Italy. He entered the Franciscan Order

about 1238 and subsequently studied at the University of Paris under Alexander of Hales, whom he calls his father and master. He himself taught at the university from 1248 to 1255, commenting on Peter Lombard's *Sentences* from 1248 to 1251. On October 23, 1256, both he and St. Thomas Aquinas were appointed to chairs of theology, but because of opposition of the university to the Mendicant Friars (Franciscans, Dominicans), the doctoral degrees of both men were withheld and their right officially to occupy their chairs was deferred until October 1257. The same year St. Bonaventure was elected Minister General of the Franciscans and his teaching career at the university came to an end. However, he continued to take an active interest in the doctrinal controversies of the time and influenced them by his writings and sermons. In 1273 he was made a Cardinal. The Order flourished under his administration, so that he became known as its second founder. He died in 1274, the same year as St. Thomas. He was canonized on July 14, 1482, and raised to the rank of Doctor of the Church in 1587.

WORKS. Main works: *Commentary on the Sentences, Itinerarium Mentis in Deum, De Reductione Artium ad Theologiam, Collationes in Hexaemeron,* contained in *Opera Omnia,* 10 vols., Quaracchi, 1882–1902. *Tria Opuscula (Breviloquium, Itinerarium, De Reductione),* Quaracchi, 1911. *Collationes in Hexaemeron* (a different redaction from that in the *Opera Omnia*), Quaracchi, 1934.

TRANSLATIONS. *Commentary on the Sentences,* I, 3, 1, in R. McKeon, *Selections,* II, pp. 118–148. *The Works of St. Bonaventura,* ed. P. Boehner and Sister M. Frances Laughlin: I. *De Reductione Artium ad Theologiam,* Latin text and trans. by Sister Emma Therese Healy, Saint Bonaventure, N.Y., 1955; II. *Itinerarium Mentis in Deum,* Latin text and trans. by P. Boehner, Saint Bonaventure, N.Y., 1956. *The Ascent of the Mind to God,* Prologue and ch. 5–7, trans. by A. C. Pegis, *The Wisdom of Catholicism,* New York: Random House, 1949, pp. 272–288. *The Works of Bonaventure,* trans. by J. de Vinck, vol. I, Paterson, N.J.: St. Anthony Guild Press, 1960.

STUDIES. C. J. O'Leary, *The Substantial Composition of Man According to St. Bonaventure,* Washington, D. C.: The Catholic University of America, 1931. A. C. Pegis, *St. Thomas and the Problem of the Soul in the Thirteenth Century,* ch. 2: St. Bonaventure and the Problem of the Soul as Substance, Toronto: St. Michael's College, 1934. E. Gilson, *The Philosophy of St. Bonaventure,* trans. by Dom Illtyd Trethowan and F. J. Sheed, London: Sheed & Ward, 1938. *A Gilson Reader,* ed. A. C. Pegis, ch. xv: The Spirit of St. Bonaventure, New York: Doubleday, 1957, pp. 105–126. G. Klubertanz, "*Esse* and *Existere* in the Philosophy of St. Bonaventure," *Mediaeval Studies,* 8 (1946), 169–188. A. C. Pegis, "St. Bonaventure, St. Francis and Philosophy," *Mediaeval Studies,* 15 (1953), 1–13.

3. *Sent.,* II, 1, 1, 1, 2; vol. 2, p. 22.

(References are to Quaracchi edition of 1882–1902.)

4. *Sermo IV*, 18–19; vol. 5, p. 572.

5. *Sent.*, III, 35, 1; vol. 3, p. 775.

6. *In Hexaemeron*, coll. 22, 21; vol. 5, p. 440.

7. *Breviloquium*, Prol. 3; vol. 5, p. 205. "Philosophical science is nothing else than certain knowledge of the truth as an object of investigation; theological science is the devout knowledge of the truth as an object of belief." *De Donis Spiritus Sancti*, coll. 4, 5; vol. 5, p. 474.

8. *Sent.*, II, 18, 2, 1; vol. 2, pp. 447–448.

9. *In Hexaemeron*, coll. 6, 2–4; vol. 5, pp. 360–361.

10. *Ibid.*, coll. 7, 3–12; vol. 5, pp. 365–367.

11. *De Donis Spiritus Sancti*, coll. 4, 12; vol. 5, p. 476.

12. *In Hexaemeron*, coll. 1, 17; vol. 5, p. 332.

13. *Sent.*, II, 1, 1, 1, 2; vol. 2, pp. 20–22.

14. *Ibid.*, I, 8, 1, 2, 2; vol. 1, pp. 160–161.

15. *Ibid.*, II, 13, 2, 2; vol. 2, pp. 320–321.

16. *Ibid.*, II, 7, 2, 2, 1, ad 6^m; vol. 2, p. 199.

17. *Ibid.*, II, 17, 1, 2; vol. 2, pp. 414–415.

18. *Ibid.*, I, 3, 2, 1, 3; vol. 1, p. 86.

19. *Ibid.*, II, 19, 1, 1; vol. 2, p. 460.

20. *Ibid.*, II, 17, 2, 2, ad 6^m; vol. 2, p. 423. *In Hexaemeron*, coll. 2, 2; vol. 5, p. 336.

21. *Sent.*, II, 16, 1, 2, fund. 4; vol. 2, p. 397.

22. *In Hexaemeron*, coll. 1, 13; vol. 5, p. 331; *Sermo IV*, 18; vol. 5, 572.

23. *In Hexaemeron*, coll. 2, 23; vol. 5, p. 340.

24. *Breviloquium*, II, 12; vol. 5, p. 230.

25. *Sent.*, I, 8, 1, 1, 2; vol. 1, pp. 153–155.

26. *De Mysterio Trinitatis*, I, 1, 29; vol. 5, p. 48.

27. *Sent.*, I, 8, 1, 1, 2, concl.; vol. 1, p. 154. See Hugh of St. Victor, *De Sacramentis*, I, 3, 1.

28. *Itinerarium Mentis in Deum*, I, 6; vol. 5, p. 297. See St. Augustine, *Ennaratio in Psalmum 145*, 5; PL 37, 1887.

29. *De Reductione Artium ad Theologiam*, 8; vol. 5, p. 322.

30. *Sent.*, II, 24, 1, 2, 4; vol. 2, pp. 568–571.

31. *Ibid.*, II, 39, 1, 2; vol. 2, p. 904. *De Mysterio Trinitatis*, I, 1; vol. 5, p. 49. *Itinerarium Mentis in Deum*, III, 1; vol. 5, p. 303.

32. *De Scientia Christi*, IV; vol. 5, p. 23. *Sermo IV*, 6–10; vol. 5, pp. 568–570.

33. *De Scientia Christi*, ibid.

34. Matthew of Aquasparta, Quaestio I (*De Humanae Cognitionis Ratione*), Quaracchi, 1933, p. 96; ad 4^m, p. 103. See E. Gilson, *The Unity of Philosophical Experience*, New York: Scribner's, 1947, p. 56.

35. Quaestio II, *ed. cit.*, p. 118. See E. Gilson, *The Spirit of Mediaeval Philosophy*, trans. by A. H. C. Downes, London: Sheed & Ward, 1936, pp. 230–235; A. C. Pegis, "Matthew of Aquasparta and the Cognition of Non-Being," *Scholastica ratione historico-critica instauranda* (*Acta congressus scholastici internationalis*), Rome, 1951, pp. 463–480.

36. *In Hexaemeron*, coll. 6, 7–32; vol. 5, pp. 361–364.

37. See F. Van Steenberghen, *Aristotle in the West*, Louvain: E. Nauwelaerts, 1955, pp. 160–162. For the contrary view, see E. Gilson, *History*, pp. 339–340.

XII. St. Albert the Great

1. LIFE. ST. ALBERT was born in the southern German town of Lauingen about 1200. He studied the liberal arts at Padua, and after joining the Dominicans in 1223 he was sent to Cologne to study theology. From 1228 to 1240 he taught theology at Cologne and other German cities. From *c.* 1242 to 1248 he was at Paris, studying and teaching theology. He may have taught St. Thomas at Paris; he certainly had him as a pupil at Cologne, where he lectured from 1248 to 1260. After serving as bishop of Ratisbon for two years (1260–1262), he spent the remainder of his life teaching, writing, doing scientific research, and performing diplomatic missions. He died at Cologne in 1280. He was canonized and declared a Doctor of the Church in 1931. WORKS. *Opera Omnia*, ed. A. Borgnet, 38 vols., Paris: Vivès, 1890–1899. A new critical edition has been begun by the Albertus Magnus Institute in Cologne. To date, 4 vols. have appeared, published in Münster in Westphalia, 1951–1958. Albert's main writings include: *Summa de Creaturis* (1236–1243) in five parts: *De Quattuor Coaevis, De Homine, De Bono, De Sacramentis,* and *De Resurrectione* (the last three parts are contained in the new critical edition); *Commentary on the Sentences* (1243–1249); Commentaries on the works of Dionysius (1247–1256); Commentaries on Aristotle's logical works, the *Metaphysics, Physics, De Anima* (probably between 1256–1275); *De Unitate Intellectus contra Averroem* (1256–1257); *De*

Intellectu et Intelligibili (1258); *Summa Theologiae* (1270–1280). TRANSLATION. *On the Intellect and the Intelligible*, Bk. I; R. McKeon, *Selections*, I, pp. 326–375. STUDIES. P. G. Meersseman, *Introductio in Opera Omnia B. Alberti Magni*, Bruges, 1931. M.-H. Laurent and M.-J. Congar, *Essai de bibliographie albertinienne, Revue Thomiste,* 36 (1931), 422–468. U. Dähnert, *Die Erkenntnislehre des Albertus Magnus gemessen an den Stufen der "abstractio"* (Leipzig, 1933). A. C. Pegis, *St. Thomas and the Problem of the Soul in the Thirteenth Century*, Toronto, 1934, ch. 3: St. Albert the Great and the problem of the soul as form and substance. E. Gilson, "L'Ame raisonnable chez Albert le Grand," *Archives,* 14 (1943–1945), 5–72. R. Miller, "An Aspect of Averroes' Influence on St. Albert," *Mediaeval Studies,* 16 (1954), 57–71. L. Ducharme, "'Esse' chez saint Albert le Grand," *Revue de l'Université d'Ottawa* (Oct.–Dec. 1957), 1–44. L. Kennedy, "The Nature of the Human Intellect according to St. Albert the Great," *Modern Schoolman,* 37 (1960), 121–137.
2. In Epistolas Dionysii Areopagitae, VII, 2; vol. 14, p. 910.
3. Ernst Meyer, *Geschichte der Botanik,* 9–84. Cited by H. Wilms, *Albert the Great,* London: Burns Oates & Washbourne, 1933, p. 21.
4. Cited by H. Wilms, *op. cit.,* p. 59.
5. De Vegetabilibus et Plantis, VI, 1, 1; vol. 10, pp. 159, 160.
6. Summa Theol., II, 69, 2, ad 2; vol. 33, p. 16.
7. Nemesius, *Peri Phuseos Anthro-*

pou liber a N. Alfano in Latinum translatus, 2; ed. C. Burkhard, Leipzig: Teubner, 1917, pp. 24–25, 39.

8. *Summa Theol.*, II, 2, 9; vol. 32, pp. 140, 141.

9. *De Anima*, II, 1, 4; vol. 5, pp. 198, 199.

10. *Summa de Creaturis*, I, 2, 5; vol. 34, pp. 333, 334. *Summa Theol.*, II, 3, 2; vol. 32, p. 29. See p. 160.

11. *De Intellectu et Intelligibili*, I, 1, 6; vol. 9, p. 486.

12. *Summa Theol.*, II, 14, 2; vol. 32, p. 196.

13. *Sent.*, I, 2, 5; vol. 25, pp. 59, 60.

14. *Summa Theol.*, I, 15, 3; vol. 31, pp. 110, 111.

15. *De Intell. et Intell.*, II, 5; vol. 9, pp. 510, 511; ch. 8, pp. 515, 516.

16. *Summa Theol.*, II, 77, 3; vol. 33, p. 78. The agent intellect,

which is by nature immortal, being simple and unchangeable, imparts to the possible intellect both being and immortality. *Summa de Creaturis*, II, 55, 5; vol. 35, p. 474.

17. *Sent.*, I, 46, 14; vol. 26, p. 450.

18. *Summa de Creaturis*, II, 81, 3; vol. 35, p. 661.

19. *Sent.*, I, 5, 6; vol. 25, p. 184.

20. *De Bono*, I, 1, 1 (Münster i. W., 1951), p. 1.

21. *Ibid.*, a. 6, p. 12. See Augustine, *De Doctrina Christiana*, I, 32; PL 34, 32.

22. *Ibid.*, a. 10, p. 20.

23. For St. Albert's notion of beauty, see H. Pouillon, "La beauté, propriété transcendantale chez les scolastiques (1220–1270)," *Archives*, 15 (1946), 293–301.

24. *Sent.*, I, 8, 15; vol. 25, p. 242.

XIII. St. Thomas Aquinas

1. LIFE. For the life of ST. THOMAS, see A. Walz, *Saint Thomas Aquinas, A Biographical Study*, trans. by S. Bullough, Westminster, Md.: Newman Press, 1951. He was born, probably in 1225, at Roccasecca, near Aquino, between Rome and Naples. His father was Count Landulf of Aquino and his mother was Theodora, sister of the Emperor Frederick Barbarossa. In 1230 he was placed in the Abbey of Monte Cassino. Nine years later he was sent to the University of Naples to study the arts and philosophy. He took the Dominican habit in 1243 against the wishes of his parents, who had him confined until 1245. After his release he went to Paris and then to Cologne, where he studied under St. Albert.

From 1252 to 1255 he studied at Paris, receiving the degree of Master of Theology in 1256. After teaching for several years there he returned to Italy in 1259, where he taught theology until 1268. From 1269 to 1272 he was teaching again in Paris. In 1272 he became Regent of the Dominican House of Studies at Naples. He died at Fossanuova on March 7, 1274. He was canonized in 1323, declared a Doctor of the Church in 1567 and the Patron of Catholic schools in 1880.

WORKS. For a complete list of his works, with their chronology, editions, and translations, see I. T. Eschmann, "A Catalogue of St. Thomas's Works," in E. Gilson, *The Christian Philosophy of St. Thomas Aquinas*, New York:

Random House, 1956. Among the more important editions and works are: *Opera Omnia*, 25 vols., Parma, 1862–1870, reprinted by the Musurgia Press, New York, 1948–1950. In the Leonine edition, 16 vols. have appeared to date: *Opera Omnia*, Rome, 1882–1948. This includes the *Summa Theologiae* (vols. 4–12), and the *Summa Contra Gentiles* (vols. 13–15). The Leonine text of these two works has been published in manual editions by Marietti. *Scriptum super Sententiis*, ed. P. Mandonnet and M. F. Moos, 4 vols., Paris: Lethielleux, 1929–1947. *Quaestiones Disputatae*, ed. R. Spiazzi, 2 vols., Turin: Marietti, 1949. *Quaestiones Quodlibetales*, ed. R. Spiazzi, Turin: Marietti, 1949. *Opuscula Omnia*, ed. P. Mandonnet, 5 vols., Paris: Lethielleux, 1927; new edition by J. Perrier, vol. 1, Paris: Lethielleux, 1949. *Le "De Ente et essentia," texte établi d'après les manuscrits parisiens*, ed. M. D. Roland-Gosselin, Paris: J. Vrin, 1926. *In Aristotelis Librum De Anima Commentarium*, ed. A. M. Pirotta, Turin: Marietti, 1948. *In X Libros Ethicorum Aristotelis Expositio*, ed. R. Spiazzi, Turin: Marietti, 1949. *In XII Libros Metaphysicorum Aristotelis Expositio*, ed. M. R. Cathala, R. Spiazzi, Turin: Marietti, 1950. *In Librum B. Dionysii De Divinis Nominibus Expositio*, ed. C. Pera, Turin: Marietti, 1950. *In VIII Libros De Physico Auditu sive Physicorum Aristotelis Commentaria*, ed. A. M. Pirotta, Naples: M. d'Auria Pontificius Editor, 1953. *Expositio super Librum De Causis*, ed. H. D. Saffrey, Fribourg: Société Philosophique, 1954. *Expositio*

super Librum Boethii De Trinitate, ed. B. Decker, Leiden: E. J. Brill, 1955.

TRANSLATIONS. *Summa Theologiae*, trans. by the English Dominicans, 22 vols.; 2nd ed., New York: Benziger, 1912–1936. *On the Truth of the Catholic Faith (Summa Contra Gentiles)*, trans. by A. C. Pegis (I), J. F. Anderson (II), V. J. Bourke (III), Charles O'Neil (IV); 5 vols., New York: Doubleday Image Books, 1954–1956. *Basic Writings of Saint Thomas Aquinas*, ed. A. C. Pegis, 2 vols., New York: Random House, 1948. *Introduction to Saint Thomas Aquinas*, by A. C. Pegis, New York: Random House, 1948. *The Compendium of Theology*, trans. by C. Vollert, St. Louis: Herder, 1947. *On Spiritual Creatures*, trans. by M. G. Fitzpatrick and J. J. Wellmuth, Milwaukee: Marquette University Press, 1949. *On Being and Essence*, trans. by A. Maurer, Toronto: Pontifical Institute of Mediaeval Studies, 1949. *The Division and Methods of the Sciences. Questions V and VI of the commentary on the De Trinitate of Boethius*, trans. by A. Maurer, Toronto: Pontifical Institute of Mediaeval Studies, 1953. *Truth*, trans. by R. Mulligan, R. Schmidt, J. McGlynn, 3 vols., Chicago: Regnery, 1952–1954. *On Kingship to the King of Cyprus*, trans. by G. B. Phelan and I. T. Eschmann, Toronto: Pontifical Institute of Mediaeval Studies, 1949. *The Soul*, trans. by J. P. Rowan, St. Louis: Herder, 1949. *Commentary on the De Anima*, trans. by K. Foster and S. Humpfries, London: Routledge and Kegan Paul, 1951. *The Pocket Aquinas, Se-*

lected from the Writings of St. Thomas, ed. V. J. Bourke, New York: Washington Square Press, 1960. *Treatise on Separate Substances*, trans. by F. J. Lescoe, West Hartford, Conn.: St. Joseph College, 1959. *Commentary on the Metaphysics*, trans. by J. P. Rowan, 2 vols., Chicago: H. Regnery, 1961.

STUDIES. Useful bibliographies: V. J. Bourke, *Thomistic Bibliography*, St. Louis: University Press, 1945. P. Wyser, *Thomas von Aquin*, in *Bibliographische Einführungen in das Studium der Philosophie* 13/14, Bern: A. Franke, A. G. Verlag, 1950. P. Mandonnet and J. Destrez, *Bibliographie thomiste*, 2nd ed., Paris: J. Vrin, 1960.

A. D. Sertillanges, *The Foundations of Thomistic Philosophy*, trans. by G. Anstruther, St. Louis, 1931. J. Maritain, *St. Thomas Aquinas, Angel of the Schools*, trans. by J. F. Scanlan, London: Sheed & Ward, 1933; *The Degrees of Knowledge*, trans. under the supervision of G. B. Phelan, New York: Scribner's, 1959. A. C. Pegis, *St. Thomas and the Problem of the Soul in the Thirteenth Century*, Toronto, 1934; *St. Thomas and the Greeks*, Milwaukee: Marquette University Press, 1939. M.-D. Chenu, *Introduction à l'étude de saint Thomas d'Aquin*, Paris: J. Vrin, 1950. G. Smith, *Natural Theology*, New York: Macmillan, 1951. V. J. Bourke, *Ethics. A Textbook in Moral Philosophy*, New York: Macmillan, 1951. G. Klubertanz, *The Philosophy of Human Nature*, St. Louis: Herder, 1951. G. K. Chesterton, *St. Thomas Aquinas (The Dumb Ox)*, ed. A. C. Pegis, New York: Doubleday

Image Books, 1955. E. Gilson, *The Christian Philosophy of St. Thomas Aquinas*, trans. by L. Shook, New York: Random House, 1956; *Elements of Christian Philosophy*, New York: Doubleday, 1960. L. M. Régis, *Epistemology*, New York: Macmillan, 1959. *A Latin-English Dictionary of St. Thomas Aquinas based on the Summa Theologica and selected passages of his other works*, Boston: St. Paul Editions, 1960.

2. *Summa Contra Gentiles*, I, 2, #2 (henceforth cited as *SCG*). See St. Hilary, *De Trinitate*, I, 37; PL 10, 48.

3. *SCG*, I, 4.

4. *Summa Theologiae*, I, 1, 3 (henceforth cited as *ST*). For St. Thomas' notion of theology, see E. Gilson, *The Christian Philosophy of St. Thomas Aquinas*, pp. 7–25; *Elements of Christian Philosophy*, pp. 22–42.

5. *SCG*, II, 4, #5.

6. *ST*, I, 2, 3. See *SCG*, I, 13; *Compendium of Theology*, I, 3. For the sources of the five ways, see R. Arnou, *De Quinque Viis Sancti Thomae ad Demonstrandam Dei Existentiam apud Antiquos Graecos et Arabes et Judaeos Praeformatis vel Adumbratis*, Rome: Pontificia Universitas Gregoriana, 1932.

7. *SCG*, I, 13, #4.

8. This is particularly evident in the causation of being (*esse*), which is the proper effect of God (for he is Being itself: *Ipsum Esse*). Creatures cause being only as instruments of God and through his power. See *De Potentia*, III, 4.

9. *SCG*, *I*, 30, #4; *ST*, I, 4, 3.

10. *De Veritate*, 23, 7, ad 9.

11. *De Potentia*, VII, 5, ad 14; *In*

Dionysii De Divinis Nominibus, VII, 4, #732.

12. SCG, I, 18.

13. Ibid., I, 21.

14. Ibid., I, 22, #10.

15. On Being and Essence, V; trans. p. 51.

16. SCG, I, 42.

17. Ibid., II, 15, 16.

18. ST, I, 25, 6.

19. De Potentia, II, 1.

20. ST, I, 15, 2; *De Veritate*, III, 8.

21. ST, I, 25, 6, ad 3.

22. Ibid., I, 48, 1 and 3; 49, 2. See J. Maritain, *Saint Thomas and the Problem of Evil*, Milwaukee: Marquette University Press, 1942.

23. ST, I, 46, 2; *SCG*, II, 38; *De Aeternitate Mundi*.

24. ST, I, 47, 1.

25. Since accidents do not possess their own being, they are not really composed of essence and being. The real composition is found only in substances. See *De Veritate*, 27, 1, ad 8. For the meaning of essence, quiddity, and nature, see *On Being and Essence*, I; trans. pp. 27, 28.

26. De Potentia, III, 5, ad 2.

27. Ibid., VII, 2, ad 9.

28. ST, I, 8, 1.

29. SCG, I, 25, #10; *ST*, III, 77, 1, ad 2.

30. Sent., I, 23, 1, 1; vol. 1, p. 555; *ST*, I, 29, 3.

31. ST, I, 50, 2, ad 3; *De Substantiis Separatis*, VI, #45.

32. SCG, II, 55.

33. Qu. Disp. De Anima, I, ad 2. See E. Gilson, *The Christian Philosophy of St. Thomas Aquinas*, p. 470, 10.

34. ST, I, 50, 4.

35. Ibid., I, 76, 4.

36. SCG, II, 73; *De Unitate Intellectus contra Averroistas*.

37. ST, I, 76, 1; *Qu. Disp. De Anima*, I, 1.

38. See A. C. Pegis, "St. Thomas and the Unity of Man," *Progress in Philosophy*, Milwaukee: Bruce, 1955, pp. 153–173.

39. Qu. Disp. De Anima, I, ad 1; *ST*, I, 75, 6; *SCG*, II, 55.

40. Qu. Disp. De Anima, ibid.; *ST*, I, 76, 1, ad 5.

41. De Spiritualibus Creaturis, X, ad 8.

42. For truth and falsity in sense knowledge, see *De Veritate*, I, 9 and 11.

43. ST, I, 84, 5.

44. Ibid., I, 85, 1.

45. In De Trinitate, V, 3; trans. pp. 26–27.

46. In Perihermenias, I, lect. 5, #8 and 12; Leonine ed., vol. 1, pp. 25, 28.

47. Sent., I, 19, 5, 1; vol. 1, p. 486. See G. B. Phelan, "Verum Sequitur Esse Rerum," *Mediaeval Studies*, I (1939), 11–22.

48. ST, I–II, 57, 5, ad 3.

49. SCG, III, 19, 20.

50. ST, I–II, 26, 2.

51. Ibid., II–II, 27, 4.

52. De Veritate, 22, 6.

53. ST, I–II, 19, 5; 64, 1.

54. Ibid., I–II, 90, 4.

55. ST, I–II, 91, 2. See J. Maritain, *The Rights of Man and Natural Law*, trans. by Doris C. Anson, New York: Scribner's, 1947.

56. SCG, III, 48, #15.

XIV. Latin Averroism

1. De Anima Intellectiva, 3; ed. P. Mandonnet, vol. 2, p. 154.

2. Ibid., 7, p. 164.

3. LIFE. SIGER was born about 1240 in Brabant (in what is now Belgium). He was a Canon of St.

Paul's in Liége and a teacher of philosophy at the Faculty of Arts at Paris by 1266. His heterodox teachings were condemned in 1270 by Stephen Tempier, the bishop of Paris. In 1276 he was summoned, along with two other masters from Brabant, Goswin of La Chapelle and Bernier of Nivelles, to appear before the Inquisitor of France, Simon du Val, to answer the charge of heresy. Siger fled from France and laid his case before the papal tribunal in Italy. A further and more extensive condemnation of his doctrines followed in 1277 at Paris. Siger died in Orvieto before Nov. 10, 1284, stabbed to death by his demented secretary. Agostino Nifo, writing about 1500, calls him the founder of the Averroist sect.

WORKS. C. Baeumker, *Die Impossibilia des Siger von Brabant*, *Beiträge*, II, 6, Münster i. W., 1898. P. Mandonnet, *Siger de Brabant et l'averroïsme latin au XIIIe siècle*, vol. 2, *Les philosophes belges*, VII, Louvain: Institut Supérieur, 1908: contains *Quaestiones Logicales*; *Quaestio Utrum haec sit vera: Homo est animal, nullo homine existente*; *Impossibilia*; *Quaestiones Naturales*; *De Necessitate et Contingentia Causarum*; *De Aeternitate Mundi*; *De Anima Intellectiva*. M. Grabmann, "Neuaufgefundene 'Quaestionen' Sigers von Brabant zu den Werken des Aristotelen (Clm. 9559)," *Miscellanea Fr. Ehrle*, Rome, 1924. F. Stegmüller, "Neugefundene Quaestionen des Siger von Brabant," *Revue de théol. ancienne et médiévale*, 3 (1931), 158–182: contains five questions on ethics. F. Van Steenberghen, *Siger de Brabant d'après ses oeuvres in-*

édites, I. *Les philosophes belges*, XII, Louvain: Institut Supérieur, 1931: contains *Quaestiones de Anima* of doubtful authenticity. W. J. Dwyer, *L'Opuscule de Siger de Brabant "De Aeternitate Mundi*," Louvain: Institut Supérieur, 1937. C. A. Graiff, *Siger de Brabant, Questions sur la Métaphysique*, Louvain: Institut Supérieur, 1948. P. Delhaye, *Siger de Brabant, Questions sur la Physique d'Aristote*, Louvain: Institut Supérieur, 1941, of doubtful authenticity. A. Zimmermann, *Die Quaestionen des Siger von Brabant zur Physik des Aristoteles*, Cologne, 1955.

STUDIES. P. Mandonnet, *Siger de Brabant et l'averroïsme latin au XIIIe siècle*, 2 vols., *Les philosophes belges*, VI, VII, Louvain: Institut Supérieur, 1911–1908. F. Van Steenberghen, *Siger de Brabant d'après ses oeuvres inédites*, 2 vols., *Les philosophes belges*, XII–XIII, Louvain: Institut Supérieur, 1931–1942. B. Nardi, *Sigieri di Brabante nel pensiero del Rinascimento italiano*, Rome: Edizioni italiani, 1945. F. Van Steenberghen, "Siger of Brabant," *The Modern Schoolman*, 29 (1951), 11–27. A. Maurer, "Esse and Essentia in the Metaphysics of Siger of Brabant," *Mediaeval Studies*, 8 (1946), 68–85. J. J. Duin, *La doctrine de la providence dans les écrits de Siger de Brabant*, Louvain: Institut Supérieur, 1954: contains text of *De Necessitate et Contingentia Causarum* and selected Questions. L. Kendzierski, "Eternal Matter and Form in Siger of Brabant," *The Modern Schoolman*, 32 (1955), 223–241.

4. *Paradiso*, X, 133–138. For the interpretation of these lines, see

E. Gilson, *Dante the Philosopher*, trans. by D. Moore, London: Sheed & Ward, 1948, pp. 257–281; 317–327.

5. For Siger's doctrine of free will, see O. Lottin, *Psychologie et Morale aux XIIe et XIIIe siècles*, I, Louvain: Abbaye du Mont César, 1942, pp. 262–271.

6. *Metaphysics*, ed. Graiff, p. 155, line 22.

7. For Siger's doctrine of being, see E. Gilson, *Being and Some Philosophers*, Toronto: Pontifical Institute of Mediaeval Studies, 1952, pp. 61–70.

8. *De Anima Intellectiva*, ed. P. Mandonnet, vol. 2, pp. 146–150.

9. *Ibid.*, p. 163.

10. *Ibid.*, p. 154. See the texts of Siger's *De Intellectu* in B. Nardi, *op. cit.*, p. 19.

11. B. Nardi, p. 26. In an early work, *Quaestiones in tertium de Anima*, Siger describes the agent and possible intellects as two parts of the intellectual soul. See F. Van Steenberghen, *op. cit.*, vol. 2, p. 631.

12. LIFE. BOETIUS OF DACIA was born in Sweden in the first half of the thirteenth century. He was probably a canon of the diocese of Linkoping, Sweden. Like Siger of Brabant, he was a master of arts at Paris and a leader of the Averroist movement there. His teachings were condemned along with those of Siger. He seems to have joined the Dominican Order at some unknown date. This accounts for his name "Boetius of Dacia," for the Dominican province of Dacia included both Denmark and Sweden. The date of his death is unknown.

WORKS. M. Grabmann, *Neuaufgefundene Werke des Siger von Bra-bant und Boetius von Dacien*, Munich, 1924; *Die Opuscula De Summo Bono sive de Vita Philosophi und De Sompniis des Boetius von Dacien*, *Archives*, 6 (1931), 287–317, reprinted in *Mittelalterliches Geistesleben*, 2 (1936), pp. 200–224; *Die Sophismataliteratur des 12. und 13. Jahrhunderts, mit Textausgabe eines Sophisma des Boetius von Dacien . . .*, *Beiträge*, 36, 1, Münster, 1940. Géza Sajó, *Un traité recemment decouvert de Boèce de Dacie, De Mundi Aeternitate*, Budapest: Akademia Kiado, 1954.

STUDIES. P. Doncoeur, "Notes sur les averroistes latins. Boèce le Dace," *Revue des sciences philosophiques et théologiques*, 4 (1910), 500–511. P. Mandonnet, "Note complémentaire sur Boèce de Dacie," *Revue des sciences phil. et théol.*, 22 (1933), 246–250. E. Gilson, "Boèce de Dacie et la double vérité," *Archives*, 30 (1955), 81–99. A. Maurer, "Boetius of Dacia and the Double Truth," *Mediaeval Studies*, 17 (1955), 233–239. G. Sajó, "Boèce de Dacie et les commentaires anonymes inédits de Munich sur la physique et sur la génération attribués à Siger de Brabant," *Archives*, 33 (1958), 21–58.

13. *De Aeternitate Mundi*, ed. G. Sajó, p. 119.

14. *De Summo Bono, Archives*, p. 307.

15. P. Mandonnet, "Note complémentaire sur Boèce de Dacie," p. 250.

16. *De Summo Bono*, p. 300.

17. *Ibid.*, pp. 303, 304.

18. For this condemnation, see E. Gilson, *History*, pp. 402–410; F. Van Steenberghen, *Aristotle in the West*, trans. by L. Johnston, Lou-

vain: E. Nauwelaerts, 1955, pp. 235–238.

19. Giles of Rome, *Errores Philoso-* *phorum,* ed. J. Koch, with trans. by J. O. Riedl, Milwaukee: Marquette University Press, 1944.

xv. The Reaction to Thomism

1. Acta Sanctorum, March 7, vol. 7, p. 661, n. 15.

2. John Pecham, *Registrum Epistolarum,* ed. C. T. Martin (Rolls Series), London, 1885, vol. 3, p. 901.

3. Theoremata de Esse et Essentia, ed. E. Hocedez, Louvain: Museum Lessianum, 1930; trans. by M. Murray, *Theorems on Existence and Essence,* Milwaukee: Marquette University Press, 1952.

4. Quodlibet, I, 9 (Paris, 1518). See J. Paulus, *Henri de Gand, essai sur les tendances de sa métaphysique,* Paris: J. Vrin, 1938, pp. 284–291.

5. See J. Owens, "The Number of Terms in the Suarezian Discussion of Essence and Being," *The Mod-* *ern Schoolman,* 34 (1957), 161.

6. Comm. in 1, 3, 4; ed. L. Urbano, Madrid, 1934, vol. 1, p. 141.

7. Summa Theologiae, I, 76, 3.

8. Ibid., I, 76, 4.

9. See D. Callus, *The Condemnation of St. Thomas at Oxford,* Westminster, Md.: Newman Bookshop, 1946.

10. Reg. Epist., vol. 3, pp. 871, 901.

11. Acta Apostolicae Sedis, 6 (1914), p. 385.

12. De Veritate, XI, 1.

13. Contra Gentiles, III, 69, #15. See E. Gilson, "Pourquoi saint Thomas a critiqué saint Augustin," *Archives,* I (1926–1927), 5–127.

xvi. John Duns Scotus

1. LIFE. JOHN DUNS SCOTUS, called the Subtle Doctor, was born about 1266, according to most historians in the town of Maxton, Scotland. C. Balić recently presented evidence that his birthplace was the nearby town of Duns ("Note di un viaggio al 'natio loco' del beato Giovanni Duns Scoto," *Vita Minorum,* 6 [1953], 1–7). In any case, Duns was his family name. At the age of eleven he was placed in the Franciscan convent at Dumfries, and he took the Franciscan habit in 1281. After studying at Oxford, he was ordained a priest in 1291. From 1292 to 1296 he was a student at Paris. On returning to Oxford he lectured on the *Sentences* of Peter Lombard. These lectures took final shape in his chief work, the *Opus Oxoniense* (1297–1301). He lectured again on the *Sentences* at Paris, and the students' reports of these lectures are called *Reportata Parisiensia* (1302–1307). In 1303 he was banished from France for siding with Pope Boniface VIII in his quarrel with Philip the Fair. The next year he was back in Paris, where he became Master of Theology in 1305. In 1307 he was sent to Cologne, where he died in 1308. Although not solemnly beatified, he is traditionally called Blessed.

WORKS. Besides the *Opus Oxoniense* and *Reportata Parisiensia,* his major works include commentaries on Aristotle's logic, *Quaestiones in Metaphysicam, Quaestiones Quodlibetales, De Primo*

Principio. These are published in *Opera Omnia*, 26 vols., Paris: Vivès, 1891–1895. This collection also contains spurious works, such as *De Rerum Principio, Expositiones in Metaphysicam,* commentaries on the *Physica* and *De Anima* (the latter probably by Antonius Andreas, Scotus' secretary, expressing Scotus' thought). The *Theoremata* is of doubtful authenticity. C. Balić thinks Scotus sketched its outlines while someone else completed it. E. Gilson shows that the first 16 theorems agree with Scotus' thought on what pure reason can demonstrate about God. (See below, STUDIES.) Arguments against its authenticity will be found in F. Copleston, *A History of Philosophy,* II, pp. 478–481. New edition of *De Primo Principio* by E. Roche, with Latin text and translation, St. Bonaventure, N.Y.: Franciscan Institute, 1949. A critical edition of Scotus' *Opera Omnia* is being prepared under C. Balić; 4 vols. have appeared to date, containing the *Opus Oxoniense* (called *Ordinatio* because published by Scotus himself) to Bk. I, d. 10, Vatican, 1950–1956. TRANSLATIONS. *Opus Oxoniense,* I, d. 3, q. 4, trans. by R. McKeon, *Selections,* II, pp. 313–350. *De Primo Principio,* trans. by E. Roche, St. Bonaventure, N.Y., 1949. *Opus Oxon.,* I, d. 1, q. 1, trans. by N. Micklem, *Reason and Revelation: A Question from Duns Scotus,* London: Nelson, 1953. STUDIES. C. R. S. Harris, *Duns Scotus,* 2 vols., Oxford, 1927. E. Gilson, "Avicenne et le point de départ de Duns Scot," *Archives,* 2 (1927), 89–149. J. Kraus,

Die Lehre des Johannes Duns Scotus der natura communis, Paderborn, 1927. E. Gilson, "Les seize premiers Theoremata et la pensée de Duns Scot," *Archives,* 11 (1937–1938), 5–86. C. L. Shircel, *The Univocity of the Concept of Being in the Philosophy of Duns Scotus,* Washington, D.C.: Catholic University Press, 1942. E. Bettoni, *L'ascesa a Dio in Duns Scoto,* Milan: Vita e Pensiero, 1943. M. Grajewski, *The Formal Distinction of Duns Scotus,* Washington, D.C.: Catholic University Press, 1944. A. W. Wolter, *The Transcendentals and Their Function in the Metaphysics of Duns Scotus,* St. Bonaventure, N.Y.: Franciscan Institute, 1946. E. Gilson, *Jean Duns Scot. Introduction à ses positions fondamentales,* Paris: J. Vrin, 1952.

2. *Opus Oxon.,* Prol., p. 1, q. 1; ed. Balić, I, p. 1. (References are to the Vivès edition unless otherwise indicated.)

3. According to Avicenna, reason can prove that man's final end is the vision of spiritual substances. On Scotus' interpretation of Avicenna, see E. Gilson, *Jean Duns Scot,* pp. 22–29.

4. *In Metaph.,* I, vol. 7, p. 11. For the objects of theology and metaphysics, see *Opus Oxon.,* Prol., p. 3, q. 1–3.

5. See J. Owens, "Up to What Point Is God Included in the Metaphysics of Duns Scotus?" *Mediaeval Studies,* 10 (1948), 163–177.

6. *Opus Oxon.,* I, d. 2, p. 1, q. 1–2. Another version of the proof is in the *De Primo Principio.*

7. For the knowability of God, see *Opus Oxon.,* I, d. 3, p. 1, q. 1–2.

8. *Super libros Elenchorum,* q. 15,

n. 6, vol. 2, p. 22; q. 16, n. 4, p. 24.
9. *Opus Oxon., ibid.*, n. 58; ed. Balić, III, p. 40; *Quodl.*, V, 3–4; vol. 25, pp. 199–200.
10. *De Primo Principio*, 4; ed. Roche, pp. 146–148.
11. *Opus Oxon.*, I, d. 8, q. 4, vol. 9, p. 636.
12. On formal non-identity, see *Rep. Par.*, I, d. 45, q. 2, vol. 22, p. 500; *Opus Oxon.*, I, d. 2, p. 2, q. 1–4, n. 403; ed. Balić, II, p. 356.
13. *Opus Oxon.*, I, d. 8, a. 4, n. 23, vol. 9, p. 671.
14. See E. Gilson, *Jean Duns Scot*, pp. 209, 235, 251.
15. *Opus Oxon.*, I, d. 35, qu. unica, n. 10, vol. 10, p. 548. On Scotus' notions of being and the divine Ideas, see E. Gilson, *Being and Some Philosophers*, Toronto, 1952, pp. 84–94.
16. *Opus Oxon.*, I, d. 36, qu. unica, vol. 10, p. 564.
17. *Ibid.*, I, d. 39, qu. unica, n. 14, vol. 10, p. 626.
18. *Ibid.*, II, d. 3, q. 1, n. 2, vol. 12, p. 7.
19. The object of the sense is always an individual, but the sense primarily and properly perceives in it an essence (e.g., greenness) which of itself is neither individual nor universal. The individual as such is perceived by the senses only through common-sense objects such as position and place. *Ibid.*, n. 4; *In Metaph.*, I,

q. 6, n. 9–11, vol. 7, pp. 75–77.
20. *Opus Oxon.*, II, d. 3, q. 4–5, vol. 12, pp. 91–127.
21. *Ibid.*, II, d. 3, q. 6, n. 15, vol. 12, p. 144. The term *haecceitas* appears several times in the printed works of Scotus, although its authenticity has been questioned. In any case, it was used widely by followers of Scotus. See E. Gilson, *op. cit.*, p. 464, note 2.
22. *Rep. Par.*, II, d. 12, q. 8. n. 8, vol. 23, p. 39; *Opus Oxon.*, II, d. 3, q. 6, n. 15, vol. 12, p. 144.
23. *Rep. Par.*, II, d. 1, q. 2, n. 3, vol. 22, p. 523.
24. *Quodl.* I, q. 1, n. 4, vol. 25, p. 9.
25. *Opus Oxon.*, IV, d. 11, q. 3, n. 46, vol. 17, p. 429.
26. *In Metaph.*, VII, q. 18, n. 11, vol. 7, pp. 460–461. See E. Gilson, "Avicenne et le point de départ de Duns Scot," *Archives*, 2 (1927), p. 146.
27. *Opus Oxon.*, I, d. 1, p. 1, q. 2, n. 32; ed. Balić, II, p. 21; II, d. 3, q. 9, n. 6–7, vol. 12, pp. 212–213; III, d. 14, q. 3, n. 4, vol. 14, p. 524.
28. *Rep. Par.*, III, d. 14, q. 3, n. 12, vol. 23, p. 359.
29. *Opus Oxon.*, I, d. 3, q. 4; ed. Balić, III, p. 123.
30. *Ibid.*, II, d. 25, qu. unica, n. 22, vol. 13, p. 221.
31. *Ibid.*, III, d. 37, qu. unica, n. 8, vol. 15, p. 827.

PART 4 THE MODERN WAY

XVII. The New Logic and Physics

1. For the history of medieval logic, see C. Prantl, *Geschichte der Logik im Abendlande*, 4 vols., Leipzig, 1927; P. Boehner, *Medieval Logic. An Outline of Its Development from 1250 to c.*

1400, Chicago: University Press, 1952; E. A. Moody, *Truth and Consequence in Mediaeval Logic*, Amsterdam: North-Holland Pub. Co., 1953.

2. Peter of Spain, *Summulae Logicales*, ed. I. M. Bochenski, Rome: Marietti, 1947. Tracts VI–XII have been edited, with an English translation, by J. P. Mullally, Notre Dame, Ind., 1945.

3. *Ibid.*, ed. Mullally, pp. 4–6.

4. See E. Synan, "The Universal and Supposition in a *Logica* attributed to Richard of Campsall," *Nine Mediaeval Thinkers*, Toronto: Pontifical Institute of Mediaeval Studies, 1955, p. 201; "The Universal in an Anti-Ockhamist Text," *An Etienne Gilson Tribute*, Milwaukee: Marquette University Press, 1959, p. 304. For a discussion of the authenticity of this Logic, see E. Synan, "Richard of Campsall, an English Theologian of the Fourteenth Century," *Mediaeval Studies*, 14 (1952), 1–8.

5. Peter of Spain, *op. cit.*, p. 10.

6. See St. Thomas, *In Perihermenias*, I, lect. 5; Leonine ed., I, p. 28, n. 22; E. Gilson, *The Christian Philosophy of St. Thomas Aquinas*, New York: Random House, 1956, p. 42.

7. See J. R. O'Donnell, "The Syncategoremata of William of Sherwood," *Mediaeval Studies*, 3 (1941), 70–71.

8. For the place of grammar in the universities, see L. J. Paetow, *The Arts Course at Medieval Universities, with special Reference to Grammar and Rhetoric*, Champaign, Ill., 1910.

9. *Ibid.*, p. 35.

10. *The Battle of the Seven Arts; a French Poem by Henri d'Andeli, Trouvère of the Thirteenth Cen*tury, ed. and trans. by L. J. Paetow, Berkeley: University of California Press, 1914.

11. Siger's *Summa Modorum Significandi* has been edited by G. Wallerand, *Les oeuvres de Siger de Courtrai* (*Les philosophes belges*), VIII, Louvain, 1913, pp. 93–125; also, with an English translation, by Sister John Marie Riley, *The "Summa Modorum Significandi" of Siger of Courtrai*, St. Louis: Sisters of St. Joseph of Carondelet, 1943. Perhaps the most perfect specimen of speculative grammar is that of Thomas of Erfurt (about 1350), published among the works of Duns Scotus, *Opera Omnia*, Paris: Vivès, 1891, vol. 1.

12. See Siger of Courtrai, *op. cit.*, ed. G. Wallerand, p. 108.

13. For the history of medieval science, see P. Duhem, *Système du Monde; histoire des doctrines cosmologiques de Platon à Copernic*, 7 vols., Paris, 1913–1956. L. Thorndike, *A History of Magic and Experimental Science*, 8 vols., New York, 1923–1958. A. Maier, *An der Grenze von Scholastik und Naturwissenschaft*, Essen, 1943; A. Maier, *Die Vorläufer Galileis im 14. Jahrhundert*, Rome, 1949; A. Maier, *Zwei Grundprobleme der scholastischen Naturphilosophie*, Rome, 1951; A. Maier, *Metaphysische Hintergründe der spätscholastischen Naturphilosophie*, Rome, 1955; A. Maier, *Zwischen Philosophie und Mechanik*, Rome, 1958. A. C. Crombie, *Augustine to Galileo: the History of Science. A.D. 400–1650*, London: Falcon Press, 1957; A. C. Crombie, *Medieval and Early Modern Science*, 2 vols., New York: Doubleday Anchor

Books, 1959. (Excellent bibliography.) M. Clagett, *The Science of Mechanics in the Middle Ages*, Madison: University of Wisconsin Press, 1959.

14. C. Dawson, *Medieval Essays*, ch. 8: The Scientific Development of Medieval Culture, New York: Doubleday Image Books, 1959, p. 127.

15. See G. Leff, *Bradwardine and the Pelagians*, Cambridge: University Press, 1957.

16. Quoted by J. Weisheipl, "The Place of John Dumbleton in the Merton School," *Isis*, 50 (1959), 446. The following pages on Oxford physics draw heavily upon this excellent article.

17. See H. L. Crosby, Jr., *Thomas of Bradwardine, His* Tractatus de Proportionibus, *Its Significance for the Development of Mathematical Physics*, Madison: University of Wisconsin Press, 1955.

18. See C. Wilson, *William Heytesbury. Medieval Logic and the Rise of Mathematical Physics*,

Madison: University of Wisconsin Press, 1956.

19. Ockham, *Sent.*, IV, 4, G; *Summa Logicae*, I, 44.

20. Ockham, *Sent.*, II, 9; *Quodl.*, I, 5.

21. Ockham, *Sent.*, II, 26, M; *The Tractatus de Successivis Attributed to William Ockham*, ed. P. Boehner, St. Bonaventure: Franciscan Institute, 1944, p. 45.

22. Ockham, *Tractatus de Successivis, ibid.*

23. *Maistre Nicole Oresme, Le Livre du Ciel et du Monde*, II, 8; ed. A. D. Menut and A. J. Denomy, *Mediaeval Studies*, 4 (1942), p. 205. Two of the propositions condemned in 1277 were: (34) "The First Cause could not create many worlds"; (49) "God cannot move the heavens with a rectilinear movement because this would leave a vacuum." See *Chartularium Universitatis Parisiensis*, ed. H. Denifle and A. Chatelain, Paris, 1889, I, pp. 545–546.

24. *Le Livre du Ciel et du Monde*, II, 25; p. 273.

XVIII. William of Ockham and Fourteenth-Century Nominalism

1. LIFE. For OCKHAM's life and works, see Léon Baudry, *Guillaume d'Occam, sa vie, ses oeuvres, ses idées sociales et politiques*, I: *L'homme et les oeuvres*, Paris: J. Vrin, 1949. Ockham was born about 1290, or perhaps a little earlier, in the village of Ockham, in the county of Surrey, England. In Winchelsey's episcopal register his name is given as Guilielmus de Okam, indicating that Ockham was his place of birth. Having entered the Franciscan Order, he came to Oxford about 1310, where

he commented on the *Sentences* from about 1319 to 1320. He completed his studies for the degree of Master of Theology and even gave his inaugural lecture, thus becoming an *inceptor* (beginner), but he was not assigned a teaching post at the university, probably because in 1324 he was summoned to Avignon by Pope John XXII to answer the charge of heresy. His trial lasted three years, and although a commission censured a list of propositions taken from his works, there was no formal condemnation. In 1328 he escaped from Avignon with the Franciscan Minister General, Michael of Cesena, who opposed the pope on the questions of the poverty of Christ and the temporal power of the Church. The two were excommunicated and took refuge with the pope's adversary, the Emperor Louis of Bavaria. While living with the emperor at Munich, Ockham wrote his treatises on Church and State. Before his death in 1349 or 1350, steps were taken for his reconciliation with the Church, but it is not known whether he made his submission.

WORKS. Earliest logical treatise: *Expositio Aurea super Artem Veterem*, Bologna, 1496, of which *Perihermenias*, I, was edited by P. Boehner, *Traditio*, 4 (1946), 320–335. His main logical work is *Summa Logicae*, ed. P. Boehner, St. Bonaventure, N.Y.: Franciscan Institute, 1951. Three works in physics, of which *Summulae in Libros Physicorum* has been published, Bologna, 1494. Theology: *Commentary on the Sentences*, Lyons, 1495. P. Boehner edited Question 1 of the Prologue, Paderborn, 1939; B. I, d. 2, q. 8, *The New Scholasticism*, 16 (1942), 224–240; B. II, q. 14–15, *Traditio*, 1 (1943), 245–275. *Quodlibetal Questions*, Strasbourg, 1491. Minor theological works: *De Sacramento Altaris*, ed. T. Birch, Burlington, Iowa, 1930; *Tractatus de Praedestinatione et Praescientia Dei et de Futuris Contingentibus*, ed. P. Boehner, St. Bonaventure, N.Y.: Franciscan Institute, 1945. His political writings are listed in L. Baudry, *op. cit.*, pp. 288–294. *Tractatus de Successivis Attributed to William Ockham*, ed. P. Boehner, St. Bonaventure, N.Y.: Franciscan Institute, 1944. The *Centiloquium Theologicum* is of doubtful authenticity; ed. P. Boehner, *Franciscan Studies* (1941–1942). Its authenticity is defended by E. Iserloh, "Um die Echtheit des Centiloquium . . . ," *Gregorianum*, 30 (1949), 78–103, 309–346. TRANSLATIONS. Selected *Quodlibets*, trans. by R. McKeon, *Selections*, II. P. Boehner, *Ockham, Philosophical Writings*, London: Nelson, 1957.

STUDIES. F. Hochstetter, *Studien zur Metaphysik und Erkenntnislehre Wilhelms von Ockham*, Berlin, 1927. P. Vignaux, *art.* "Nominalisme," *Dictionnaire de théologie catholique*, XI (1931), 733–784; E. Amann and P. Vignaux, *art.* "Occam," *op. cit.*, 864–903. Ernest Moody, *The Logic of William of Ockham*, New York: Sheed & Ward, 1935. A. C. Pegis, "Concerning William of Ockham," *Traditio*, 2 (1944), 465–480; A. C. Pegis, "Some Recent Interpretations of Ockham," *Speculum*, 23 (1948), 458–463. M. C. Menges, *The Concept of the Univocity of Being regarding the Predication of God and Creature According to William Ockham*, St. Bonaventure, N.Y.: Franciscan Institute, 1958. R. Guelluy, *Philosophie et théologie chez Guillaume d'Ockham*, Louvain: E. Nauwelaerts, 1947. P. Boehner, *Collected Articles on Ockham*, St. Bonaventure, N.Y.: Franciscan Institute, 1958. A. Maurer, "Ockham's Conception of the Unity of Science," *Mediaeval Studies*, 20 (1958), 98–112. L. Baudry, *Lexique philosophique de Guillaume d'Ockham*, Paris: Lethielleux, 1958. V. Heynck, "Ockham-Literatur 1919–1949," *Franziskanische Studien*, 32 (1950), 164–183.

2. *Sent.*, Prologue, 7, E.

3. *Ibid.*, 8, C.

4. *Ibid.*, 1, F.

5. *Ibid.*, 1, H–L; *Physics*, Prologue, ed. P. Boehner, *Ockham, Philosophical Writings*, p. 7.

6. *Physics*, pp. 9, 10.

7. *Sent.*, I, 2, 4, M. See *Physics*, p. 11.

8. *Sent.*, I, 2, 10, O.

9. *Quodlibet*, I, 1.

10. *Ibid.*, IV, 1. See *Quodl.*, II, 9; *Sent.*, II, 15, ed. Boehner, p. 254. See H. R. Klocker, "Ockham and Efficient Causality," *The Thomist*, 23 (1960), 106–123.

11. *Quodl.*, II, 1. The immateriality and immortality of the soul are certain only through faith: *Quodl.*, I, 10.

12. *Ibid.*, IV, 2.

13. *Summa Logicae*, I, 64.

14. *Sent.*, I, 2, 1, F.

15. Ockham accepts the formal distinction only when faith compels him to do so. For example, there is a formal distinction between the three Persons of the Trinity. See *Sent.*, I, 2, 1, D, F; I, 2, 3, B.

16. *Sent.*, I, 2, 1, D; I, 2, 2, G.

17. See St. Thomas, *Sent.*, I, 22, 1, 3, ad 3m; ed. Mandonnet, p. 539.

18. *Sent.*, I, 2, 1, BB.

19. *Ibid.*, I, 6, 1, P.

20. *Ibid.*, I, 35, 5, Q–R.

21. *Ibid.*, I, 2, 7, B.

22. *Ibid.*, I, 2, 6, B.

23. *Ibid.*, KK–LL.

24. See above, p. 247.

25. *Sent.*, I, 2, 7.

26. See F. Pelster, "Heinrich von Harclay und seine Quästionen,"

Miscellanea Fr. Ehrle, I, Rome, 1924, p. 337; A. Maurer, "Henry of Harclay's Question on the Univocity of Being," *Mediaeval Studies*, 16 (1954), 1–18.

27. *Sent.*, I, 2, 7, M.

28. *Ibid.*, I, 2, 8, Q. Ockham rejects the theory, attributed to Roscelin, that universals are conventional signs or words. *Ibid.*, E.

29. *Sent.*, I, 2, 8; *Commentary on Perihermenias*, I.

30. *Quodl.*, IV, 19; *Summa Logicae*, I, 12; *Quaestiones super Libros Physicorum*. See P. Boehner, "The Realistic Conceptualism of William Ockham," *Traditio*, 4 (1946), 317.

31. *Sent.*, Prologue, I, X–Z; II, 15, E.

32. *Sent.*, Prologue, I, HH; *Quodl.*, I, 14.

33. *Sent.*, Prologue, I, GG.

34. *Ibid.*, HH. See E. Gilson, *The Unity of Philosophical Experience*, New York: Scribner's, 1941, pp. 81–82.

35. *Quodl.*, VI, 6.

36. *Sent.*, Prologue, I, Z; *Quodl.*, V, 5.

37. *Sent.*, I, 27, 3, H–I. Besides the intellect and its object, abstractive knowledge requires a habit in the intellect. *Sent.*, II, 15, Q.

38. *Comm. on Perihermenias*, I, Q–R; pp. 331–333.

39. *Sent.*, II, 15, T.

40. *Ibid.*, II, 24, Q.

41. *Ibid.*, II, 25, A, O; II, 15, XX.

42. *Ibid.*, I, 2, 7, CC.

43. See G. de Lagarde, *La naissance de l'esprit laïque au déclin du moyen âge*, VI, Paris: E. Droz, 1946; T. Davitt, *The Nature of Law*, St. Louis: Herder, 1951, Part I, ch. 3, pp. 39–54; A. P. D'Entrèves, *Natural Law, an In-*

troduction to Legal Philosophy, London: Hutchinson House, 1951, pp. 68–71, 76.

44. Sent., II, 4–5, H; 19, P; IV, 8–9, E.

45. Ibid., Prol., 1, BB.

46. Ibid., II, 19, O; III, 12, AAA; IV, 14, D.

47. Ibid., I, 41, 1, K; III, 13, C.

48. Le Tractatus de Principiis Theologiae attribués à Guillaume d'Occam, ed. L. Baudry, Paris: J. Vrin, 1936.

49. For Luther's relation to Ockham, see P. Vignaux, *Luther, Commentateur des Sentences*, Paris: J. Vrin, 1935.

50. Nicholas' treatise *Exigit Ordo Executionis* has been edited by J. R. O'Donnell, *Mediaeval Studies*, 1 (1939), 181–280. For his thought, see J. R. O'Donnell, "The Philosophy of Nicholas of Autrecourt and his Appraisal of Aristotle," *Mediaeval Studies*, 4 (1942), 97–125; J. R. Weinberg, *Nicolaus of Autrecourt, a Study in Fourteenth-Century Thought*, Princeton: University Press, 1948.

The position of Gregory of Rimini (d. 1358) with regard to nominalism is still in dispute. The latest discussion of this subject is found in G. Leff, *Gregory of Rimini, Tradition and Innovation in Fourteenth Century Thought*, Manchester: University Press, 1961.

XIX. Master Eckhart and Speculative Mysticism

1. LIFE. JOHN ECKHART was born about 1260 at Hochheim, near Gotha, Germany. He joined the Dominican Order, probably at Erfurt, and studied and taught at Paris, obtaining the degree of Master of Theology in 1302. On his return to Germany he was chosen Provincial of Saxony and later Vicar-General of his Order. From 1311 to 1314 he was once again at Paris, lecturing and writing. He was then appointed to Cologne, where in 1326 the Archbishop accused him of heresy. His trial took place at Avignon, and in 1329, two years after his death, 28 propositions taken from his works were condemned by Pope John XXII.

WORKS. Eckhart's main work is the unfinished *Opus Tripartitum*, whose prologues have been edited by H. Denifle, *Meister Eckeharts lateinische Schriften und die Grundanschauung seiner Lehre, Archiv für Literatur und Kirchengeschichte des Mittelalters*, II, Berlin, 1886, pp. 417–652. This also contains Scriptural commentaries. New editions in preparation: *Magistri Eckhardi Opera Latina*, Leipzig: F. Meiner: I, *Super Oratione Dominica*, ed. R. Klibansky, 1934; II, *Opus Tripartitum, Prologi*, ed. H. Bascour, 1935; III, *Quaestiones Parisienses*, ed. A. Dondaine, 1936. *Meister Eckhart, die deutschen und lateinischen Werke*, Stuttgart-Berlin: Verlag von W. Kohlhammer, 1936 ff.

TRANSLATIONS. F. Pfeiffer, *Meister Eckhart*, trans. by C. de B. Evans, 2 vols., London, 1924, 1931: contains sermons and tractates. R. Blakney, *Meister Eckhart*, New York: Harper, 1941: contains Talks of Instruction, The Book of Divine Comfort, The Aristocrat,

About Disinterest, and Sermons. *Meister Eckhart, Selected Treatises and Sermons Translated from Latin and German with an Introduction and Notes*, by J. M. Clark and J. V. Skinner, London: Faber and Faber, 1958.

STUDIES. B. J. Muller-Thym, *The Establishment of the University of Being in the Doctrine of Meister Eckhart of Hochheim*, New York: Sheed & Ward, 1939 (contains a bibliography, pp. 117–137). J. M. Clark, *The Great German Mystics, Eckhart, Tauler and Suso*, Oxford: Basil Blackwell, 1949; *Meister Eckhart, An Introduction to the Study of His Works, with an Anthology of His Sermons*, London: Nelson & Sons, 1957. J. Ancelet-Hustache, *Master Eckhart and the Rhineland Mystics*, trans. by Hilda Graef, New York: Harper Torchbooks, 1957.

2. This saying, also quoted by Pascal, is taken from *The Book of the Twenty-Four Philosophers*, ed. C. Baeumker, *Festgabe Georg Freiherrn von Hertling*, Freiburg im Breisgau, 1913, p. 31.

3. See M. De Wulf, *The History of Mediaeval Philosophy*, II, p. 288. The latest discussion of this problem is in V. Lossky, *Théologie négative et connaissance de Dieu chez Maître Eckhart*, Paris: J. Vrin, 1960, pp. 207–220, especially note 164.

4. *Quaestiones Parisienses*, ed. A. Dondaine, pp. 7, 8. This is also the interpretation of some modern biblical scholars. See A.-M. Dubarle, "La signification du Nom de Iahweh," *Revue des sciences philosophiques et théologiques*, 35 (1951), 3–21; M. M. Bourke, "Yahweh, the Divine Name," *The Bridge*, 3, New York: Pantheon Books, 1958, pp. 271–287.

5. *Quaestiones Parisienses*, p. 7.

6. Text quoted by G. della Volpe, *Il misticismo speculativo di Maestro Eckhart nei suoi rapporti storici*, Bologna, 1930, p. 155. See E. Gilson, *Being and Some Philosophers*, Toronto: Pontifical Institute of Mediaeval Studies, 1952, p. 39.

7. *Meister Eckhart, die deutschen und lateinischen Werke*, ed. Stuttgart, II, p. 24.

8. *Opus Tripartitum, prologi*, ed. H. Bascour, p. 21.

9. *Meister Eckhart, die deutschen und lateinischen Werke*, I, p. 39.

10. See V. Lossky, *op. cit.*, p. 213.

11. *Sermon 17*, trans. by J. M. Clark, *Meister Eckhart, an Introduction to the Study of His Works, with an Anthology of His Sermons*, pp. 206–208.

12. *Opus Tripartitum*, ed. H. Bascour, pp. 15–16, 25.

13. *Ibid.*, p. 15.

14. See text in R. Blakney, *Meister Eckhart*, p. 264, n. 5. See also B. J. Muller-Thym, *The Establishment of the University of Being in the Doctrine of Meister Eckhart of Hochheim*, pp. 84 ff.

15. See B. J. Muller-Thym, *op. cit.*, pp. 21 ff.

16. See J. M. Clark, *op. cit.*, pp. 44, 202–203.

17. *Sermon V*, trans. by J. M. Clark, *op. cit.*, pp. 150–151.

18. *Ibid.*, p. 149.

19. *Ibid.*, p. 151.

20. See text in R. Blakney, *op. cit.*, p. 282, n. 13.

21. The text of the 28 condemned propositions has been translated by J. Clark, *op. cit.*, pp. 253–258. Eckhart's defense has been translated by R. Blakney, *op. cit.*, pp. 258–305.

22. See J. M. Clark, *The Great*

German Mystics, Eckhart, Tauler and Suso, p. 37.

23. See J. Ancelet-Hustache, *Master Eckhart and the Rhineland Mystics*, p. 150.

24. See J. M. Clark, *Henry Suso, Little Book of Eternal Wisdom and Little Book of Truth*, translated with an Introduction and Notes, London: Faber and Faber, 1953.

25. For Ruysbroeck's life and thought, see A. Wautier D'Aygalliers, *Ruysbroeck the Admirable*, trans. by F. Rothwell, London: Dent and Sons, 1925. His *The Adornment of the Spiritual Marriage, The Sparkling Stone*, and *The Book of Supreme Truth* have been translated by C. A. Wyn-

schenk, with Introduction and Notes by E. Underhill, New York: E. P. Dutton, 1916.

26. *The Spiritual Marriage*, III, 6.

27. On the authorship of this work, see L. Baudry, *L'Imitation de Jésus-Christ*, trans. with an introduction, Paris: Aubier, 1950, pp. 1–78. Fr. Baudry concludes that Thomas à Kempis very probably wrote it. See also A. Hyma, *The Brethren of the Common Life*, Grand Rapids: W. B. Eerdmans Pub. Co., 1950, p. 166. According to A. Hyma, Thomas à Kempis is the author in the sense that he wrote a portion of it and worked over devout exercises of his confrères.

xx. Nicholas of Cusa

1. LIFE. NICHOLAS KREBS was born at Kues, Germany, in 1401. He attended the school of the Brothers of the Common Life in Deventer, Holland, and then studied at Heidelberg, Padua, and Cologne. Ordained a priest in 1426, he spent several years doing pastoral work. In 1432 he was sent to the Council of Basle, where he supported the claim of the supremacy of the Church Council over the pope. Later he changed his view and went over to the side of the pope. He worked for the reconciliation of the Hussites with the Church and undertook a number of missions for the Holy See. He went to Constantinople to arrange for the reconciliation of the Eastern Church with Rome. In 1450 he was created a Cardinal and given the bishopric of Brixen (in the Italian Tyrol). He died in 1464.

WORKS. *Nicolai de Cusa Opera*

Omnia, 7 vols., ed. E. Hoffmann and R. Klibansky, Leipzig: F. Meiner, 1932–1953. *Nicolaus von Cues, Philosophische Schriften*, vol. 1, ed. A. Petzelt, Stuttgart: W. Kohlhammer, 1949.

TRANSLATIONS. *The Vision of God*, trans. by E. G. Salter, New York: Frederick Ungar, 1960. *On Learned Ignorance*, trans. by G. Heron, London: Routledge & Kegan Paul, 1954.

STUDIES. E. Vansteenberghe, *Le cardinal Nicolas de Cues*, Paris: H. Champion, 1920. E. Cassirer, *Individuum und Kosmos in der Philosophie der Renaissance*, Leipzig: Teubner, 1927. H. Bett, *Nicholas of Cusa*, London, 1932. M. de Gandillac, *La philosophie de Nicolas de Cues*, Paris: Aubier, 1941. J. Koch, *Nicolaus von Cues und seine Umwelt*, Heidelberg, 1948. E. Zellinger, *Cusanus-Konkordanz unter Zugrundelegung der philosophischen und der be-*

deutendsten theologischen Werke,
Munich: Max Hueber, 1960.
2. *De Docta Ignorantia,* I, 1.
3. *Ibid.,* I, 3.
4. *Apologia Doctae Ignorantiae,*
ed. R. Klibansky, vol. 2, p. 6.
5. *De Docta Ignorantia,* I, 2.
6. *Ibid.,* I, 4.
7. *Ibid.,* I, 11.
8. *Ibid.,* I, 13.
9. *Ibid.,* I, 14.
10. *Ibid.,* I, 6.
11. *Ibid.,* II, 1.
12. *De Venatione Sapientiae,* 9.

13. *De Ludo Globi,* 1.
14. *De Visione Dei,* 12; *De Docta
Ignorantia,* II, 2.
15. *De Docta Ignorantia,* II, 3.
16. *Ibid.,* II, 5.
17. *Ibid.,* II, 4.
18. *Ibid.,* II, 9.
19. *Ibid.,* II, 6.
20. *Ibid.,* III, 3.
21. *Ibid.,* III, 3–4; *De Visione Dei,*
19–21.
22. *De Docta Ignorantia,* II, 11–12.
23. *De Conjecturis,* I, 2; ed. A.
Petzelt, pp. 123–124; I, 13, p. 146.

PART 5   THE MIDDLE AGES AND RENAISSANCE PHILOSOPHY

XXI. Marsilio Ficino and Pietro Pomponazzi

1. For the history of the notion of the Renaissance and the conflicting opinions on its meaning, see W. K. Ferguson, *The Renaissance in Historical Thought, Five Centuries of Interpretation,* Boston: Houghton Mifflin Co., 1948. A good sketch of Renaissance philosophy will be found in J. Collins, *A History of Modern European Philosophy,* Milwaukee: Bruce, 1954, pp. 13–50. For a fuller account, see F. Copleston, *A History of Philosophy,* vol. 3, pp. 207–405.
2. See D. Bush, *The Renaissance and English Humanism,* Toronto: University Press, 1939, p. 68.
3. Petrarch (1304–1374), for example, wrote bitterly against Aristotelianism, especially in its Averroist interpretation, but he acknowledges his great debt to St. Augustine. See the selections from Petrarch's works translated by H. Nachod in *The Renaissance Philosophy of Man,* ed.

E. Cassirer, P. O. Kristeller, and J. H. Randall, Jr., Chicago: University Press, 1948, pp. 34–143.
4. See E. Gilson, *La philosophie au moyen âge,* Paris: Payot, 1944, pp. 720–753; "Humanisme médiévale et Renaissance," *Les idées et les lettres,* Paris: J. Vrin, 1932, pp. 171–196. P. Renucci, *L'aventure de l'humanisme européen au moyen âge (IVᵉ–XIVᵉ siècle),* Paris: Les Belles Lettres, 1953.
5. LIFE. FICINO was born in 1433 in Figline, near Florence. After studying at Florence and perhaps at Bologna, he met Cosimo de' Medici, who became his patron. Cosimo gave him a villa at Careggio, near Florence, and encouraged him to pursue Platonic philosophy. The villa became a center of research and study in Platonism. At Cosimo's request Ficino translated the works of Plato and many Neoplatonists. His principal work, the *Theologia Platonica,* was written between 1469 and

1474. In 1473 he was ordained a priest. In later life he translated the *Enneads* of Plotinus and some of the works of Porphyry, Proclus, and Dionysius the Pseudo-Areopagite. He died in 1499. WORKS. For the list and chronology of Ficino's works, see P. O. Kristeller, *Supplementum Ficinianum*, I, Florence: L. S. Olschki, 1937, pp. lxxvii–clxvii. *Opera Omnia*, 2 vols., Basel, 1561. *Marsilio Ficino's Commentary on Plato's Symposium*, Latin text with a translation and Introduction by S. R. Jayne, Columbia: University of Missouri, 1944. *Marsile Ficin, Commentaire sur le Banquet de Platon*, ed. R. Marcel, Paris: Guillaume Budé, 1956. TRANSLATIONS. *Commentary on Plato's Symposium* (see above). *Five Questions concerning the Mind*, trans. by J. L. Burroughs in *The Renaissance Philosophy of Man*, pp. 193–212. STUDIES. P. O. Kristeller, *The Philosophy of Marsilio Ficino*, trans. by V. Conant, New York: Columbia University Press, 1943. J. Festugière, *La philosophie de l'amour de Marsile Ficin*, Paris: J. Vrin, 1941. P. O. Kristeller, *Studies in Renaissance Thought and Letters*, Part II: Marsilio Ficino and His Circle, Rome: Edizioni di storia e letteratura, 1956; same author, "The Scholastic Background of Marsilio Ficino," *Traditio*, II (1944), 257–318. R. Marcel, *Marsile Ficin*, Paris: "Les Belles Lettres," 1958.

6. *Epistola dedicatoria in Librum de Vita*, p. 493. (Unless otherwise noted, the references are to the Basel edition of 1561.)

7. *Epist.* IX, p. 899.

8. *Epist.* VIII, p. 872.

9. *Commentarium in Parmenidem*, 50, p. 1165.

10. Pico della Mirandola, *Of Being and Unity*, 3; trans. by V. M. Hamm, Milwaukee: Marquette University Press, 1943, p. 17.

11. *Comm. in Parmen.*, 49, p. 1164.

12. *Theologia Platonica*, V, 7, p. 140.

13. *Ibid.*, XVII, 2, p. 387.

14. *Ibid.*, XII, 7, p. 282.

15. *Ibid.*, VIII, 2, pp. 184–186.

16. *Ibid.*, XIV, 2, pp. 307–309. See Ficino's *Five Questions concerning the Mind*, p. 207.

17. *Ibid.*, V, 8–9, pp. 140–143. For St. Thomas' influence on Ficino, see E. Gilson, "Marsile Ficin et le Contra Gentiles," *Archives*, 24 (1957), 101–113.

18. See J. Coquelle's introduction to his edition of Cajetan's *Commentaria in De Anima Aristotelis*, Rome: Institutum Angelicum, 1938, I, pp. xxi–xxxvi. Also E. Gilson, "Cajétan et l'humanisme théologique," *Archives*, 22 (1955), 113–136.

19. *Commentary on Plato's Symposium*, Oratio tertia, ch. 3; ed. S. R. Jayne, p. 56. In the *Platonic Theology* the bond of love uniting all the parts of the universe is called the World Soul. See *Theologia Platonica*, III, 2, p. 121.

20. *Epist. I*, p. 635.

21. *Comm. on Symposium*, Oratio prima, ch. 4; ed. S. R. Jayne, p. 40.

22. *Ibid.*, Oratio sexta, chs. 18–19, pp. 101–103.

23. LIFE. POMPONAZZI was born at Mantua in 1462. After studying philosophy and medicine at Padua he taught there with great success until 1488. Afterward he taught at Ferrara and Bologna. He was a layman and married three times. He died in 1524.

WORKS. *De Naturalium Effectuum Admirandorum Causis, seu De Incantationibus Liber*, Basel, 1567. Extracts from Pomponazzi's unedited *Commentary on the De Anima* have been published by L. Ferri, *La Psicologia di Pietro Pomponazzi secondo un manoscritto inedito dell'Angelica di Roma* (Estratto dal Tomo 3° Serie IIª degli Atti della Reale Accademia dei Lincei, Rome, 1876). *De Immortalitate Animae*, ed. G. Morra, Bologna: Nanni & Fiammenghi, 1954. *Libri Quinque De Fato, De Libero Arbitrio et De Praedestinatione*, ed. R. Lemay, Lucani: In Aedibus Thesauri Mundi, 1957.

TRANSLATION. *On the Immortality of the Soul*, trans. by W. Hay II, revised by J. H. Randall, Jr., in *The Renaissance Philosophy of Man*, pp. 280–381.

STUDIES. A. H. Douglas, *The Philosophy and Psychology of Pietro Pomponazzi*, Cambridge: University Press, 1910. B. Nardi, "Gli scritti del Pomponazzi," *Giornale Critico della Filosofia Italiana*, 29 (1950), 207–216; "Le opere inedite del Pomponazzi," *Giornale Critico della Fil. Ital.* (1950), 427–442. B. Nardi, art. "Pomponazzi," *Enciclopedia Cattolica*, IX, 1731–1734. P. O. Kristeller, "Two Unpublished Questions on the Soul of Pietro Pomponazzi," *Medievalia et Humanistica*, 1955, 76–101.

24. *On the Immortality of the Soul*, IV.

25. *Ibid.*, VIII. For Pomponazzi's relation to St. Thomas on the subject of the soul, see A. C. Pegis, "Some Reflections on *Summa Contra Gentiles* II, 58," *An Eti-*

enne Gilson Tribute, ed. C. J. O'Neil, Milwaukee: Marquette University Press, 1959, 172–177.

26. *On the Immortality of the Soul*, VIII.

27. *Ibid.*, IX.

28. In his *De Immortalitate Animae*, written against Pomponazzi in 1518 at the request of Pope Leo X, Nifo attempts the impossible task of showing how, according to St. Thomas, the soul is both a subsistent reality and the form of the body without alluding to the Thomistic doctrine of being (*esse*). (See ch. 69.) This reflects the brand of Thomism taught in Italy around 1500.

29. *On the Immortality of the Soul*, XV.

30. *Ibid.*, XIV. See J. S. Mill, *Utilitarianism*, ch. 2: "It is better to be a human being dissatisfied than a pig satisfied; better to be Socrates dissatisfied than a fool satisfied."

31. *On the Immortality of the Soul*, XIV.

32. *Ibid.* For the influence of Stoicism in the sixteenth century, see L. Zanta, *La renaissance du Stoïcisme au XVIᵉ siècle*, Paris, 1914.

33. See A. Maurer, "Between Reason and Faith: Siger of Brabant and Pomponazzi on the Magic Arts," *Mediaeval Studies*, 18 (1956), 1–18.

34. *De Incantationibus*, 12, pp. 231–232.

35. *Ibid.*, 10, p. 201.

36. *Ibid.*, 12, p. 243.

37. M. de Andrea defends the orthodoxy of Pomponazzi in "Fede e ragione nel pensiero del Pomponazzi," *Rivista di filosofia neoscolastica*, 38 (1946), 278–297. W. Betzendörfer maintains that

he was a rationalist in *Die Lehre von der zweifachen Wahrheit bei Petrus Pomponatius*, Tübingen, 1919.

38. De Incantationibus, 12, p. 286.

39. See A. Gewirth, *Marsilius of Padua and Medieval Political Phi-losophy*, New York: Columbia University Press, 1951.

40. See Stuart MacClintock, *Per-versity and Error, Studies on the "Averroist" John of Jandun*, Bloomington: Indiana University Press, 1956.

XXII. Renaissance Scholasticism. Francis Suarez

1. For Spanish Jesuit political theorists of the Renaissance, see J. N. Figgis, *Studies of Political Thought from Gerson to Grotius, 1414–1625*, 2nd ed., Cambridge: University Press, 1923, pp. 146–166. C. Giacon, *La seconda sco-lastica*. Vol. 1: *I grandi Commen-tatori di san Tommaso;* vol. 2: *Precedenze teoretiche ai problemi giuridici;* vol. 3: *I Problemi giuridico-politici*, Milan: Fratelli Bocca, 1944–1950.

2. John Capreolus, *Defensiones Theologiae Divi Thomae Aqui-natis*, edited by Paban-Pègues, 7 vols., Turin: Alfred Cattier, 1900–1908. See M. Grabmann, "Johan-nes Capreolus, O.P., der 'Princeps Thomistarum' (gest. 7 April, 1444) und seine Stellung in der Geschichte der Thomistenschule," *Divus Thomas* (Fribourg), 22 (1944), 85–109, 145–170.

3. Capreolus, *op. cit.*, vol. 1, pp. 301–315. See N. J. Wells, "Capre-olus on Essence and Existence," *The Modern Schoolman*, 38 (1960), 1–24. J. Hegyi, *Die Bedeu-tung des Seins bei den klassischen Kommentatoren des heiligen Thomas von Aquin: Capreolus, Silvester von Ferrara, Cajetan*, Pullach: Verlag Berchmanskol-leg, 1959, pp. 19–24.

4. Capreolus, *op. cit.*, vol. 1, pp. 302–305; vol. 3, pp. 73–75.

5. Ibid., vol. 3, p. 76. See St. Thomas, *De Potentia*, 3, 5.

6. Commentaria in De Ente et Essentia D. Thomae Aquinatis, ed. M.-H. Laurent, Turin: Mari-etti, 1934. *De Nominum Ana-logia*, ed. N. Zammit, Rome: Angelicum, 1934. *The Analogy of Names, and the Concept of Be-ing*, trans. by E. A. Bushinski, with H. J. Koren, Pittsburgh: Duquesne University Press, 1953.

7. See E. Gilson, "Cajétan et l'Existence," *Tijdschrift voor Phi-losophie*, 15 (1953), 267–286; "Cajétan et l'humanisme théolo-gique," *Archives*, 30 (1955), 113–136. C. Fabro, "L'obscurcissement de l'esse dans l'école thomiste," *Revue Thomiste*, 58 (1958), 443–472.

8. In De Ente et Essentia, 5, p. 161.

9. Ibid., p. 159.

10. Commentaria in libros Aris-totelis de Anima, Compluti: F. Ramirez, 1583, fol. 150v. See E. Gilson, "Cajétan et l'humanisme théologique," p. 122, note 2.

11. Text quoted by M.-H. Laurent in his Introduction to Cajetan's *Commentaria in de Anima*, ed. I. Coquelle, Rome: Angelicum, 1938, p. xxxv. See E. Gilson, *art. cit.*, pp. 114, 115.

12. See A. Maurer, "St. Thomas and the Analogy of Genus," *The New Scholasticism*, 29 (1955),

127–144; R. J. Masiello, "The Analogy of Proportion according to the Metaphysics of St. Thomas," *The Modern Schoolman*, 35 (1958), 91–105.

13. For the difference between St. Thomas' and Scotus' notions of analogy, see E. Gilson, *Jean Duns Scot*, Paris: J. Vrin, 1952, p. 101.

14. See Cajetan, *Commentaria in Summa Theologiae*, III, 2, 2; Leonine ed., vol. 11, pp. 25–29; III, 4, 2, pp. 74–81.

15. *In De Ente et Essentia*, Prooemium, I, n. 5, pp. 6, 7.

16. See B. Roth, *Franz von Mayronis, O.F.M., sein Leben, seine Werke, seine Lehre vom Formalunterschied in Gott*, Werl in Westfalen: Franziskus Druckerei, 1936.

17. Francis of Meyronnes, *In I Sent.*, d. 47, q. 3, Venice, 1520, fol. 134 F.

18. *Ibid.*, C–D.

19. See B. Roth, *op. cit.*, pp. 563–564.

20. See I. Brady, "The *Liber de Anima* of William of Vaurouillon O.F.M.," *Mediaeval Studies*, 10 (1948), 225–297; 11 (1949), 247–307.

21. See J. B. Scott, *The Catholic Conception of International Law. Francisco de Vitoria, Founder of the Modern Law of Nations: Francisco Suarez, Founder of the Philosophy of Law in general and in particular of the Law of Nations*, Washington, D.C., 1934.

22. D. Bañez, *Scholastica commentaria in Primam Partem Summae Theologiae D. Thomae Aquinatis*, ed. L. Urbano, Madrid-Valencia, 1934, vol. I, p. 141. Quoted by E. Gilson, "Remarques sur l'expérience en métaphysique," *Actes du XIème congrès international de philosophie*, Brussels, 1953, p, 8. Same author, "Cajétan et l'humanisme théologique," p. 119.

23. See C. Fabro, *art. cit.*, pp. 457, 458.

24. John of St. Thomas, *Cursus Philosophicus Thomisticus*, ed. B. Reiser, 3 vols., Turin: Marietti, 1930–1937; *Cursus Theologicus*, 4 vols. to date, Paris, Tournai, Rome: Desclée, 1931–1953; *The Material Logic of John of St. Thomas*, trans. by Y. R. Simon, J. J. Glanville, G. D. Hollenhorst, Chicago: University Press, 1955.

25. See *Jesuit Thinkers of the Renaissance. Essays presented to John F. McCormick, S.J.*, ed. G. Smith, Milwaukee: Marquette University Press, 1939.

26. Vasquez, *Commentaria ac Disputationes in primam partem S. Thomae*, Lyons, 1631, disp. 50, cap. 6. See J. Maritain, *The Dream of Descartes*, New York: Philosophical Library, 1944, pp. 144–145.

27. Vasquez, *op. cit.*, disp. 57, cap. 2, n. 8; disp. 75, cap. 3, n. 15–16. For the medieval sources of the Cartesian doctrine, see R. Dalbiez, "Les sources scolastiques de la théorie cartésienne de l'être objectif (à propos du Descartes de M. Gilson)," *Revue d'histoire de la philosophie*, 3 (1929), 464–472; E. Gilson, *Etudes sur le rôle de la pensée médiévale dans la formation du système cartésien*, Paris: J. Vrin, 1930, pp. 203–207.

28. LIFE. SUAREZ, called the *Doctor Eximius*, was born in Granada, Spain, in 1548 and died in Lisbon in 1617. He studied at Salamanca and taught philosophy and theology at Avila, Segovia, Valladolid, Rome, Alcalá, Salamanca, and Coimbra.

WORKS. Published in 28 volumes in the Paris, Vivès edition of 1856–1878. His most important philosophical work is his *Disputationes Metaphysicae* (vols. 25, 26). His *Tractatus de Anima* was published posthumously in 1621.

TRANSLATION: *Francis Suarez, On the Various Kinds of Distinctions* (*Disputationes Metaphysicae, 7*), trans. by C. Vollert, Milwaukee: Marquette University Press, 1947. STUDIES. L. Mahieu, *François Suarez, sa philosophie et les rapports qu'elle a avec sa théologie*, Paris: Desclée, 1921. C. Giacon, *Suarez*, Brescia: "La Scuola," 1945. M. Grabmann, "Die Disputationes Metaphysicae der Franz Suarez in ihrer methodischen Eigenart und Fortwirkung," *Mittelalterliches Geistesleben*, Munich: Max Hueber, 1926, vol. 1, pp. 525–560. J. F. McCormick, "The Significance of Suarez for a Revival of Scholasticism," *Aspects of the New Scholastic Philosophy*, ed. C. A. Hart, New York: Benziger Bros., 1932, pp. 32–39.

29. Vita Leibnitii a seipso, in Foucher de Careil, *Nouvelles lettres et opuscules inédits de Leibniz*, Paris, 1857, p. 382. Quoted by J. Maréchal, *Précis d'histoire de la philosophie moderne*, Louvain: Museum Lessianum, 1933, p. 155.

30. Sämtliche Werke, ed. E. Grisebach, III, 20, and IV, 70. Quoted by M. Grabmann, *art. cit.*, p. 535.

31. C. Wolff, *Philosophia prima sive Ontologia*, I, 2, cap. 3, art. 169, Verona, 1789, p. 72. Quoted by E. Gilson, *Being and Some Philosophers*, Toronto: Pontifical Institute of Mediaeval Studies, 1952, p. 117.

32. Disp. Meta. l, 1, 5; vol. 25, p. 3.

33. Ibid., 2, 1, 9, p. 68.

34. Ibid., 2, 1, 14, pp. 69, 70.

35. Ibid., 2, 4, 9, p. 90. For Suarez' notion of being, see E. Gilson, *op. cit.*, pp. 97–107.

36. Ibid., 31, 2, 1; vol. 26, p. 229; *ibid.*, 31, 2, 10, p. 232.

37. See J. Owens, "The Number of Terms in the Suarezian Discussion of Essence and Being," *The Modern Schoolman*, 34 (1957), 147–191. J. G. Caffarena, "Sentido de la composicion de ser y esencia en Suarez," *Pensamiento* (Madrid), 15 (1959), 135–154.

38. Disp., 31, 1, 3, p. 225.

39. Ibid., 31, 1, 11, p. 228.

40. Ibid., 31, 1, 13, p. 228.

41. Ibid., 31, 4, 3, p. 235.

42. Ibid., 7, 1, 4–5; vol. 25, p. 251.

43. Ibid., 31, 6, 23; vol. 26, p. 250.

44. See J. Owens, *art. cit.*, 178–187.

45. Disp. 6, 1, 1–2; vol. 25, pp. 201, 202.

46. Ibid., 6, 1, 11–12, p. 204.

47. Ibid., 6, 2, 1, p. 206.

48. For a defense of Suarez against the charge of nominalism, see J. M. Alejandro, *La gnoseologia del Doctor Eximio y la acusacion nominalista*, Comillas [Santander]: Universidad Pontificia, 1948.

49. Disp. 6, 2, 14, p. 210.

50. Ibid., 6, 5, 3, p. 223.

51. Ibid., 5, 6, 15, p. 186.

52. Ockham, *Sent.*, I, 2, 6; G.J.

53. Disp. 29, 1, 7; vol. 26, p. 23. For Suarez' proof for the existence of God, see A. Breuer, *Der Gottesbeweis bei Thomas und Suarez. Ein wissenschaftlichen Gottesbeweis auf der Grundlage von Potenz und Aktverhältnis oder Abhängigheitsverhältnis*, Fribourg, Switzerland, 1930. For his doctrine of motion, see N. Junk, *Die Bewegungslehre des Franz Suarez*, Innsbruck, Leipzig: F. Rauch, 1938.

54. Disp. 29, 1, 20–22, pp. 27, 28.

55. *Disp.*, 29, 1, 35, p. 32.
56. *Ibid.*, 29, 2, 5, p. 35.
57. *Ibid.*, 29, 2, 37, p. 42.
58. *Ibid.*, 29, 3, 11, p. 51.
59. For Suarez' doctrine of law, see T. E. Davitt, *The Nature of Law*, St. Louis: Herder, 1951, pp. 86–108. E. Jombart, "Le volontarisme de la loi d'après Suarez," *Nouvelle revue théologique*, 59 (1932), 34–44. J. de Blic, "Le volontarisme juridique chez Suarez," *Revue de philosophie*, 10 (New Series [1930]), 213–230.
60. *De Legibus*, I, 1, 1; vol. 5, p. 1. See St. Thomas, *Summa Theologiae*, I–II, 90, 1.
61. *De Legibus*, I, 1, 7–8, pp. 2, 3.

62. *Ibid.*, I, 5, 24, p. 22.
63. *Ibid.*, I, 12, 3, p. 53. See St. Thomas, *Summa Theologiae*, I–II, 90, 4.
64. See St. Thomas, *op. cit.*, I–II, 90, 1, ad 3.
65. *De Legibus*, I, 4, 11, p. 16.
66. *Ibid.*, I, 5, 5–11, pp. 18, 19.
67. *Ibid.*, II, 3, 11, p. 95.
68. *Ibid.*, II, 3, 5–6, pp. 93, 94.
69. *Ibid.*, II, 3, 9, p. 94. See St. Thomas, *op. cit.*, I–II, 91, 1.
70. *De Legibus*, II, 4, 8, p. 99.
71. *Ibid.*, I, 3, 10, p. 9. See St. Thomas, *op. cit.*, I–II, 91, 2.
72. *De Legibus*, II, 5, 14, p. 103.
73. *Ibid.*, I, 5, 8, pp. 18, 19.
74. *Ibid.*, II, 6, 12, p. 108.

CONCLUSION

1. See F. Copleston, *A History of Philosophy*, vol. 3, p. 1.

2. See the works of Jacques Maritain and Gabriel Marcel.

ADDENDA

Page 144 at note 20:

J. Quinn offers evidence that St. Bonaventure posits only one substantial form in man and indeed in any living body. There is in that body, however, a plurality of substantial dispositions that prepare the way for the reception of the substantial form. See J. Quinn, *The Historical Constitution of St. Bonaventure's Philosophy* (Toronto, 1973), pp. 219-319.

Page 147 at note 26:

J. Quinn shows that, although St. Bonaventure posits in the soul an innate knowledge of God from His image in the soul, this is not to be understood as an innate idea of God. See J. Quinn, *The Historical Constitution of St. Bonaventure's Philosophy* (Toronto, 1973), pp. 428-434.

Page 192 at note 1:

The statement of Siger of Brabant "At present we have nothing to do with the miracles of God, since we treat natural things in a natural way" is an echo of the remark of St. Albert (who was one of Siger's teachers): *nihil ad me de Dei miraculis, cum ego de naturalibus disseram.* See St. Albert, *De Generatione et Corruptione*, lib. 1, tract. I, c. 22; ed. Borgnet, IV, p. 363. But St. Albert's attitude towards faith and reason was not the same as Siger's. Siger like St. Albert defended the autonomy of philosophy, but unlike him he held philosophical positions contrary to Christian doctrine. See F. Van Steenberghen, *Maitre Siger de Brabant* (Louvain, 1977), p. 230. On Albert's relations to Siger, see F. Van Steenberghen, *La philosophie au XIIIe siècle* (Louvain, Paris, 1966), p. 304.

Page 195 at note 5:

In the Cambridge manuscript of Siger's *Metaphysics* (V, 8) man's free will is described as a self-determination to act, and in his Commentary on the *Liber de Causis* (25) man is said to be master of his acts. See C. J. Ryan, "Man's Free Will in Siger of Brabant," *Mediaeval Studies*, 45 (1983).

Page 386: BOETHIUS

It is usually said that Boethius studied in Athens, but the evidence for this is not conclusive. He may have received his entire education in Italy. See P. Courcelle, *Les lettres grecques en Occident, de Macrobe à Cassiodore*, Paris: E. de Brocard, 1943, pp. 259-260. J. Satorowicz, "De Boethii in Graecam Itinere," *Divus Thomas* (Piacenza), 72 (1969), 430-440.

BIBLIOGRAPHIC SUPPLEMENT

i. St. Augustine

LIFE. F. Van der Meer, *Augustine the Bishop*, trans. B. Battershaw and C. R. Lamb, London and New York: Sheed & Ward, 1961. P. Brown, *Augustine of Hippo. A Biography*, London: Faber & Faber, 1967.

WORKS. Bibliographical information in: *Répertoire bibliographique de saint Augustin 1950-1960*, ed. T. Van Bavel and F. Van der Zande, Steenbrugge: Abbey of St. Peter, 1963; *Bibliographia Augustiniana*, ed. C. Andresen, Darmstadt: Wissenschaftliche Buchgesellschrift, 1973. A new critical edition of the works of St. Augustine is appearing in the series *Corpus Christianorum*, Turnholt: Brepols, 1956 ff.

TRANSLATIONS. *The Fathers of the Church* continues to issue translations of the works of St. Augustine. The series is now published in Washington, D.C. by Fathers of the Church, Inc. It includes: *The Confessions*, trans. V. J. Bourke (1953); *The Trinity*, trans. S. McKenna (1963), *The Retractations*, trans. M. I. Bogan (1968); *The Teacher, The Free Choice of the Will, Grace and Free Will*, trans. R. P. Russell (1968).

OTHER TRANSLATIONS. *The Problem of Free Choice*, trans. M. Pontifex, Westminster, Md.: Newman Press, 1955. *Confessions*, trans. J. K. Ryan, New York: Garden City, 1960. *The Essential Augustine*, V. J. Bourke, New York: New American Library, 1964. *Concerning the City of God against the Pagans*, trans. H. Bettenson, Harmondsworth: Penguin Books, 1972.

STUDIES. P. Courcelle, *Les Confessions de saint Augustin dans la tradition littéraire, antécédents et postérité*, Paris: Etudes Augustiniennes, 1963. R. J. O'Connell, *St. Augustine's Early Theory of Man, A.D. 386-391*, Cambridge, Mass.: Harvard University Press, 1968; *Art and the Christian Intelligence in St. Augustine*, Cambridge, Mass.: Harvard University Press, 1978. R. A. Markus, *Saeculum: History and Society in the Theology of St. Augustine*, Cambridge: University Press, 1970.

ii. Boethius

WORKS. *De Hypotheticis Syllogismis*, Testo, traduzione di L. Orbertello, Brescia: Paideia, 1969. New revised edition of *The Theological Tractates*, with trans. by H. F. Stewart, E. K. Rand, S. J. Tester, Cambridge, Mass.: Harvard University Press, 1973.

TRANSLATIONS. *The Consolation of Philosophy*, trans. R. Green, Indianapolis: Bobbs Merrill, 1962. *De Topicis Differentiis*, trans. E. Stump, Ithaca: Cornell University Press, 1978.

STUDIES. K. Dürr, *The Propositional Logic of Boethius*, Amsterdam: North-Holland, 1951. B. L. Jefferson, *Chaucer and the Consolation of Philosophy of Boethius*, New York: Haskell House, 1965. G. Schrimpf, *Die Axiomenschrift des Boethius (De Hebdomadibus) als philosophisches*

Lehrbuch des Mittelalters, Leiden: Brill, 1966. P. Courcelle, *La Consolation de Philosophie dans la tradition littéraire, antécédents et postérité de Boèce*, Paris: Etudes Augustiniennes, 1967. L. Obertello, *Severino Boezio*, 2 vols., Genoa: Accademia Ligure di Scienze e Lettere, 1974; vol. 2 contains a bibliography. J. Gruber, *Kommentar zu Boethius De Consolatione Philosophiae*, Berlin, New York: de Gruyter, 1978. J. Shiels,

"Boethius' Commentaries on Aristotle," *Medieval and Renaissance Studies*, 4 (1958), 217-244. L. Minio-Paluello, "Les traductions et les commentaires aristotéliciennes de Boèce," *Texte und Untersuchungen zur Geschichte der altchristlichen Literatur*, 64 (1957), 358-365. *Boethius, His Life, Thought and Influence*, ed. M. Gibson, Oxford: Blackwell, 1981.

III. John Scotus Erigena

WORKS. *Periphyseon (De Divisione Naturae)*, ed. and trans. I. P. Sheldon-Williams, with L. Bieler, Dublin: Dublin Institute for Advanced Studies, vol. 1, 2, 1968. *Homélie sur le Prologue de Jean*, ed. and trans. E. Jeauneau, Paris: Editions du Cerf, 1969. *Commentaire sur l'évangile de Jean Scot*, ed. and trans. E. Jeauneau, Paris: Editions du Cerf, 1972. *Expositiones in Ierarchum Coelestem*, ed. J. Barbet (*CCCM*, 31), Turnholt: Brepols, 1975. *De Divina Predestinatione Liber*, ed. G. Madic (*CCCM*, 50), Turnholt: Brepols, 1978.

TRANSLATION. *Periphyseon. On the Division of Nature*, trans. by M. L. Uhlfelder, with summaries by J. A. Potter, Indianapolis: Bobbs-Merrill, 1976.

STUDIES. J. J. O'Meara, *Eriugena*, Cork: Cultural Relation Committee of Ireland, 1969. *The Mind of Eriugena.*

Papers of a Colloquium, Dublin 14-18 July, 1970, ed. J. J. O'Meara and L. Bieler, Dublin: Irish University Press for Royal Irish Academy, 1973. C. Allegro, *Giovanni Scoto Eriugena*, 3 vols., Rome: Citta Nuova Editrice, 1974. R. Roques, *Libres sentiers vers l'Erigénisme*, Rome: Edizioni dell'Ateneo, 1975. *Jean Scot Erigène et l'histoire de la philosophie* [*Actes du Colloque*], Laon, 7-12 juillet 1975, Paris: Editions du Centre National de la Recherche Scientifique, 1977. E. Jeauneau, *Quatre thèmes Erigéniens*, Montréal: Institut d'Etudes Médiévales Albert-le-Grand; Paris: Vrin, 1978. *Eriugena. Studien zu seinen Quellen. Vorträge des III. Internationalen Eriugena-Colloquiums*, Freiburg im Breisgau, 27.-30. August, 1979, Heidelberg: Carl Winter Universitätsverlag, 1980.

III. Dionysius the Pseudo-Areopagite

WORKS. The various Latin versions of his writings are contained in *Dionysiaca*, 2 vols., Paris: Desclée de Brouwer, 1937.

TRANSLATIONS. *Œuvres complètes du Pseudo-Denys l'Aréopagite*, trans. into French by M. de Gandillac, Paris:

Aubier, 1943. *The Divine Names*, trans. by the editors of the Shrine of Wisdom, Fuitry Brook: Shrine of Wisdom, Wisconsin, 1957. *The Mystical Theology and the Celestial Hierarchies*, 2nd ed. trans. by the editors of the Shrine of Wisdom,

Fuitry Brook: Shrine of Wisdom, Wisconsin, 1965. STUDIES. R. Roques, *L'univers dionysien, structure hiérarchique du monde selon le Pseudo-Denys*, Paris: Aubier, 1954. J. Vannest, *Le mystère de Dieu. Essai sur la structure rationnelle de la doctrine mystique du Pseudo-Denys l'Aréopagite*, Brussels: Desclée de Brouwer, 1959. M. Schiavone, *Neoplatonismo e Christianesimo nello Pseudo Dionigi*, Milan: Marzorati, 1963. D. Rutledge, *Cosmic Theology; the Ecclesiastical Hierarchy of Pseudo-Denys. An Introduction*, London: Routledge & K. Paul, 1964. P. Scazzoso, *Ricerche sulla struttura del linguaggio dello pseudo-Dionigi Areopagita. Introduzione alla letteratura delle opere pseudo-dioniziane*, Milan: Vita e Pensiero, 1967. R. F. Hathaway, *Hierarchy and the Definition of Order in the Letters of Pseudo-Dionysius; a study in the form and meaning of the Pseudo-Dionysian Writings*, The Hague: Nijhoff, 1969 [1970].

iv. St. Anselm

LIFE. *The Life of St. Anselm, Archbishop of Canterbury*, ed. Eadmer, ed. with trans. by R. W. Southern, Oxford: Clarendon Press, 1962.
TRANSLATIONS. *Proslogium, with a Reply on Behalf of the Fool by Gaunilo and the Author's Reply to Gaunilo*, trans. with philosophical commentary by M. J. Charlesworth, Oxford: Clarendon Press, 1965. *Truth, Freedom and Evil: three Philosophical Dialogues by Anselm of Canterbury*, ed. and trans. by J. Hopkins and H. Richardson, New York: Harper and Row, 1967. Anselm of Canterbury, vol. 1: *Monologion, Proslogion, Debate with Gaunilo, and a Meditation on Human Redemption*, trans. J. Hopkins and H. Richardson; vol. 2: *Philosophical Fragments, De Grammatico, On Truth, Freedom of Choice, The Fall of the Devil, The Harmony of the Foreknowledge, the Predestination and the Grace of God with Free Choice*; vol. 3: *Two Letters concerning Roscelin, The Incarnation of the Word, Why God became a Man, The Virgin Conception and Original Sin, The Procession of the Holy Spirit, Three Letters on the Sacraments*; vol. 4: *Hermeneutical and Textual Problems on the Complete Treatises of St. Anselm*, by J. Hopkins, Toronto and New York: Edwin Mellen Press, 1974-1976.
STUDIES. Studies in *Spicilegium Beccense. I. Congrès International du IXe centenaire de l'arrivée d'Anselme au Bec*, Paris: Vrin, 1959. R. W. Southern, *Saint Anselm and his Biographer, a Study of Monastic Life and Thought, 1059-c. 1130*, Cambridge, University Press, 1963. D. P. Henry, *The De Grammatico of St. Anselm; the Theory of Paronymy*, Notre Dame, Ind.: University of Notre Dame Press, 1964. C. Hartshorne, *Anselm's Discovery; a Re-examination of the Ontological Proof for God's Existence*, La Salle, Ill.: Open Court, 1965. A. C. Pegis, "St. Anselm and the Argument of the 'Proslogion'," *Mediaeval Studies*, 28 (1966), 228-267. D. P. Henry, *The Logic of St. Anselm*, Oxford: Clarendon Press, 1967. *Memorials of St. Anselm*, ed. R. W. Southern and F. S. Schmitt, London: Oxford University Press, 1969. J. Vuillemin, *Le Dieu d'Anselme et les apparences de la raison*, Paris: Aubier, 1971. R. P. LaCroix, *Proslogion II and III: a Third Interpretation of St. Anselm's Argument*, Leiden: Brill, 1972. J. Hopkins,

A Companion to the Study of St. Anselm, Minneapolis: University of Minnesota Press, 1972. K. Jaspers, Anselm and Nicholas of Cusa. The Great Philosophers, vol. 2, The Original Thinkers, ed. H. Arendt, trans. R. Manheim, New York: Harcourt Brace, 1974. D. P. Henry, Commentary on De Grammatico: the Historical-Logical Dimensions of a Dialogue of St. Anselm's, Dordrecht: Reidel, 1974. R. D. Shafner, Anselm Revisited. A Study of the Role of the Ontological Argument in the Writings of Karl Barth and Charles Hartshorne, Leiden: Brill, 1974. G. R. Evans, Anselm and Talking about God, Oxford: Clarendon Press, 1978. G. R. Evans, Anselm and a New Generation, Oxford: Clarendon Press, 1980.

v. Peter Abelard

WORKS. Historia Calamitatum, ed. J. Monfrin, Paris: Vrin, 1959. Petri Abaelardi Opera Theologica, 2 vols., ed. E. M. Buytaert (CCCM, 11-12), Turnholt: Brepols, 1969. Dialectica, ed. L. M. De Rijk, 2nd rev. ed., Assen: Van Gorcum, 1970. Dialogus inter Philosophum, Judaeum et Christianum, ed. R. Thomas, Stuttgart-Bad Cannstatt: Fr. Fromann, 1970. Ethics, ed. and trans. D. E. Luscombe, Oxford: University Press, 1976-78.

TRANSLATIONS. Du Bien suprème (Theologia Summi Boni), trans. J. Jolivet, Montréal: Bellarmin; Paris: Vrin, 1978. A Dialogue of a Philosopher with a Jew and a Christian, trans. P. J. Payer, Toronto: Pontifical Institute of Mediaeval Studies, 1979.

STUDIES. R. Thomas, Der philosophisch-theologische Erkenntnisweg Peter Abaelards im Dialogus inter Philosophum, Judaeum et Christianum, Bonn: Rohrscheid, 1966. A. V. Murray, Abélard and St. Bernard: a Study in Twelfth Century 'Modernism', Manchester: Manchester University Press, New York: Barnes & Noble, 1967. J. Jolivet, Arts du langage et théologie chez Abélard, Paris: J. Vrin, 1969. D. E. Luscombe, The School of Peter Abelard; the Influence of Abelard's Thought in the Early Scholastic Period, Cambridge: University Press, 1969. M. T. Beonio-Broccopieri Fumagalli, The Logic of Abelard, trans. S. Pleasance, 2nd ed., Dordrecht: Reidel, 1970. R. E. Weingart, The Logic of Divine Love. A Critical Analysis of the Soteriology of Peter Abelard, Oxford: Clarendon Press, 1970. D. W. Robertson, Abelard and Heloise, New York: Dial Press, 1972. T. M. Tomasic, William of Saint-Thierry against Peter Abelard: a Dispute in the Meaning of Being a Person, Rome: Editiones Cistercienses, 1972. Peter Abelard, Proceedings of the International Conference, Louvain, May 10-12, 1971, ed. E. M. Buytaert, Louvain: University Press, 1974. L. Urbani Olivi, La Psichologia di Abelardo e il Tractatus de Intellectibus, Rome: Edizioni di Storia e Letteratura, 1976 (contains an edition of the Tractatus de Intellectibus). M. M. Tweedale, Abailard on Universals, Amsterdam, New York: North-Holland, 1976. P. L. Williams, The Moral Philosophy of Peter Abelard, Lanham, Md.: University Press of America, 1980. Pierre Abélard. Pierre le Vénérable. Les courants philosophiques, littéraires et artistiques en Occident au milieu du XIIe siècle, Paris: Editions du Centre National de la Recherche Scientifique, 1975.

VI. The School of Chartres

GENERAL. E. Jeauneau, *Lectio Philosophorum; recherches sur l'Ecole de Chartres*, Amsterdam: Hakkert, 1973.

CHALCIDIUS. *Timaeus/Plato; a Calcidio translatus commentarioque instructus*, ed. J. H. Waszink, 2nd ed., London: Warburg Institute; Leiden: Brill, 1975. J. H. Waszink, *Studien zum Timaioskommentar des Calcidius*, Leiden: Brill, 1964. J. C. M. Winden, *Calcidius on Matter, his Doctrine and Sources*, Leiden: Brill, 1965. J. Boeft, *Calcidius on Fate, his Doctrine and Sources*, Leiden: Brill, 1970. J. Boeft, *Calcidius on Demons*, Leiden: Brill, 1977.

WORKS AND STUDIES.

a) *Gilbert of Poitiers. The Commentaries on Boethius by Gilbert of Poitiers*, ed. N. M. Haring, Toronto: Pontifical Institute of Mediaeval Studies, 1966. H. Elswijk, *Gilbert Porreta, sa vie, son œuvre, sa pensée*, Louvain: Spicilegium sacrum Lovaniense, 1966.

b) *William of Conches. Glosae super Platonem*, ed. E. Jeauneau, Paris: Vrin, 1965. H. E. Rodnite, "The Doctrine of the Trinity in Guillaume de Conches' Glosses on Macrobius: Texts and Studies," Ph.D. thesis, Columbia University, 1974. J. H. Newell, *The Dignity of Man in William of Conches and the*

School of Chartres in the Twelfth Century, Durham, N.C.: Duke University Press, 1978.

c) *Thierry of Chartres. Commentaries on Boethius by Thierry of Chartres and his School*, ed. N. M. Haring, Toronto, Pontifical Institute of Mediaeval Studies, 1971. "A Commentary on Boethius' *De Trinitate* by Thierry of Chartres," ed. N. M. Haring, *Archives*, (23), 1956, 257-325.

d) *Bernard Silvester. Cosmographia*, ed. P. Dronke, Leiden, Brill, 1978. B. Stock, *Myth and Science in the Twelfth Century. A Study of Bernard Silvester*, Princeton, N.J.: Princeton University Press, 1972.

e) *Clarenbaud of Arras*. N. M. Haring, *Life and Works of Clarembald of Arras*, Toronto: Pontifical Institute of Mediaeval Studies, 1965.

f) *John of Salisbury. John of Salisbury's Entheticus de Dogmate Philosophorum*, ed. D. J. Shurin, Chapel Hill, N.C., 1970.

g) *Alain of Lille* (d. 1202). *Anticlaudianus, or the Good and Perfect Man*, trans. J. J. Sheridan, Toronto: Pontifical Institute of Mediaeval Studies, 1973. *The Plaint of Nature*, trans. J. J. Sheridan, Toronto: Pontifical Institute of Mediaeval Studies, 1980.

VII. Introduction to Scholasticism

THE NEW TRANSLATIONS. The medieval Latin translations of the works of Aristotle are appearing in the series *Aristoteles Latinus*, ed. L. Minio-Paluello et al., Bruges-Paris: Desclée de Brouwer, 1961 ff.; Leiden: Brill, 1968 ff.

For the new translations, see L. Minio-Paluello, *Opuscula: the Latin Aristotle*, Amsterdam: Hakkert, 1972. J. Isaac, *Le Peri Hermeneias en Occident de Boèce à saint Thomas*, Paris: Vrin, 1953.

VIII. Arabian and Jewish Philosophy

1. ARABIAN PHILOSOPHY: GENERAL. R. Walzer, *Greek into Arabic. Essays in Islamic Philosophy*, Oxford: Bruno Cassirer, 1962. *A History of Muslim Philosophy*, 2 vols., ed. M. M. Shariff, Wiesbaden: Otto Harrassowitz, 1963. S. H. Nasr, *An Introduction to Islamic Cosmological Doctrines*, Cambridge, Mass.: Harvard University Press, 1964. E. A. Myers, *Arabic Thought and the Western World in the Golden Age of Islam*, New York: Ungar, 1964. A. Badawi, *La transmission de la philosophie grecque au monde arabe*, Paris: Vrin, 1968. M. Fakhry, *A History of Islamic Philosophy*, New York: Columbia University Press, 1970. A. Badawi, *Histoire de la philosophie en Islam*, 2 vols., Paris: Vrin, 1972. G. C. Anawati, *Etudes de philosophie musulmane*, Paris: Vrin, 1974. *Essays on Islamic Philosophy and Science*, ed. G. F. Hourani, Albany: State University of New York Press, 1975.

2. AVICENNA

LIFE: *The Life of Ibn Sina*, trans. W. E. Gohlman, Albany: State University of New York Press, 1974.

WORKS. The Latin translation of the works of Avicenna is appearing in the series *Avicenna Latinus*. *Liber de Anima seu Sextus de Naturalibus*, ed. S. Van Riet, 2 vols., Louvain: E. Peeters; Leiden: Brill, 1968, 1972. *Liber de Philosophia Prima sive Scientia Divina*, 2 vols., ed. S. Van Riet, Louvain: E. Peeters; Leiden: Brill, 1977, 1980. *Avicenna's Treatise on Logic*, ed. and trans. F. Zabeek, The Hague: Nijhoff, 1971.

TRANSLATIONS. *The Propositional Logic of Avicenna*, trans. N. Shehaby, Boston: Reidel, 1973. *The Metaphysica of Avicenna: a Critical Translation, Commentary and Analysis of the Fundamental Arguments in Avicenna's Metaphysics*, by P. Morewedge, London: Routledge & K. Paul, 1973. *Avicenna's Commentary on the Poetics of Aristotle; a Critical Study with an Annotated Translation*, by I. M. Dahiyat, Leiden: Brill, 1974. *La Métaphysique du Shifa*, French trans. by G. C. Anawati, Paris: Vrin, 1978.

STUDY. O. Chahine, *Ontologie et théologie chez Avicenne*, Paris: Adrien Maisonneuve, 1962.

3. AVERROES:

WORKS. *In Aristotelis Librum II (α) Metaphysicorum Commentarius*, Freiburg: Paulus Verlag, 1966. *In Librum V (Δ) Metaphysicorum Aristotelis Commentarius*, ed. P. Ruggero, Bern: Franke, 1971. *Das neunte Buch (θ) des lateinischen Grossen Metaphysik-Kommentars von Averroes*, ed. B. Bürke, Bern: Franke, 1969.

TRANSLATIONS. *Commentary on Plato's Republic*, trans. E. I. J. Rosenthal, Cambridge: University Press, 1956. *Averroes on Aristotle's De Generatione et Corruptione, Middle Commentary and Epitome*, trans. S. Kurland, Cambridge, Mass.: Harvard University Press, 1958. *On the Harmony of Religion and Philosophy*, trans. G. F. Hourani, London: Luzac, 1961. *Averroes' Epitome on Parva Naturalia*, trans. H. Blumberg, Cambridge, Mass.: Medieval Academy of America, 1961. *Averroes' Middle Commentary on Porphyry's Isagoge and on Aristotle's Categoriae*, trans. H. A. Davidson, Cambridge, Mass.: Medieval Academy of America, 1969. *Averroes on Plato's Republic*, trans. R. Lerner, Ithaca, N.Y.: Cornell University Press, 1974. *Averroes' Three Short Commentaries on Aristotle's Topics, Rhetoric and Poetics*, trans. C. E. Butterworth, Albany: State University of New York Press, 1977.

STUDY. B. S. Kogan, "Averroes and the Theory of Emanation," *Mediaeval Studies*, 43 (1981), 384-404.

4. ALKINDI. N. Rescher, *Al-Kindi. An Annotated Bibliography*, Pittsburgh: University of Pittsburgh Press, 1965. *Al-Kindi's Metaphysics*, trans. A. L. Ivry, Albany: State University of New York Press, 1974. J. Jolivet, *L'intellect selon Kindi*, Leiden: Brill, 1971.

5. ALFARABI. *Al-Farabi's Short Commentary on Aristotle's Prior Analytics*, trans. N. Rescher, Pittsburgh: University of Pittsburgh Press, 1963.

6. ALGAZEL. W. M. Watt, *The Faith and Practice of Al-Ghazali*, London: Allen & Unwin, 1953. W. M. Watt, *Muslim Intellectual. A Study of Al-Ghazali*, Edinburgh: University Press, 1963. M. A. Quasem, *The Ethics of Al-Ghazali, a Composite Ethics in Islam*, Peninsular Malaysia by Central Printing, Sendirian Berhad, Petaling Jaya, Selangor, 1975.

7. JEWISH PHILOSOPHY: GENERAL. Bibliography: G. Vajda, *Jüdische Philosophie. Bibliographische Einführungen in das Studium der Philosophie*, ed. I. M. Bochenski, Bern: Francke, 1950. M. Eisler, *Vorlesungen über die jüdischen Philosophen des Mittelalters*, 3 vols., Vienna, 1876 (reprint: New York: Burt Franklin, n.d.). J. Guttmann, *Die Philosophie des Judentums*, Munich: Reinhardt, 1933. I. I. Efros, *The Problem of Space in Jewish Medieval Philosophy*, New York: Columbia University Press, 1917 (reprint: W. C. Brown). I. I. Efros, *Studies in Medieval Jewish Philosophy*, New York and London: Columbia University Press, 1974.

8. ISAAC ISRAELI. *Isaac Israeli. His Works*, trans. by A. Altmann and S. M. Stern, Oxford: University Press, 1958.

9. IBN GABIROL. *The Fountain of Life* (*Fons Vitae*), specially abridged ed., trans. by T. E. James, London: Peter Owen, 1962. *Livre de la Source de Vie* (*Fons Vitae*), trans. J. Schlanger, Paris: Aubier, 1970. J. Schlanger, *La philosophie de Salomon Ibn Gabirol*, Leiden: Brill, 1968.

10. MAIMONIDES. *The Guide of the Perplexed*, trans. S. Pines, Chicago: Chicago University Press, 1963. W. Backer, M. Brown, D. Simonsen, *Moses ben Maimon, sein Leben, seine Werke und sein Einfluß*, 2 vols., Leipzig: Gustav Fock, 1908-1914. *Maimonide, sa vie, son œuvre, son influence* (Cahiers Juifs, 10, no. 16/17, juillet-octobre 1935). C. Klein, *The Credo of Maimonides*, New York: Philosophical Library, 1958. S. H. Atlas, *From Critical to Speculative Idealism. The Philosophy of Solomon Maimon*, The Hague: Nijhoff, 1964. D. J. Silver, *Maimonidean Criticism and the Maimonidean Controversy 1180-1240*, Leiden: Brill, 1965 (good bibliography). *Studies in Maimonides and St. Thomas Aquinas*, ed. J. I. Dienstag, New York: Ktav, 1975.

ix. Early Philosophy at Paris and Oxford

UNIVERSITIES. C. H. Haskins, *The Rise of Universities*, New York: Holt, 1923. L. J. Daly, *The Medieval University, 1200-1400*, New York: Sheed & Ward, 1961. H. Wierwzowski, *The Medieval University: Masters, Students, Learning*, Princeton: Van Nostrand, 1966. *The University in Society*, vol. 1, *Oxford and Cambridge from the 14th to the early 19th Century*, ed. L. Stone, Princeton: University Press, 1974. A. B. Cobban, *The Medieval Universities: their Development and Organization*, London: Methuen, 1975. *The Universities in the Late Middle Ages*, ed. J. Ijsewijn and J. Paquet, Louvain: University Press, 1978. G. Leff, *Paris and Oxford Universities in the Thirteenth and Fourteenth Centuries*, New York: John Wiley & Sons, 1968. N. Orme, *English Schools in the Middle Ages*, London: Methuen, 1973.

WILLIAM OF AUVERGNE. *De Trinitate*, ed. B. Switalski, Toronto: Pontifical Institute of Mediaeval Studies, 1976. A. Quentin, *Naturkenntnisse und Naturanschauungen bei Wilhelm von Auvergne*, Hildesheim: Gerstenberg, 1976 (summary in English).

ROBERT GROSSETESTE. *Commentarium in VIII Libros Physicorum Aristotelis*, ed. R. C. Dales, Boulder, Col.: University of Colorado Press, 1963.

x. Roger Bacon

STUDIES. E. Westacott, *Roger Bacon in Life and Legend*, New York: Philosophical Library, 1953. C. Bérubé, *De la philosophie à la sagesse chez saint Bonaventure et Roger Bacon*, Rome: Istituto Storico del Cappuccini, 1976. N. W. Fisher and S. Unguru, "Experimental Science and Mathematics in Roger Bacon's Thought," *Traditio*, 27 (1971), 353-378. K. M. Fredborg, L. Nielsen and J. Pinborg, "An Unedited Part of Roger Bacon's *Opus Maius*: De Signis," *Traditio*, 34 (1978), 75-136. H. G. Molland, "Medieval Ideas of Scientific Progress," *Journal of the History of Ideas*, 39 (1978), 561-577. V. Foley and K. Perry, "In Defense of *Liber Igneum*: Arab Alchemy, Roger Bacon and the Introduction of Gunpowder into the West," *Journal for the History of Arabic Science*, vol. 3 (1979), 200-218.

xi. St. Bonaventure

TRANSLATIONS. *The Works of Bonaventure*, trans. J. de Vinck, 5 vols., Paterson, N.J.: St. Anthony Guild Press, 1960-1970. *Bonaventure – The Soul's Journey into God; The Tree of Life; The Life of St. Francis*, trans. E. Cousins, New York: Paulist Press, 1978. *Disputed Questions on the Mystery of the Trinity*, trans. Z. Hayes, St. Bonaventure, N.Y.: Franciscan Institute, 1979.

STUDIES. A. C. Pegis, "The Bonaventurian Way to God," *Mediaeval Studies*, 29 (1967), 206-242. J. F. Quinn, *The Historical Constitution of St. Bonaventure's Philosophy*, Toronto: Pontifical Institute of Mediaeval Studies, 1973 (the most thorough study of the philosophy of St. Bonaventure, including a comparison with that of St. Thomas). *S. Bonaventura 1274-1974*, 5 vols., Rome: Grottaferrata, 1972-1973 (studies in commemoration of the 700th anniversary of his death). *Bonaventure and Aquinas: Enduring Philosophers*, ed. R. W. Shahan and F. J. Kovach, Norman: University of Oklahoma Press, 1976 (studies in commemoration of the 700th anniversary of his death). *Actes du colloque saint Bonaventure, 12-15 septembre 1971, Orsay, Etudes franciscaines*, 21 (1971), supplément annuel. *Proceedings of the Seventh Centenary Celebration of the Death of Saint Bonaventure*, ed. P. F. Foley, St. Bonaventure, N.Y.: Franciscan Institute, 1975. *Atti del Congresso Internazionale per il VII Centenario di San Bonaventura da Bagnoregio, Rome 19-26 settembre 1974*, ed. A. Pompei, 3 vols., Rome: Pontificia Facoltà Teologica 'San Bonaventura', 1976. C. Bérubé, *De la philosophie à la sagesse chez saint Bonaventure et Roger Bacon*, Rome: Istituto Storico dei Cappuccini, 1976.

XII. St. Albert the Great

BIBLIOGRAPHIES. Useful bibliographies, continuing that of M. H. Laurent and Y. Congar: F. J. Catania, "Bibliography of St. Albert the Great," *The Modern Schoolman*, 37 (1959), 11-28; M. Schooyans, "Bibliographie philosophique de Saint Albert le Grand – 1931-1960," *Revista da Universidade Católica de Saõ Paulo*, 21 (1961), 36-88.

LIFE AND WORKS. J. A. Weisheipl, "The Life and Works of St. Albert the Great," *Albertus Magnus and the Sciences. Commemorative Essays 1980*, Toronto: Pontifical Institute of Mediaeval Studies, 1980, pp. 13-51; "Albert the Great and Medieval Culture," *The Thomist*, 44 (1980), 481-501. The Cologne edition of Albert's works consists of the following volumes to 1978: *De Caelo et Mundo* (VI); *De Anima* (VII); *De Natura et Origine Animae, De Principiis Motus Progressivi, Quaestiones super De Animalibus* (XII); *Super Ethica* (XIV); *Metaphysica* (XVI.1, 2); *De Unitate Intellectus, De XV Problematibus, Problemata Determinata, De Fato* (XVII.1); *Postilla super Isaiam, Ieremiam, Ezeckielem* (XIX); *De Natura Boni* (XXV.1); *De Sacramentis, De Incarnatione, De Resurrectione* (XXVI); *De Bono* (XXVIII); *Summa Theologiae, Lib. I, p. 1, q. 1-50A* (XXXIV.1); *Super Dionysium De Divinis Nominibus* (XXXVII.1); *Super Dionysii Mysticam Theologiam et Epistulas* (XXXVII.2).

TRANSLATION. *Book of Minerals*, trans. D. Wyckoff, Oxford: Clarendon Press, 1967.

STUDIES. *Albertus Magnus and the Sciences. Commemorative Essays 1980*, ed. J. A. Weisheipl, Toronto: Pontifical Institute of Mediaeval Studies, 1980. Fr. Ruello, *La notion de vérité chez saint Albert le Grand et saint Thomas d'Aquin de 1243 à 1254*, Louvain: Nauwelaerts, 1969. *Albert the Great. Commemorative Studies*, ed. F. J. Kovach and R. W. Shahan, Norman: University of Oklahoma Press, 1980. *Albert the Great: Theologian. Essays in Honor of Albertus Magnus 1280-1980. The Thomist*, 44 (1980). *Albert van Lauingen 700 Jahre†, Albertus Magnus. Festschrift 1980*, Lauingen: Leo-Druck KG Gundelfingen/Donau, 1979. *Albertus Magnus, Doctor Universalis 1280/ 1980*, ed. G. Meyer and A. Zimmermann, Mainz: Matthias-Grünewald, 1980. L.-B. Geiger, "La vie, acte essentiel de l'âme – l'*esse*, acte de l'essence d'après Albert-le-Grand," in *Etudes d'histoire littéraire et doctrinale*, Montréal: Institut d'études médiévales; Paris: Vrin, 1962, pp. 49-116. G. Wieland, *Untersuchungen zum Seinsbegriff im Metaphysikkommentar Alberts des Großen*, Münster: Aschendorff, 1972. L. Sweeney, "The Meaning of *Esse* in

Albert the Great's Texts on Creation in *Summa de Creaturis* and *Scripta Super Sententias*," *Southwestern Journal of Philosophy*, 10.2 (Fall, 1979), 65-95. L. Sweeney, "*Esse Primum Creatum* in Albert the Great's *Liber de Causis et Processu Universitatis*," *The Thomist*, 44 (1980), 599-646.

XIII. St. Thomas Aquinas

LIFE. J. A. Weisheipl, *Friar Thomas d'Aquino. His Life, Thought and Work*, New York: Doubleday, 1974. This excellent biography contains an updated catalogue of the works of St. Thomas.

WORKS. The Leonine edition of the works of St. Thomas continues to be published; the following volumes have appeared since 1965: vol. 22: *Quaestiones Disputatae De Veritate* (1970-1975); vol. 26: *Expositio super Job* (1965); vol. 28: *Expositio super Isaiam* (1974); vol. 40: *Contra Errores Graecorum, De Rationibus Fidei, De Forma Absolutionis, De Substantiis Separatis, Super Decretalem* (1969); vol. 41: *Contra Impugnantes Dei Cultum et Religionem, De Perfectione Spiritualis Vitae, Contra Doctrinam Retrahentium a Religione* (1970); vol. 42: *Compendium Theologiae, De Articulis Fidei et Ecclesiae Sacramentis, Responsio de 108 Articulis, Responsio de 43 Articulis, Responsio de 36 Articulis, Responsio de 6 Articulis, Epistola ad Ducissam Brabantiae, De Emptione et Venditione ad Tempus, Epistola ad Bernardum Abbatem Casinensem, De Regno ad Regem Cypri, De Secreto* (1979); vol. 43: *De Principiis Naturae, De Aeternitate Mundi, De Motu Cordis, De Mixtione Elementorum, De Operationibus Occultis Naturae, De Iudiciis Astrorum, De Sortibus, De Unitate Intellectus, De Ente et Essentia, De Fallaciis, De Propositionibus Modalibus* (1976); vol. 47: *Sententia Libri Ethicorum* (1969); vol. 48: *Sententia Libri Politicorum. Tabula Libri Ethicorum* (1971). Also published: *Liber de Causis et Sancti Thomae de Aquino super Librum de Causis Expositio*, ed. V.-M. Pouliot, Kyoto: Institutum Sancti Thomae de Aquino, 1967.

TRANSLATIONS. *Aristotle on Interpretation. Commentaries by St. Thomas and Cajetan*, trans. J. T. Oesterle, Milwaukee: Marquette University Press, 1962. *Commentary on Aristotle's Physics*, trans. R. J. Blackwell et al., New Haven: Yale; London: Routledge & K. Paul, 1963. *Summa Theologiae*, Latin and English, ed. T. Gilby, 60 vols., London, New York: Eyre and Spottiswoode-McGraw Hill, 1964-1974. *Aquinas On Being and Essence. A Translation and Interpretation*, by J. Bobik: Notre Dame, Ind.: Notre Dame University Press, 1965. *Commentary on the Nicomachean Ethics*, trans. C. I. Litzinger, 2 vols., Chicago: Regnery, 1964. *St. Thomas Aquinas, Siger of Brabant, and St. Bonaventure. On the Eternity of the World*, trans. C. Vollert, L. A. Kendzierski and P. M. Byrne, Milwaukee: Marquette University Press, 1964. *On the Unity of the Intellect against the Averroists*, trans. B. Zedler, Milwaukee: Marquette University

Press, 1968. *Commentary on the Posterior Analytics of Aristotle*, trans. F. R. Larcher, Albany, N.Y.: Magi, 1970. *An Aquinas Reader, Selections from the Writings of Thomas Aquinas*, ed. M. T. Clark, Garden City, N.Y.: Doubleday Image, 1972.
STUDIES. V. J. Bourke has continued his bibliography of St. Thomas to 1978: *Thomistic Bibliography, 1940-1978*, complied by T. L. Miethe and V. J. Bourke, Westport, Conn. and London: Greenwood Press, 1980. *Index Thomisticus. Sancti Thomae Aquinatis Operum Omnium Indices et Concordantiae*, 49 vols., ed. R. Busa, Stuttgart-Bad Cannstatt: Frommann-Holzborg, 1974-1980. This comprehensive index of the works of St. Thomas contains three sections: 1 (in 10 vols.) covers "Indices of Distributions," "Summaries of the Dictionary," and "Indices of Frequency." 2 (in 31 vols.), contains a complete concordance for all the works of St. Thomas. 3 (in 8 vols.) is devoted to terms in other authors. Some of the commemorative volumes published on the occasion of the 700th anniversary of the death of St. Thomas are: *Centenary of St. Thomas Aquinas 1274-1974. The Thomist*, 38 (4 vols.), 1974. *The Review of Metaphysics, a Commemorative Issue. Thomas Aquinas 1274-1974*, 27 (1974). *St. Thomas Aquinas 1274-1974. Commemorative Studies*, ed. A. A. Maurer, 2 vols., Toronto: Pontifical Institute of Mediaeval Studies, 1974. *Thomas von Aquin 1274/1974*, ed. L. Oeing-Hanhoff, Munich: Kösel, 1974. *Colloque commémoratif saint Thomas d'Aquin, 1274-1974. Eglise et Théologie*, 5, n. 2, 1974. *Tommaso d'Aquino nel suo Settimo Centenario. Atti del Congresso Internazionale* (Rome-Naples, 1974), ed. B. D'Amore, 9 vols., Naples: Edizioni Domenicane Italiane; Rome:

Herder, 1974-1978. *Bonaventure and Aquinas: Enduring Philosophers*, ed. R. W. Shahan and F. J. Kovach, Norman: University of Oklahoma Press, 1976. *Aquinas and Problems of his Time*, ed. C. Verbeke and D. Verhelst, Louvain: University Press; The Hague: Nijhoff, 1976. *Calgary Aquinas Studies*, ed. A. Parel, Toronto: Pontifical Institute of Mediaeval Studies, 1978. *Celebrating the Medieval Heritage: a Colloquy on the Thought of Aquinas and Bonaventure*, ed. D. Tracy, *The Journal of Religion*, 58, supplement, 1978. F. C. Copleston, *Aquinas*, Penguin Books, 1955. R. McInerny, *The Logic of Analogy. An Interpretation of St. Thomas*, The Hague: Nijhoff, 1961. F. J. Kovach, *Die Aesthetik des Thomas von Aquin*, Berlin: de Gruyter, 1961. J. Pieper, *Guide to Thomas Aquinas*, trans. R. and C. Winston, New York: Pantheon, 1962. A. C. Pegis, *At the Origin of the Thomistic Notion of Man*, New York: Macmillan, 1963. E. Gilson, *The Spirit of Thomism*, New York: Kenedy & Sons, 1964. E. Gilson, *Le Thomisme. Introduction à la philosophie de saint Thomas d'Aquin*, 6th ed., Paris: Vrin, 1965. M. D. Chenu, *Toward Understanding St. Thomas*, trans. A. M. Landry and D. Hughes, Chicago: Regnery, 1964. V. J. Bourke, *Aquinas' Search for Wisdom*, Milwaukee: Bruce, 1965. R. Schmidt, *The Domain of Logic according to Saint Thomas Aquinas*, The Hague: Nijhoff, 1966. G. B. Phelan, *Selected Papers*, ed. A. G. Kirn, Toronto: Pontifical Institute of Mediaeval Studies, 1967. J. Owens, *An Interpretation of Existence*, Milwaukee: Bruce, 1968. A. Kenny, *The Five Ways. St. Thomas Aquinas' Proofs of God's Existence*, London: Routledge & K. Paul, 1969. C. Fabro, *Exegesi Tomistica*, Rome: Editrice della Pontificia Università

Lateranense, 1969. C. Fabro, *Tomismo e Pensiero Moderno*, Rome: Editrice della Pontificia Università Lateranense, 1969. U. Eco, *Il Problema Estetico in San Tommaso d'Aquino*, 2nd ed., Milan: Bompiani, 1970. L. Elders, *Faith and Science. An Introduction to St. Thomas' Expositio in Boethii de Trinitate*, Rome: Herder, 1974. B. Mondin, *St. Thomas Aquinas' Philosophy in the Commentary on the Sentences*, The Hague, Nijhoff, 1975. J. Owens, *St. Thomas on the Existence of God. Collected Papers of Joseph Owens, C.Ss.R.*, ed. J. R. Catan, Albany: State University of New York Press, 1980. F. Van Steenberghen, *Le problème de l'existence de Dieu dans les écrits de S. Thomas d'Aquin*, Louvain-la-Neuve: Editions de l'Institut Supérieur, 1981.

XIV. Latin Averroism

1. SIGER OF BRABANT:

WORKS. New and revised editions of the works of Siger are being published in the Louvain series *Philosophes Médiévaux*. Already printed: *Siger de Brabant. Quaestiones in Tertium De Anima, De Anima Intellectiva, De Aeternitate Mundi*, ed. B. Bazán, Louvain: Publications Universitaires, 1972; *Siger de Brabant. Ecrits de Logique, de Morale et de Physique*, ed. B. Bazán, Louvain: Publications Universitaires, 1974. Siger's *Quaestiones in Metaphysicam* will appear in two volumes, ed. by W. Dunphy and A. Maurer, revising the edition of C. Graiff and containing two unedited manuscripts of the work.

The recently discovered Commentary on the *Liber de Causis* is edited by A. Marlasca: *Les Quaestiones super Librum de Causis de Siger de Brabant*, Louvain: Publications Universitaires, 1972. The authenticity of the work, which is placed at the end of Siger's career (1275-6) is attested by two ascriptions to Siger in the Vienna manuscript, but serious problems remain concerning the compatibility of its doctrine with the previously known works of Siger. The influence of St. Thomas on this commentary is extensive. The editor concludes: "Il faudrait donc admettre une nouvelle évolution de Siger en ce domaine, sans doute sous l'influence de saint Thomas. Mais la doctrine du commentaire n'est pas très claire sur ce point" (p. 21). Though the work contains theses condemned in 1277, some parts are summaries of articles from St. Thomas' *Summa Theologiae* (Van Steenberghen, *Maître Siger de Brabant*, p. 134).

STUDIES. F. Van Steenberghen, *Maître Siger de Brabant*, Louvain: Publications Universitaires, 1977. On Siger's relation to Dante in light of the new discoveries, see A. Zimmerman, "Dante hatte doch Recht. Neue Ergebnisse der Forschung über Siger von Brabant," *Philosophisches Jahrbuch*, 7 (1967-68), 206-217; "Thomas von Aquin und Siger von Brabant in Licht neuer Quellentexte," *Literatur und Sprache im europaischen Mittelalter. Festschrift für Karl Langosch zum 70. Geburtstag*, Darmstadt, 1973, 417-447. E. Mahoney, "Saint Thomas and Siger of Brabant Revisited," *The Review of Metaphysics*, 27 (1974), 531-553.

Siger borrows liberally from St. Thomas in determining the relations between metaphysics and the theology of Sacred Scripture; see W. Dunphy and A. Maurer, "A Promising New Discovery for Sigerian Studies," *Mediaeval Studies*, 29 (1967), 364-369. A. Maurer, "Siger of Brabant on Fables and Falsehoods in Religion," *Mediaeval Studies*, 43 (1981), 515-530.

2. BOETIUS OF DACIA:

    LIFE. New evidence indicates that Boetius was of Danish, not of Swedish, origin; so he should be called Boetius of Denmark. See S. Skovgaard Jensen, "On the National Origin of the Philosopher Boetius of Dacia," *Classica et Mediaevalia*, 24 (1963), 232-241.

    WORKS. The works of Boetius of Denmark are appearing in the series *Corpus Philosophorum Danicorum Medii Aevi: Boethii Daci Opera*, Copenhagen: G. E. C. Cad, 1974 ff. Vol. IV.1: *Modi Significandi sive Quaestiones super Priscianum Maiorem*. Vol. V.1: *Quaestiones De Generatione et Corruptione*. Vol. V.2: *Quaestiones super libros Physicorum*. Vol. VI.1: *Topica*. Vol. VI.2: *De Aeternitate Mundi, De Summo Bono, De Somniis*. Vol. VIII: *Quaestiones super IV^m Meteorologicorum*. H. Roos, "Das Sophisma des Boetius

van Dacien 'Omnis homo de necessitate est animal' in doppelter Redaktion," *Classica et Mediaevalia*, 23 (1962), 178-197; "Ein unbekanntes Sophisma des Boetius de Dacia," *Scholastik*, 38 (1963), 378-391.

    STUDIES. G. Sajó, "Boèce de Dacie et les commentaires anonymes inédits de Munich sur la Physique et sur la Génération attribués à Siger de Brabant," *Archives*, 25 (1958), 21-58.

3. THE CONDEMNATION OF 1277:

    R. Hissette, *Enquête sur les 219 articles condamnées à Paris le 7 mars 1277*, Louvain: Publications Universitaires, 1977. J. F. Wippel, "The Condemnation of 1270 and 1277 at Paris," *The Journal of Medieval and Renaissance Studies*, 7 (1977), 169-201. E. H. Wéber, *La controverse de 1270 à l'Université de Paris et son retentissement sur la pensée de S. Thomas d'Aquin*, Paris: Vrin, 1970.

4. JOHN OF JANDUN:

    See L. Schmugge, *Johannes von Jandun (1285/89-1328). Untersuchungen zur Biographie und Sozialtheorie eines lateinischen Averroisten*, Stuttgart: Anton Hiersemann, 1966.

xv. The Reaction to Thomism

STUDIES. F. J. Roensch, *Early Thomistic School*, Dubuque, Iowa: The Priory Press, 1964 (contains valuable information about the early followers of St. Thomas). Recent essays on the literature of the "Correctives" of St. Thomas and the Dominican replies: L. Hödl, "Geistesgeschichtliche und literarkritische Erhebungen zum Korrektorienstreit (1277-1287)," *Recherches de théologie ancienne et médiévale*, 33 (1966), 81-114; P. Glorieux,

"Pro et contra Thomam. Un survol de cinquante années," in T. W. Kohler, ed., *Sapientiae Procerum Amore. Mélanges médiévistes offerts à Dom Jean-Pierre Muller*, Rome: Ed. Anselmiana, 1974 (*Studia Anselmiana*, 63), 255-287. On John of Rodington, see M. Tweedale, *John of Rodynton on Knowledge, Science and Theology*, Ann Arbor, University of Michigan photocopy, 1978.

xvi. John Duns Scotus

LIFE. For the life of Duns Scotus see A. B. Emden, *A Biographical Register of the University of Oxford to A.D. 1500*, Oxford: Clarendon Press, 1957, I, pp. 607-610; C. Balić, "The Life and Works of John Duns Scotus," in *John Duns Scotus, 1265-1965*, ed. J. K. Ryan and B. M. Bonansea, Studies in Philosophy and the History of Philosophy, 3, Washington, D.C.: Catholic University of America Press, 1965, pp. 1-27; C. K. Brampton, "Duns Scotus at Oxford, 1288-1301," *Franciscan Studies*, 24 (1964), 5-20.

According to C. Balić, Scotus was born *c.* 1265, likely in Duns, Scotland. He took the Franciscan habit at Dumfries *c.* 1278 and was ordained priest in 1291. From 1291 to 1293 he studied in Scotland and England; in 1293 he was sent to study at Paris until 1297. From 1297 to 1300 he was lecturing on the *Sentences* at Cambridge; from 1300 to 1302 he lectured on the same work at Oxford. From 1302 to 1303 he lectured at Paris. In 1303 he was banished from France by Philip IV and he returned to Oxford to continue his lectures on the *Sentences*. In 1304 he returned to Paris where he received the doctorate in 1305. From 1306 to 1307 he was *magister regens* at Paris. In 1307 he was sent to Cologne, where he died Nov. 8, 1308.

WORKS. The critical edition of Scotus' works is being prepared by the Scotist Commission. Seven volumes of the *Ordinatio*, to Book II, dist. 3, have appeared to 1973. The *Lectura in librum primum Sententiarum*, ed. C. Balić, to dist. 45, has been published (2 vols., Vatican, 1966). The *Lectura* is Scotus' first reading of the *Sentences* at Oxford.

TRANSLATION. *John Duns Scotus, God and Creatures. The Quodlibetal Questions*, trans. F. Alluntis and A. B. Wolter, Princeton, N.J.: Princeton University Press, 1975.

STUDIES. R. Effler, *John Duns Scotus and the Principle "Omne quod movetur ab alio movetur,"* St. Bonaventure, N.Y.: Franciscan Institute, 1962. Important essays in *De Doctrina Ioannis Duns Scoti. Acta Congressus Scotistici Internationalis Oxonii et Edimburgii 11-17 Sept. 1966 celebrati*, 4 vols., Rome: Cura Commissionis Scotisticae, 1968; *Deus et Homo ad Mentem I. Duns Scoti. Acta Tertii Congressus Scotistici Internationalis Vindebonae, 28 Sept. 1970*, 2 vols., Rome, 1972. R. P. Prentice, *The Basic Quidditative Metaphysics of Duns Scotus as Seen in his De Primo Principio*, Rome: Antonianum, 1970.

xvii. The New Logic and Physics

Essays on the *antiqui* and *moderni* in *Antiqui und Moderni. Traditionsbewußtsein und Fortschrittsbewußtsein im späten Mittelalter*, ed. A. Zimmermann, Berlin, New York: de Gruyter, 1974.

THE NEW LOGIC AND GRAMMAR. P. V. Spade, *The Mediaeval Liar: a Catalogue of the Insolubilia-Literature*, To-ronto: Pontifical Institute of Mediaeval Studies, 1975. *William Heytesbury on "Insoluble" Sentences. Chapter One of his Rules for Solving Sophisms*, trans. P. V. Spade, Toronto: Pontifical Institute of Mediaeval Studies, 1979. *Johannes Buridanus. Sophismata*, ed. T. K. Scott, Stuttgart-Bad Cannstatt: Frommann-Holzboog, 1977. *Radul-*

phus Brito, Quaestiones super Priscianum Minorem, ed. H. W. Ender and J. Pinborg, 2 vols., Stuttgart-Bad Cannstatt: Frommann-Holzboog, 1980. G. L. Bursill-Hall, *Speculative Grammars of the Middle Ages*, The Hague: Mouton, 1971. J. Pinborg, *Logik und Semantik im Mittelalter: ein Überblick*, Stuttgart-Bad Cannstatt: Frommann-Holzboog, 1972. D. P. Henry, *Medieval Logic and Metaphysics*, London: Hutchinson University Library, 1972. E. J. Ashworth, *The Tradition of Medieval Logic and Speculative Grammar*, Toronto: Pontifical Institute of Mediaeval Studies, 1978.

THE NEW PHYSICS: EDITIONS. Nicole Oresme, *De Proportionibus Proportionum. Ad Pauca Respicientes*, ed. and trans. by E. Grant, Madison: University of Wisconsin Press, 1966. *Nicole Oresme and the Medieval Geometry of Qualities and Motions. A Treatise on the Uniformity and Difformity of Intensities known as Tractatus de Configurationibus Qualitatum et Motuum*, ed. and trans. with commentary by M. Clagett, Madison: University of Wisconsin Press, 1968. *John Pecham and the Science of Optics. Perspectiva Communis*, ed. with trans. by D. C. Lindberg, Madison: University of Wisconsin Press, 1970. *Nicole Oresme and the Kinematics of Circular Motion. Tractatus de Commensurabilitate vel Incommensurabilitate Motuum Celi*, ed. and trans. by E. Grant, Madison: University of Wisconsin Press, 1971. Robert Kilwardby, *De Ortu Scientiarum*, ed. A. G. Judy, London: The British Academy; Toronto: Pontifical Institute of Mediaeval Studies, 1976.

THE NEW PHYSICS: STUDIES. W. A. Wallace, *Causality and Scientific Explanation*, vol. 1: *Medieval and Early Classical Science*, Ann Arbor: University of Michigan Press, 1972. M. Clagett, *Archimedes in the Middle Ages*, vol. 1, Madison: University of Wisconsin Press, 1964; vols. 2-4, Philadelphia: The American Philosophical Society, 1976-1980. R. C. Dales, *The Scientific Achievement of the Middle Ages*, Philadelphia: University of Pennsylvania Press, 1973. *A Source Book in Medieval Science*, ed. E. Grant, Cambridge, Mass.: Harvard University Press, 1974. D. C. Lindberg, *Theories of Vision from Al-Kindi to Kepler*, Chicago: University of Chicago Press, 1976. *Science in the Middle Ages*, ed. D. C. Lindberg, Chicago: University of Chicago Press, 1978.

XVIII. William of Ockham

LIFE. A. B. Emden, *A Biographical Register of the University of Oxford to A.D. 1500*, Oxford: Clarendon Press, 1958, II, pp. 1384-1387. J. A. Weisheipl, "Ockham and some Mertonians," *Mediaeval Studies*, 30 (1968), 163-213.

WORKS. The critical edition of Ockham's theological and philosophical writings is being prepared by the Franciscan Institute, St. Bonaventure, N.Y. Already published: *Scriptum in Librum Primum Sententiarum. Ordinatio*, dist. 1-41, vols. I-IV (1967-1979). *Summa Logicae* (1974). *Expositio in Libros Artis Logicae Prooemium et Expositio in Librum Porphyrii De Praedicabilibus; Expositio in Librum Praedicamentorum Aristotelis; Expositio in Librum Perihermenias Aristotelis; Tractatus De Praedestinatione et De Praescientia Dei respectu Futurorum*

Contingentium (1978). *Expositio super Libros Elenchorum* (1979). *Quodlibeta Septem* (1980).
TRANSLATIONS. *Predestination, God's Foreknowledge, and Future Contingents*, trans. M. M. Adams and N. Kretzmann, New York: Appleton-Century-Crofts, 1969. *Ockham's Theory of Terms. Part I of the Summa Logicae*, trans. M. L. Loux, Notre Dame: Notre Dame University Press, 1974.
STUDIES. A. S. McGrade, *The Political Thought of William of Ockham. Personal and Institutional Principles*, Cam-

bridge: Cambridge University Press, 1974. G. Leff, *William of Ockham. The Metamorphosis of Scholastic Discourse*, Manchester: Manchester University Press; Totowa, N.J.: Rowman and Littlefield, 1975. K. Bannach, *Die Lehre von der Doppelten Macht Gottes bei Wilhelm von Ockham*, Wiesbaden: Franz Steiner, 1975.
For Adam Wodeham, an early follower of Ockham, see W. J. Courtenay, *Adam Wodeham. An Introduction to his Life and Writings*, Leiden: Brill, 1978.

XIX. Master Eckhart

TRANSLATIONS. *Parisian Questions and Prologues*, trans. A. A. Maurer, Toronto: Pontifical Institute of Mediaeval Studies, 1974. R. Schürmann, *Meister Eckhart, Mystic and Philosopher; Translations with Commentary*, Bloomington: Indiana University Press, 1978.
STUDIES. M. A. Lücker, *Meister Eckhart und die Devotio Moderna*, Leiden: Brill, 1950. K. Kertz, "Meister Eckhart's Teaching on the Birth of the Divine Word in the Soul," *Traditio*, 15 (1959), 327-363. H. Wackerzapp, *Der Einfluß Meister Eckharts auf die philosophischen Schriften des Nickolaus von Kues*, Münster: Aschendorff,

1962. J. D. Caputo, "The Nothingness of the Intellect in Meister Eckhart's Parisian Questions," *The Thomist*, 39 (1975), 85-115. J. D. Caputo, *The Mystical Element in Heidegger's Thought*, Athens: Ohio University Press, 1978 (a study of Heidegger's relations with Eckhart). C. F. Kelley, *Meister Eckhart on Divine Knowledge*, New Haven: Yale University Press, 1977. *Meister Eckhart of Hochheim 1327-28-1978. The Thomist*, 43 (1978) (contains commemorative essays, including E. Colledge, "Meister Eckhart: his Times and his Writings" and bibliography, pp. 313-336).

XX. Nicholas of Cusa

TRANSLATIONS. *Unity and Reform; Selected Writings*, ed. J. P. Dolan, Notre Dame, Ind.: Notre Dame Press, 1962. *Nicholas of Cusa on God as Non-other: a Translation and Appraisal of De Li Non Aliud*, by J. Hopkins, Minneapolis: University of Minnesota Press, 1979. *Idiota de Mente. The Layman: About Mind*, trans. C. L. Miller, New York: Abaris Book, 1979.

STUDIES. *Nicolas de Cusa en el V Centenario de su Muerte (1464-1964)*, Madrid: Instituto 'Luis Vives' de Filosofia, 1967. *Mitteilungen und Forschungsbeiträge der Cusanus-Gesellschaft*, 14 vols., Mainz: Mattias-Grünewald, 1968-1980. K. Jaspers, *Anselm and Nicholas of Cusa. The Great Philosophers*, vol. 2: *The Original Thinkers*, ed. H. Arendt, trans. R.

Manheim, New York: Harcourt Brace, 1974. E. Colomer, *De la Edad Media al Renacimento: Ramon Lull, Nicolas de Cusas, Juan Pico della Mirandola*, Barcelona: Herder, 1975. J. E. Biechler, *The Religious Language of Nicholas of Cusa*, Tallahassee, Flor.: American Academy of Religion, Scholars Press, 1975. J.

Hopkins, *A Concise Introduction to the Philosophy of Nicholas of Cusa*, Minneapolis: University of Minneapolis Press, 1978. P. M. W. Trinkaus, *Disjunction and Metaphor: the Development of Nicolaus Cusanus' Philosophy of Man*, Ann Arbor: University of Michigan photocopy, 1976.

XXI. Marsilio Ficino and Pietro Pomponazzi

1. RENAISSANCE PHILOSOPHY AND THE MEDIEVAL TRADITION:

E. Gilson, *Les idées et les lettres*, Paris: Vrin, 1932. P. O. Kristeller, *Studies in Renaissance Thought and Letters*, Rome: Editioni di Storia e Letteratura, 1956. N. W. Gilbert, *Renaissance Concepts of Method*, New York: Columbia University Press, 1960 (chapter 1 treats of ancient and mediaeval sources of Renaissance methodology). P. O. Kristeller, *Eight Philosophers of the Italian Renaissance*, California: Stanford University Press, 1964 (includes chapters on Ficino and Pomponazzi). P. O. Kristeller, *Renaissance Philosophy and the Mediaeval Tradition*, Latrobe, Penn., 1966. P. O. Kristeller, *Le Thomisme et la pensée italienne de la Renaissance*, Paris: Vrin; Montréal: Institut d'Etudes Médiévales, 1967. A. della Torre, *Storia dell'Accademia Platonica di Firenze*, Turin: Bottega d'Erasmo, 1968. *Renaissance Philosophy. New Translations*, ed. L. A. Kennedy, The Hague, Paris: Mouton, 1973. N. G. Siraisi, *Arts and Sciences at Padua. The Studium of Padua before 1350*, Toronto: Pontifical Institute of Mediaeval Studies, 1973. *Medieval Aspects of Renaissance Learning. Three Essays*, ed. and trans. E. P. Mahoney, Durham, N.C.: Duke University Press, 1974.

2. FICINO:

WORKS. *Théologie platonicienne de l'immortalité des âmes*, ed. and trans. R. Marcel, 3 vols., Paris: Les Belles Lettres, 1964-1970. *De Vita Libri Tres*, ed. F. K. Franke, New York: G. Olms, 1978. *Marsilio Ficino: the Philebus Commentary*, ed. and trans. M. J. B. Allen, Berkeley: University of California Press, 1975.

TRANSLATION. *The Letters of Marsilio Ficino*, trans. by members of the Language Department of the School of Economic Science, London: Shepheard-Walwyn, 1975.

STUDIES. A. Chastel, *Marsile Ficin et l'art*, Geneva: E. Droz, 1954. M. Schiavone, *Problemi Filosofici in Marsilio Ficino*, Milan: Marzorati, 1957. A. Collins, *The Secular is Sacred: Platonism and Thomism in Marsilio Ficino's Platonic Theology*, The Hague: Nijhoff, 1974.

3. POMPONAZZI:

WORKS. *Corsi Inediti dell'Insegnamento Padovano*, ed. A. Poppi, Padua: Antenore, 1966 (contains editions of *Super Libello de Substantia Orbis, Expositio et Quaestiones Quattuor, Quaestiones Physicae et Animasticae Decem*).

STUDIES. J. H. Randall, *The School of Padua and the Emergence of Modern Science*, Padua: Antenore, 1961. B. Nardi, *Studi su Pietro Pomponazzi*, Florence: Felice le Monier, 1965. A. Poppi, *Saggi sul Pensiero inedito di Pietro Pomponazzi*, Padua: Antenore, 1970. G. Zanier, *Ricerche sulla Diffusione e Fortuna del 'De Incantationibus di Pomponazzi*, Florence: La Nuova Italia, 1975.

4. ACHILLINI:
H. S. Matsen, *Alessandro Achillini (1463-1512) and his Doctrine of 'Universals' and 'Transcendentals'. A Study in Renaissance Ockhamism*, Lewisburg: Bucknell University Press; London: Associated University Presses, 1974.

XXII. Renaissance Scholasticism

1. CAJETAN:
Aristotle: On Interpretation. Commentaries by St. Thomas and Cajetan, trans. J. T. Oesterle, Milwaukee: Marquette University Press, 1962. *Commentary on Being and Essence*, trans. L. H. Kendzierski and F. C. Wade, Milwaukee: Marquette University Press, 1964. A. Maurer, "Cajetan's Notion of Being in his Commentary on the *Sentences*," *Mediaeval Studies*, 28 (1966), 268-278. J. Reilly, *Cajetan's Notion of Existence*, The Hague: Mouton, 1971.

2. SUAREZ:
On Formal and Universal Unity, trans. J. F. Ross, Milwaukee: Marquette University Press, 1964. *Defensio Fidei III*, ed. E. and L. Pereña, Madrid: Instituto Francisco de Vitoria, 1965. T. J. Cronin, *Objective Being in Descartes and in Suarez*, Rome: Gregorian University Press, 1966. J. P. Doyle, "Suarez on the Reality of the Possibles," *The Modern Schoolman*, 45 (1967), 29-48. J. P. Doyle, "Suarez on the Analogy of Being," *The Modern Schoolman*, 46 (1968), 219-249. H. Siegfried, *Wahrheit und Metaphysik bei Suarez*, Bonn: H. Bouvier, 1967. *De Legibus*, ed. L. Pereña et al., vols. 1–, Madrid: Instituto Francisco de Vitoria, 1971 –. N. J. Wells, "Suarez on the Eternal Truths," *The Modern Schoolman*, 58 (1981), 73-104; 159-174.

Index

Italic numbers indicate main references

Abelard, Peter, *59-70*, 76, 77, 79, 90, 154, 246, 250, *391-393*.
Abraham, 69.
Academics, 4-6.
Achillini, Alexander, 341.
Adam, 48, 69.
Adam of Marsh, 130, 136.
Adelard of Bath, 255.
Afnan, S. M., 396.
Albert, St., 127, 128, *153-162*, 194, 215, 245, 255, 292, 298, 299, 348, 359, *403-404*.
Albert of Saxony, 262.
Alcuin, 35, 36, 389.
Alejandro, J. M., 425.
Alexander of Alexandria, 360.
Alexander of Aphrodisias, 28, 29, 86, 87, 330, 338.
Alexander of Hales, 127, *137-138*, 209, 352, *400-401*.
Alfarabi, 87, 94, 97, 100, 329.
Alfred, King, 34.
Algazel, 86, 101, 205, 397.
Alhazen, 131.
Alkindi, 86, 94, 205.
al-Ma'mūn, Caliph, 94.
Amann, E., 415.
Amaury of Bène, 46.
Ambrose, St., 384.
Anaxagoras, 319, 320.
Ancelet-Hustache, J., 418.
Anderson, J. F., 405.
Andrea of Florence, 104.
Anselm, St., 4, 11, *48-58*, 61, 111, 147, 154, 226, 295, 314-316, 376, *390-391*.
Anson, D. C., 407.
Anstruther, G., 406.
Antoninus, St., 329.
Antonio de la Madre de Dios, 354, 355.
Antonius Andreas, 351, 411.

Apuleius, 71, 329, 393.
Arberry, A. J., 396.
Aristotle,
  attitude toward: Abelard, 60; St. Albert, 155, 156, 159, 160; Boethius, 27, 29; St. Bonaventure, 139-142, 145, 146, 148, 149, 152; Duns Scotus, 221-223, 226; Ficino, 329; Francis of Meyronnes, 352; Latin Averroists, 192-193; Nicholas of Autrecourt, 289; Nicholas of Cusa, 313, 322; Mystics of 14th century, 308; Pomponazzi, 339-340, 342, 344; Roger Bacon, 128; Siger of Brabant, 194, 196; St. Thomas, 183, 184, 189, 194; William of Auvergne, 115-117.
  commentators: 28, 261, 349, 353, 355, 392.
  condemnations and prohibitions: 88-90, 153, 205-207.
  doctrine transformed by St. Thomas: 166, 179, 190.
  errors and deficiencies: 101, 140, 141, 205, 257-258.
  influence: 21, 28-29, 72, 85-88, 93-94, 110, 111, 121, 134, 137, 180, 192-193, 202, 206, 213, 215, 217, 245, 251, 255, 284, 337, 373.
  translations: 33, 85-88.
Arnou, R., 406.
Augustine, St., *3-21*, 22, 23, 36, 37, 41, 48, 49, 51, 53-55, 57, 58, 67, 70, 71, 100, 105, 111, 116, 118 127-129, 132, 134, 136, 137, 139, 143, 144, 148, 152, 159, 161, 171, 182-184, 190, 207-209, 217-219, 254, 256, 282, 288, 299, 306-308, 310, 315, 323, 327-329, 330, 333, 334, 372, 375, 376, *384-386*, 390, 391, 400, 404, 420.
Augustine of Canterbury, St., 36.